An Archaeology of Doings

James F. Brooks

General Editor

An Archaeology of Doings

SECULARISM AND THE STUDY OF PUEBLO RELIGION

Severin M. Fowles

SAR
PRESS

School for Advanced Research Press

Santa Fe

School for Advanced Research Press
Post Office Box 2188
Santa Fe, New Mexico 87504-2188
www.sarpress.org

Managing Editor: Lisa Pacheco
Editorial Assistant: Ellen Goldberg
Design and Production: Cynthia Dyer
Manuscript Editor: Merryl Sloane
Proofreader: Dianne Nelson
Indexer: Margaret Moore Booker

Library of Congress Cataloging-in-Publication Data
Fowles, Severin M.
 An archaeology of doings : secularism and the study of Pueblo religion / Severin M. Fowles. — 1st ed.
    p. cm.
 Includes bibliographical references and index.
 ISBN 978-1-934691-56-4 (alk. paper)
 1. Taos Indians—Religion. 2. Taos Indians—Rites and ceremonies. 3. Taos Indians—Antiquities.
 4. Pueblo Indians—Religion. 5. Pueblo Indians—Antiquities. 6. Indian Catholics—New Mexico—Taos
 Pueblo. 7. Christianity and other religions—New Mexico—Taos Pueblo. 8. Taos Pueblo (N.M.)—Religious
 life and customs. 9. Taos Plateau (N.M.)—Antiquities. 10. Taos Pueblo (N.M.)—Antiquities. I. Title.
 E99.T2F68 2012
 978.9004'97496—dc23
                              2012018025

Library of Congress Catalog Card Number: 2012018025
International Standard Book Number: 978-1-934691-56-4
First edition 2013.

All illustrations and photographs by Severin M. Fowles unless otherwise noted.

Cover illustration: Drawing by Severin M. Fowles, based on kiva murals at Picurís Pueblo.

The School for Advanced Research on the Human Experience (SAR) promotes the furthering of scholarship on—and public understanding of—human culture, behavior, and evolution. SAR Press publishes cutting-edge scholarly and general-interest books that encourage critical thinking and present new perspectives on topics of interest to all humans. Contributions by authors reflect their own opinions and viewpoints and do not necessarily express the opinions of SAR Press.

Contents

Figures and Tables

Preface

The following chapters respond to a set of archaeological conversations about premodern religion that have been intensifying and show no sign of weakening in the years to come. Generally speaking, these conversations are themselves a collective response to a congeries of late twentieth- and early twenty-first-century stimuli, some located within the narrow intellectual currents of archaeological debate, others impacting the discipline from the outside as archaeologists respond to changes in the weather of their wider political surroundings.

Within the discipline, the recent interest in religion has been a response, first, to the interpretive turn in archaeology, which since the start of the 1980s has been challenging prehistorians to read material remains, if not exactly as texts, then at least as semiotically dense phenomena affording access to past cultural understandings of the world. Insofar as religion is commonly treated as an especially symbolic human phenomenon, it has emerged as a natural focus for interpretive studies, and much of this research is now moving beyond questions of meaning to explore the role of religion in the transformation of past societies (e.g., Cauvin 2000; Hodder 2010). Archaeologists of a more scientific persuasion have also been contributing to the interest in premodern religion. Stimulated by developments in neurology and cognitive science, they have come to understand religion as an effect of biology and have been resuscitating long-dormant inquiry into the origins of religiosity both in the deep past of our species (e.g., Mithen 1996) and as an ongoing "origin-in-process," anchored in the structure of the human mind, that has been with us throughout history (e.g., Lewis-Williams 2010). There have even been efforts to marry these seemingly divergent humanistic and scientific approaches (e.g., Renfrew and Morley 2009).

Forces outside the discipline are clearly having their effect as well. More and more social analysts in the West have convinced themselves, rightly or wrongly, that religion is again on the rise. "God is back," reads the blunt title of one volume (Micklethwait and Wooldridge 2009). Ours is a postsecular age, add others (Berger 1999). Whether one greets such remarks with open arms or clenched fists, there is no denying the new imperative to take religion's place in society, past and present, more seriously. Given the media storm surrounding fundamentalist and evangelical movements, it makes sense that a number of archaeologists have become especially interested in the history of world religions (e.g., Assman 2010; Fogelin 2006; Insoll 2001), particularly Islam (e.g., Insoll 1999; Lape 2005; Straughn 2006). Interest in the so-called traditional religions has grown in response to political concerns as well, however. As indigenous communities throughout the colonized world continue to fight for greater control over the sites, landscapes, and artifacts of their ancestors, they have frequently done so in the explicit language of religion, stressing the sanctity of particular places and things as a means of building their cases for certain rights and protections. In the United States in particular, the passage of the Native American Graves Protection and Repatriation Act (NAGPRA) in 1990 prompted a large archaeological literature on sacred places and ritual objects (e.g., Gulliford 2000; Hall 1997; Reilly and Garber 2007; VanPool et al., eds. 2006). These days, knowing what is sacred and what is not in the archaeological record can be as much a matter of legal necessity as intellectual curiosity.

The tangled relations between these varied late twentieth-century developments—in archaeological theory, social critique, native law, neuroscience, geopolitics, and more—and their convergence within the study of religion are fascinating subjects, and while I hope to make a contribution to contemporary thought on such matters, my chief aim in writing this book has been to complicate the way archaeologists increasingly rely upon "religion" as an organizing concept in their analyses of other worlds in distant times and places. Certainly there is widespread acknowledgment that religion is an awkward and imprecise cross-cultural category, difficult to define in ethnographic contexts and even more difficult to excavate. By and large, however, archaeologists have been reluctant to follow this critical project forward into a more radical unpacking. There has never been, for instance, any meaningful archaeological debate about the implications of post-Geertzian critiques of religion as a profoundly secular category within anthropology (in the sense of Asad 1993, 2003). I find this both surprising and unfortunate. If we should be worried about the nontranslatability of "religion" in, say, medieval European contexts, if we must be vigilant about the many questionable premises the term smuggles in even there (for instance, that religion is a matter of private belief, a means of engaging the transcendent, a set of mystifications legitimizing a particular distribution of nonreligious power, and so on), are these worries not massively amplified when we begin to make claims about precolonial religions in non-Western worlds? How are we, as students of deeply *premodern* religion, to respond when we are told that religion is a historically contingent category underwriting a distinctly *modern* agenda? The most common response, regrettably, has been to shut our ears, cite Geertz rather than Asad, and be done with it.

This book explores an alternative strategy. Rather than ignore the problem of translation, I have sought to make nontranslatability the very focus of my analysis. Rather than treat definitional matters as a beginning point that, once muddled through, permits us to go about our business using phrases like "prehistoric religion" and "ancient rituals" with relative impunity, my goal is to embrace the critical unpacking of religion as a genuine methodology, permitting it to structure my investigations from start to finish. In practice, this means that I have not laid at the reader's feet a corpus of initially inexplicable archaeological phenomena with the intent of gradually making them legible through a demonstration of their relationships to some sort of universal understanding of what religion is. On the contrary, I have drawn on the category of religion to probe the depths of its illegibility, inserting it into a non-Western setting precisely in order to document the extent and nature of its dissonance. I regard this as akin to a laboratory experiment in which a known chemical is mixed with an unknown substance to produce a bubbling, brewing reaction that is regarded as diagnostic—a disturbance that reveals something significant about the phenomenon of interest.

If the modern, secular category of religion is my known chemical, as it were, the ancestral world of the Northern Tiwa communities in the American Southwest is my unknown substance. The Northern Tiwas today comprise two Pueblo communities, Taos and Picurís; their ancestors have resided in the Taos region of northern New Mexico for at least a thousand years and perhaps much longer. Like most other non-Western peoples, the Northern Tiwas have no indigenous term for religion, and I am interested in what reaction takes place when this foreign category is introduced into an account of their past. Following an initial consideration of the challenges presented by postsecular critiques to an archaeology of premodern religion (chapter 1), each chapter proceeds to explore the poorness of fit between the modern category of religion and a different period in Northern Tiwa history. In chapters 2 and 3, this amounts to a process of deliberate dismantling: beginning with the common anthropological claims that the ancestral Northern Tiwas "were religious," "practiced rituals," and conceived of an order set apart as "the sacred," I pick and scrape at the viability of these assumptions, eventually concluding that our use of such terms reveals much more about our own tendency to situate Pueblo society within a Western evolutionary narrative than it does about the Pueblos themselves.

The discussion then pivots in chapter 4, at which point the critique of religion as an analytical category gives way to the search for alternative understandings more in line with ancestral Pueblo practices and indigenous sensibilities. Like many other Native American communities, the Pueblos commonly refer to their ceremonies as "doings," and as far as I know there has never been any anthropological effort to explore just what this term means in a native context, how it is used, or why it so frequently surfaces precisely in those moments when ethnographers think they are hearing something about native religion. The word "doings," in other words, has been pushed to the side as a quaint vernacular expression, an unsystematic way of talking about a subject that we, as anthropologists, explore using more precise analytical terms. I redress this situation in the second half of the book, arguing that the very commonness of the word "doings" may be its greatest virtue. Indeed, if we seek an alternative to the modernist category of religion, there is no better place to look than in the local vernacular and in ways of talking that, from our perspective, seem semantically empty but from the native perspective clearly are not. Chapters 4, 5, and 6, then, progressively move away from an analysis of religion per se and toward an analysis of ancestral Northern Tiwa doings, using the impressive thirteenth- and early fourteenth-century archaeological remains of the Taos region as a means of focusing the discussion. This is where an archaeology of doings takes shape.

The final chapter returns to the problem of religion but now more specifically to the Pueblo communities' strategic engagement with this foreign category during the colonial period. Both Spanish and American colonialisms, each in its own way, were Christian undertakings; consequently, the question of whether the Pueblos did or did not have an indigenous religion, comparable to Christianity, has always been a loaded one, with on-the-ground implications in the tug and pull of colonial power struggles. Tracing this history highlights just what is at stake when one argues, as I do, that prior to the missionary project, the Pueblos did not have a religion but rather something else, something that escapes straightforward translation into Western categories. Well aware of the dangers involved, I suggest there is more to be gained than lost by a serious consideration of this argument, both for indigenous communities and for American society more generally, the latter of which has much to learn from the logic of Pueblo doings and the social worlds these doings make possible. In response, then, to the central question posed in chapter 1—What would a postsecular archaeology of premodern religion look like?—the final chapter offers two conclusions. First, a postsecular archaeology of premodern religion would not be an archaeology of religion at all; in the case of the Pueblos, it would be an archaeology of doings. Second, a postsecular archaeology would struggle against the use of ancestral Pueblo doings as a proxy for the developmental past of Western society; it would, in contrast, explore the alterity and coevalness (in the sense of Fabian 1983) of doings with an eye toward the possibilities this opens up for the novel transformation of Western society in the years to come.

Let me stress, then, that the object I have placed under the microscope is the Western archaeological tradition and its ties to the secular project. Insofar as this project has repeatedly implicated non-Western groups like the Northern Tiwas, it is essential that any effort to excavate archaeology's secular orientation also attend to the specific empirical claims this orientation has generated in local contexts. Not in order to assess whether the existing evidence supports contemporary models of premodern religion in the pre-Columbian Southwest, in Iron Age Africa, in Neolithic

Europe, or anywhere else, nor as a means of determining whether our models could be strengthened through the collection of additional ethnographic or archaeological data. Plenty of scholarship within the archaeology of religion, traditionally conceived, busily works toward such ends already. Here, I attempt something different, an exercise in critical theory in which specific archaeological claims about the religiosity of non-Western Others are themselves treated as evidence. I am interested in the intellectual orientation that prompts these claims and in the deeper secular imaginaries that, in turn, make this orientation seem logical and necessary. Whatever else this book may accomplish, my hope is that it will convince the reader that there is ample room to question both the logic and the necessity of "premodern religion" as a subject of inquiry in the Pueblo Southwest and anywhere else archaeologists have sought to dig up the sacred.

Acknowledgments

Research for this book began in 1996, the final edits were completed fifteen years later, and along the way I benefited from the kindness of many individuals and institutions. The archaeology faculty at the University of Michigan provided a continuous thread of intellectual guidance. I am grateful in particular to Richard Ford for his model efforts to transcend the subdisciplinary divide between archaeological and sociocultural anthropology and for his unwavering emphasis on the virtues of ecological thought, the influence of which will be plainly evident in the following pages. Norman Yoffee's scholarship has had a similarly deep impact, notably as a model of how to undertake a critical archaeology that does not shy away from the grand narrative but rather works toward the construction of equally grand counternarratives. I thank John Speth for the many lessons he has provided over the years regarding the logic of archaeological interpretation and the mobilization of field data to address anthropological questions.

The fieldwork and laboratory studies discussed in chapters 3–6 would not have been possible but for the extraordinary generosity of Southern Methodist University's extension campus in Taos, New Mexico. Michael Adler, the current director of SMU-in-Taos, has played an especially significant role, providing mentorship throughout my study of Taos archaeology as well as access to local sites, artifact collections, and research facilities. Paul Williams of the Bureau of Land Management went out of his way to facilitate my rock art research in the Rio Grande gorge, which has proven instrumental in reinterpreting the Taos katsina tradition. I am also grateful to Richard Aspenwind of Taos Pueblo, who has consulted on the research reported herein and offered many reflections that will continue to guide my understanding of ancestral Pueblo history.

On the interpretation of northern Rio Grande history and ethnography, I have benefited from conversations and correspondence with Kurt Anschuetz, Risa Arbolino, Jeffrey Boyer, Elizabeth Brandt, Donald Brown, Sam Duwe, Sunday Eiselt, Matthew Liebmann, Maxine McBrinn, Scott Ortman, James Snead, Paul Williams, and the members of the Taos Archaeological Society. On archaeological approaches to religion, secularism, and ontology, I have learned much from discussions with Ben Alberti, Brian Boyd, Rodney Campbell, Zoe Crossland, Terry D'Altroy, Lars Fogelin, Ian Straughn, and Christopher Witmore. On how to live a happy life away from such matters, I am grateful for the daily kindness of Ellen and Jules Morris, surely the best teachers I will ever know.

One or more chapters of the book were read by Rodney Campbell, Lars Fogelin, Ellen Morris, Nan Rothschild, Ian Straughn, and Darryl Wilkinson; all offered valuable feedback that improved the text. Scott Ortman and an anonymous reviewer read a complete draft for SAR Press, and I am especially grateful to both for their thoughtful commentaries. If I did not follow all their good suggestions or address all their well-reasoned critiques, it is only because I have been convinced to undertake additional writing projects that will do so with greater care in the near future.

Financial support for research and writing was provided by a dissertation improvement grant from the National Science Foundation, a presidential research award from Barnard College, and a Hunt Fellowship from the Wenner-Gren Foundation.

o n e
Archaeology after Secularism

Man constructs according to an archetype.
— *Mircea Eliade*, The Myth of Eternal Return

Prognoses of religion's future are different today than they were just a few decades
ago. In the early twenty-first century, still reeling from the eschatological swirl
of anxieties and doubts that accompanied the turn of the millennium, one finds
respected scholars writing that they were wrong about modernity and the decline
in religiosity it was meant to entail. In 1929, Walter Lippmann famously wrote of
modernity as an acid—one touch, it seemed, and our religious dispositions begin to
corrode. Such a claim could hardly be made today. The acids of modernity, we are
now told, are weaker than once thought and religion much more durable. Indeed,
the contemporary moment appears to be one in which fear of an increasingly godless
world by the godly has been replaced in many quarters by fear of an increasingly
godly world by the godless. Secularization theory is giving way to talk of resurgent
religion. And, astonished, scholarship blinks and rubs its eyes at the *"desecularization*
of the world," at the new *"post-secular* world" (Asad 2003; Berger 1999). "Remember
the good old days," mocks Bruno Latour (2004:154), "when university professors
could look down on unsophisticated folks because those hillbillies naively believed
in church, motherhood, and apple pie? Things have changed a lot."

The surprise is familiar. For as long as scholars have talked about secularization as an undeniable trend, they have also observed that secularization is, in fact,
quite deniable, even in its European and Euro-American homelands (e.g., Greeley

1972; Smith 1978[1962]:3). Recall Durkheim's position at the start of the twentieth century. Despite two hundred years of philosophical argument that both condemned religion as mere illusion and prophesied the coming of an enlightened and fully secular world, Durkheim's discussion of the elementary forms of religious life sprang instead from the observation that religion has been far stronger than its critics and cultured despisers have been wont to acknowledge. If religion is mere illusion, he asked, if it is a grand disastrous fallacy, a flawed and ineffective science or the means of mass enslavement, how are we to explain its persistence once revealed for what it is? Why have so many chosen to keep their illusions? For that matter, why did pre-modern peoples not only develop but also commit themselves so fully to a mistake in the first place? If we begin by condemning religion as empty illusion or, worse yet, as a failed attempt at rationality, then "it is impossible to explain how it was able to survive the first attempts made, and the persistence with which it has maintained itself becomes unintelligible" (Durkheim 1965[1915]:98). "It is hard to understand," wrote Durkheim, "how men have continued to do certain things for centuries with-out any object" (101). "How could a vain fantasy have been able to fashion the human consciousness so strongly and so durably?...how has this extraordinary dupery been able to perpetuate itself all through the course of history?" (87). Set aside Durkheim's way out of this Enlightenment quandary: his influential thesis that religion, far from being flawed philosophy, is how a community sacralizes and thereby strengthens itself. The point is that Durkheim's question at the start of the twentieth century—if religion is illusory, obfuscating, and indeed "wrong," why does it persist?—is not all that different than the question being posed at the start of the twenty-first.

The tone and urgency of contemporary worries over religion's vitality, however, feel different. In place of the comparative detachment of Durkheim's sociological meditations, today's concerns echo an earlier moment at the birth of modernity when many social critics sought explicitly to drag society out from beneath the thumb of papal authority. In the seventeenth and eighteenth centuries, scholarly concern in Europe was with the *political* power of religious institutions and ideologies, a power that was thought to corrupt fair and proper governance as well as religion's suppos-edly true nature as a private matter of salvation. Religion and the political had to be wrenched apart, and a major tactic in this violent bifurcation involved the construc-tion of new universal categories of "religion" and "politics" that could be etched onto the past. As Asad (1993) has carefully argued, our current understanding of "religion" as a matter of belief rather than action is an inheritance of such early modern battles.

But the secularist struggle today is not so much to wrench religion and politics apart as it is to prevent the two from reuniting. This, at least, is how the struggle is frequently presented. Ominous signs are everywhere noted that religion, like a virus (a "virus of faith," as science warrior Richard Dawkins [2006] puts it), is once again penetrating political bodies, national and international alike. In England, much was made of Tony Blair's very un-British attendance at Catholic mass while prime min-ister (not to mention his alleged prayer sessions with George W. Bush). In France,

Nicolas Sarkozy's endorsement of the church as fundamental to European ethics and morality was viewed as more worrisome yet (Sciolino 2008). America's secularity has always been of a different sort; Americans have traditionally wanted their politicians to be strongly but privately religious. Nevertheless, following the 2004 presidential election, many American secular liberals stared in queasy disbelief at electoral maps in which the vast sea of Republican "red" states had been relabeled "Jesusland"— dark satire that played off the left's impression that a born-again president had been voted in primarily on religious grounds. Wringing their hands, they reiterated Durkheim's query with added emphasis: if religion is an illusion, why does it both persist *and seem to spread*? The desecularization of US politics is not merely commented upon; it is marked with a special opprobrium.

If Republican red is the color of secular concern at home, Islamic green is the color of fear abroad. From the reassertion of theocracy in Iran to the subsequent intensification of militant Islamic organizations more broadly, the melding of religious convictions and political action is considered to dangerously contaminate and radicalize both. Of course, much US political discourse uses the label of Islamic "extremism" to present entirely rational Middle Eastern struggles in an irrational— that is, an overly religious—framework, diverting attention from the larger motivations behind those struggles. Be that as it may, the "green" international worries of neoconservatives broadly mirror the "red" domestic worries of many American secular liberals. In each case, the desecularization of politics is regarded as a dangerous regression. Again, many onlookers ask: whatever happened to the Enlightenment?

This question reverberates not only in the northern Atlantic, but among those with a broadly secular orientation in the Middle East as well. Saba Mahmood reflects on the reaction by "progressive leftists" in the Arab world—she considered herself a member—to the late twentieth-century Islamic revival movements, noting her "profound dis-ease with the appearance of religion outside of the private space of individualized belief":

> For those with well-honed secular-liberal and progressive sensibilities, the slightest
> eruption of religion into the public domain is frequently experienced as a dangerous
> affront, one that threatens to subject us to a normative morality dictated by mullahs
> and priests. This fear is accompanied by a deep self-assurance about the truth of the
> progressive-secular imaginary, one that assumes that the life forms it offers are the
> best way out for these unenlightened souls, mired as they are in the spectral hopes
> that gods and prophets hold out to them. (Mahmood 2004:xi)

That this self-assurance has fallen apart is widely apparent. Now one reads that it is by becoming more intensely Islamic that Algerian women are able to make significant strides in modernizing their country (Slackman 2007). And that as South Korea reaches new heights of industrialization and technological sophistication, the popularity of shamanism seems also to be on the rise (Sang-Hun 2007). And that businesspeople in China are turning to Christianity to become more effective capitalists on the global stage (Micklethwait and Wooldridge 2009:8). Modernity and religiosity, once antithetical, now appear to be anything but.

To speak of postsecularism, then, is to speak of a palpable phenomenon, a widespread perception and subject of global debate. One might say, more precisely, that postsecularism, like postmodernism, is a condition, a falling away of one's bedrock belief in the progressive disenchantment of the world and its replacement by a growing concern over the world's reenchantment. Which is also to say that postsecularism marks yet another crisis of narratives, one that begins with the worry that contemporary social actors have simply forgotten their lines in the great drama of civilization's progress and ends with an unsettling realization that the world may actually be acting out the script of a very different play. If secularism was once understood to stand outside culture and history, if it was understood to rise above individual cultures by providing rational, universal standards by which individual cultures might be judged, if it was thought to transcend individual histories by standing at the end of history, then postsecularism marks a mounting denial of these claims. It represents a new appreciation of secularism's historical and cultural specificity—as well as, for secularism's apologists, its worrisome fragility.

I regard both secularism and postsecularism, then, as a set of claims about plotlines, rather than a set of social configurations per se. Whether or not the world is becoming more religious is a spurious question that cannot be addressed precisely because religion is an unstable category that does not translate from one historical moment to the next with fidelity. But this is not to say that the problem of postsecularism is a trivial matter, that it is merely a set of claims about plotlines. On the contrary, cultural understandings of the relationship between past, present, and future comprise the very ground from which we leap into action. Narratives are powerful, and secularization is perhaps the most potent narrative of the past half millennium.

A Postsecular Archaeology of Premodern Religion?

This book is an archaeological response to the challenge of postsecularism and to the growing literature that questions the secular orientation of scholarship in the humanities and social sciences. It is motivated especially by conversations within anthropology that have used the continued prominence of world religions as a springboard for a new wave of critical reflection both on the secular as a specifically Western ontology and on the implicitly Protestant or post-Reformation assumptions underwriting the discipline's ostensibly universal analytical categories (Calhoun et al. 2011; Fitzgerald 2007; Scott and Hirschkind 2006). The most prominent participant in these conversations has been Talal Asad (1993, 2003), whose critique of anthropological figurations of religion as a matter of meaning and belief rather than discipline and power not only has led anthropologists to confront the historic specificity of religion as a discursive domain, but also has forced the discipline to unpack "religion" in non-Western and nonmodern societies generally. While the targets of his critique differ from Asad's, Bruno Latour (1993) has developed a related analysis of what he refers to as the modernist project of purification in which an ideological commitment to separating religion, politics, science, economics, and so on obscures and, indeed, facilitates the increasing interweaving of these categories. For Latour, as for Asad, a rigid boundary simply cannot be drawn around "religion" except within a very specific secular modern imaginary.

As the broader implications of postsecular critiques are debated, the marked absence of archaeological voices has become increasingly curious. Archaeology, after all, would seem to be centrally implicated: its primary objects of study are the premodern and non-Western societies in which universalist notions of religion presumably face especially severe problems of translation. Ironically, though, at the precise intellectual moment when classic definitions of religion began to fall apart, the "archaeology of religion" emerged as a major project (e.g., Barrowclough and Malone 2007; Biehl and Bertemes 2001; Fogelin 2007, 2008; Glowacki and Van Keuren 2011; Hayden 2003; Hays-Gilpin and Whitley 2008; Hodder 2010; Insoll 2001; Renfrew and Morley 2009). Indeed, since the 1990s, a growing body of work has drawn on archaeological remains to explicitly model ancient religions, and nearly all of this work is founded upon secularist understandings of religion as a universal phenomenon centered on questions of meaning, symbolism, and belief in the supernatural. As one collection of archaeological essays begins, "Religion is universal in human societies.... [It] is unifying and pervasive" (VanPool et al. 2006:1).

Which is to say that archaeology has yet to meaningfully engage with the broader reevaluation of religion in the discipline, and I contend that this is a significant problem for more than just archaeologists. Indeed, it was precisely in its portrayals of the premodern that twentieth-century anthropology most directly contributed to modernist understandings of the natural or intended place of religion in social life. Early anthropologists devoted considerable energy to theorizing religion's putative origins—origins that often looked surprisingly secular. Primitive religion was frequently presented as having been born of private reflection on the meaning of life, death, and the soul, or it was said to have evolved out of an original stage of magic, reckoned as a kind of quasi-scientific study of cause-and-effect relationships in nature. Such models naturalized Enlightenment principles: because religion was originally a private matter, so must it be today; because religion was originally born of an effort (albeit a flawed effort) to explain cause-and-effect relationships in nature, so must modern science return us to a basic materialist orientation that centuries of corruption by priests and theologians have obscured. I will have more to say about the entangling of modernist futures with primitive origins in a moment. For now, I will merely underscore the observation that models of premodern religion have been and continue to be especially prominent as the space of secular ideology building, and archaeologists—as the only anthropologists who continue to study premodernity—must therefore participate in any meaningful revisionist effort in the discipline. Pruning weeds only goes so far; at some point, one must dig up the roots.

What is needed is a postsecular archaeology that sets its sights on unpacking the anthropological category of premodern religion. This is the challenge taken up in this book.

Such an undertaking is bound to encounter resistance on two fronts. First, there is the simple fact that contemporary sociocultural anthropologists have largely brushed aside the premodern—and along with it, their archaeological colleagues. Few are willing to entertain the possibility that those studying the stones and bones of hoary antiquity might have anything novel to say about secularism. I am under no illusions that this book will overcome such resistance, but a one-sided effort at disciplinary rapprochement is better than none at all. Second, there will surely be some in the archaeological community who will resist what they regard as an unproductive deconstructionist assault on one of their most promising analytical categories. After all, many are of the opinion that it is something of a big deal that we are now able to legitimately study ancient religion alongside ancient politics and economics. One is lectured repeatedly on the manner in which the archaeology of religion used to be marginalized on two grounds. First, it was thought that archaeology, with its materialist methods, lacked the tools to reconstruct past meaning and belief (infamously, Hawkes 1954); second, it was assumed that religion was a superstructure anyway, a "misty realm," as Marx (1990[1865]:65) put it, so why bother? Modern archaeologists have freed themselves of both these shackles, both the methodological and the theoretical attitudes that prevented serious inquiry into past religious experience. These days, most archaeologists willingly accept not only that we have the means to study ancient religions, but also that religion, insofar as it was a core motivation in the past, must be a core focus of inquiry among scholars in the present. And shouldn't we be grateful for these developments? Now that we've cleared space for an archaeology of religion, do we really want to undercut it by saying that "religion"—as defined by secular theorists—is a historically contingent product of the Reformation? Do we really want to say that religion, as such, didn't exist in premodern and non-Western times and places? Wouldn't it be embarrassing to discover that having just drawn the baby a bath, there's no longer any baby to bathe?

I can only respond by saying that whereas I once supported these new movements with enthusiasm, I now find it increasingly difficult to quiet the nagging feeling that the archaeology of religion has come to us as a stillbirth. Perhaps there is yet time to administer a cure. Perhaps the child can be saved by nuancing definitions or by further emphasizing that ancient religions were more matters of practice than belief. Perhaps we need only be more diligent in pointing out the close interpenetration of religion, politics, and economics in the premodern world. In the end, I suspect, such efforts are bound to fail. "Religion" has become a secular category through and through. The acids of modernity have done their work, not through corrosion, but through transfiguration, a transfiguration that makes translation entirely fraught.

Consider the incoherence of religion as an archaeological category when dealing with a premodern context in which, we are told, the spheres of religion, politics, and economics were all fully interwoven. What does this really mean? What does it mean to interweave categories that, from the perspective of the modern analyst, have been defined in contrast to one another? Nearly all archaeological commentary on the subject implicitly builds from the position that they (the premoderns) like us (the moderns) did indeed have spheres of action called "religion," "politics," "economics," and the like. It is simply that these spheres bled into one another. They were "enmeshed" (Bertemes and Biehl 2001:15), "hopelessly intertwined" (Garwood et al. 1991:viii), fused into a "creative *amalgam*, a seamless conceptual fabric, of what Westerners see as 'sacred' and 'secular'" (Lewis-Williams and Pearce 2005:105). Premoderns lived in blurred worlds of mixed-up categories that we have only recently learned to separate. Back then, the actions of priest, president, and profiteer could hardly be distinguished.

Not surprisingly, the problem of legibility is an overwhelming preoccupation of archaeological writing on religion. What is ritual? What is not? When is a building a temple rather than an elite residence? How is one to pull from the tangled categories of premodernity some strands of behavior that can serve as the special subject matter of an archaeology of religion? "How," ask François Bertemes and Peter Biehl (2001:14), "can we discuss the functions and meanings of cult and religion within a society before we have any clear criteria for recognizing it at all or for documenting it archaeologically?" "How are researchers to identify what behaviors in the past were 'ritual,' as opposed to some other social or economic practices?" seconds Ian Kuijt (2002:81). Or as Colin Renfrew puts it:

> How…does one recognize the archaeological evidence of religious behavior, of cult practice, for what it is? On what grounds, for instance, is one pit, with animal bones and a few artifacts, dismissed as domestic refuse, while another is seen as a ritual deposit with evidence of sacrifice? In what circumstances shall we regard small terracotta representations of animals and men as figurines, intended as offerings to the deity, and when shall we view them as mere toys for the amusement for children? (1985:2)

The desire expressed here is for a coherent definition of ritual and religion that will sort out the tangle in all times and places—precisely the kind of universal definition that has undergone sustained critique within sociocultural anthropology.

None of the archaeological attempts to clarify these matters have been successful. The most common archaeological strategy is to hold fast to a Geertzian definition of religion that vaguely links religion to matters of symbolism: "It is the problem of symbolism and meaning which seems, above all, to distinguish prehistoric and historic approaches to [religious] ritual in archaeology," wrote Garwood et al. (1991:ix) in the early 1990s, and the situation has changed little since (e.g., Henshilwood 2009; J. Renfrew 2009). Colin Renfrew, arguably the archaeologist with the most sustained intellectual commitment to the issue, has reiterated this position, proposing that religious ritual is distinct not just in being composed of invariant sequences of formal acts and utterances (in the sense of Rappaport 1999:24) but also because it involves distinctively *expressive* action. In this way, concludes Renfrew (2007:9), we should at least be able to say that work on an assembly line—however repetitive it may be—is not ritual, for there is nothing particularly expressive about it. But of course, there is no logic to this sort of statement. The worker always performs for the foreman; minimally, she always expresses her fulfillment of a contract, asserting that she has indeed earned her wages. How is this any less expressive than lighting candles in a church to ensure one's prayers are heard? Similar arguments can be made in prehistoric contexts. Were repetitive practices like flint knapping and field clearance any less expressive than prayer? What aspect of culture is not expressive, symbolic, and a matter of meaning?

Partly in response to such concerns, many archaeologists have fallen back upon even older anthropological definitions of religion as belief in the supernatural (e.g., Mithen 2009:123). In the introduction to another volume on the archaeology of religion, the editors opt to "define religion as systems of notions about the supernatural and the sacred, about life after death and related themes" with rituals being the practices that make these notions concrete (Malone et al. 2007:1). Such definitions are slippery not only because of the inclusion of unspecified "related themes" but also because they conflate the supernatural with the sacred, despite long-standing anthropological cautions against such a conflation. More significantly, the notion of the supernatural itself has been the target of repeated criticism over the past century. Put bluntly, the division between natural and supernatural realms is a loaded modernist notion, a product of the post-Reformation division between the this-worldly concerns of science and politics and the otherworldly concerns of religion. How could non-Western and nonmodern peoples believe in a worldly division with which they had no experience and of which they had no conception?

This is when archaeologists begin to throw up their hands in frustration. Here is where they begin to wish they could shift the conversation to questions of archaeological methods instead of definitional matters. "Fine," they will say, "if the notion of the supernatural has too much baggage, let us follow William James and simply define religion as belief in an unseen order." This is the approach taken by David Lewis-Williams and David Pearce in *Inside the Neolithic Mind*, one of the most important studies of prehistoric religion yet produced. "All religions have some orientation to unseen realms, beings and powers," they claim (Lewis-Williams and Pearce 2005:26). Their text deserves extended consideration, more than I can offer here. For now, it is enough to note that Lewis-Williams and Pearce consider religion to be a neurological phenomenon, grounded in the physiological experience of altered states of consciousness: "perceptions of [religion's] invisible realms," they argue, "derive from the electro-chemical functioning of the brain," which leads humans to see patterns, objects, people, and places that do not exist (285). The careful reader will have already noted a basic paradox at the heart of Lewis-Williams and Pearce's position. In what sense can religion be construed as a belief in "unseen realms [and] beings" when the authors' own research into altered states reveals the impressive degree to which these things are, in fact, *seen*? Are not religion's realms and beings *regularly* seen in the course of shamanic journeys, dreams, vision quests, near-death experiences, and the like? Is it not self-evident that shamans believe in the existence of (what to them is) a visible and quite sensuously experienced realm? Isn't the fact that we might not see or experience this realm—that we might consider it an illusion—entirely beside the point?

This critique opens onto a room cluttered with subsidiary worries. If we define religion as belief in an unseen order, how is Western physics to be separated out? And how are we to find space within religion for all those devout Christians who claim to see God in every plant and animal? Moreover, are we really to conclude that Native Americans "see" Father Sun traveling across the heavens any less clearly than Anglo American scientists "see" a stationary mass of hydrogen and helium? Is Father Sun any less empirical than a nuclear fusion reaction perceived from a million kilometers away?

Those archaeologists who had not previously walked out on the conversation are now probably heading for the door. Perhaps there is one closet Dawkins fan left who is willing to argue that, in the end, archaeology must settle upon a definition of religion as belief in beings and powers that science has now shown to be complete illusions. Religion is the mystified component of past belief systems. Yes, this is where archaeology ends up when it is honest with itself. The unpleasant reality is that when we as archaeologists—particularly, prehistoric archaeologists—write about religion, we still tend to fall back on some core notion of the irrational. When an artifact or trace of an activity can be directly linked with the quest for food, bodily comfort, or safety then it passes as economic (which is to say, rational). But when an artifact defies a crudely materialist interpretation, when it seems bizarre or inexplicable or non-utilitarian, or—better yet—when it smacks of belief in gods, the afterlife, or some other fanciful sphere, only then does it enter into discussions of religious ritual. Needless to say, this is an overwhelmingly secular position, for it places all of religion in the past by stigmatizing it as a fallacy that humankind is gradually correcting.

The critique is obvious. No one has ever believed in illusions; everyone believes in the real world as they perceive it really to be. Moreover, no one acts irrationally; everyone's actions are performed for reasons that are, from the actor's perspective, entirely reasonable. Within archaeology, Joanna Brück (1999) provides an especially frank consideration of the implications of this critique, noting how the analytical division between secular and ritual spheres slips into a division between rationality and irrationality that has been mapped onto the division between Western and non-Western societies as part of the legitimizing discourse of European colonialism. The situation is irredeemable, she concludes. Rather than study ritual, Brück advises archaeologists to devote their energies to the study of alternative rationalities.

A few archaeologists are exploring a more radical escape strategy. Ben Alberti and colleagues (Alberti and Bray 2009; Alberti and Marshall 2009; Alberti et al.

2011) have proposed that we abandon epistemological questions of religious belief altogether and turn instead toward more fundamental matters of ontology. What might be gained, they ask, were we to seek out alternative worlds in the past as opposed to alternative worldviews? This is not a simple proposition. Alberti intends it as an explicit provocation aimed to uproot a paired set of premises that have always underwritten the secular modern project. First premise: there is one reality, a singular nature, defined by Western scientists. Second premise: there is a multiplicity of cultural perspectives on that single reality, a multiplicity of belief systems (i.e., religions) that inevitably cloak nature in illusions to a greater or lesser degree. Alberti rejects these premises; he rejects the use of Western understandings of causation, agency, personhood, and the like as the standards by which the relative irrationality of non-Westerners and premoderns is to be judged. His pluralization of ontology marks a purposeful effort to cut anchor and set us adrift, stripped of the secular modern rudders (prominently, the category of religion) that have always guided us back toward familiar waters.

Practically speaking, this approach effectively does away with religion as an analytical endpoint. Rather than seeking insight into Neolithic Levantine religion or Aztec religion or Mississippian religion, we are now encouraged to develop understandings of Neolithic or Aztec or Mississippian *worlds*, each with its own sorts of agents, powers, relations, and structures, each with its own understandings of what it means to act practically, rationally, and effectively. The archaeology of religion in this way becomes a project of registering the dissonance between the modernist category of religion and the nonmodern world into which it has been inserted. It becomes a project of successively moving away from "religion" toward some other, historically specific category that maps out the social relations between people and things in some other, overtly nonmodern and nonsecular fashion.

A postsecular archaeology of premodern religion, then, might be imagined as an entirely parochial endeavor that seeks, quite deliberately, to scrape and pick away at its own founding premise—religion's universality—by underscoring the non-translatability of modernist categories, eventually arriving at a new, locally defined category made legible by the ways in which it is "not religion." Broadly speaking, this is the methodology followed in the present study. My goal, however, is neither particularism nor relativism nor local understanding. Nor is it a clearer portrayal of the past, per se. Each time we tamper with religion in premodern times, we intervene in modernist understandings of religion's future in the most general terms, which is to say that to unpack premodern religion as an archaeological category, even in individual case studies, is to help unpack secularism itself. I hope, in the end, to make a small contribution to this larger project.

Again, archaeologists have important—even essential—contributions to make to anthropology's critical analysis of secularism precisely because they are the only members of the discipline whose research continues to focus on premodernity. There was a time when sociocultural anthropologists spent a great deal of time talking about the premodern, the traditional, and the primitive. They classified and compared premodernities, assigned evolutionary positions to non-Western peoples, and critically engaged Western grand narratives outlining the rise of civilization. In hindsight, it is easy to look down our noses at such work. Certainly, many early and mid-twentieth-century ethnographers were caught up in colonial logics to a degree they must not have appreciated at the time. But the subsequent critiques of this disciplinary heritage have resulted in a fresh crop of problems. Is it not the case, for instance, that the wholesale rejection of older evolutionary typologies—from Lewis Henry Morgan's savagery-barbarism-civilization scheme to the egalitarian-ranked-stratified-state model of Morton Fried—has led many sociocultural anthropologists to fall back upon an even cruder narrative of human social development? Having washed their hands of serious inquiry into the world as it was prior to European colonialism and the rise of global capitalism, many now seem fated to write and rewrite a much simplified book with only two chapters: chapter 1, the premodern; chapter 2, the modern. Once, all the world was premodern (precapitalist, precolonial, pre-nation-statist). Then, it became modern (capitalist, colonial, filled with nation-states). The two terms stand at arm's length just as ethnographers and archaeologists stand at arm's length in anthropology departments. Regardless of whether the rupture of modernization is presented in tragic or even dystopian terms, is this not its own blunt form of unilineal evolutionism? Are two evolutionary stages really better than four?

Unilineal evolutionism, ironically, is implicit in a great deal of contemporary anthropology, even among those who have been especially harsh critics of mid-twentieth-century evolutionary theory. Time and again I have heard anthropologists critique modernity through a vague comparison with the premodern world, as if premodernity were a kind of totality about which one could generalize, a totality that need not be interrogated beyond the simple conclusion that it is (or was) everything the modern is not. Even Asad, one of our most subtle critics of great divides and grand narratives, is not free from such statements. "Secularism," he has written,

> is not simply an intellectual answer to a question about enduring social peace and toleration. It is an enactment by which a *political medium* (representation of citizenship) redefines and transcends particular and differentiating practices of the self that are articulated through class, gender, and religion. In contrast, the process of mediation enacted in "premodern" societies includes ways in which the state mediates local identities without aiming at transcendence. (Asad 2003:5)

I want to put to the side what Asad is claiming in positive terms about secularism as well as his larger critique of the rhetoric of religious tolerance and focus instead on what he sets up as secularism's foil. Secularism is defined, in part, through a negative comparison with premodern societies, a category Asad uses with visible discomfort. Premodern is put in scare quotes, and Asad hedges by observing that the process of mediation in premodern societies merely includes ways of exerting state control without redefining and transcending difference. This is a strange statement. First, we are presented with an image of premodernity in the singular, insofar as Asad talks of a premodern "process of mediation" rather than an array of variable processes. Second, we are left wondering whether this premodern process, which is said to employ different strategies, also includes state modes of mediation that *do* aim at the transcendence of local identities. Presumably not, for this would introduce the possibility of a species of premodern secularism, an oxymoron for most commentators on the subject (but see chapter 3). One can only conclude, then, that Asad's hedging and ambiguity signal his discomfort at relying upon the very divide between modern and premodern that he elsewhere seeks to question.

It should go without saying that "modern" and "premodern," while ideologically linked, are not in the slightest way comparable categories on the ground. The modern may have diverse local manifestations, but it is still drawn into a kind of historical singularity through the insidious effects of colonialism, global capitalism, industrialization, nation-state building, and international warfare. The premodern is a radically heterogeneous congeries of historically unrelated phenomena. To compare modern and premodern is not to compare apples and oranges. It is to compare apples with vast orchards of oranges, plums, pomegranates, kiwis, strawberries, and any number of other fruits that no one alive today has ever seen or tasted. And it is this fact of radical premodern pluralism that sociocultural anthropology has generally ceased to consider in any depth. In Asad's work, for instance, the premodern often seems to be synonymous with medieval Christian and Islamic societies—these, at least, are his primary foils to the modern. However, it is at precisely this point that archaeologists need to raise their hands and remind the discipline not only that premodernity includes a great deal more than just the Abrahamic traditions, but also that the modernist discourse of the West has always, in practice, *relied upon* particular understandings of premodern heterogeneity to construct its master narratives of secularization.

The Myth of Eternal Return

Here is the crux of the problem as I see it: we have misrepresented the narrative structure of Western storytelling about the emergence of the modern world. We have wrongly concluded, first, that the modernist master narrative is linear, and second, that the narrative is premised upon a single great divide marking the emergence of the modern out of the premodern, of us out of them. As Webb Keane (2007:48) puts it, "[T]he idea of modernity commonly seems to include two distinctive features: rupture from a traditional past, and progress into a better future." One rupture (A → B), marking a great leap of human progress. Not surprisingly, this rupture is typically positioned somewhere during the early modern period: in the sixteenth-century religious reforms of the Protestants, in the rationalism of the seventeenth-century philosophers, or in the eighteenth-century humanism of Enlightenment scholars. "The European history of ecclesiastical withdrawal from secular politics and from secular intellectual problems to specialised religious spheres is the history of this whole movement from primitive to modern," observes Mary Douglas (1988[1966]:92), expressing a common position.

For Douglas, as for so many others, the movement from premodern to modern involved a process of differentiation in which formerly unified societies became fragmented into a number of incommensurable realms. Modern societies, generally speaking, aspire toward a world in which religious authority is kept separate from political authority; political interests are kept out of the objective production of scientific knowledge; the economic marketplace is kept free from state intervention; and the renouncing of idolatry keeps the boundary between people and things sharply drawn. Thus has modernization become equated with specialization, compartmentalization, and the purification of categories to the point that modern individuals are said to regard thinking and knowing as a matter of pulling apart wholes into discrete elements (Douglas 1988[1966]:78). "Break it down for me," says the CEO to his team of analysts in an epistemological mode that has not changed significantly since the eighteenth-century efforts of Linnaeus to know nature by parsing it into ever-finer taxonomic divisions.

Latour (1993) offers the most ambitious critique of this narrative of modernization, not by challenging the intimate link between modernity and purification but by arguing that purification must be understood as ideology rather than practice. On the ground, he suggests, modernity has been characterized by the *intensified* blurring of categories. This is the great paradox of modern society in Latour's reading: the more we tell ourselves that religion, politics, and economics are discrete, the more we mix them with impunity. It is a brilliant analysis, but a brilliant analysis of only half the story for it directs all its critical attention toward the triumphalist account of modernity's emergence from premodernity.

What is missing is an appreciation of all the ideological work the notion of premodernity has traditionally performed. Indeed, if modernist narratives really were as clear-cut as many suggest, if they really were built upon notions of forward flight and the wholesale sloughing off of the illusions of the past, then it would be difficult to understand how these narratives became so potent. How has modernity come to appear natural and necessary if its links to the past have been severed? Upon what grounds have modernist narratives succeeded in countering alternative narratives asserting different sorts of futures? If modernists claim that history is a progression from A to B, how have they fended off altermodernists who have instead claimed $A \rightarrow C$ or $A \rightarrow D$? Such questions highlight the limitations of a historical imaginary that truly is linear, that truly does privilege the new.

This is why modernist narratives, in practice, rarely are linear. On the contrary, most adhere to a tripartite structure characterized by *two* great divides in which an original condition, a deep past, anticipates a future condition to which society is now returning: $A^1 \rightarrow B \rightarrow A^2$ with A^1 representing the primitive or natural condition,

B a period of deviation, and A^2 the emerging present or future condition that has been made to appear legitimate insofar as it reinstates a supposedly natural order of things. There is always, in other words, a third chapter. Premodernity is necessarily divided in two. And it is through circularity and the logic of return—return to the primitive, albeit in updated or perfected form—that most modernist narratives have gained rhetorical purchase.

Consider one of anthropology's founding texts: Lewis Henry Morgan's *Ancient Society* (1974[1877]). Disdained by many anthropologists as a relic of the discipline's colonialist past, Morgan's account of humanity's development from savagery to barbarism to civilization is typically considered one more example of the Victorian infatuation with progress and linear evolutionary development. Those who take this position have their reasons. A great deal of *Ancient Society* is devoted to inventorying the gradual accumulation of technological and institutional know-how that led to the emergence of ever more civilized societies: stone tools, fire, dugout canoes, civil law, coinage, poetry, religious freedom, common schools, the use of coal, the electric telegraph, and on and on. Civilization, for Morgan, was an additive process, to be sure. Society advanced by building upon the achievements of the former age, and modern man was a giant because he stood on the shoulders of primitives.

But this is not what made *Ancient Society* into an instant classic. The linearity of Morgan's account was hardly the source of its appeal. Rather, it was the powerfully circular manner in which he framed his conclusions that caused such a stir. Indeed, Morgan was one of the key architects of the teleological position that liberal democracy was both humankind's original condition and its future destiny. "Democracy," he wrote in *Ancient Society*, "once universal in a rudimentary form and repressed in many civilized states, is destined to become again universal and supreme" (Morgan 1974[1877]:351).

> A mere property career is not the final destiny of mankind, if progress is to be the law of the future as it has been of the past. The time which has passed away since civilization began is but as a fragment of the past duration of man's existence; and but a fragment of the ages to come. The dissolution of society bids fair to become the termination of a career of which property is the end and aim, because such a career contains the elements of self-destruction. Democracy in government, brotherhood in society, equality in rights...and universal education, foreshadow the next higher plane of society to which experience, intelligence and knowledge are steadily tending. It will be a revival, in a higher form, of the liberty, equality and fraternity of the ancient gentes. (Morgan 1974[1877]:562)

The deployment of circularity here is profound. As in the past, so too in the future; statements such as these resonated with many nineteenth-century intellectuals. Engels, for example, concluded *The Origin of the Family, Private Property and the State* by quoting the same passage: "It will be a revival, in a higher form, of the liberty, equality and fraternity of the ancient gentes. The End" (Engels 1902[1884]:217). It was a kind of "amen" endorsement that others were quick to second. Morgan, in short, was considered to be completing Marxist thought by providing an image of primitive communism that pre-echoed the anticipated future ($A^1 \rightarrow B \rightarrow A^2$).

Morgan and his followers were hardly unique in their reliance upon circular histories to advance a progressive politics. Any number of other chroniclers of modernity's emergence out of premodernity could be used to illustrate the same point, from the philosophes of the eighteenth century to the posthumanists of the present. There is a more important observation to be made, though. While the logic of return is common to many modernist narratives, its earliest and most profound expression appeared in accounts of the history of religion. Beginning with the initial Protestant critiques of the papacy, many theologians and scholars have promoted particular visions of "true religion" both through a contrast with the "false religion" of the recent past (the logic of rupture) *and* through an exposition on the purity, innocence, and naturalness of religion as it was in the deep past (the logic of return). Indeed, the very structure of $A^1 \rightarrow B \rightarrow A^2$ might be regarded as having been modeled on much older Abrahamic notions of human transgression followed by a renewed covenant with God. Be that as it may, one can hardly overestimate the insidious influence of the simple claim that a true and original religion, long since corrupted, must now be reestablished.

To appreciate the impact of this claim, we must know something about its history. Wilfred Cantwell Smith has traced the genealogy of the Western concept of "true religion" with care, documenting the key shift during the seventeenth century from an earlier understanding of religion (*religio*) as Christian piety to a subsequent pluralization of religion in which there were many different systems of belief, directed toward different deities, that could be critically compared. "The plural arises," argues Smith (1978[1962]:40), "when one contemplates from the outside, and abstracts, depersonalizes, and reifies, the various systems of other people of which one does not oneself see the meaning or appreciate the point." To pluralize religion is to externalize the world itself and to assume the position of the objective outside observer with the transcendent authority to evaluate the relative truth or falsity of other peoples' ways of life. Thus did the pluralization of religion—particularly within the Protestant tradition—play a key role in the emergence of a distinctively secular worldview (Smith 1978[1962]:44; see also Asad 1993; Masuzawa 2005).

Assessments of the truth or falsity of other peoples' religions were never based on conviction alone, however, but also on particular constructions of religion's original nature. "Since at least the Reformation," notes David Haycock (2002:140), "religious practice at its most ancient was widely considered by Protestant theologians and apologists to have been 'more' true—or at least less corrupt—than modern religious practice, and that by examining ancient texts and chronologies, this true state of worship could be rediscovered, modern corruptions and adhesions removed, and true Christian worship re-established." Again, there is nothing linear about this strategy.

To break with the medieval past and inaugurate a reformed or enlightened present ($...B \rightarrow A^2$), one depended on conceptions of a prior rupture between an original inviolate religion and the corrupted forms that succeeded it ($A^1 \rightarrow B...$).

For Protestants, deists, and other anti-clerical critics of the early modern period, the protagonists in this first great historical rupture were, without question, the priests. "I suppose none will deny but that Priests have introduced Superstition and Idolatry, as well as sown Quarrels and Dissentions where-ever they came," wrote Lord Cherbury in 1663 (quoted in Haycock 2002:144). Born in the perfect light of God's revelation, humanity fell into idolatrous corruption only at a later stage, through priestcraft, and this must be undone to return society to the divine fold.

The narrative of corruption did more than simply build a compelling case for clerical reform. It also served as an ideological space where Western intellectuals hammered out the tenets of secularism itself. It was here that Locke built his argument for the necessary separation of church and commonwealth, arguing that state governance is one thing, but "the business of true religion is quite another thing." True religion, he argued, is an entirely private matter that individuals come to only through persuasion and inward reflection, never by force, and the true church should therefore be understood as a voluntary association of freely choosing believers focused on heaven, not on earthly influence and power. "Who sees not how frequently the name of the Church, which was venerable in [the] time of the apostles, has been made use of to throw dust in the people's eyes in the following ages?" (Locke 2003[1685]:408). Such statements operated on multiple levels. First, they drew a sharp conceptual line between religion and politics. Second, they further parsed religion into true and false variants: true religion looked inward and heavenward, unsullied by power struggles on earth; false religion was in bed with politics. Third, and for my purposes most important, both distinctions were mapped onto a tripartite historical narrative: in the beginning, religion and politics were distinct, each attending to its own concerns; in the middle period, both were corrupted by their dangerous miscegenation; today, in the modern era, religion and politics are again returning to their true and discrete positions as a result of Protestant reforms and the spread of liberal democracy.

By the latter half of the eighteenth century, the modernist account of religious history had gained considerable clarity. In 1779, Thomas Jefferson wrote Locke's ideas on tolerance and church-state separation into law, establishing the United States as a model for the new age of secular governance. Powerful arguments in both Enlightenment philosophy and Christian theology added intellectual gravity. Kant's portrayal of religion "within the limits of reason alone" was, of course, particularly influential, but related positions were soon developed in Christian theology itself, notably in the writings of Friedrich Schleiermacher, who wedded the Enlightenment emphasis on individual autonomy with the emotive thrust of German Romanticism. Schleiermacher's *On Religion: Speeches to Its Cultured Despisers* (1996[1799]) was a strange but important defense of religion in which he argued that Christianity was in its truest form in early times before it attained a rigid structure. "Thus it was religion when the ancients…regarded every unique type of life throughout the whole world as the work and reign of an omnipresent being…. It was religion when they rose above the brittle iron age of the world, full of fissures and unevenness, and again sought the golden age on Olympus among the happy life of the gods" (1996[1799]:25). But when the church emerged and instituted orthodox ways of believing and acting, it was, in Schleiermacher's estimation, "a complete departure from its [religion's] characteristic ground" (ibid.). He concluded: "the systematizers have caused all this. Modern Rome, godless but consistent, hurls anathemas and excommunicates heretics; ancient Rome, truly pious and religious in a lofty style, was hospitable to every god and so it became full of gods" (28). In Schleiermacher's theology, ancient polytheism was, ironically, more genuinely Christian than contemporary Catholicism—a response, perhaps, to Hume (1976[1757]), one of the most prominent "cultured despisers" of religion, who had previously offered a much less flattering portrayal of ancient polytheism as the beginning of a long dark history of religious irrationality. But Schleiermacher's praise of a primitive world that was "hospitable to every god" must also be read as part of the evolving Enlightenment discourse on religious tolerance. Indeed, Schleiermacher legitimized the modern struggle for tolerance by claiming that it marked a return to an original state of tolerance, a natural condition of open-armed polytheism prior to the fall into monotheistic dogma.[1]

During the late nineteenth and early twentieth centuries, modernist accounts of religion's history gained further clarity, largely through the tremendous impact of Darwinism and the rush to use an evolutionary approach, broadly conceived, to organize the rapidly expanding archive of world peoples. Major texts by Tylor, Frazer, Durkheim, Malinowski, and others became part of an influential anthropological project to explore the historical implications of ethnographic diversity. As Tylor (1913[1871]:2:408) put it, the anthropological ambition was to replace an older theological speculation on religious origins with a new "ethnographic method in theology" involving empirical observations of the living representatives of ages long past.

However novel its methodology, however expanded its data set, the anthropology of religion nevertheless continued to address long-standing Protestant concerns. Earlier debates over the nature of "true religion" resurfaced as anthropological debates over the essential or fundamental qualities of "primitive religion." In part, this took the form of a great preoccupation with definitions: What, at its heart, is religion? How does it differ from magic? And how do both differ from science? What was religion's original relationship to politics and to the running of society? These were not just academic questions. Early anthropology quite explicitly looked to the primitive to build support for particular claims about the proper course of society in the future. "The science of culture is essentially a reformer's science," wrote Tylor (1913[1871]:2:410). "A return to older starting-points may enable [the anthropologist] to find new paths, where the modern track seems stopped by impassable barriers" (2:402).

Early anthropologists thus struck a delicate balance between praise and condemnation of the primitive world, a reflection of the complex discursive role that primitivity was required to play in the effort to find these new paths. Tylor might write:

> The onward movement from barbarism has dropped behind more than one quality of barbaric character, which cultured modern men look back on with regret, and will even strive to regain by futile attempts to stop the course of history, and restore the past in the midst of the present. So it is with social institutions. The slavery recognized by savage and barbarous races is preferable in kind to that which existed for centuries in late European colonies. The relation of the sexes among many savage tribes is more healthy than among the richer classes of the Mohammedan world. As a supreme authority of government, the savage councils of chiefs and elders compare favourably with the unbridled despotism under which so many cultured races have groaned. The Creek Indians, asked concerning their religion, replied that where agreement was not to be had, it was best to "let every man paddle his canoe his own way"; and after long ages of theological strife and persecution, the modern world seems coming to think these savages not far wrong. (Tylor 1913[1871]:1:26)

But he also was quick to reassure the reader that this was not to say that the primitive world was as moral or enlightened as the modern world. On one hand, then, Tylor's reassertion of the superiority of modernity might be read as buying into the post-Darwinian ideology of inexorable human advance in which the unfolding present is regarded as an inevitable improvement on the past. On the other hand, it is clear that however much the modern stood above the primitive, the primitive somehow still stood above the medieval world. Indeed, the apparent civility of the primitive only arose in comparison to "late European colonies," to the "Mohammedan world," and to the "long ages of theological strife" Europe had just left behind. There is no straight and simple arrow of progress in such statements. Far from it. Tylor was drawing on a familiar trope of historical return: the modern, once again, was presented as breaking with the recent past through a restoration of and improvement upon primitive principles of gender equality, democratic governance, and religious tolerance that had been forsaken.[2]

Needless to say, such claims were subject to ongoing debate. A few decades later, Durkheim offered his own critiques of those who, like Tylor and Morgan, drew unwarranted comparisons between primitive and modern contexts. Durkheim saw no grounds for conceptually equating, for instance, "primitive democracy and that of to-day, the collectivism of inferior societies and actual socialistic tendencies, the monogamy which is frequent in Australian tribes and that sanctioned by our laws, etc." (1965[1915]:114). And yet, when it suited his purposes, Durkheim was entirely willing to make his own circular equations between past and present, notably in his repeated mention of the affinity between the religious aspects of revolutionary populism in France and the totemism of Australian Aborigines. For Durkheim, both were examples of the same effervescent wellspring of religion, sui generis. Note that

Durkheim was not simply making a claim about the universality of the urge toward religion. His claim was more specific and had to do with the comparable "nudity" (Durkheim's term) of the primitive Aborigines and modern political revolutionaries, both of whom were shorn of the "luxuriant vegetation" (presumably, a reference to priestly excesses) that had grown up around and obscured religion's essence in the recent past (1965[1915]:17).

In other contexts, early twentieth-century anthropologists critiqued their predecessors' tendency to discuss primitives as if they were ancient savage philosophers soberly mulling over the metaphysical implications of death and dreams. "Belief in immortality," wrote Malinowski (1948[1925]:51), "is the result of a deep emotional revelation, standardized by religion, rather than a primitive philosophic doctrine." Here, too, we might imagine that Malinowski was registering his opposition to the unwarranted conflation of present and past and to the imposition of modern modes of intellectual thought on a world that had no such traditions. But if Malinowski did away with the image of the primitive philosopher, he was altogether willing to people humanity's origins with a range of other modern professionals. The savage community, he argued elsewhere, contained "both the antiquarian mind" and the "naturalist." Malinowski even claimed that every savage community had its "sociologists" as well—and not just any sort of sociologists, but *functionalists* (like Malinowski) who analyzed and could explain the underlying structure of their tribe's institutions (1948[1925]:35). What was the point of these statements? On the surface, Malinowski clearly sought, in good anthropological fashion, to encourage a sympathetic attitude toward non-Western tribal peoples by translating the unfamiliar into familiar terms. At a deeper level, however, he was participating in the naturalization of historically specific modes of modern intellectual inquiry by presenting them as human enterprises that were present at the very beginning.

Of all the modern professions Malinowski found in the primitive world, the most notable was that of the scientist. "Every primitive community is in possession of a considerable store of knowledge, based on experience and fashioned by reason," he observed (1948[1925]:16). From this, Malinowski concluded that all human communities, past and present, have engaged in scientific inquiry of one sort or another. But Malinowski took this observation a step further by portraying magic—the sine qua non of life "among the Stone Age savages"—as having an especially close kinship with science. Magic, he argued, is "a body of purely practical acts" that draws upon theories, systems of principles, and specific methodologies in a means-ends fashion (1948[1925]:70). It is, as he put it, a sort of pseudo-science, guided by an entirely rational orientation to the world that simply builds from false premises. This was a position Malinowski had inherited from Sir James Frazer, who was more explicit on the subject and had argued at length that primitive magic was "next of kin to science" (or, less flatteringly, "the bastard sister of science") (Frazer 1955[1911–1915]:57).

In pointing to the affinity between magic and science, Malinowski and Frazer simultaneously underscored the difference between magic and religion. For

Malinowski, while magic and religion were both responses to certain life stresses, they operated in very distinct registers. Magic filled technical gaps in knowledge by creating new methods to accomplish entirely straightforward goals, such as hunting or sea travel, whereas religion responded to life crises by positing the presence of supernatural spirits and realms. Magic looked to immanent cause-and-effect relationships, whereas religion posited the existence of another, transcendent world. Hence, Malinowski praised the evolutionary contributions of magic, "which has yet been the best school of man's character" (1948[1925]:90). He offered no comparable praise for religion.

Frazer also privileged magic over religion due to the former's greater similarity to science. In disambiguating magic, religion, and science, he wrote:

> If religion involves, first, a belief in superhuman beings who rule the world, and, second, an attempt to win their favour, it clearly assumes that the course of nature is to some extent elastic or variable, and that we can persuade or induce the mighty beings who control it to deflect, for our benefit, the current of events from the channel in which they would otherwise flow. Now this implied elasticity or variability of nature is directly opposed to the principles of magic as well as of science, both of which assume that the processes of nature are rigid and invariable in their operation...both of which take for granted that the course of nature is determined, not by the passions or caprice of personal beings, but by the operation of immutable laws acting mechanically. (Frazer 1955[1911–1915]:58–59)

Thus when Frazer (65–66) wrote of a progression from an original age of magic to a subsequent age of religion that is now giving way to an age of modern rationality, he charted a complicated back-and-forth motion: from quasi-science to anti-science to true science, from materialism to spirituality to materialism, from the rational to the irrational to the rational.

Such arguments had an air of prophecy about them that drew upon deep Christian themes of original innocence, transgression/corruption, and rebirth/reform. Nowhere is this clearer than in the work of Durkheim, whose implicit anti-clericalism was coupled with a studied respect for religion's contributions to social life generally. Durkheim lamented the fact that religion rang false for modern society and that religious abuses had led many critics toward an empty atheism. Christianity's failings must not be taken as an indictment of religion as a general phenomenon, he argued, for to indict religion is to indict society itself. Rather, we must await religion's rebirth in new form: "In a word, the old gods are growing old or already dead, and others are not yet born.... [But this situation] cannot last forever. A day will come when our societies will know again those hours of creative effervescence, in the course of which new ideas and new formulae are found which serve for a while as a guide to humanity" (Durkheim 1965[1915]:475).

Suffice it to say that the basic notions defining secular modernity—democracy, universal human rights, gender equality, materialism, scientific rationality, and especially the privatization and depoliticization of religion—were all crafted through a particular historical discourse that was much more than the simple unidirectional story of liberation and successive enlightenment. The modern world was rendered natural and legitimate through a more complicated narrative involving the corruption of an original, quasi-modern project that must now be reestablished and perfected. The individual plotlines have varied: eighteenth-century Protestants may have claimed to be purging religion of its recent corruptions in an effort to reestablish a pure and original form of Christianity, while nineteenth-century anthropologists may have claimed that modern science was shedding religious illusions altogether and returning humanity to its original quasi-scientific, quasi-secular agenda. Either way, a common underlying structure prevailed. By and large, modernist narratives saw history as a progression from true to false to true, $A^1 \rightarrow B \rightarrow A^2$.

Let me leap now to the issue that perplexes me in all this. Where, I find myself asking, is the supposed linearity of the modernist historical imaginary? Where is the myth of progress? Where are the "mainline narratives of simple, cost-free supersession" that are commonly said to have dominated storytelling since the Enlightenment (Taylor 2007:772)? In the examples just considered, we are clearly not looking at a Hegelian model of history with its relentless movement forward toward an unprecedented future (divinely ordained or not). The tripartite division of history into a primitive origin, a corrupted middle period, and a reformed present is not a classic dialectical process. We might even describe it as a movement from thesis to antithesis to *anti-antithesis*—a movement forward that is simultaneously a movement backward. Why has this patently circular narrative structure not been given greater attention?

Part of the answer may have to do with the tendency in contemporary criticism to lump premodernity into a single category and to focus exclusively on claims of an early modern rupture that has liberated us from the shackles of the premoderns. More often than not, the critic attempts to undercut certain perceived dualisms in modernist narratives—past versus present, enchantment versus disenchantment, intolerance versus tolerance, tyranny versus democracy—by asserting either that these dualisms do not exist or that, if they do, it would be wrong to read them as a triumphal progression from a lesser to a more enlightened condition. Either the division between premodern and modern is challenged or the historical movement from one to the other is recoded as an undesirable and alienating fall from grace. Regardless, the critique is typically directed at a stereotyped Whig history.

When the logic of return *is* acknowledged, it tends to be presented as an antimodern gesture rather than one that is fundamentally modern. There is, of course, a significant literature discussing the manner in which constructed images of enlightened primitives or noble savages have been used to critique Western society or to express cynicism regarding its trajectory (Ellingson 2001; Pagden 1982). But I am arguing something different. It was not just the anti-moderns who turned their gaze backward toward the primitive, the pagan, and the primordial. The past was not merely a source of romantic nostalgia. And neo-paganism or neo-tribalism cannot be reduced to a simple case of the return of the repressed, as Charles Taylor (2007:612–613) has made it out to be. On the contrary, the logic of return lies at the heart of the logic of progress. Primitivists go backward to go backward. Modernists go backward to go forward.

Ironically, we are left with an understanding of the modern historical imagination that is strikingly close to that of the natives in so many early twentieth-century assessments. Consider Mircea Eliade's (1974) classic description of the "archaic man" who rejects history, devalues the passage of time, and lives his life as an endless reenactment of mythical archetypes. He does so, Eliade tells us, to overcome the existential terror of history, to overcome the fear of losing himself in the endless cascade of new moments and altered essences. To acknowledge history, in other words, is to accept constant change and to risk undermining being itself, insofar as history robs the individual of stable forms and a stable self. This is why the primitive indulged in rituals of cosmic rebirth and why he repressed memories of the past as a series of unique events. "Archaic humanity...defended itself, to the utmost of its powers, against all the novelty and irreversibility which history entails" (1974:48). Primitives were people without history by design, deploying eternal archetypes as a strategy to preserve the self (cf. Lévi-Strauss 1966:233–234). "Hence we are justified," argues Eliade (1974:91–92), "in speaking of an archaic ontology, and it is only by taking this ontology into consideration that we can succeed in understanding—and hence in not scornfully dismissing—even the most extravagant behavior on the part of the primitive world; in fact, this behavior corresponds to a desperate effort not to lose contact with *being*."

Exactly who is Eliade talking about in such statements, "archaic man" or "twentieth-century man"? Who stands trembling before the terror of history, the primitive or the modern intellectual writing in the wake of two devastating world wars and the first apocalyptic deployment of nuclear weaponry? Who is consumed with archetypes, the savage or the anthropologist who pores over travelers' reports like tea leaves, searching for that which is elemental, natural, or original in the human experience?

There is a core paradox here. We regularly assume that the modernist conception of history is progressive and linear. We may mark the beginnings of this conception differently: with Judaism's reinterpretation of history as God's progressive intervention in the world, with Enlightenment renderings of universal history as a process of successive liberation, or with Darwin's radically non-teleological account of the origin of the species. Regardless, the claim that the modernist temporality is linear goes unquestioned. And yet, as we have seen, there is nothing linear about many of the specific historical narratives that this intellectual tradition has produced. Quite the contrary. Modernist histories promote an ideology of progress by providing us with ironic accounts of a future return to human origins in which something natural—that is, something essential and unchanging—is recovered.

The incongruity is not between the ideology of progress and the real, on-the-ground history it claims to represent, however incongruous these two things may be. The incongruity plays itself out *within the ideology of progress itself.* Primitives, we are told, suffer historical events in a linear, irreversible fashion and yet they seek to deny this irreversibility through myths of eternal return. But the modernist alternative does not present us with a temporality in which real and imagined histories have become any more aligned. Instead, we seem to be presented with a picture of a modern world that experiences history in a circular fashion and yet struggles to deny this circularity by promoting its own myths of progress. Our history is circular, but we somehow manage to convince ourselves it is linear; their history is linear, but they tell themselves, again and again, it is circular.

For the time being, it is enough to emphasize that there have always been two great divides in the modernist master narrative, and the emergence of modern secular society has always been presented as a return to an original, quasi-secular, quasi-modern project. We are not faced with a linear progressivist evolution, then, but with a classic myth of eternal return, reliant on tropes of reformation and renewed covenants that are obscured when, in a critical mode, we focus solely on the latter half of the story. Dazzled by the violent lunge of the tiger (the logic of rupture), we blind ourselves to the fact that the tiger is chasing its own tail (the logic of return) (figure 1.1).

Primitive Religion and the Burden of Archaeology

Let us turn to consider archaeology's participation in all of this. If much is at stake in accounts of deep antiquity, if this has always been the space where the modern secular project grounded and naturalized its visions of the future, what happened when curiosity drove scholars to put spade in soil and sift through the actual material remains of the ancient world?

To adequately address this question we must go back to archaeology's antiquarian beginnings in England and its links to the larger Enlightenment project.[3] In a superb study, David Haycock (2002) has outlined not only the extent to which Protestant scholarship in seventeenth-century England was invested in writing a religious history of Britain that was independent of Roman Catholic ties, but also the notable role played by antiquarians such as William Stukeley in this project. It was they, notes Haycock, who sought to lend archaeological support to Protestant notions of a true and original Christianity that had existed prior to its corruption by the Catholic Church—a true and original Christianity that was indigenous, not to Israel or Rome, but to the British Isles. Thus arose a deep English fascination with ancient Druidic religion at sites like Stonehenge and Avebury that has persisted into the present.

For many seventeenth- and eighteenth-century antiquarians, ancient Druidic religion stood as an exemplar of the pure and original form of Christianity to which Protestants were now returning. Their thinly veiled agenda was to solidify the critique of papal authority by demonstrating that the ancient Britons had known the

The narrative of rupture

Premodern	⟹	Modern
Religious ontology		Scientific ontology
Religion as public theater		Religion as private belief
Politicized religion		De-politicized religion
Religious intolerance		Religious tolerance
Theocratic despotism		Secular democracy

The narrative of return

Primitive	⟹	Premodern	⟹	Modern
Magical ontology		Religious ontology		Scientific ontology
• world-embracing (fetishistic)		• world-renouncing (theistic)		• world-embracing (naturalistic)
• materialism		• spiritualism		• materialism
• immanence		• transcendence		• immanence
• rational (though flawed)		• irrational		• rational
Religion as private reflection		Religion as public theater		Religion as private belief
• "ancient savage philosophers"		• orthodox clergy		• modern philosophers
Pre-political religion		Politicized religion		De-politicized religion
• religion as effervescence		• religion as exploitation		• religion as effervescence
Polytheism		Religious intolerance		Religious tolerance
Primitive democracy		Theocratic despotism		Secular democracy

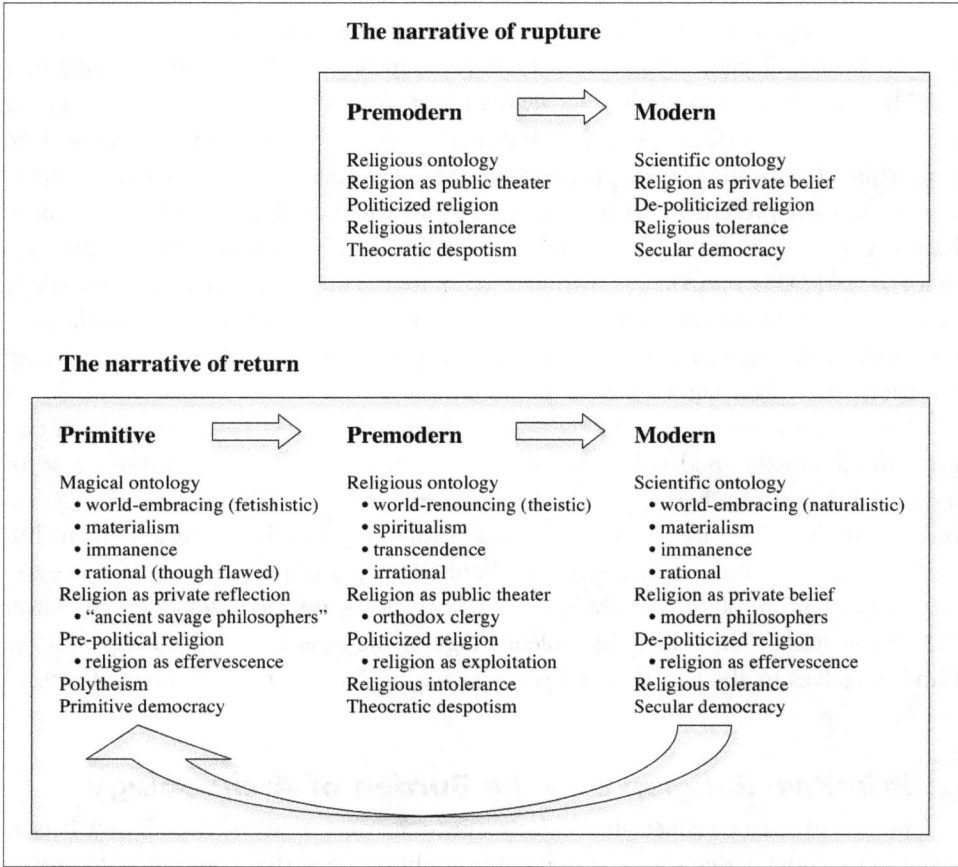

Figure 1.1. Two metanarratives of modernization and secularization. The first, emphasizing rupture, is linear. The second, emphasizing return, is circular.

gospel, as Henry Rowlands put it in 1723, "in the earliest Years of Christianity, even before *Rome* itself," and this task was to be accomplished through, among other methods, investigation into "Erections, Monuments, and Ruins; Idifices and Inscriptions" (quoted in Haycock 2002:113, 135). In this way, Protestantism, nationalism, and an emergent study of archaeology all became intimately linked. "The study of British history," observes Haycock (114), "was significant in the early modern period on at least two grounds: it served to prove and defend the independence and antiquity of the Church of England, and it returned true Christian (i.e., Protestant) worship to the original dictates of Christianity at its very earliest date."

The antiquarians kept good company. No less a figure than Sir Isaac Newton mused over the significance of archaeological sites as evidence of a lost Eden of sorts in which spirituality and scientific knowledge flourished in true and pure forms. "It's certain that ye old religion of the Egyptians," he wrote, "was ye true [Noachian] religion tho corrupted before the age of Moses by the mixture of fals Gods with that of ye true one" (quoted in Gaukroger 1991:192). Newton, quite clearly, did not hold a linear conception of historical progress; in no way did he regard the ancient remains of Egypt and other parts of the world as primitive relics underscoring the theological and scientific advances made by the modern age. Rather, Newton looked to archaeological sites as evidence of a past sophistication, long since degraded, that he and his colleagues were struggling to reestablish. He was convinced, for instance, that the heliocentric understanding of the universe—that most jarring of scientific revelations during the sixteenth and seventeenth centuries—must have been known to the earliest civilizations, and he claimed to find evidence of this in ancient sites like Stonehenge and Solomon's Temple (Haycock 2002:154–156).

It was Stukeley, however, who pioneered the study of British monuments and used this research to promote a circular view of history in which pre-Roman and post-Reformation Britain were conceptually equated. The Druids, in Stukeley's analysis, were Phoenician colonists who brought the "true, patriarchal religion," as originally revealed by God, to England during the time of Abraham: "Therefore they brought along with them the patriarchal religion, which was so extremely like Christianity, that in effect it differ'd from it only in this; they believed in a Messiah who was to come into the world, as we believe in him that is come...the Druids were of *Abraham's* religion intirely, at least in the earliest times, and worshipp'd the supreme Being in the same manner as he did" (Stukeley 1740:2). Elsewhere, Stukeley (1763:8) even went so far as to refer to Abraham as a Druid—indeed, as the "first Druid."

There are two important points to make in regard to Stukeley's thesis. First, he was among the first to collect archaeological data in response to pointed research questions. Stukeley excavated and took careful measurements of Stonehenge, for instance, to demonstrate that it was laid out using an Egyptian cubit measuring system, and this explicit deployment of material evidence permits us to speak of him as among the world's first archaeologists in the modern sense. Second, Stukeley's research conformed very closely to the modernist narrative structure in which, as we have seen, the intended reforms of the present are cast as a grand return to the purity of origins. Stukeley's archaeological model of patriarchal religion, in this sense, was very much in keeping with the writings of anti-papal critics such as Voltaire, who outlined the history of religion in bolder (and more acerbic) terms:

> Men are surely blind and singularly unfortunate to prefer an absurd and bloody religion, supported by hangmen and surrounded with pyres; a religion that can only be approved by those to whom it gives power and riches; a restricted religion that is received in only a part of the world, to a simple and universal religion, that the *chris-ticoles* themselves confess was the religion of mankind in the time of Seth, Enoch, and Noah. *If the religion of the first patriarchs is true, then the religion of Jesus is false.* (Voltaire 1974:213, emphasis added)

Voltaire, like Stukeley, was a deist and a Freemason, and both were wedded to the tripartite vision of history that dominated eighteenth-century thought in Europe. Both, in other words, took for granted that there were two great divides that structured the evolution of religion and society. As Stukeley put it in his monograph on Avebury: "in all accounts of the first beginnings of nations, they had the first religion: 'till as every where, time, richness, politeness and prosperity bring on corruption in church and state" (quoted in Haycock 2002:184). A fall into corruption, then, marked the first divide. The second divide involved a more recent—indeed, an emergent— return to the fold, a return to a true religion, purged of political machinations.

Needless to say, Stukeley's archaeological research into the history of religion cannot be divorced from its British context. In the United States, where modern Euro-Americans and the region's ancient inhabitants were historically separated by a gulf of colonialism, the nationalistic interest in archaeological remains necessarily led in different directions. And yet, there too the logic of return repeatedly structured commentary on the archaeological past. Thus it was repeatedly insisted that ancestral Native Americans originally descended from the lost tribes of Israel, that they had since degenerated, and that they must now return to the true faith through European and Euro-American guidance. By the early nineteenth century, speculation about actual archaeological sites gave rise to a more insidious narrative in which the monumental earthen mounds of the Ohio and Mississippi valleys were interpreted as the remains of a glorious original civilization (more often than not an originally white civilization) that had, at some point in the late pre-Columbian period, fallen before the savage ancestors of the modern Native Americans (Silverberg 1986). Indian removal policies and expanding Euro-American colonialism were thereby justified as a return to white, Christian control of the continent.

As Anglophone archaeology became increasingly empirical during the middle and late nineteenth century, these sorts of arguments came under repeated attack. Well distanced from the bloody religious battles of the seventeenth century, still unaware of the world wars that would create an existential crisis in the twentieth century, dazzled by the scientific and economic gains of industrialization and colonialism, Victorian scholarship reached new heights of confidence in the inevitable march of human progress. If ever there was a time when modernist narratives actually were linear, it was during this period, particularly following the publication of *On the Origin of Species* in 1859. Countering early modern models of human degeneration briefly became a major charge for both anthropologists and archaeologists. Among the latter, Sir John Lubbock offered one of the most influential critiques. First published in 1865 and reprinted many times, his *Pre-Historic Times* wove together ethnographic and archaeological evidence to argue—more in the style of Herbert Spencer than Darwin—that humanity has consistently progressed and will continue to progress toward not only more sophisticated technology but also greater happiness and moral virtue (Lubbock 1892[1865]:599–601). (Not incidentally, Lubbock was a banker by profession during an extended period of economic growth and prosperity in Britain.)

Lubbock's argument for linear and uniform human progress shone brightest when he discussed technology and the age-by-age growth of knowledge regarding materials and techniques. It was he who first introduced terms like "Paleolithic," "Mesolithic," and "Neolithic" into archaeological discourse. When it came to the history of religion, however, his faith in the inexorability of progress wavered. Lubbock's position on the history of religion was clearly modeled on Comte's (1880[1830]) positive philosophy, and Lubbock made the same convoluted effort to fit the entire history of religion into a single uniform movement toward an ever more transcendent conception of the divine. For Lubbock, as for Comte, the most primitive Paleolithic societies lived in a world of pure immanence; every object was naively imagined to be its own god or spirit and to be coercible as such (Lubbock 1892[1865]:206). The evolution of religion, then, was understood as the process by which these fetishistic object-gods gradually became more abstract, more powerful, and more withdrawn from the physical world, ultimately becoming the arbiters of morality and the afterlife rather than agents who interfered with the mechanical and scientifically predictable running of things on earth. Comte had argued that religion and science are two sides of a common evolutionary coin: it is only as God becomes truly supernatural that the natural world is liberated of fetishism and becomes available to true scientific study (cf. Gauchet 1999). Lubbock concurred (cf. Lubbock 1892[1865]:373).

And yet, the old Protestant story of corruption and reform lived on in the margins, showing its face in Lubbock's occasional references to striking deviations from the ideal progression of events. Pre-Columbian Mexico and Peru—in short, all of the New World's indigenous state societies—had strayed from the path, leading them instead "to a religion of terror, which finally became a terrible scourge of humanity" (Lubbock 1892[1865]:385). So too had medieval Europe lapsed back into "the dark belief in witchcraft, which led to thousands of executions, and hung like a black pall over the Christianity of the middle ages" (386–387). Such statements remind us that much of the talk of linear progress during the late nineteenth century was simultaneously haunted by an imperial nightmare of the inevitable cycle of civilization's growth, spiritual corruption, and collapse. This is especially apparent in the morbid fascination with ancient ruins that was widespread among both Europeans and Euro-Americans of the period. In the shadow of the crumbling facade of a Mayan temple or a Mississippian mound, white colonial societies found both mysterious civilizations of the past as well as gloomy harbingers of a future in which another collapse into barbarism seemed unavoidable (Miller 1994). Even when it was not embraced, the logic of return clung to the modernist imaginary as ruins cling to the land.

Compared with the largely speculative and romantic musings of the preceding two centuries, twentieth-century archaeology might reasonably be described as an altogether novel scholarly pursuit. This, of course, was the period of archaeology's professionalization in academic departments and, later, in cultural resource management firms. It was also, more significantly, the heady period when a great many methodological advances led to the collection of a vast array of new types of data.

While remarkable in and of itself, the expansion of archaeological data sets becomes all the more so when compared with simultaneous trends in sociocultural anthropology, which could be said to have *lost* its evolutionary data sets over this same period as critiques of ethnology's primitivist underpinning led many scholars to question whether contemporary non-Western peoples could really provide any insight at all into humanity's prior evolutionary stages (see Fabian 1983). Indeed, by the 1980s, archaeologists had fully replaced ethnographers as the anthropological specialists of the premodern, and their claims were increasingly bolstered by an ever-expanding arsenal of analytical techniques.

What effect did this have on the way archaeologists theorized religion? Ironically, the rise of a truly scientific archaeology and the amassing of new data did little to alter the well-worn anti-clerical story line in which an originally pure religious life came to be progressively corrupted by priests seeking political gain. And it did little to change the overall message of the history of religion: first, that modern society has been right to depoliticize the church and return religion to a matter of private belief, and second, that secularization is the natural fulfillment of a primitive—that is, an originary—agenda.

The idiom, however, was increasingly Marxist rather than Protestant. This is most clearly seen in the widely read work of V. Gordon Childe, whose sweeping early to mid-twentieth-century accounts of Old World prehistory and history firmly established terms like superstructure, ideology, contradiction, and revolution in the archaeological vernacular. Childe did not foreground the history of religion in his work—that position was reserved for the history of technology and economic organization—but his position on the matter was hardly hidden. Childe's understanding of religion's origins combined insights from Frazer and Durkheim. Paleolithic peoples, he argued, deployed principles of sympathetic magic as a pragmatic means of intervening in natural processes, and they also developed the first "germs of religion" (e.g., "sacrifice," "totemic ceremonies and abstinences," and the like) as a means of promoting solidarity among society's members (Childe 1964[1942]:54). Only later, following the development of agriculture, did such "useful illusions" become the monopolies of secret societies and priesthoods, which unleashed their latent potential as tools of economic and political exploitation. Thus did "nebulous and fluid superstitions" come to be transformed into "more rigid forms of theological dogmas, backed up by organized 'churches' and supporting the vested interests of priesthoods, their royal patrons and divine kings" (145).

Like his Victorian predecessors, Childe (1944) wrote of unidirectional human progress as an inevitable reality. Nevertheless, the logic of return remained foundational to his historical reconstructions. Take, for instance, the symmetry in Childe's emphasis on the two great emancipatory struggles in human history, the first of which was undertaken during Paleolithic and early Neolithic times as individuals sought to liberate themselves from subservience to their natural environment. This first struggle sought to separate humanity from animality, a feat that was accomplished partly through technological innovations (stone tools, fire, clothing, domesticated plants) and partly through illusions of spiritual power (principally, sympathetic magic), both of which gave humans control over that which had previously enslaved them: nature. The "Neolithic revolution," in Childe's account, marked the consummation of this emancipatory project (1948[1936]:49, 56). But in good Marxist fashion, Childe also regarded each historical solution as the source of new contradictions. Hence, the very strategies that had liberated human beings from the natural environment ended up enslaving them in the ensuing social environment. On the heels of the Neolithic revolution, technological innovations revealed their vulnerability to monopolization, and religion, for its part, soon slipped from an innocuous source of social solidarity and individual empowerment into a grand ideology legitimizing the elites' control of the masses. In this way, the state became its own hostile and oppressive environment with which the individual was forced to contend. As Paleolithic peoples sought liberation from the processes of nature, so must modern peoples seek liberation from the ideologies and structures of the state.[4]

A similar position was simultaneously developed within American anthropology by Leslie White, also a card-carrying Marxist. Though White primarily drew upon ethnographic rather than archaeological data, his portrayal of the history of religion was, for all intents and purposes, identical to Childe's. Again we are presented with a story in three acts. The history of religion, we are told, began with an initial "tribal" period during which religion offered illusions of control over nature for individuals and promoted social solidarity within human groups. Significantly, the most primitive religions stayed out of politics altogether: "primitive peoples felt for the most part that they could manage [their social affairs] themselves without the interference or the help of the gods" (White 1959:218). All this changed after the agricultural revolution, however, which for White, as for Childe, is the key fulcrum on which human history has teetered. As agricultural communities produced increasing surpluses to be fought over, the community members who had previously served as mere intermediaries between humans and the spirit world gradually asserted themselves as demigods. Shaman became priest and then divine king as religious beliefs released their hidden potential to serve as an ideological tool for political and economic oppression. This dangerous miscegenation of religion and politics—this "marked intrusion of the deities into the social affairs of mankind" (White 1959:218)—is what White referred to as the "state-church," humanity's great transgression that the modern age is finally learning to overthrow.

Most now regard Leslie White as a marginal figure in the intellectual history of sociocultural anthropology, but his influence on American archaeology has been profound, both directly, in the case of key archaeologists, such as Lewis Binford, who studied under him, and indirectly via anthropologists, such as Marshall Sahlins, Elman Service, and Roy Rappaport, who extended aspects of White's evolutionary project and continue to be common reference points for contemporary archaeological theory. Regardless, the important point is that the combined writings of Childe and

White effectively repackaged the old Protestant narrative of religion's historical progression, updating its terminology but not fundamentally altering its overall structure. Rather than speaking in theological terms about an original "true religion" that became corrupted or "false" and that must, through reformation, be returned to its true form, anthropologists were now able to speak more scientifically about "adaptive" early religions that became "maladaptive" and that must, in some sense, become adaptive again. Or they could speak of early religions focused on private matters of concern (shamanism) that became institutionalized and politicized over time by a priestly class (theocracy) and that now, in the modern age, are returning to their private forms once again. Or they could speak of early religions as having been a means of social "integration" that evolved to become a means of elite "legitimization" and that are now returning to the innocuous matter of cultural "integration" (in the sense, for instance, that Christianity is often said to form a common and unifying cultural background for an otherwise secular Europe).

This is not to say that subsequent anthropologists have always discussed the history of religion in precisely these terms. On the contrary, since the 1970s, the discipline has more or less eschewed the very genre of the grand narrative, religious or otherwise. Still, as we have seen, such narratives continue to quietly propagate in the shadows, receiving little or no comment precisely because anthropology's overall account of the history of religion has become fragmented: archaeologists are charged with explaining the evolutionary progression from human origins to the rise of theocratic regimes (i.e., the rise of the archaic state); sociocultural anthropologists are given the task of writing the genealogy of modernity's emergence out of the medieval (i.e., the rise of the liberal democratic state). To the extent that these two histories are kept separate—to the extent, for instance, that archaeologists and sociocultural anthropologists do not contribute to each other's edited volumes—the discipline as a whole is able to replicate the overarching story line without ever confronting it.

But the situation is more complicated yet, because the archaeology of religion has itself become internally specialized and subdivided. Renfrew (1994:50) hinted as much in the early 1990s, observing that during the latter half of the twentieth century, two divergent views of religion emerged within archaeology: a functionalist view that "saw religion as useful in ensuring the smooth functioning of society by ensuring some considerable degree of community of belief, some acceptance of the social system, and hence some general social solidarity among members of the community," and a "Marxist" view that took religion to be "a means, developed by the elite, for the manipulation of the masses." The archaeology of religion has broadened somewhat since then, but the division still captures the lion's share of contemporary research. What Renfrew failed to mention, however, is that these two positions clearly map onto an evolutionary division as well. There is no question that functionalist or Durkheimian theories of religion are far more frequently drawn upon in the study of small-scale band and early village societies while Marxist approaches, loosely conceived, almost always characterize the study of chiefdoms and archaic states. Social scale and complexity, in other words, largely determine the sort of theory archaeologists draw upon to think about religion.

Why is this so? Why are Marxist analyses of hunter-gatherer religions so rare in twentieth-century archaeology? And why are Durkheimian analyses of state religions unheard of?

The answer leads us back to the deep fraternity between archaeology, secularism, and modernity's dominant myth of eternal return. In its portrayal of religious experiences among small-scale prehistoric societies, archaeology continues to produce visions of an original, natural condition—visions upon which secularist narratives have always depended, as we have seen. This is where the discipline has kept alive nineteenth-century discussions of sympathetic magic as a matter of cause-and-effect relations in nature (a proto-science) and of religious ritual as a kind of benign communalism (a proto-nationalism) that integrates the group while staying well clear of the political machinations of individuals (e.g., Coulam and Schroedl 2004; Lipe and Hegmon, ed. 1989). Not surprisingly, discussions of power and ideology rarely occur in the archaeology of simple hunter-gatherers or early agriculturalists. Such matters are reserved for the archaeology of more complex polities, where an extensive literature examines the growth of ancestor cults, ritual violence, the restriction of access to sacred objects and spaces, the transformation of the shaman into a religious elite, and the like (e.g., Bauer 1996; Brumfiel 1998; DeMarrais et al. 1996; Emerson 1996; Knapp 1988; Miller and Tilley 1984).

There are two observations to make regarding the archaeological texts just cited. First, all of them accept without examination the premise that religion is a universal category, an aspect of the human experience with certain fundamental, if difficult to specify, qualities and concerns that can be found in all societies, past and present. Second, they assume that the process of social evolution has not entailed substantial changes to religion's fundamental qualities and concerns (they are, after all, fundamental). "Religion," from this perspective, does not truly evolve; rather, it is religion's relationship with other aspects of the human experience—notably, with politics and economics—that changes. This is how it becomes possible for archaeologists to say, over and over again, that something called religion came to be "intertwined" with something called politics with the rise of complex society.

In the following chapters, I develop a general critique of these assumptions. Here, it will suffice to highlight one text that stands out among archaeological offerings insofar as it explicitly reengages the grand narrative. Brian Hayden's *Shamans, Sorcerers, and Saints: A Prehistory of Religion* (2003) is an ambitious book, designed for a wide readership, that draws upon an ecological approach to chart the history of religion over the past half million years. Hayden's analysis builds from the premise that religion is a strategy used by individuals to promote their self-interest as they seek access to food, shelter, defense, reproduction, comfort, political power, and so on: whatever else it might also be, religion is an effort to derive personal benefits from the world, the study of which Hayden refers to as a "political ecology" of religion.

To be sure, Hayden's approach to religion cannot be used to represent contemporary archaeological research writ large; its materialism is clearly at odds with certain currents of idealism within European archaeological circles, for instance. But those casting stones at ecological approaches such as Hayden's often do so hypocritically, the vehemence of their critiques stemming from an unwillingness to own up to the materialist premises that quietly underwrite their own work. Hayden's special crime, if it can be considered such, is that he is explicit. Regardless, he is perhaps the only modern anthropologist to tackle the full sweep of human religious history and so deserves special attention.

Here are the brief outlines of Hayden's argument. We are told that religious ritual originally evolved during the Middle Paleolithic (if not before) as an adaptation to a dangerous and uncertain natural environment in which there would have been strong selective pressure for practices that enhanced mutual aid. The ecstatic experiences of collective religious ritual, reasons Hayden, would have promoted social bonding, and this would have given evolving human societies a competitive edge early on (see also Hayden 1987). "People that pray together, stay together," he argues in a basically Durkheimian mode (Hayden 2003:32). Alongside the collectivism of early religion, however, were the more individualistic practices of shamans. Early shamans, he suggests, were many things, but their primary function was to serve as "technicians of ecstasy" who managed vital forces that were "much like electricity" and helped sustain the community at large (2003:50–57). There is a familiar comparison between shamanism and modern science—"at the extremes, science and traditional religions that view the world as full of sacred forces seem to have many points in common" (401)—but it is especially interesting that Hayden also draws a comparison between early shamans and modern businessmen. Shamanic rituals, we learn, are pragmatic and goal-oriented; they "sometimes even take on the flavor of business contracts" (10). Echoing descriptions of the entrepreneurial energy of free-market systems, Hayden claims that "shamanism is always about the release of one's wild genius." Of course, he is also careful to distinguish shamanism "from the priestly attempts to control economics and politics that characterize hierarchical religions" (57).

During the Upper Paleolithic, hunter-gatherers in a few regions became more sedentary and hierarchical, and it is at this evolutionary point—at the transition from generalized to complex hunter-gatherers, also known as the rise of "transegalitarian" societies—that Hayden first finds evidence of aspiring elites seeking to monopolize religious experience in an effort to build and legitimize political power:

> What seems to occur as transegalitarian societies become more complex is that shamans begin to specialize and create hierarchies; only those at the top are authorized to conduct the most important initiations or other ceremonies and thus collect the most lucrative fees or favors. In all this, we can see the dilution or subordination of the original ecstatic spiritual nature of the shaman in order to accommodate political

goals of the families or groups that sponsor their own shamans and underwrite their training. (2003:151)

These processes continued into the Neolithic, when, Hayden claims, "religion took a decisive turn." As "communities gradually evolved toward chiefdom-level societies, aspiring elites undoubtedly attempted to extend the influence of their own lineage ancestral cults to veneration by the entire community" (209). Enter the priest. Enter public cults and temple economies. Enter the ideological fount of oppression that would plague the masses for thousands of years to come.

The details of Hayden's account become predictable after this point. We are told that European megaliths like Stonehenge were orchestrated by priests who "were only using religion and their ancestors as a means to express their wealth and success while simultaneously pumping up their claim to ancestral sources of preternatural power" (2003:235). From there, it was a short journey to the emergence of priest-kings. With the rise of archaic states, "the king became god" and sought to eliminate all means of accessing the spiritual realm that were not under official state control (378). While originating in populist movements in opposition to state hierarchies, the Abrahamic religions nevertheless proved to be equally detrimental to the masses, ultimately giving rise to religiously motivated wars and newly expanded forms of imperialism (384–385). By medieval times, by the end of Hayden's account, Western religions had grown radically intolerant, a far cry from humanity's earliest Paleolithic communities, which had embraced religious diversity and were even accepting of relatively high levels of atheism and agnosticism (10–11).

The dominant arc of Hayden's prehistory of religion, as in much Protestant scholarship since the sixteenth century, is a bleak one. Primordial religion sits upon a kind of moral pedestal as having been practical, tolerant, democratic, ecologically adaptive, and supportive of both the individual and the community. Since the Neolithic, however, things seem to have generally worsened rather than improved: religion has become increasingly political, destructive, ideological, and oppressive. But if the old narrative of corruption is strongly present in Hayden's account, so too is the Protestant vision of a modern world that is throwing off clerical corruption, returning to the fold, and reinstating a pure form of original spirituality. The difference is that Hayden sees this return to the past as having been inaugurated by the Industrial Revolution rather than the Protestant Reformation and by capitalists rather than theologians. Modern economics, liberal democracy, and the empowerment of the individual, he argues, have undercut older religions, setting them adrift. And this has cleared space for a return to the individually satisfying and ecologically responsible spirituality that characterized Paleolithic shamanism millennia ago. It has cleared space, as Hayden (2003:413) puts it, for the "rediscovery" of "the ancient roots of traditional religion...long-suppressed."

Perhaps after a long detour of some 30,000 years during which aspiring elites sought to monopolize control of the supernatural, religion is finally returning to its popular and more universal roots. Just as industrialization freed the slaves, eliminated crushing workloads for many workers, and made politics more democratic, so it seems to be reconstituting religious life. I would predict that religious control, too, is returning to the hands of people in general, but only time will tell how far this trend will go and what forms it will take. (414)

Herewith ends modern archaeology's most sustained examination of the evolution of religion, but not before Hayden offers up a sixteen-point checklist designed to help students decide which neo-pagan cult might be right for them!

Hayden is hardly alone in looking kindly upon the shaman. Shamanic ritual and the experience of altered states are by far the most intensely studied phenomena within the archaeology of religion at the moment (e.g., Lewis-Williams and Pearce 2005; Price 2001; VanPool 2003; Whitley 2000), and many of the scholars involved in this research seem to regard shamanism with special admiration, particularly when compared with their negative portrayals of the bloody priestcraft of state religions. Some have gone further and explicitly argued that we have much to learn from modern neo-shamans and neo-pagans who, like archaeologists, visit prehistoric sites in search of communion with the ancients (see Rountree 2002, 2007; Wallis 2003).

Be that as it may, I suspect the large majority of European and American archaeologists would agree that *organized* religions—that is, religions with priesthoods, orthodox teachings, inflexible codes of behavior, and political aspirations—are anachronistic relics that have little role to play in a modernizing world. Most would probably also agree that the "long detour of some 30,000 years" has finally run its course. Just as some political economists claim that Western liberal democracy has ushered in the end of history, many archaeologists accept that modern science is presiding over the end of belief. "There is probably no way to turn back, no matter how fiercely reactionary some believers may be," argue Lewis-Williams and Pearce in one of the few monograph-length studies of prehistoric religion that rivals Hayden's in scope. They continue: "True, the rise of fundamentalism with its desire to control scientific research in some parts of the West must give us pause, but it seems unlikely that, in the long run, scientific advance with its rejection of supernatural agency can be stopped. Attempts to achieve a rapprochement between science and religion are today common, but they inevitably end in adjustments to religious belief, not to scientific findings" (2005:290). Such unblinking faith in secularization, rare though it may be in other humanities and social sciences, is common among archaeologists. In the opening chapter of yet another volume dedicated to the subject, David Whitley and Kelley Hays-Gilpin (2008:20) argue that earlier archaeologists generally avoided discussions of prehistoric religion "because, initially at least, science and religion were competing modes of thought." But the situation has now changed, they contend: "it now seems safe to say that in the West we are freed from the shackles of religious thought and authority" (Whitley 2008:86). "Science is now sufficiently mature as a mode of thought to turn its gaze towards its former rival, in order to understand religion as one of the universals of human social life" (Whitley and Hays-Gilpin 2008:20). There is a distinctly secular irony in such statements: now that we in the West are no longer religious, we are free to examine religion as a "universal" human endeavor. This is what Haraway (1988:582) acerbically referred to as the "god trick," whereby the scientist somehow convinces his audience that he stands fully outside the world and so is able to examine it in an unsituated, politically neutral, ahistorical, and entirely authoritative fashion.

The Challenge of Postsecularism

Needless to say, one never does stand outside the world, and god tricks are only able to expose the illusions of others by hiding the illusions of one's own. The more deeply invested we become in the logic of rupture and in modernity's distinction vis-à-vis the recent past, the more we paradoxically rely on narratives of return to an ancient past with which we have some essential, if long dormant, affinity. Secular futures, in other words, have always been fashioned out of quasi-secular pasts in which magic was like science, shamans were like surgeons, religion was private, society was tolerant, and spirituality had nothing at all to do with politics. In the mythos of secular scholarship, modernity has always been a second coming.

But secularism's myth of eternal return, in its outlines at least, has been borrowed from a Christian tradition that still has uses for it. Indeed, reformation continues to be a pressing concern for many Protestants in the United States, although the target of reform has now become secularism itself, and the "true religion" they seek to reinstate, ironically, is an earlier Christianity that had much more direct control over the state. History must be made again; fresh pasts must be created to accommodate hoped-for futures. After studying the new historiography of the Christian right, Jeff Sharlet observed that while the "theocentric" governance they dream of is a long way off, the creation of a Christian origin story for America is already well under way. It is not to be found in the standard American histories, of course—which the fundamentalists claim have all been whitewashed by liberal, secular scholarship—"but in another story, one more biblical, one more mythic and more true. Secularism hides this story, killed the Christian nation, and tried to dispose of the body. Fundamentalism wants to resurrect it, and doing so requires revision: fundamentalists, looking backward, see a different history" (Sharlet 2006:34). They see a different history in which the separation of church and state was never the intent of the founding fathers. America, the new religious historians emphasize, was established as a necessarily Christian nation; secularization was a perversion of this original mandate; and the future, therefore, must seek to reunite church and state, religion and politics, Christianity and national identity once again. $A^1 \rightarrow B \rightarrow A^2$. Sharlet keenly observes that this fundamentalist narrative is proving especially potent because, while making its truth claims like all histories, it never denies its mythic structure. On the contrary, it embraces it.

There is something to be learned from this, particularly for a discipline like anthropology whose reconstructions of human social development have always been much more than a cold parade of facts. Mythic structures are easily obscured when history is written by specialists one piece at a time. When archaeologists study the progressive politicization of "religion" from Paleolithic to medieval times ($A^1 \rightarrow B$), when sociocultural anthropologists examine the alleged depoliticization or privatization of "religion" from medieval to modern times ($B \rightarrow A^2$), and when both ignore the work of their subdisciplinary colleagues just down the hall, it is easy to slip into the mistaken conclusion that the Western historical imaginary is linear and progressive. It is easy to reify the claim that we are unique in this regard, that we are revolutionary in our focus on revolutionary breaks with the past. This is a strange species of purification in which anthropology—recent anthropology—has been especially complicit. We have internalized the logic of rupture through a rupture of our own within the discipline, through the erection of a great divide between archaeology and sociocultural anthropology, between the study of premodernity and the study of modernity. But the more the West tells itself it has broken with the past, the more invested it becomes in narratives of a return to the past. Like the bodies of the undead in a B-grade horror film, the chopped-up fragments of our cultural myths pull themselves together whether we like it or not, which is undoubtedly why the culture wars have come to focus so intensely on which historical details are or are not to be included in classroom textbooks (see Shorto 2010), those remaining (undead) bastions of the grand narrative within a contemporary intellectual scene that is otherwise hostile toward such things.

This is what postsecularism exposes. And this is why it presents such important challenges for both sociocultural anthropology and archaeology. My interests are primarily in the latter, so I will not push further my plea that sociocultural anthropologists seriously unpack their reliance on "premodernity" as an analytical category, which is silently implied, of course, whenever conversations about secular modernity are on the table. Pointing to the history of Islam as a counter to the overly Christian moorings of most Western accounts of the emergence of the secular age (see Warner et al. 2010) does not sufficiently address the problem. The premodern always maps out a far vaster ideological terrain, one that sociocultural anthropologists will only be able to navigate once they have at least a passing familiarity with contemporary archaeological scholarship.

As archaeologists, we must take on a symmetrical task. We must be willing to undertake a critical evaluation of how our individual research projects—restricted in time and space though they may be—articulate with the broader cultural vision of secularization as a historical process. To what extent does our use of "religion" as an analytical category in the study of premodernity smuggle in an implicit set of oppositions (between church and state, belief and action, rationality and irrationality, immanence and transcendence, religion and the secular) that makes the secular modern appear natural and inevitable? Once we have addressed this issue, once we have gained perspective on the persistent interpenetration of reconstructed pasts and desired futures, once we have come to terms with the mythic current flowing through our research, the challenge then expands. If our secularization narratives are breaking down, if we are becoming resigned to a future that will be as enchanted as ever, how will this alter our understandings of premodern worlds? Will we dig in our heels and continue to promote secularism through our portrayals of the ancient past? Will we search out alternative narratives that clear spaces for alternative futures? Or might we work toward archaeological accounts that escape the dual logic of rupture and return altogether?

t w o
The Paradox of the Priest

Here there seems to be nothing but earth and vast mountains and sky with clouds...and a bunch of people who seem to have survived merely to perform a necessary ceremony.
—*Jaime de Angulo*, Jaime in Taos, *writing of Taos Pueblo in the 1920s*

TAOS NEW MEXICO. Retreat from the modern day.
—*Contemporary travel advertisement*

The Pueblo communities of the American Southwest, those encountered by the Spanish in the sixteenth century at least, were "Neolithic." Their technologies were of ceramic, fiber, stone, and bone. Domesticated plants, while present in some parts of New Mexico and Arizona for three millennia, had only dominated Pueblo economies for seven centuries or so at the time of European conquest. And residence in dense sedentary villages of up to a few thousand souls was more recent still—only in the thirteenth century CE did communities across the Southwest make a universal commitment to village life. Relatively speaking, then, the Pueblos at the time of contact were "newly Neolithic."

It was with such an evolutionary orientation that anthropologists of the late nineteenth and early twentieth centuries visited the Pueblos to glimpse what life had been like in early times, prior to metallurgy, writing, cities, standing armies, kings and queens. Lewis Henry Morgan (1974[1877], 1965[1881]), one of the earliest and most prominent anthropological visitors, saw in Pueblo social and economic organization—their "communism in living," as he put it—a key ethnographic example of an "ancient universal prevalence," one that Marx and Engels, building upon Morgan's work, later popularized as an original condition of primitive communism. A steady stream of European and Euro-American ethnographers soon followed, each journeying west into Indian country under the vague impression that their movement through geographic space was simultaneously a movement backward in time. To stand before Pueblo people was to look into prelapsarian eyes and see an original condition: Rousseau's natural man.

Ancient society was precisely what the well-known German art critic Aby Warburg sought when he visited the Pueblos at the close of the nineteenth century. "To what extent," he wrote two decades later from a sanatorium, "does this pagan world view, as it persists among the [Pueblo] Indians, give us a yardstick for the development from primitive paganism, through the paganism of classical antiquity, to modern man?" (1995:4). Warburg, like so many other early anthropologists and tourists, was led to the Pueblos by a trail of nostalgia, prompted not only by scientific curiosity into the supposed origins of society, but also by a hazy desire to recapture the authentic social experiences that the modern world had lost. A strange mix of respect and condescension characterized such encounters; regardless, these early visitors, and the formal ethnographies that shortly followed, rapidly cast the Pueblos as "ancient ones," ancestors to us all.

I am powerfully reminded of this complex construction of ancientness, authenticity, and ancestry each time I visit Taos Pueblo, that highly photographed holdout of adobe architecture in north-central New Mexico (figure 2.1). Taos is and for at least seven centuries has been an extraordinarily resilient indigenous community, but over the course of its history the pueblo has undergone tremendous change. From the predation of conquistadors, Catholic clerics, and Comanche raiders during the early colonial period, to Taos's political subordination to the United States since the mid-nineteenth century, to the daily onslaught of tourists and New Age sycophants in recent decades—in each of these encounters, the pueblo has been prompted to reinvent itself. This is to say that the past five hundred years have been a time of intense and turbulent history making for the resident community. Still, during a UNESCO review in the 1980s, Taos was identified as the "best preserved" (a dubious honor) of the indigenous villages in the American Southwest. And in 1992 it officially became a World Heritage Site, one of only twenty such sites in the United States and the only one that monumentalizes a living settlement. The only one that monumentalizes a people in addition to a place.

Understandably, the resident community is proud of this recognition of global significance. But what does it mean that Taos Pueblo, as a World Heritage Site, is now ranked among those cosseted points on the landscape that "belong to all the peoples of the world, irrespective of the territory on which they are located"? Laudable though UNESCO's broader efforts at conservation may be, is this not very strange? Is Taos Pueblo really now to be viewed on some level as part of the collective heritage of not only the United States, but also England and Germany? Is it not surreal that an international organization in Paris has written a report praising the occupants of Taos Pueblo, halfway across the world, for their efforts to ensure that "discordant elements, such as inappropriate doors, have been replaced using more harmonious designs and materials" (UNESCO 1992:2)?

Figure 2.1. Taos Pueblo, northside roomblock.

One can ignore or plaster over discordant elements and inappropriate doors in the present, but archaeology doggedly testifies that change and instability, not stasis and stability, are the more traditional elements of the Puebloan past, even (and, in some senses, especially) prior to the coming of Europeans. This was as true in the Pueblos' "religion" as it was in their "economic" and "political" organization. Indeed, strong arguments can be leveled against any temptation to view the Pueblos as Stone Age survivals, latter-day representatives of premodernity, of a tribal or village stage that characterized the Old World many millennia ago.

And yet, this book is premised upon a conviction that the historical sequence of the Pueblos *does* tell us something important about the hoary debate over religion and its evolutionary history, not just as a matter of Western discourse but also on the ground, in the human past, as it was actually experienced. How can one say such a thing without becoming tangled in a bramble of primitivist arguments? Primitivism persists in a variety of guises—not least in the discourse of world heritage—but to say that a village like Taos Pueblo has things to tell us about what life was or, more accurately, was *not* like in small-scale societies of other times and places need not entail any such position. This is especially the case when one's sights are set on critiquing deeply held assumptions about these societies and the sorts of religions they practiced, as mine are here.

Put bluntly, my aim in the following discussion of the Pueblos is to draw critical attention to the chimera of "true religion"—to the image of a purified religion that stands fully apart from politics—which was and, in many cases, continues to be constructed around a certain set of societies, once called primitive and now more commonly referred to as traditional, tribal, small-scale, or indigenous. As I will emphasize, I regard the functionalist notion that religion initially evolved as a solidarity-building alternative to real political action to be, in large part, a reification of a post-Reformation Western agenda and so to have little or no basis in any sort of empirical observation. Some will surely regard this as a stale critique. Functionalism, after all, has had a bad name in the discipline since the early 1970s when sociocultural anthropologists began to shift their focus from the study of how societies hold together to how they are fragmented, inconsistent, idiosyncratic, or even dysfunctional. But there is no denying that functionalism (and with it, an implicit notion of true religion) has proven more resilient within archaeology.

I will avoid an extended discussion of why this is so. Some would undoubtedly claim that archaeological theory *always* walks ten paces behind sociocultural anthropology, like a private eye following a suspicious character. However, the reasons are more complex than this and involve both the nature of archaeological research and the subjects under investigation. Functionalist theory was developed to understand especially tribal milieus, formerly the bread and butter of early- to mid-twentieth-century ethnography. It is hardly surprising, therefore, that the widespread rejection of functionalism in sociocultural anthropology came just as interest shifted away from small-scale "traditional" societies and toward postcolonial contexts variously entangled with a globalizing modernity. Nor is it surprising that archaeologists, who continue to study premodern contexts, should continue to promote functionalist theories. Functionalism is linked to the study of premodernity (or nonmodernity), not archaeology per se, although this is often overlooked.

Be that as it may, there are certain key areas of anthropological research where long-standing functionalist interpretations of religion must be critically reassessed, and the American Southwest is prominent among them. In the eyes of generations of scholars, artists, and other seekers who have been discontented with a disenchanted post-Enlightenment world, true religion lies hidden among the mesas of New Mexico and Arizona, secreted away behind weathered adobe walls and sinuous veils of piñon smoke. Recall that Aldous Huxley's character John the Savage—foil to the dehumanized denizens of the World State in *Brave New World*—was expressly raised on the "savage" reservation by Pueblo Indians who taught John to experience God in an authentic, emotive, and radically apolitical mode. Savage religion, in Huxley's rendering, was the grease of mechanical solidarity. With minor modifications, the same idealized image of the Pueblos continues to serve as a paradigmatic contrast to more hierarchical societies whose religions are presented as having been disfigured by the ideological manipulation of elites, transformed from metaphysical purity into a mere extension of the political. The story of corruption by an emergent "church-state," of the progressive "intrusion of the deities into the social [i.e., political] affairs of mankind" (White 1959:218–219), of the supposed loss of a spiritual innocence that must be reclaimed—these are, as I suggested in the previous chapter, primarily Protestant beliefs.

I will have more to say about this broad evolutionary story later in this book. Before that discussion, however, I want to trace the contours of a much more localized narrative, a particular archaeological sequence in the Pueblo region that will set the stage for a general critique. Taos Pueblo lies at the end of that narrative, and it is tempting, therefore, to follow UNESCO's lead and claim that, localized though the discussion may be, it is nevertheless the entire world's heritage that is at issue. As I hope to make clear by the close of this book, there are both truths and falsities in this claim.

Red Willow People

Tucked in the northeastern corner of the Pueblo world, modern Taos Pueblo is the larger of two Northern Tiwa–speaking communities. Its nearest linguistic and cultural relative, Picurís Pueblo, is located roughly twenty miles to the south (figure 2.2). The residents of both Taos and Picurís descend from native peoples, some of whom have occupied this region for at least a millennium, and both villages contend for the title of "oldest continuously inhabited settlement" in North America. Limited archaeological testing suggests that Taos Pueblo may have occupied its current location since the thirteenth or fourteenth century, and excavations during the 1960s raised the possibility that Picurís Pueblo has been inhabited more or less continuously since the eleventh century, notwithstanding a brief sojourn on the Plains during the colonial period (Ellis and Brody 1964; Dick et al. 1999). Additional research has documented extensive Pueblo settlements dating as early as the tenth century that are directly ancestral to the modern Northern Tiwas (Fowles 2004:194–200), which is to say that the antiquity of their presence in the region is impressive.

When the Spanish arrived, Taos and Picurís were among the largest villages in the Southwest, each housing thousands of people in dense architectural compounds five or more stories high. Both were major trade centers, both were widely known for their hunting and hide working, and both had close ties to the Apaches and Utes who had recently entered the Southwest from the north and east. Both villages were, in other words, strategic middlemen in an emergent network of interregional interdependency. Indeed, most of the coveted bison hides at Hopi, nearly three hundred miles to the west, probably passed through Northern Tiwa hands.

But the two pueblos did not fare equally well following the sixteenth century as they were forced to submit to Spanish, then Mexican, then American rule. At Picurís, waves of disease, colonial violence, and outmigration, among other forces, reduced the population early on, and much tribal land was lost to encroachment by Hispano settlers. By the early twentieth century, ethnographers were predicting that the remaining community would soon disappear completely. Although reports of the death of Picurís were greatly exaggerated, the effect was that twentieth-century ethnography largely passed the pueblo by, and we are left to rely upon what is known of post-contact Taos Pueblo for our primary ethnographic insight into pre-Columbian Northern Tiwa patterns. From the outset, then, we are working with only half the story.

Of course, the ethnographic literature on Taos itself is not particularly detailed. Jaime de Angulo wrote in 1924 of "mysterious Taos, Taos out of which

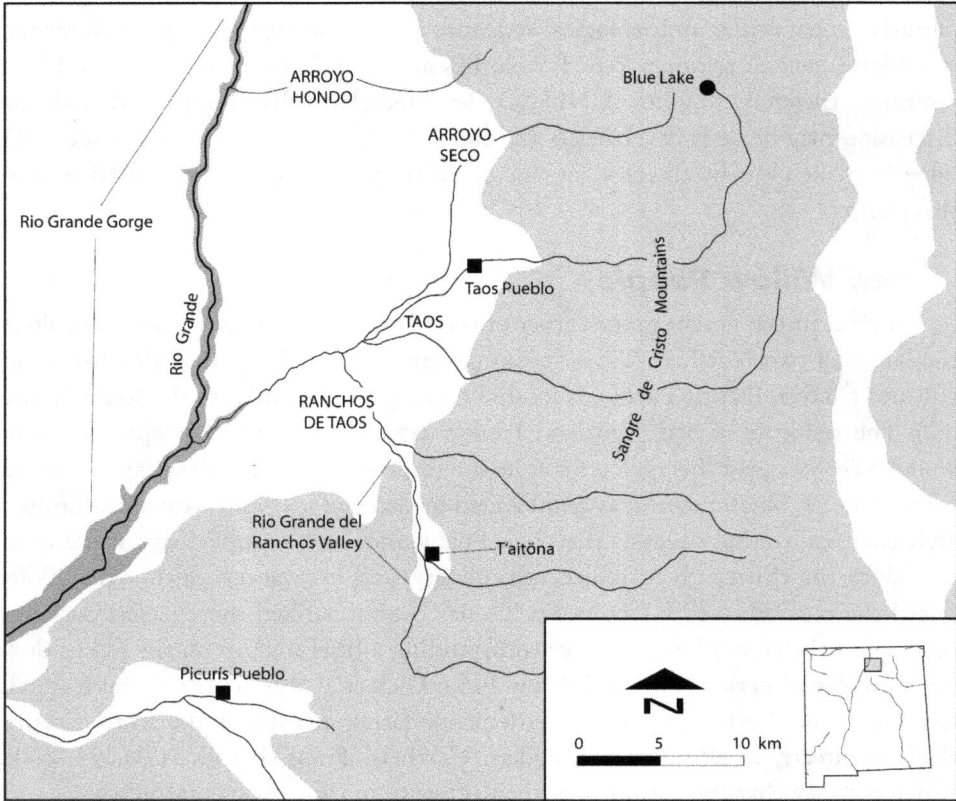

Figure 2.2. Map of the Taos region.

the anthropologists have never been able to get any information" (1985:36), and he could have been referring to any number of heavyweights of early Pueblo ethnography, including Matilda Cox Stevenson (1906–1907), Ruth Benedict (see de Angulo 1985:91–93), Leslie White (see Parsons 1996a[1940]), and Elsie Clews Parsons (1936, 1996a[1940], 1996b[1939]). All encountered fierce opposition at Taos, particularly when they broached subjects that touched upon the religious sphere. White went so far as to conclude that the pueblo had a coordinated scheme to deal with nosy investigators. "As a matter of fact," he wrote, "Taos has actually employed 'stool pigeons'—i.e., persons who pretend to be 'writing a book about their religion'— to discover journalists and ethnologists; once discovered they were avoided like a plague" (1937:199). Anecdotal stories can still be heard to this effect; however, the more recent variants have been transformed into morality tales, in which the native archivist of tribal secrets is said to have had his house raided and his papers destroyed.

The most extensive ethnographic account of Taos Pueblo has never been published and was for many years lost to anthropology. During 1906 and sporadically in the years that followed, Stevenson hounded the Taos community, pushing her way into ceremonies and interviewing those she could entice away from the pueblo. To say her work was controversial would be a vast understatement (see Parsons 1936:14–15) for it galvanized Taos into a unified and almost unconditional opposition to anthropologists. Thirty years later, for instance, Parsons found it necessary to dedicate her brief monograph to "My best friend in Taos, the most scrupulous Pueblo Indian of my acquaintance, who told me nothing about the pueblo and who never will tell any white person anything his people would not have him tell, which is nothing" (Parsons 1936:3).[1]

Stevenson's aggressive insensitivity did not help matters, of course, but the community's acrimony toward anthropologists sprang from a deeper source. The efficacy of ritual knowledge throughout the Pueblo world (and perhaps at Taos especially; see Brandt 1980) was and is dependent on tightly regulated layers of secrecy. Prayers, songs, languages, formulas, and so on were not part of a general store of cultural knowledge; only those who had been properly trained in the appropriate kiva or clan society gained access to such powerful secrets. "In Taos we don't tell anything," said Tony Luhan (quoted in de Angulo 1985:37). "We don't show anything. It's all secret. It's all under." Under wraps, underground, under priestly control—a key pattern to which I will return presently. Regardless, when security was breached, when a non-initiate gained access to esoteric knowledge, that knowledge lost its power, and the community as a whole suffered. Hence the common Pueblo practice in which an interloper was forced to join a ritual society after unwittingly stumbling upon a private ceremony. Stevenson, of course, was a very worrisome interloper, but Taos was not about to initiate her. The secrets she carried away thus became the focus of lingering anxiety.

It is fitting, in this sense, that Stevenson's notes were never published,[2] and one might legitimately argue that unpublished is just how they should remain. Nevertheless, I have chosen to reintroduce certain portions of her work here, partly because a century has passed and many of the ethnographic details are no longer as controversial as they once were, but also because they provide extraordinarily important insights into indigenous Northern Tiwa social organization and historiography. Indeed, Stevenson's notes are currently our *only* means of reading the region's past not as the faceless prehistory of the archaeologist but as the history of named groups whose descendants continue to live with and reflect deeply upon their past.

North American archaeology has renewed its engagement with indigenous oral histories, prompted by the passing of NAGPRA legislation as well as the strong advocacy of native critics (e.g., Deloria 1997; Echo-Hawk 2000; Mann 2003). After many dark decades in which native people's knowledge of their ancestry was put to the side as subjective, mythological, and, hence, largely irrelevant to the scientific reconstruction of the past, this is long overdue. That said, there is no escaping the reality that history is primarily composed among the Pueblos in what we would call a sacred idiom, and this can result in a tension between the desire for public acknowledgment of the authority of oral histories and the desire to keep the details of those histories private. One evening, after I had presented on the archaeological and ethnohistoric evidence of his ancestors, a Taos leader offered the following commentary: "You went back and forth," he said. "Some parts got pretty close. Other parts were really wrong. But I can't tell you which is which." Fair enough. For many centuries, the old men of Taos and Picurís have been the only legitimate arbiters of the Northern Tiwa past. Until they choose otherwise, the existing corpus of twentieth-century ethnography at least permits us to aspire toward a history that is "pretty close" (rather than wildly off the mark) and that makes explicit the vital links between the modern indigenous communities and their ancestors, whose remains are the object of archaeological inquiry.

In the early twentieth century, Taos Pueblo housed some five to seven hundred residents (Bodine 1979), and my goal for the remainder of this chapter is to establish the key lines of social division within the population at that time. (Hence my use of the past tense, even though many of the ethnographic details continue to characterize the community today.) Like so many communities whose histories lie outside the era of nation-states, the members of Taos Pueblo typically referred to themselves simply as "the people." But they also had a more complex name for themselves that roughly translates as the "Red Willow People," derived from the Red Willow Creek that flows clear and strong through the middle of their village. From the perspective of Taos oral history, the Red Willow People were a heterogeneous bunch, composed of a number of named social groups with diverse backgrounds, each of which figured into a variety of narrative dramas. Most of these groups are described as different *tai'na*, or "peoples"; however, the generic use of this term obscures a much more complicated migration history and set of social reorganizations. Here, I adopt slightly different terms for the sake of clarity. Early twentieth-century Taos, for my purposes, can be viewed as having been divided into two *moieties*, each of which was divided into three *kivas*, which were in turn composed of a number of different subgroups, or *peoples*, who participated in one or more *ritual societies*. Together, these structural divisions combined to form the elaborate tapestry that anthropologists have alternately referred to as Pueblo "religion" or "government" but that I will temporarily discuss here as Pueblo "hierocracy," simply to avoid unwanted baggage. Five interwoven terms, then, rise to the surface and demand our attention: moieties, kivas, peoples, societies, and hierocracy.

Moieties

Among the major findings of twentieth-century ethnography in the American Southwest was a tendency for clanship to be pronounced among the Western Pueblos and for a ceremonial (i.e., non-kin-based) moiety system to more often structure social life among the Eastern or Rio Grande Pueblos. As a member of the latter, historic Taos Pueblo followed this broad pattern: notions of clanship were muted and a dual division structured much of the community's ritual life. The Taos moiety system lacked the explicit ideology of moiety interdependence and complementarity so elegantly documented by Alfonso Ortiz (1969) among the neighboring Tewas.

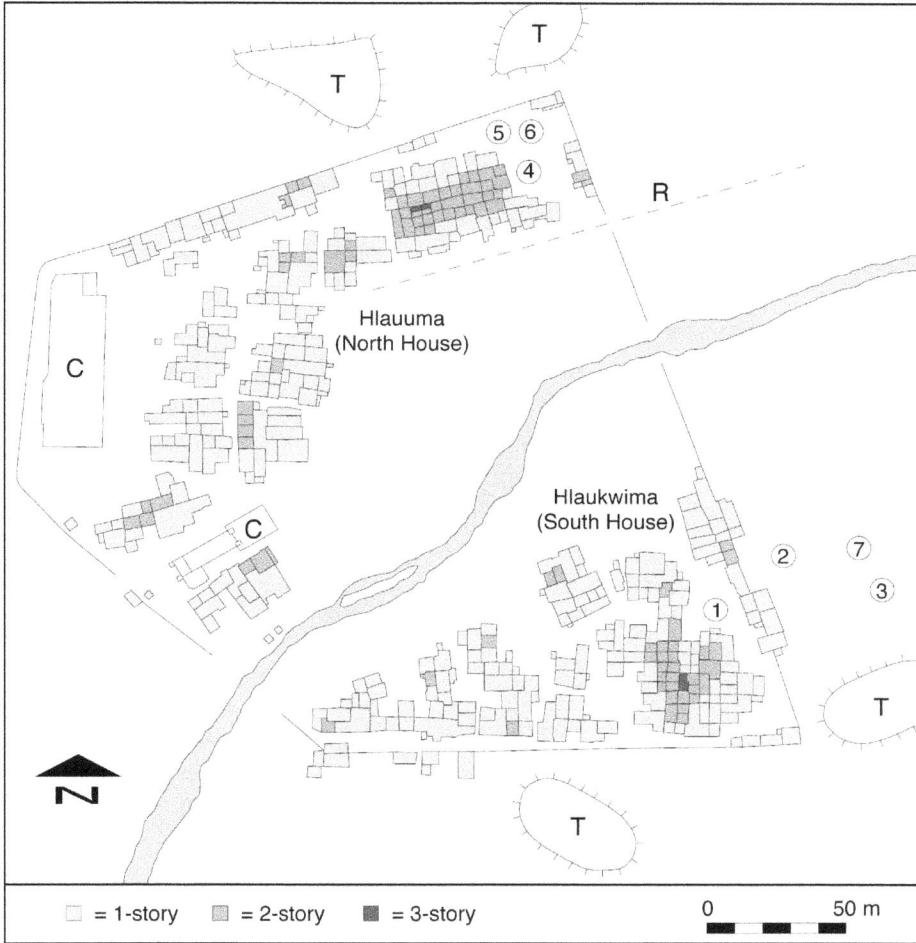

Figure 2.3. Map of Taos Pueblo (based on Bodine 1979). Southside kivas: 1 = Feather, 2 = Water, 3 = Old Axe, 7 = "disused," or Earth Mother; northside kivas: 4 = Big Earring, 5 = Day, 6 = Knife; T = trash pile, R = race course, C = Catholic church.

Nevertheless, dualism was conspicuous in many aspects of Taos's social organization and cosmic symbolism. North was to south as winter was to summer, as hunting was to agriculture, as men were to women, and so on; such oppositions appear to have saturated indigenous understandings of the world.

Dualism was also mapped out spatially. Running east to west through the heart of the community, Red Willow Creek physically divided Taos into two architectonic masses: the North House (Hlauuma) and the South House (Hlaukwima) (figure 2.3). Three active kivas and two refuse mounds mirrored each other on the two sides of the river, the entire layout serving as a spatial reification of a ceremonial order that emphasized balance and duality. Individual rituals underscored this spatial division, most publicly in the annual relay races when north ran against south along a racetrack that paralleled the river. The races were community-wide events; everyone participated either by running, officiating, or actively encouraging the runners. And while they were far from adversarial—both sides had the common goal of assisting the sun in its course across the sky (Parsons 1936:96)—the races were nevertheless a highly visible context in which the division became palpable.

In the early twentieth century, moiety affiliation appears to have followed naturally from one's kiva membership, which more properly stood at the core of an individual's identity. Initiated into the Feather Kiva, for instance, one was a de facto member of the southside moiety. The Taos moieties may not even have been formally named, although it is entirely possible that this information was simply hidden from ethnographers (see Parsons 1936:77n38). Regardless, the highest echelons of community leadership were explicitly linked to the moiety division. The Big Earring Man of the north group and the cacique (and/or Water Man)[3] of the south group were the two principal leaders of the community (Parsons 1936; Stevenson 1906–1907:file 3.1), and it was largely through these parallel positions that a degree of balance in the distribution of power was achieved. As Adolph Bandelier (1984[1885–1888]:247) observed in 1888, "each one of the two great buildings [the north and south houses] has its cacique, and they call him *Te-cla-pa*."

Kivas

Whereas moiety organization only surfaced in particular contexts, kiva membership suffused most aspects of social life at Taos. All members of the community, both male and female, were given to a particular kiva soon after birth. For boys, association with a kiva typically involved a lengthy initiation process, during which they were secluded from the greater community for training in various secret rituals, sacred knowledge, and ceremonial prescriptions (Bodine 1979; Parsons 1936:45–46). This process began at roughly age nine and lasted about eighteen months for the full initiation, culminating with the boy's participation in the ceremonial pilgrimage to Blue Lake, the sacred body of water high in the mountains to the east of the village where some say the Northern Tiwas originally emerged from the lower world (Bodine 1988; Stevenson 1906–1907). For girls, no formal initiation took place; religious matters relevant to particular rituals were instead taught in the home as needed prior to a girl's participation in kiva events.

The first truly ethnographic comment on the Taos kivas was made in 1885 by Bandelier, who initially reported seven active "estufas" (1984[1885–1888]:80) and later noted only six (1976[1890–1892]:pt. 1): Bead, Water, Axe, Feather, Sun, and Knife. Stevenson (1906–1907:file 3.1) recorded the same six principal groups in 1906 as did Parsons (1936) in the early 1930s. All six remain active today. With the possible exception of a seventh "disused kiva" (the source of the discrepancy in Bandelier's journals), there has thus been a basic stability in kiva organization for more than a century. As I have already noted, the six kivas were organized spatially into two groups: on the northside, the Big Earring (Bandelier's Bead Clan), Day, and Knife kivas, all of which were located within the walls of the Pueblo, just north of the race course, and on the southside, the Water, Old Axe or Kwathlowúna, and Feather kivas. Among the southside kivas, only Feather was located within the Pueblo's walls; the remaining two were situated just outside the southeast corner of the village.

Stevenson learned a fair amount about the membership and ceremonial responsibilities of these kiva groups. I will not review those details here with the exception of one further point regarding the complicated relationship between kinship and kiva membership. Past scholarship has been greatly confused by this relationship, primarily due, once again, to the reticence of the Pueblos to divulge information that strays too close to their ceremonial life. I count myself among the confused, but I offer the following discussion with the hope of at least moving the subject forward.

Early on, most scholars implicitly assumed that kinship structured Taos kiva organization. Kivas were regularly referred to as "clans" (e.g., Bandelier 1976[1890– 1892]; Espinosa 1936; Grant 1976[1925]; Miller 1898), based on the erroneous assumption that *all* pueblos contained clans. Parsons (1936:38–39) was unable to elicit much more discussion on this subject than her predecessors, but during the mid-1930s she nevertheless felt confident enough to claim that the Taos kiva groups, contrary to received wisdom, were fully divorced from the kinship system. Moreover, she concluded that Taos "had no conception...of any matronymic or patronymic exogamous group" (38). Taos kivas, as far as she knew, were composed of a variety of loosely defined bilateral kin groups, and parents were free to give their child to any of the six kivas they chose.

In her efforts to document Taos clanlessness, however, Parsons may have overstated the case. Stevenson's (1906–1907:file 3.4) much more detailed notes clearly suggest that kinship was relevant to kiva membership. For instance, while Stevenson's informants noted that birth did not completely dictate the kiva in which one would participate, they also stated that one was always simultaneously linked at a general level with the kiva of one's father. Indeed, it was expected that a son given to a kiva other than that of his father would then give his own son to his father's kiva. (Such a tendency for patrilines to cluster in particular kivas is also seen in Parsons's genealogical diagrams.) It is worth noting that kiva (or, at least, moiety) membership at Picurís, the other Northern Tiwa Pueblo, appears to have been patrilineally determined (Bodine 1979:273; Fox 1967:17; Parsons 1939:216; but see Brown 1999:22), increasing the likelihood that one would have been born with kiva and moiety affiliations at Taos as well.

In practice, all Taos individuals may have had the potential to draw upon multiple kiva associations. By right of kinship, one appears to have been associated with one's father's kiva, but newborns could also be promised or given to a different kiva in which they would later participate as members. Parsons (1936:46) also learned that if an individual happened to be "doctored by a group within another kiva he promises that group his service for a stated time; he becomes their 'servant'"—pointing to yet another form of kiva association. How did such a system of multiple affiliations actually function? Consider Parsons's brief discussion of female ceremonialism: "For dance practice, a girl goes to the kiva of her father, subsequently to that of her husband except of course in dances where all may practice in the same kiva. But when there is work to be done, such as plastering in the kiva the girl was given to, she is summoned to contribute her service. According to these rules, a woman might have had associations with only one kiva, or with two, or with three" (Parsons 1936:46). I suspect this was true for most members of the community.

Peoples

Admittedly, the model of kiva-kin relations just sketched remains vague, and the situation becomes even less clear when we look to the internal divisions within the kivas themselves, for while there were only six active kivas, nearly all ethnographers at Taos have recorded a much larger number of named "peoples" (e.g., the Golden Warbler People, the Green Leaf People, etc.). Bandelier's (1984[1885–1888]:80) Taos informants told him that each of the seven kivas had more than one named group within it, and also that some named groups were split across multiple kivas. Two decades later, Stevenson was presented with a similar picture, and her notes reveal a concerted effort to clarify the complicated relationship between kivas and the varied "peoples" they included (see figure 2.3). Whereas most of the peoples had a unique relationship with a particular kiva (e.g., the Golden Warbler People were all members of the Feather Kiva), some peoples had members in a variety of kivas (Stevenson 1906–1907:file 3.1). Stevenson was told, for example: "There are 20 men of the Fialo'la tai'na gens [Big Earring People] belonging to estufa No. 1 [Feather Kiva]. Others of the same gens have allied themselves, or their fathers did so for them, to other gens in other estufas. Turtu tai'na (Day People) and Pachunona tai'na ('A fine red stone slightly blended with white' People) are scattered among the different estufas and they therefore have no gens head or father as a body, each one belonging to a gens in an estufa by adoption" (Stevenson 1906–1907:file 3.24; Stevenson's reference to people groups as "gens" and kivas as "estufas" was an early twentieth-century convention). Two additional entries in Stevenson's notes—the first in Stevenson's words, the second in those of her informant—further attest to the lack of correspondence between kivas and people groups:

> *Tócholimafia tai'na* [the Golden Warbler People] has 21 men, a number of women. The men belong as a body to kiva No. 1 [the Feather Kiva], but others are allied to other kivas. For example, Juan's youngest son joined the kiva of the gens of kiva No. 2 [the Day Kiva], he joining through the *Toltu tai'na* [the Day People], the mother's gens. And in like manner different gentes are scattered among the main bodies of gentes in the different kivas. It has been explained that it is the custom for the son to join the kiva of his father's gens. (Stevenson 1906–1907:file 3.9)
>
> My wife desired that our younger son should join the kiva of her father who belongs to the Ice People. I sent for a member of the *Harl tai'na* [Ice People in Day

Kiva], this being the name of the kiva to which my wife's father belonged, and made
known my wish that my youngest son should become allied with his kiva. My son
accompanied the man to his house and ate with him. He afterwards told the boy
when in the kiva of the *Harl tai'na* that though he belonged to the *Tocholimofia tai'na*
gens [the Golden Warbler People], he also belonged to the Harl tai'na by adoption.
The children of my boy will belong to the *Tocholimofia tai'na*, because this is his real
gens. (Quoted in Stevenson 1906–1907:file 3.11)

It appears, then, that one could have a "real" people affiliation through one's paternal
line and a secondary people affiliation as a result of ceremonial adoption.

As organizational entities, people groups were clearly distinct from kivas, and
yet, very few functions or particular rituals have been recorded in connection with
them. Certain peoples owned one or two flutes (Stevenson 1906–1907:file 3.1), presumably used in kiva ceremonies, and we also know that each kiva derived its name
from the leading people group within it. Such details, however, merely confirm the
reality of these groups; they do little to explicate their structural significance. How
are we to understand non-clan-based kivas that nevertheless had kinship overtones,
as well as peoples or subkiva groups that had few formal responsibilities?

It is at this point that structuralist approaches are left with little to say and history must raise its hand to venture an answer. Indeed, the most plausible explanation
for such organizational complexity is that it resulted from hundreds of years of social
intermixing and hybridization. As we will see in the next chapter, the archaeological
and oral historical evidence converge on an image of the ancestral Northern Tiwas
as a multicultural composite of lineages or clans with quite distinct histories. And
I have elsewhere suggested that the ethnographically recorded people groups were
remnants of these earlier clans or lineages, holdovers from a time of population mix-
ing when ethnicity and kinship would have been largely synonymous (Fowles 2005;
Bernardini and Fowles 2011). Be that as it may, Taos Pueblo, like all communities,
must be viewed as a product of history, and this means we should not seek to impose
too great a coherency upon it. Social life is inherently anachronistic in this sense—
even in the context of a "traditional society."

Societies

Beyond the kin, kiva, and moiety groups, Taos Pueblo was also served by a series
of societies, or ceremonial sodalities, with more specialized functions. These groups
comprised a sort of indigenous service industry related to curing, fertility, warfare,
hunting, and the like. Six have been recorded at Taos (Fowles 2004:appendix A;
Parsons 1936:82–83), and although we know very little about these societies, two
observations deserve comment.

First, while each society drew its leadership from a particular kiva, many contained members from multiple kivas. At the time of Parsons's fieldwork, for example,
the Black Eyes Society was dominated, as it appears always to have been, by the

Knife Kiva, but it also drew its membership from the Water and Old Axe kivas. The ceremonial societies, in other words, cut across kiva and moiety divisions, but let me quickly add that there was no overall proliferation of sodalities—curing societies, priesthoods, clans, katsina groups, and the like—with overlapping memberships such as have long been cited as the basis of social integration among the Western Pueblos (e.g., Kroeber 1917).

Second, the ceremonial societies contributed to the broader symbolic logic of the moiety system insofar as each society was dominated by either the northside or the southside kivas. The three southside societies (Bear, Corn Mother, and Fire), for instance, all had curing functions, a pattern that is consistent with the mythological description of the Summer People (the people of the south) as the keepers of powerful medicine (Parsons 1936; Stevenson 1906–1907:file 3.1). Moreover, the Old Axe Kiva dominated the Corn Mother Society, which is consistent with the general connection between the southern moiety and agriculture. In contrast, the societies dominated by the northside kivas were concerned either with snowfall (Big Hail and White Mountain), hunting (White Mountain), or social entertainment and discipline (Black Eyes), broadly in keeping with the northside associations noted earlier.

Hence, we must imagine a three-tiered structure at Taos Pueblo in which peoples were incorporated into kivas and kivas were incorporated into moieties, all of which was overlain by a system of ceremonial societies. But we should also avoid reading too great a coherence into this structure. No doubt, it made good sense to the Northern Tiwas, but it was no timeless and essential whole. The Taos social universe is probably better understood as an evolving structural patchwork composed of loosely bound elements, some inherited, some vestigial, and others in the process of becoming.

Hierocracy

The more complicated issue is how this structural patchwork, this bare skeletal apparatus, was animated and reproduced through the actions of real individuals with their own dispositions and divergent motivations. To broach this issue is to quickly shift from talking about "religion" to a discussion of strategic action, or what is traditionally classified as "politics." Indeed, just as the occupants of Taos respected and adhered to their religious traditions, they also respected and adhered to their religious leaders in the sense of granting them authority, high prestige, and decision-making power. In Pueblo studies, we have grown accustomed to discussing such religious leaders as a veritable elite, comparable to the upper echelons in much larger and more rigidly stratified societies. I will take issue with this position in later chapters, but the key point is that whenever such elitism exists, one can assume that the privileges involved will be both assiduously defended by the privileged and challenged by the disenfranchised. Thus does Pueblo religion begin to become indistinguishable from Pueblo politics.

Thus also does the analyst confront a classic tension that has always turned the wheel of historical change. On one side, leaders presumably lead because they believe it is in their interest to do so. On the other side, followers accept or submit to the leadership of others because they too believe it is in their (the followers') self-interest. The devil is in the system of interests, in the points of convergence, divergence, and contradiction, in the discourse surrounding whose interests are really being served.

We must be careful here. There is a strong temptation to simply accept that the "real interests" of a given individual or group of individuals can be identified in a forthright manner, and perhaps at a crude level this is possible: we might accept that adequate food, health, safety, and so on are, generally speaking, desirable. But my concern is with a higher set of culturally defined interests and with scenarios in which it is less clear where the benefits lie. "Who is to say who is dominated and on what basis?" asks Steven Lukes (2005:111). On what analytical authority, for instance, are Marxists able to claim that the real interests of the masses are clouded and suppressed by a false consciousness leading them to false wants? On what authority did Nietzsche write of a slave morality that makes the Christian desire the undesirable?

Such questions are hardly irrelevant to the present discussion. The stated purpose of "religion" at Taos, as at all pueblos, was to ensure the well-being of the collectivity. It was undertaken to help the rain fall and the crops grow, to grant women fertility and men success in the hunt, to protect the village from disease and attack. It was not undertaken to further the power of individual religious leaders; on the contrary, priestly office was thought to entail great personal sacrifice. The entire ceremonial edifice—all the kivas, moieties, ceremonies, priesthoods, initiations, and pilgrimages—existed purely to serve the needs of the world at large. So said the priests and much of their congregation, at least.

My first inclination, I will admit, is to read such statements as at least partly ideological, akin to the notion that modern US politicians are public servants fighting for the best interests of the populace at large. We might note, for instance, that in contrast to its explicit aims, religiously based factionalism has historically run rampant in the pueblos, leading to community disintegration at some villages and the exile of dissidents at others. That this was the case among the Northern Tiwas deep in the past is evident in their oral histories: Picurís stories talk of community disintegration stemming from an "extreme uprising of personal jealousies" among the ceremonial leaders (Brown 1973:70), leaving little doubt that Northern Tiwa priests were not above self-interest. Moreover, Pueblo religious leadership was, by its very nature, highly exclusionary. Only men of the appropriate parentage who had been properly trained over the course of their lives were able to assume positions of high authority—women and most men were marginalized in this sense. Little surprise that Pueblo ethnographies contain frequent statements by disgruntled individuals who viewed the actions of their leaders as elitist and self-aggrandizing. Even among the supposedly Apollonian pueblos, religion was frequently "a language of argument, not a chorus of harmony" (to borrow from Leach 1964[1954]:277).

Nevertheless, it remains the case that Lukes's question—"Who is to say who is dominated and on what basis?"—is not so easy to answer. Consider the following commentary by Bunzel on the situation at Zuni: "The priesthoods are the branch of religious service that carries the greatest prestige and heaviest responsibilities. Because of the heavy responsibilities the office is avoided rather than sought, and considerable difficulty is experienced in recruiting [into] the priesthoods. As one informant said, 'They have to catch the men young to make them priests. For if they are old enough to realize all that is required of them, they will refuse'" (1992[1932]:542).

How are we to understand such a situation in which the desirable (prestige) was simultaneously undesirable, in which individuals actively avoided becoming "elite"? And how are we to further evaluate the position of Pueblo women, who were, more often than not, acknowledged by both genders as the most powerful but who nevertheless had very little say in group decision making and thus, to the Western eye, seem to have been the *least* powerful? I will leave these questions unanswered and attempt neither to identify subalterns nor evaluate their degree of disempowerment. It is enough to demonstrate that Northern Tiwa ceremonialism was *about* power. Rather than a Western-style hierarchy in the strict sense, we must view it instead as a kind of circuitry through which power, at once social and spiritual, flowed like electricity—a circuitry, as we will see, that was periodically rewired by priestly electricians.

The term for these electricians among the Northern Tiwas was *lutina* (henceforth lulina), typically translated as "old men" or "Old People." Brandt (1980) has written most explicitly of the lulina and observes that they were regarded as a veritable class of the ritually initiated that was set apart from the uninitiated *'it' oysemayana*, or "New People."[4] The distinction parallels the much better known division between Made People and Dry Food People among the Tewas (Ortiz 1969); the lulina were, in effect, the Made People of Taos Pueblo. As such, they were not a body of all the elderly males in the community. "Old," in this sense, did not refer to an individual's actual age in years but rather to the extent of his religious training. An elderly man who had either failed to take an active part in, or was denied access to, kiva rituals during his youth would continue to be a member of the New People and would be referred to as a "boy" even by priestly initiates who were decades his junior (Bodine 1979:262; Brandt 1980:141). The "men" in "old men," on the other hand, may be taken literally, for women were fully excluded from priestly leadership positions.[5]

Anthropologists know little of the lulina's internal organization. Stevenson's scattered field notes demonstrate that, despite a lack of overall institutional centralization, the structure of relationships between priestly leaders was carefully defined. Arguably (see Parsons 1936:77; Smith 1967:54–55), at the sacerdotal apex was the village cacique, who appears to have been a priest so entirely consumed by his ritual observances that he lived a largely secluded life, shielded from the humdrum affairs of farming, hunting, craft production, and the like. The Northern Tiwa cacique—like the caciques of many other Pueblo groups (see French 1948:3; Hill 1982:184)—was a kind of extrahuman entity, not unlike the divine kings of many African societies in the sense that he was regarded not only as a priest, but also as a collective fetish of sorts, a possession of the community. Consequently, the cacique was not expected to have a loud voice in debates or to stridently push particular agendas; his role was to ratify and legitimize the decrees of the other lulina (see Fenton 1957:320, 342). At both Taos and Picurís Pueblos, the position was held by an individual for life and was hereditary, ideally at least, from father to son (Parsons 1936:77). Indeed, at Picurís it appears that a few children, noblesse by birth, were raised specially for the cacique-ship: "When they were teaching Augustine he was young. I remember he was young. They were teaching him for a Cacique. Cacique is the head of the pueblo, of all the doings, of everything. I remember that he was too young, but still they taught him, those other old men" (Picurís informant quoted in Brown 1973:168). The same was probably true of Taos Pueblo.

Whereas the cacique's eyes were focused on weighty matters in the kiva, the lulina with the greatest day-to-day influence seem to have been the moiety heads, each of whom was selected from the male membership of a specific kiva (Stevenson 1906–1907:file 3.1). These positions were exclusionary by design, and while they were not strictly hereditary, there was a marked tendency for particular families to dominate moiety leadership over multiple generations, thereby asserting themselves as the major players in the community. The Romero family provides a case in point. At the time of Stevenson's research in 1906, the northside moiety was effectively led by Venturo Romero, the Big Earring Man. Venturo had received religious training from his maternal great-grandfather, a "great man" and an important priest of the community who had presumably been the moiety head of the previous generation and had personally selected Venturo to be his successor (Stevenson 1906–1907:file 2.18). Interestingly, Venturo's native name was Purältláwa, Great White Mantle, "the mantle of strength and power, or the most powerful" (Stevenson 1906–1907:file 3.14). This name would have been given to him at the time of his kiva initiation (likely while he was a pre-adolescent), and it would have surely signaled the expectation that he was to become a village leader. Venturo, in other words, appears to have been born into a certain privilege, though he also benefited from his own innate charisma and leadership abilities, which were considerable. He became widely respected and was viewed by community members as the "earthly representative" of the Creator deity and as a leader who was "regarded as more than human" (Stevenson 1906–1907:file 3.25; see also file 3.26).

Venturo died in 1918, and there are suggestions that shortly thereafter his memory was well on its way to attaining semi-mythological status. Grant (1976[1925]:83–84) heard tales in the early 1920s (originally recounted by Venturo himself) of his great prowess at buffalo hunting. One such story told of his first expedition, during which Venturo, a neophyte at the age of sixteen or so, allegedly killed four buffalo while the seasoned hunters in the entourage came back empty-handed. The story may have been true, or be based in fact, but its retelling helped turn Venturo into something of a legend. Significantly, it did so following established tradition. The northside moiety at Taos, as we have seen, was symbolically associated with hunting, and it was therefore appropriate that Venturo, the leader of this moiety, distinguished himself early on as a leader of the hunt. Ritual symbolism was no mere abstract structure; it was the very stuff of which political leaders were made.

Following Venturo's death, his son and apprentice, Tomás, succeeded him as head of the northside moiety. According to Parsons (1936:77), Tomás Romero was only twenty years old when he became moiety head, highlighting once again the reality that governance at Taos was not strictly gerontocratic in nature. Pedigree rather than age was the key characteristic of leaders. As his father before him, Tomás assumed the preeminent leadership position in the community and was described as "Chief of the Houses, i.e., Town chief and Council chief" (Parsons 1936:77).

By the 1950s and 1960s, ethnographic reports on Taos Pueblo ceased to publish the names of the individuals serving as Big Earring Man or northside moiety head. Given that Tomás Romero had already begun training his sons in the Big Earring Kiva, it seems likely that the position remained within the lineage. Regardless, what clearly did continue was the preeminence of the position in the village hierarchy (Ellis 1974[1962]:49; Fenton 1957; Smith 1967:161), albeit in the face of increasing public resistance. Indeed, in the 1960s, Smith's (1967:161, 193–197) informants openly complained that the Big Earring Man acted unilaterally, aggressively inserting himself into all major decisions made at the pueblo. The disgruntled clearly felt that the Big Earring Man caused as many problems as he solved, but if a bully, he was nevertheless a bully that the community could not easily do without. As one Taos member commented: "he's the only one who knows what's going on, so everybody has to come running to him to help straighten things out and figure out what's going on. He pushes people here and there and settles everything, and then goes around saying what a great man he is, always able to keep things running smoothly when trouble comes" (quoted in Smith 1967:162).

Throughout the twentieth century, the head of the northside moiety wielded substantial power, and the position was successfully cultivated within a single hereditary line. In earlier generations, it appears that the cacique or the head of the southside moiety periodically held greater influence, and we might speculate that other kiva leaders saw their day in the sun from time to time as well. Prior to the Spanish curtailment of Pueblo warfare during the early colonial period, the war chief may well have been a priestly office of special importance, particularly when outside aggressors threatened. Suffice it to say that a variety of institutionalized offices, in variable states of cooperation or competition, existed within the corporation of priests that held sway over Northern Tiwa communities. One might conclude that the overall organization was heterarchical in the sense that the paths to governance were manifold, but it is nevertheless the case that each of these paths ran in roughly parallel fashion through a ritual sphere. Initiation into a kiva and apprenticeship to the lulina were the common denominators, the indispensable elements in any legitimate leader's development.

Despite the competition that took place in the priestly corporation itself, then, all Taos leaders were collaborators at a deeper level, rallying behind a common insistence on the specific religious prerequisites of leadership and the ritualized structure of the group's decision-making process. Indeed, elaborate and highly formalized rules dictated the process of political deliberation (Stevenson 1906–1907:file 3.22; see also file 2.32). When the lulina became aware of a matter of community concern, for example, the issue had to be officially raised by particular kiva heads and then circulated throughout the various kivas of the village in a defined order that reflected the overall ritual importance of each kiva. In fact, the deliberations themselves were viewed as rituals in that correct performance ensured a correct decision. French discussed this pattern at Isleta Pueblo, and his observations might reasonably be extended to Taos:

> The Isletas do not distinguish sharply between religion and politics; attitudes toward religion are carried over into spheres that are considered to be purely political in other societies. As a consequence, meetings are regarded in somewhat the same light that ceremonies are. If a meeting is properly called and is attended by the proper people, if the deliberations are carried on with an earnest endeavor to further the interests of the pueblo, and if the men present strive to be thoughtful and wise, then a "correct" decision is believed to follow automatically. The Isletas believe that thoughts can be supernaturally guided; and this belief is a factor leading to the acceptance of decisions which have been reached in the customary ways. (French 1948:37)

Consequently, community decision making was the natural responsibility of those with the deepest religious connections and insight.

Given the lulina's control over decision making, one would also expect them to have largely cornered the market on prestige—as it seems they did. The status of the Northern Tiwa priest derived from his extensive ritual labor (e.g., extended prayer, the making of offerings, and the like), designed to keep the world running in equilibrium. Again, we must bear in mind that such labor was simultaneously desirable, insofar as it was a source of great power, and undesirable, insofar as it involved great personal sacrifice. As at most pueblos, the very acts of ritual practice were thought to tax an individual's well-being. One informant told Parsons (1936:79) that some priests even died after assuming office, so heavy was their burden. For their labors, they received respect and gratitude. The community—indeed, the entire world— was in their debt.

Beyond being esteemed for their priestly duties, the lulina also stood atop the prestige hierarchy due to the belief that they became important otherworldly agents after death. Stevenson's (1906–1907:file 2.19) notes reveal that the Northern Tiwas had a complex cosmology involving a series of five worlds, the fifth and uppermost being the present world of the living. After death, all community members descended to one of the four lower worlds, although the destination was contingent upon an individual's position in the ceremonial organization. The more one participated in the ritual life of the community, the closer one resided to Kwathlowúna, the prime deity, in the afterlife. Apparently, those who served in the most important priestly positions (i.e., as cacique or Big Earring Man) were destined, after death, to sit *beside* Kwathlowúna, where their divine labor would continue. Thus did they become spirit beings in their own right who affected the course of natural events (Stevenson 1906–1907:file 3.25). Unlike the New People—that is, the ordinary Northern Tiwas—the lulina were also thought to be transformed by death into katsina, potent beings who affected the world in a variety of ways but most importantly by bringing or withholding rainfall (Stevenson 1906–1907:file 4.3). Their prestige in life, then, derived partly from their anticipated powers in death.

Systems of prestige and power, of haves and have-nots, do not go unchallenged for long, and those at the helm must therefore have some means of safeguarding and reproducing their advantage over time. How did the lulina perpetuate the hierocratic system? Superficially, we might point to one observation already made: certain prominent positions at Taos were effectively passed down from father to son, a classic means of promoting structural continuity. But nepotism alone says very little, for the heritability of leadership is itself an inequality that demands explanation.

Elizabeth Brandt's (1977, 1980, 1994) research takes us further in this regard. Drawing principally from her fieldwork at Taos, Brandt emphasizes that internal religious secrecy was the fundamental tool used by Pueblo priests both to perpetuate an ideology that granted them a largely unquestioned authority and to restrict entry into the system to those they had personally socialized.

> The religious knowledge possessed by the Old People [i.e., the lulina] is a source of natural power as Pueblo religion deals with the forces of the universe and nature generally; and as leaders they are required to fulfill their duties, responsibilities, and rights to the community to keep these forces in balance. Their authority...proceeds from their sacred knowledge: their power...from their coterminous positions in the political system and the religious system. By limiting access to the religious system, they limit access to the political system. (Brandt 1980:142–143)

Secrecy thus was more than a cultural practice; it was a basic organizational tenet. The members of Taos Pueblo were committed to the belief that prayers, ceremonies, objects, and places were powerful and potent only when the core knowledge about those ceremonies or objects was restricted to and managed by individuals with the appropriate training. Such secrets were protected from foreigners collectively by the village, but they were also protected by individual kiva groups within the village from *each other*. Brandt has appropriately described this as a complex system of both "internal" and "external" secrecy.

We should not pass over this observation hastily. It has, of course, become far too easy to simply nod and agree that knowledge is power. The equation has become a platitude that, when invoked in a Pueblo context, tends to stand in the way of careful analysis. It is essential, instead, that we view the logic of Pueblo secrecy as a much more tangible phenomenon—analogous, perhaps, to the manner in which we view the capitalist logic of value as a core component of modern economies. There is much to recommend such a comparison. Just as supply and demand dictate the market value of commodities in capitalist systems, the power of Pueblo sacred objects was dictated in part by the extent to which knowledge of those objects was confined to a select few. Flooding the market with a particular commodity reduces its value; so too the democratization of knowledge about a sacred object reduces its power (see Parsons 1936:117). And just as the capitalist might limit the supply of particular commodities to increase their worth (all else being equal), so too did Pueblo priests limit the public knowledge of sacred things to enhance their power—the power, that is, of the sacred objects and rituals, as well as, of course, their priestly possessors. Capitalist notions of market value and Pueblo notions of religious power, in other words, are both part of their own distinct cultural imaginary, but both also have quite concrete social influences insofar as they serve as fundamental rationales upon which agents act.

In practice, secrecy had additional consequences. Brandt (1980:142) notes that it permitted the Taos lulina to "invoke dire but unnamed supernatural sanctions on the rest of the population." The lulina could "ban anything they wish[ed] without the necessity for explanation by invoking secrecy." We need not look far afield for a comparative example to better grasp this state of affairs. Indeed, in its war on terror, the George W. Bush administration regularly employed secrecy in just this manner, effectively obscuring and rendering indisputable its actions by claiming that dire but unnamed compromises to national security would result if knowledge of governmental strategies were made public. It matters little whether danger comes in the form of shadowy terrorists or cloud-like katsina spirits descending from the skies to destroy society; the result is similar. When secrecy is made an essential component of knowledge, when breaches of secrecy are portrayed as grave dangers, the very questioning of the secret-holders becomes an act against the social good. Thus does political dissent lose its voice as the secret-holders acquire an authoritarian power that is beyond question.

At Taos, the patterns just described were reproduced through an elaborate system of kiva initiation during which ceremonial knowledge was transmitted to subsequent generations. Boys between the ages of roughly eight and twelve began their initiation with a period of up to eighteen months spent primarily in the kiva, away from their families and under the close watch of the priestly establishment (Bodine 1979:262; Stevenson 1906–1907:files 3.14, 3.23). During this time, they were instructed in such things as the speaking of archaic languages, the production of kiva objects, and the extensive recipes for ritual action, all of which comprised a body of esoteric knowledge from which the women and uninitiated males of the community were largely excluded (Brandt 1980:129; Miller 1898:38; Stevenson 1906–1907:file 2.5). Such instruction continued long after initiation, especially among the few who became apprentices to senior priests.

Ethnographic reports suggest that a fairly significant percentage of boys—during the past century at least—did not undergo initiation and that those who did varied in the length and depth of their training. The sons of important priests appear to have been specially bred for leadership from a young age. Boys with less prestigious parentage were given less attention. Such variability in childhood experiences translated directly into subsequent inequalities among men, for those who did not undergo the full kiva initiation during their youth were afterward denied positions of leadership, even if they matured into highly competent adults. How could an individual who never learned the secrets of the world be an effective leader within that world? In effect, the life possibilities of men were determined early on.

The Pueblo Paradox

There is a sense, then, in which Taos and the other pueblos conformed to a traditional model of a stratified society. One can legitimately speak of elites and non-elites. One can speak of hierarchy. One can speak of power. Status was not solely based on achievement; rather, ascription played a heavy hand. This much has been obvious to nearly all serious students of Southwestern ethnography, giving rise to the common assertion that the pueblos were theocracies (e.g., Brandt 1980; Eggan 1950:291; Hill 1982:181–182; Lange 1967:85; Pandey 1977:198; Parsons 1996b[1939]; White 1942:183–184; Whiteley 1998).

The term "theocracy" invites comparison with much larger-scale social phenomena: African polities governed by principles of divine kingship, royal monarchies of medieval Europe, pharaonic Egypt, and the like. Such comparisons are slippery exercises and, when taken too far, draw attention away from a key difference: however "elite" the priests were within the overall moral hierarchy of the pueblos, they nevertheless had no special—let alone kingly—privilege in any significant economic sense, or at least in any sense that we would immediately recognize as economic. Theirs was an elitism without grander residences, larger storehouses, or more wives. With few exceptions, the priests did not partake of privileged cuisine, nor did they wear fancy baubles signifying their status. Priests were even without exemption from hard labor. In fact, from a Pueblo perspective, it was *they* who labored most intensely; it was they who made the greatest personal sacrifice. The same appears to have been true in late pre-Columbian times. In a remarkable study of the Hawikku village mortuary assemblage, Todd Howell (2001) demonstrates that the priestly elite of the ancestral Zunis were not only no healthier than their peers; they also appear to have, on average, died earlier and suffered slightly higher levels of iron-deficiency anemia. The Pueblo priest, in other words, was not even close to being a king. This has also been obvious to serious students of Southwestern archaeology and ethnography.

The strangely blurred image of Pueblo priests as both master *and* slave, as both most *and* least powerful (depending upon the perspective taken), once fueled heated debate among Southwestern archaeologists over the nature of Puebloan social complexity—to little avail. Perhaps the final word was had by McGuire and Saitta (1996:201), who argued in an influential article that Pueblo society was at once egalitarian and inegalitarian, a complicated amalgam of contradictory principles: "Prehispanic pueblos, while not egalitarian, were not stratified either; in fact, they were simultaneously *both*" (see also Lekson 2005; Plog 1995). Whatever truth there may be to this position, it does not satisfactorily address the paradox of Pueblo leadership. Indeed, there is a sense in which McGuire and Saitta have restated, rather than answered, the quandary before us. To argue that the Pueblos simultaneously emphasized egalitarianism and stratification merely points to the inadequacy of these terms, as typically conceived, and our goal therefore must be to move beyond such contradictions toward an understanding of Pueblo leadership within its own logical universe.

One way of moving toward this goal might be to build from Pierre Clastres's (1989) seminal discussion of "powerless power," a parallel and similarly contradictory pattern that he viewed as characteristic of many tribal societies in the Americas. Clastres's concern was with the anthropological contrast between state and pre-state (or, better, non-state) societies, the latter of which, he argued, had been mischaracterized as evolutionarily undeveloped and as innocently unaware of true coercive power exerted by a few over the many. In contrast, Clastres sought to expose a form of noncoercive power (i.e., powerless power) exerted by tribal collectivities upon themselves, a power that enforced a radical egalitarianism and consciously abandoned the bullying of state societies. The tribal chief, in Clastres's vision, was a public symbol of that which had been rejected, a king in a cage whose superficial privileges were carefully managed and circumscribed by the collectivity: "Indian [i.e., indigenous New World] cultures are cultures anxious to reject a power that fascinates them: the affluence of the chief is the group's daydream. And it is clearly for the purpose of expressing both the culture's concern for itself and the dream it has of transcending itself, that power, paradoxical by its nature, is venerated in its impotence: this is the Indian chief, a metaphor for the tribe, the *imago* of its myth" (Clastres 1989:47). So too may it have been with the Pueblo cacique, the preeminent or "most powerful" figure in many villages. Confined for much of his adult life to the kiva, the cacique appears to have been curated as a kind of community fetish whose religious potency was the very foundation of his political impotence: he was regarded as far too important to engage in open debate about workaday matters, far too important to be disturbed by overt argument.

But Clastres's discussion can only take us so far; it does not adequately account for the more assertive of the Pueblo religious leaders, such as those discussed above. These were individuals whose power was hardly "powerless." Indeed, the widespread competition, factionalism, and attention to rules of secrecy indicate that there was much at stake. Nevertheless, if the priests possessed a veritable power—as it seems they did—then toward what ends was this power directed? Why does it appear that these power-holders abstained from a life of material privilege, like businessmen who amass large sums of money only to leave them unspent and in bank accounts, an unused potentiality? As Marx classically observed, to desire money for its own sake is to engage in behavior that is more "fetishistic" than "rational." Religion for religion's sake among the Pueblos might similarly be presented as fundamentally irrational. Were economic concerns really so detached from ceremonial practice? Southwestern scholars with materialist orientations have periodically tried to argue to the contrary, insisting that—here, as everywhere—economic interests must ultimately have been infrastructural (e.g., Lightfoot and Upham 1989). McGuire and Saitta (1996) adopt the position, for instance, that there were indeed pronounced material inequalities built into Pueblo religion. During periods of subsistence shortfall, they conclude, it was the priests whose survival was ensured before all others. In this way, the religious hierarchy can be understood as an "adaptation to scarcity," an insurance policy invoked only during hard times (see also Levy 1992).

Here, however, is where we must ask: what exactly was the Pueblo conception of wealth? Who were the rich and who the poor by indigenous standards? Such questions necessarily precede any anthropological interpretation of systemic inequalities. "Economism is a form of ethnocentrism" (Bourdieu 1990:112), and we cannot proceed as if the Pueblos followed our own narrow sense of economic rationality as related solely to the production and distribution of subsistence goods, craft items, and the like. Indeed, as soon as such questions are posed, we find that the Pueblos viewed things quite differently: the wealthiest Pueblo individual, it seems, was he who controlled the most valuable ceremonies. Religious knowledge and the sacred objects needed to participate in rituals served both as singular or inalienable possessions linked to a group's identity and as prime valuables that were transmitted between generations—and, in rare cases, between communities.

Take the Elk Dance. This ceremony has been performed at Taos Pueblo for many centuries, the leaders of each generation transferring the knowledge and rights of performance to the next generation in the context of ritual initiation and training. Like other intellectual property, knowledge of the dance could be considered an inalienable possession of the tribe, a gift bestowed on younger generations by older ones within the village. During the nineteenth century, however, the nearby Tewa village of Nambé came to desire or need the Taos Elk Dance. Presumably, Nambé leaders had witnessed the dance during visits to Taos and already knew something about the procedures and dance steps involved. Nevertheless, the dance was the property of Taos, and so the Nambé community was obligated to purchase the right to perform the ceremony before it could be introduced into their own ritual calendar. Selling some of their land to the Hispanos, Nambé raised sufficient funds to obtain "ten turquoises, five red beads, twelve dance blankets, and twelve deerskins," which were given to Taos in exchange for the dance (Parsons 1974[1929]:199).

This is not to say that everything had its price, nor that a purchased ceremony was ever fully alienated from its original owner. Parsons (1996b[1939]:969) was told of another late nineteenth-century case in which a contingent of Zuni chiefs traveled to the Hopi mesas to beg for initiation into the Hopi Snake-Antelope societies. In exchange, they offered "two large oxen, ten or more sheep, much wheat, rawhide moccasins, and other wealth"; however, the Hopis declined the offer, worrying that the "medicine"—that is, the corpus of Snake-Antelope ceremonies—might "lose its virtue." Be that as it may, the fact that the offer was made underscores the broader observation that "buying a ceremony," as Parsons put it, was a familiar practice. And it also underscores the important observation that esoteric knowledge, ritual objects, and the rights to engage in ceremony were conceptualized not only as means of cultural reproduction and worldly maintenance, but simultaneously as forms of wealth that marked a distinction between haves and have-nots.

Indeed, this wealth function of sacred objects and rituals helps us to understand an otherwise curious pattern surrounding the outcomes of major factional disputes that, prior to the reservation system, appear to have regularly led to the fragmentation of Pueblo communities. I will have more to say about the sources of Pueblo factionalism in later chapters, but for the time being let me simply draw attention to the remarkable observation made by a number of ethnographers that when irresolvable disputes arose, it was the "traditionalist" or "conservative" faction in control of key ceremonies that typically emigrated: "When a factional split becomes so intense as to cause village fission, it is the conservatives who leave, taking their information with them. They have the ability and the techniques to reconstitute a complete new village, but those who are left behind are in the same position as an American community might be if all the utilities were abandoned and the trained personnel were gone as well as all the religious and political leadership" (Brandt 1980:144; see also Parsons 1996b[1939]:1094). In other words, agricultural fields, hunting areas, storehouses filled with corn, and the like—all the things that Western materialists tend to assume were the Pueblos' core economic holdings—were considered expendable providing one maintained control of one's ceremonies. To take such a pattern seriously is to acknowledge the basic failure of traditional Western strategies of analytic reductionism; one simply cannot argue that the Pueblos used religion to legitimize the political or that, in turn, they used the political to secure access to the economic—unless, of course, one entirely reconceives the meanings of these categories.

Historic Pueblo religion, let me reiterate, cannot be said to legitimize political or economic inequalities if one has in mind some notion of political economy as a discrete analytical sphere. If we are to talk of legitimization at all, then we must begin with the acknowledgment that Pueblo religion primarily existed to legitimize *itself*, that differential access to and knowledge of the sacred was both means and end, and that ceremonial life was simultaneously superstructure and base.

This is not a common argument in archaeological studies of the Pueblos. Scholarship has tended toward two somewhat different positions, which I will gloss as the integration thesis and the legitimation thesis. The former, dominant throughout most of the latter half of the twentieth century but waning significantly in popularity in recent years, presents Pueblo religion fundamentally as a means of building community solidarity and social integration, as a natural adaptation to organizational demands within more or less egalitarian communities that lacked the strong political leaders who, in more complex societies, would have done the organizing themselves. Consider three late twentieth-century statements:

> The change in ritual architecture [at Grasshopper Pueblo] suggests expansion of ritualism with population aggregation as a principal means of accommodating different coresident ethnic groups, facilitating decision making within the community, and developing a latticework of ritual organizations, all of which ultimately had the effect of integrating social groups. (Reid and Montgomery 1999:24)

> During the period of Arroyo Hondo's most rapid expansion, new arrivals to the pueblo must have been relatively frequent. Ritual systems, represented architecturally by kivas, may have played an important role both in integrating settlements at the regional level and in assimilating the new population into existing settlements. (Creamer 1993:107)

> Ritual systems, always important for holding Anasazi communities together, became critical in preventing fission of the large pueblos [on the Pajarito Plateau], thereby providing avenues for redistribution of food, and streamlining decision-making hierarchies. (Van Zandt 1999:386)

Each author had a different late pre-Columbian village in mind, but each asked a common question—how were newly aggregated villages integrated, how were they held together?—and each drew a common conclusion: that religious ritual was the binding force. "Ritual systems" here become veritable agents, integrating society, negotiating between ethnic groups, redistributing food, and so on, and religion is understood as addressing issues that would otherwise have been the bread and butter of political contestation.

Is religion, then, cast *as* politics? Not at all. In the integration thesis, Pueblo religion is given a profoundly apolitical (one might even say anti-political) inflection, the entire emphasis being placed on the building of solidarity, on that which keeps a society functioning as a leaderless whole. Indeed, religious ritual is explicitly presented as existing to cure, prevent, or do away with the precise interpersonal competition that one would identify as "political" in the first place. This bias pervades the literature at deep levels. One need only note the remarkably widespread tendency in Southwestern archaeology to label all religious buildings as "integrative architecture" or as "communal structures" (see, in particular, Lipe and Hegmon, eds. 1989). Such terminology is slippery, for it implies not only that solidarity and the avoidance of competition were the intention of those who built the structures, but also that social integration was the necessary outcome of the structures' subsequent use.

Ethnography, however, knows no perfectly integrated system, no society characterized by such interpersonal purity of either intent or outcome. Anthropologists have critiqued functionalism on this very point for over half a century (e.g., Kroeber and Kluckhohn 1952:159). As Steven Lukes put it: "'what holds society together'—the so-called 'problem of order'—is an exceedingly complicated problem.... The first question is whether, to what extent, and in what ways, a society *does* 'hold together.' That question must be answered first, before one can seek to determine what factors are responsible for its putative integration: specifying the *explanandum* must precede seeking explanations" (1975:297). Archaeologists, particularly those of us excavating the tribal heartland of functionalist studies, would do well to keep such questions in mind. What integration was there? Did society really "hold together"? How are we to explain social disorganization? What about the problem of *disorder*? And in regard to the Pueblo case: to what extent might we read ritual structures as *disintegrative* architecture; to what extent can Pueblo religion be read as a species of political opposition even as it stressed ideological themes of communalism and balanced holism?

For students of Southwestern ethnography, such questions arise naturally. As I have already observed, the historic Pueblos hardly conform to a utopian image of perfect integration. Nevertheless, in the heat of archaeological study, analytical skill tends to be measured by one's ability to reveal order rather than disorder, to show how the pieces fit together rather than how they fall apart. And so the integration thesis is perpetuated, despite the reality that it is little more than the old Durkheimian model of primitive religion, filtered through British structural functionalism and American neo-evolutionary theory, and subsequently imposed uncritically upon the Pueblo past. Functionalism, the persistent weed in the garden of Southwestern archaeology, continues to dispatch its spores.

I am hardly alone in my dissatisfaction with the integration thesis. Beginning in the 1980s, many have sought to cast political light on precolonial Pueblo religion (notably, McGuire and Saitta 1996; Mills, ed. 2000; Plog 1995; Potter and Perry 2000; Saitta 1997; Upham 1982, 1989). Out with Durkheim, in with Marx. Consider the commentary of two of the earliest and most vociferous critics of functionalism in Southwestern archaeology: "One obtains a feeling from reading these current [integrationist] studies that...ceremonial activities operate in a social framework that is largely divorced from 'hard-core' political factors such as decision-making, the distribution of goods, social differences, and the relations of power" (Lightfoot and Upham 1989:18). For many scholars who participated in this critique, the politicization of Pueblo religion notably went hand in hand with a sort of social complexification—an evolutionary "bumping up"—by which the precolonial Pueblos came to be presented as chiefdoms rather than tribes, ranked or stratified rather than egalitarian, and, for a bold few, regional "states" rather than a congeries of pre-state communities. The implicit assumption was that the politicization of religion must characterize evolutionarily *later* rather than evolutionarily prior societies. And here we meet the same discourse of degeneration in which an original "true" religion came to be progressively corrupted by politics and rendered "false." We meet, that is, the first of the two great divides in secularism's master narrative.

Be that as it may, my present interest lies in the proposed relationship between Pueblo religion and the "hard-core" political factors referred to in Lightfoot and Upham's statement. There is no question that Lightfoot and Upham considered decision making, the distribution of goods, social differences, and the relations of power to comprise that hard political core. Also note that by "decision-making" they clearly had in mind nonreligious decisions (e.g., who gets which plots of agricultural land, who has access to which trade goods, how social transgressors are punished, etc.); by "power" they meant the ability to make those nonreligious decisions and to derive economic benefit accordingly; and by "social differences" they meant the disparities of prestige and authority that make such a system of nonreligious power possible. Their critique of the integration thesis, then, was that Pueblo religion always served some deeper set of objectives. Religion and politics were intertwined.

I am not unsympathetic to their position. Nevertheless, to proclaim that religion and politics are closely related—even so closely related as to be inseparable—is to reify a questionable division of Pueblo society into conceptually distinct sacred and profane or secular realms. The trap is easily sprung, for it lies quivering behind the very use of religion and politics as analytical categories:

> "Political," that is, secular power concerns relationships of control within and
> between social groups, and it tends to be ultimately reducible to control of mate-
> rial production—"strategic resources."... Structures of political power are, then,
> empirical—somehow solid, measurable, and susceptible to analytical scrutiny: They
> conform to "our" concepts of rational activity. "Religious" power, on the other hand,
> concerns conceptions and experience of the numinous—power as an immanent mysti-
> cal entity, inaccessible to direct analysis. "Religious" practices must be transfigured
> into schemes of "symbolism," which only affect political practice indirectly, and are
> typically treated as devices of legitimation...expressions rather than instruments of
> social action. (Whiteley 1998:83–84)

Whiteley's commentary on this matter, written in the course of his critical re-appraisal of Hopi ethnography, is invaluable, but there is a certain advantage to putting things more bluntly: to the extent that we, in the West, view political power as a real and efficacious medium of worldly practice, we relegate "religious power" (if, indeed, the phrase is not considered oxymoronic) to an *imaginary* or *symbolic* medium of action. Religious power is either political power in disguise—a wolf in sheep's clothing—or it is not power at all. Hence what I refer to as the legitimation thesis: Pueblo religion existed not only to entice rain from the heavens, to encourage animals to submit to hunters, and to build social harmony; it also (and more importantly, it is argued) existed to sanction or render legitimate a system of inequality vis-à-vis access to hard-core political and economic resources.

Is this not a step in the right direction? Does it not move us away from modernist dichotomies, bringing religion and politics into greater intimacy? Quite the opposite. To say that religion and politics are analytically distinct modes of social practice that are nevertheless so closely related as to frequently overlap is to condition us to forever see two things where there is but one. Confronted with a total social fact, the analyst sees two separate facts, as if suffering from a kind of double vision. This perceptual ailment—call it anthropological diplopia—causes us to carve up the meaningful practices of social actors into opposed realms of religious meaning and political practice, the result of which is that any evidence of competitive or strategic interpersonal action in a sacral chamber is immediately taken as the doing of something called "politics" with something called "religion." Religion is relegated to a kind of symbolic raw material, a reservoir of belief that, while innocuous in and of itself, becomes noxious when drawn into the (nonreligious) agendas of politicians. Proponents of the legitimation thesis, in their effort to draw religion and politics together, only succeed in moving them further apart.

Severe cases of anthropological diplopia can lead to headaches, and I suggest that the Pueblo paradox with which this chapter has been centrally concerned is precisely this sort of headache. As a case in point, recall Howell's (2001) discovery that the priestly leaders of the ancestral Zuni at Hawikku ate no better than the greater population and that they therefore lacked privileged access to "basic economic resources." The challenge posed should be clear: the alleged device of legitimation is present, but without evident purpose. In puzzlement, the Western scholar is left squinting for the missing politico-economic image that is expected just to the side of the religious image, searching for the missing base beneath the superstructure.

The solution, it would seem, is singularity of vision: we must accept the totality of social action as a totality. Four centuries of Protestant critiques have made us cross-eyed to the point that we have real difficulty doing without our illusory dichotomies. Pueblo religion wasn't merely related to hard-core political factors; if anything, it *was* that hardened core. Sacred things were staples. These are simple observations, but they have a sufficiently powerful alchemy to turn the study of Pueblo religion into the study of political economy (and vice versa). More important, as our secular analytical categories begin to collapse in upon themselves, a clearing emerges in which Pueblo society can begin to be reimagined using indigenous concepts. This is the project reserved for chapters 4 and 5. For now, however, we are not yet through with the category "Pueblo religion."

three
Belief and Unbelief
in a Pueblo Society

> [I]f the anthropological study of religious commitment is underdeveloped, the anthropological study of religious noncommitment is nonexistent. The anthropology of religion will have come of age when some more subtle Malinowski writes a book called "Belief and Unbelief (or even "Faith and Hypocrisy") in a Savage Society."
>
> —*Clifford Geertz, "Religion as a Cultural System"*

> The people did Indian dances.
> BUT THEY DIDN'T DO THEM ALL THE TIME.
> —*Vine Deloria Jr.,* Custer Died for Your Sins

Were I to reduce the previous chapter to a single plea—that we take religion as seriously as the ancestral Pueblos did—then the present chapter might be considered an extended qualification of that plea.

The qualification is really a set of caveats, some of which have been anticipated. I have already petitioned, for instance, that we avoid succumbing to the temptation of producing yet another meditation on the extent to which premodern religions were intertwined with "real" political and economic power. If this is how religion's explanatory position is elevated, then we have failed in our task, for the very positing of an analytical division between religion, politics, and economics obscures more than it clarifies. Moreover, we must dodge the well-camouflaged trap of speaking about religion as an ideological buttress legitimating some other system of inequalities. It is, for instance, a common anthropological argument that one segment of ancient society may have held political authority and decision-making power over another due to the former's monopoly of certain sacred objects or prayers upon which the latter was dependent. Such propositions merely dodge the more fundamental question of why unequal distributions of sacred things were accepted in the first place. If religious inequalities legitimize political inequalities, what legitimizes religious inequalities? Might the relationship be inverted? Why not view nonreligious decision-making power as a kind of superstructure legitimizing differential access to the sacred? Our difficulty in answering such questions underscores the limitations of legitimation discourse and of reductionist explanations generally. "What I mean by taking religion 'seriously' is to take it *religiously*" (Latour 2009:460)—not politically or economically.

For the moment, however, my concern is with a different caveat: if we are to take premodern religion seriously as a mode of social action, if we are to acknowledge that it may have been an end in itself and not a means toward some other nonreligious goal, then we must not slip into the assumption that the past was necessarily brimming over with spiritual vim and vigor. Ironically, we must struggle to explore a contrary position, for taking religion seriously means not taking it for granted, not regarding it as a premodern default mode. Taking religion seriously means viewing it as a contingent construction rather than a biological given, a construction that, in different times and places, may have ranged from weak to strong, informal to highly formal, insignificant to hegemonic. We must even be prepared to acknowledge that some premodern cultures or subcultures may not have been religious at all, or at least that they may have lacked anything we would feel comfortable labeling a religion.

How readily we assume—typically without even a moment's reflection—that secularity and skepticism (here, I am drawing upon popular understandings of "secularity" and "skepticism") are uniquely modern inventions and that primitivity and pronounced magico-religious credulity inevitably go hand in hand. Some anthropologists have been explicit in this assumption, referring to all "primitive societies" as necessarily "sacred societies" (e.g., Yinger 1970). Others, even while acknowledging that each of us is "admittedly a *homo religious*," still maintain that religiosity was most profoundly the domain of "the man of traditional societies" (Eliade 1961[1957]:15). "From many ethnographic accounts we know that life in 'small-scale,' 'tribal' and 'non-western' societies is permeated with religion" (Verhoeven 2002:7; see also Pauketat 2011), argues modern archaeology, echoing the early twentieth-century assumptions of sociocultural anthropology, which regularly concluded that "primitive societies without religion have never been found" (Howells 1948:11). There is a remarkable conceit here, which is thrown into stark relief when communities of nonbelieving, atheistic anthropologists nod in agreement that belief in some notion of the sacred, the transcendent, or the supernatural is a universal aspect of human existence shared by all communities (present company excluded, of course). Even apathy toward things divine seems to be the prerogative of the modern West.

The present chapter attempts to wipe away this presumption of intense premodern religiosity. My focus is upon a period one millennium ago in north-central New Mexico, and my proximate goal is to survey what we are inclined to regard as the local "religious" landscape prior to the development of Northern Tiwa society as described in the previous chapter. But given my broader agenda, let me begin by placing into question whether this religious landscape existed at all.

On Being Religiously Unmusical

"Tribesmen are often quite religious, but they are not necessarily full time servants of mumbo-jumbo. Some are decidedly unconcerned about it" (Sahlins 1968:98). Marshall Sahlins offered this characteristically insightful observation solidly within a paradigm that took "being religious" to mean believing deeply in the supernatural (that is, in mumbo-jumbo). More recent anthropology has tended to draw our attention to religion as a mode of action and discipline, and it is therefore an open question whether Sahlins would have described tribal societies as potentially unfettered by religious *practice*, as by religious belief. Be that as it may, his larger message—that we must make analytical space for non-Western or premodern societies that lack interest in any sort of phenomena that can easily be called religious—is not one that more recent anthropology has considered in any sustained way. "If the anthropological study of religious commitment is underdeveloped, the anthropological study of religious noncommitment is nonexistent"—this was how Geertz (1973:109n33) summed up the matter during the early 1970s. His observation (tucked away in a footnote) of our inattentiveness to religious noncommitment was hardly a clarion call; the same observation can be made of the present.

There have been a few other voices in the wilderness, foremost among them that of Mary Douglas, who wrote passionately against the myth of the credulous native:

> The idea that primitive man is by nature deeply religious is nonsense. The truth is
> that all the varieties of scepticism, materialism and spiritual fervour are to be found
> in the range of tribal societies. They vary as much from one another on these lines
> as any chosen segments of London life. The illusion that all primitives are pious,
> credulous and subject to the teaching of priests or magicians has probably done even
> more to impede our understanding of our own civilisation than it has confused the
> interpretations of archaeologists dealing with the dead past. (Douglas 1982:x; see also
> Goody 1996)

Given the project at hand, I advise underscoring the archaeological slight at the end of Douglas's statement. She is correct of course. Archaeologists have always had difficulty believing in the unbelief of others. Textbooks present the history of the world as the history of the devout and superstitious with premodernity extending like a vast iceberg of religiosity into the depths of time and with only modern secular society—the tip of the iceberg—managing to keep its head above water. Whatever the past was, it was enchanted.

But how seriously should we take the critique of this position? Realistically, how many times and places in the past were truly disenchanted in the Weberian sense of being free from belief in "mysterious incalculable forces" (Weber 1946:139)? How common was it for ancient peoples to stop and think, "No, I don't believe in all your gods and spirits any longer—society is better off without them"? How many premodern societies really were religiously unmusical, immune to the rhythms of sacred drums, "tone deaf when it [came] to religion just as one can be oblivious to the charms of music" (Rorty 2005:30)?

Twentieth-century ethnography of non-Western peoples would seem to lead us to the conclusion that "secular tribes" (Douglas's phrase) were rare indeed. Nevertheless, Douglas's suggestion was precisely that the dearth of ethnographic examples derives less from cultural realities than from the fact that anthropology has been closed to the possibility that premodern or non-Western peoples were anything but deeply spiritual. Secular tribes, she contended, have been hammered into religious molds, even in light of strong opposing evidence. To make her point, Douglas highlighted Barth's work among the Basseri nomads of Iran in which he confronted a society with "a ritual life of unusual poverty," that was surprisingly disinterested in religion (Barth 1961:146). This is not to say that the Basseris had no concepts of the sacred or of the spirit world—they were still, as Douglas put it, "slack Moslems"— only that these concepts were neither integrated into an overarching symbolic system nor used as a basis for ritual elaboration. That is, the Basseris were religiously unmusical, and this sort of situation, she suggested, was much more common than traditionally acknowledged.

I should point out that Barth did not consider the Basseris to be "secular," nor did he accept their ritual poverty at face value. His solution to the situation was to find fault in the narrow definition of "ritual" with which he was forced to work: "In the above description, I have adopted a sort of 'common sense' view of ritual, and compiled a list of those customs or actions which are explicitly non-technical, essentially those which the Basseri themselves classify in categories translatable as 'ceremonies,' 'religion,' and 'magic.' Greater sophistication in the definition of ritual might lead to an expansion of the field of inquiry" (Barth 1961:146). Barth proposed that we instead focus on ritual's symbolic or meaning-laden aspect. Everyday activities, he argued, can be imbued with meaning, and the technical requirements of a society's ecological adaptation can provide the basis for a system of symbols that might be considered part of an expanded definition of religion. The fact that movement structured and gave meaning to Basseri life elevated it, in Barth's view, to the status of religion, and in this way the Basseris again slid back into the security of an anthropological norm. It goes without saying, however, that every cultural act is meaningful in some way, and the natural extension of Barth's line of reasoning would be to equate religion with culture itself, leaving any remaining analytic utility to slip between the arms of its encompassing embrace.

The problem, I suspect, is that we tend to view modern Western scientific rationalism as the only meaningful foil for the religious society, even though other foils can be imagined. Before they had the opportunity to become "slack Moslems," for instance, nomadic groups such as the Basseris in the Middle East might have best been characterized by what W. Montgomery Watt described as pre-Islamic "tribal humanism":

> In contrast to the archaic religion stands what may be called "tribal humanism." This was the effective religion of the Arabs of Muhammad's day.... This is the religion we find in the poets of the Jahiliyah. For the poets what gives life a meaning is to belong to a tribe which can boast notable deeds of bravery and generosity, and to have some share in these oneself. From this standpoint the realization of human excellence in action is an end in itself, and at the same time usually contributes to the survival of the tribe, which is the other great end of life. This is humanism in the sense that it is primarily in human values, in virtuous or manly conduct, that it finds significance. But it differs from most modern humanism in that it thinks of the tribe rather than the individual as the locus of these values. (1953:24)

True, Watt wrote of "tribal humanism as a vital religious force" (25), but it should be evident from his discussion that tribal humanism appears to have been more akin to a mixture of secular humanism and nationalism (*qua* tribalism) than it was to religion in the modern sense. Contributions to the honor and prestige of one's tribe—not belief in supernatural beings—marked the path of the devout.

Would we recognize tribal humanism in the archaeological record if we saw it? Would we recognize other modes of being religiously unmusical? These are not idle questions. Large portions of the human past have left us with few material residues that can easily be called religious in any traditional anthropological sense. The millennia of relatively austere life comprising the New World's Archaic and the Old World's Mesolithic leap to mind, but there is no shortage of larger, village-oriented contexts in which materialized religious ideologies seem curiously elusive. Consider how Joan Oates summarized the early Mesopotamian record: "Although there can be little doubt that religious beliefs and rituals played an important role in the societies of sixth millennium B.C. Mesopotamia, surprisingly little unequivocal evidence of religion survives in the archaeological record" (Oates 1978:122). Why did Oates have so little doubt about the importance of religion in 'Ubaid villages? Not due to empirical findings, it seems, but rather due to the profoundly modernist assumption that all premodern and prescientific societies simply must have been highly religious and that premodern religions, rather than being private affairs, must always have dictated the actions of the community and its leaders.

Or to select an archaeological example closer to home, consider the conclusion drawn by an eminent Southwestern archaeologist as he struggled to come to terms with the apparent absence of both ritual architecture and symbolic imagery on ceramics in the Gallina region of New Mexico. "As a matter of fact," noted Stewart Peckham (1990:108), "there is little in Gallina Culture to suggest the nature of their religion." One senses the same surprise here as well. That others have labored more diligently to root out Gallina religiosity (see Ellis 1988:35–45) is a separate issue (although one that demonstrates the strong underlying push to turn premodern peoples into sacred societies). The more important question remains: at what point would the absence of evidence of religious activity lead an archaeologist to conclude that she is in fact confronting a "secular tribe"?

Few anthropologists today would be willing to decouple secularity from the specific condition of modernity. Most would wisely argue that the concept is inseparable from a tangle of related notions, including the spread of democracy, the privatization of faith, the professionalization of science, tolerance, human rights, freedom, and on and on (though we might reasonably question why there seems to be a modernist taboo about exploring many of these notions in premodernity as well). Nevertheless, some language is needed to differentiate religiously unmusical societies in antiquity from those whose religious life seems to have been much more formal, elaborate, highly materialized, group-oriented, and culturally mandatory. Herein lies the real utility of Douglas's unorthodox meditation on secular tribes: it provides a clear reminder that a single model of premodern religiosity—of its form, function, and existence in society—will not do. Before investigating a particular religion, therefore, we must first unpack our anthropological notion of "religion" itself to separate the historically contingent from the universal, if indeed we are willing to cling to any universals at all. What Douglas's exposition does especially effectively is force this unpacking.

With regard to the ancestral Pueblos, then, I propose that we make analytical space for the possibility of both belief and unbelief, practice and nonpractice, enchantment and disenchantment. Indeed, belief and unbelief may well have been two sides of a common coin during certain periods in the Pueblo past—perhaps even dialectically related, for it is difficult to accept that a religious order would ever go uncontested for long. Can ceremonial hegemony ever be complete? Does strong belief ever fail to foment strong *dis*belief or, at least, *counter*belief? The relevance of these questions will be apparent soon enough.

My immediate concern in the following discussion is the eleventh- and twelfth-century occupation of the Taos district, an occupation, it must be admitted, that no one has ever considered to be the vanguard of Pueblo development. However, I want to argue that the modest Taos communities of these centuries become especially interesting when viewed as a foil to, or even as a renunciation of, the remarkably powerful engine of orthodoxy that was concurrently emerging in Chaco Canyon a short distance to the west (figure 3.1). Chaco was one of the great New World experiments in organizational complexity, and recent research has tended to paint this complexity in richly religious hues (Plog 2011). Southwestern archaeologists debate the degree to which the Taos district and the greater Rio Grande region of which it is a part were integrated into the Chacoan system. Below I suggest that the historical linkages between Chaco and Taos were significant, but not in the sense of Taos being a backward periphery or down-the-line recipient of patterns emanating from a Chacoan core. Rather, I argue that we must entertain the possibility that the

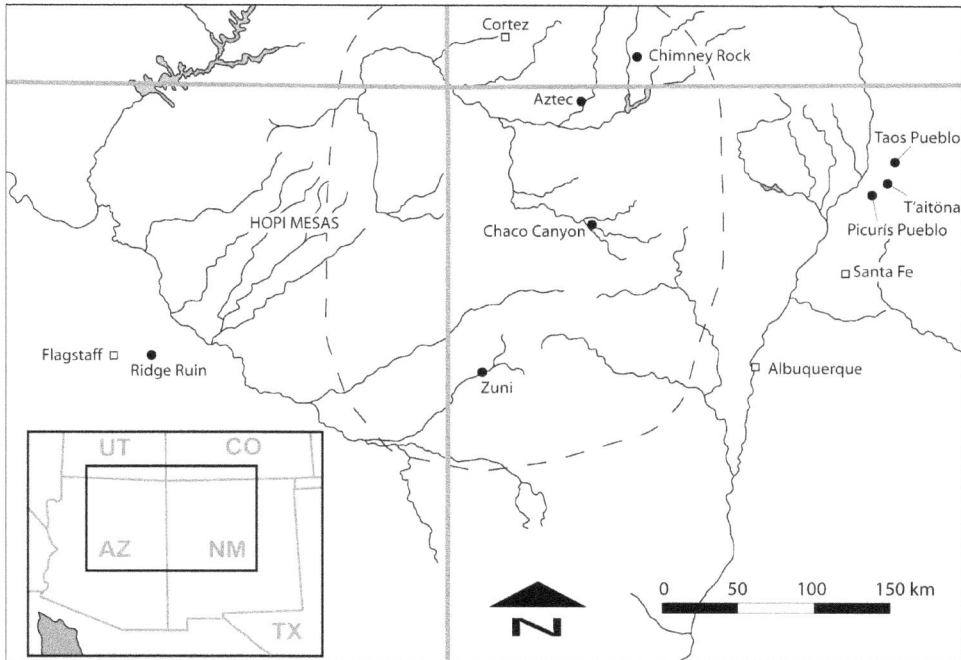

Figure 3.1. Map of the northern Southwest. Dashed line approximates the extent of Chacoan influence.

ancestral Northern Tiwas of the Taos district—along with their brethren in other parts of the Rio Grande Valley—assertively rejected belief in Chacoan orthodoxy, and I propose that we imagine Taos as its own core of reactionary non-Chaconess, as its own center of nonparticipation in the world of its western neighbors.

Chaco and the Big Idea

The "Chaco phenomenon"—as a body of scholarly writings, debates, advanced seminars, and digital archives focused on three centuries of Pueblo occupation (900–1150/1200 CE) in the San Juan basin—is a thing of cults and religious fanaticism. Colin Renfrew (2001) calls Chaco Canyon, the geographic and architectural core of the phenomenon, an LHDE (a "location of high devotional expression"), and however much this label might accurately describe the past, it is a fitting description of archaeological reverence for the canyon in the present. Summer field schools throughout the Southwest regularly make pilgrimages to honor its transcendent archaeology; objects excavated from the canyon are kept in special drawers at the American Museum of Natural History, where they are unveiled in private to VIPs by curatorial priests in white gloves. Archaeological devotion to things Chacoan is both "high" and regularly "expressed."

Along with their evident religious devotion, modern archaeologists also approach

Chaco with a certain political or ethical commitment. Chaco is important, not only for what it was, but also because it stands as an ever-present reminder of the extent and sophistication of Native American societies prior to European colonization. Tour guides in the canyon (which is now a national historical park and, like Taos Pueblo, a World Heritage Site) take obvious pleasure in suggesting that Pueblo Bonito (figure 3.2 *top*), the most impressive of the Chacoan architectural feats, was the "largest apartment complex in the world" from the late eleventh century up until the late nineteenth century, when it was finally surpassed by apartment buildings in New York City. Chaco commands respect, and this respect naturally extends to the modern indigenous peoples whose ancestors were the architects of the phenomenon.

All of this colors how archaeologists reconstruct what Chaco was, frequently prompting them to develop more extreme models than might otherwise be the case. Interpretations of Chaco Canyon have been diverse, ranging from a highly egalitarian stage for religious pilgrimage, to an economic hub of trade and redistribution, to the center of a regional state governed by dramatic shows of violence. Still, the implicit agenda bound up in these starkly divergent models is often similar. Stephen Lekson (2005, 2006, 2009), for instance, has championed a more "state"-like interpretation of Chaco—fully equipped with elites, temples, coercive power, and a pronounced command-and-obey ethic—and one of his reasons for doing so is to emphasize that the ancestral Pueblos could be just as "political," just as "complex," as Old World polities. Norman Yoffee (2001, 2005) suggests instead that we conceive of Chaco as a "rituality," an organizational development gathered around certain core rituals and beliefs that may have been quite unlike the ethnographic parallels used in normative reconstructions of the past. Both present a Chaco that cannot be cast as an early stepping-stone in an evolutionary trajectory ever marching toward the Western state. Both argue against the primitivist misconstrual of Chaco as a latter-day Çatalhöyük.

What most interests me in this literature is the tendency, once again, to parse pre-Columbian social life into post-Reformation analytical spheres. "How much of Pueblo Bonito's power was political, economic, and religious?" asks Neitzel (2003:6)—an invitation to anthropological diplopia that many have accepted. In the name of methodological clarity and rigor, the social totality is fragmented, leaving the demonstration of one's interpretive skill to emerge through the reassembling of pieces. I am reminded here of the archaeological joke about a researcher who excavated an ancient room containing a single, beautiful, whole vessel. With a wise nod to his assistant, he took the vessel in his hands and shattered it into a thousand pieces. "Now *that's* a much more significant sample size," he exclaimed with satisfaction.

We cannot escape a certain level of categorization and analytical division; neither can we fully distance ourselves from our own linguistic conventions. But we must be conscious that reassembly is a creative act. A society described as a composite entity in which religion is glued to politics and politics to economics is not the same as a society more simply viewed as a complete vessel. Reassembly, moreover, presents the researcher with an opportunity to shuffle and reglue pieces of the social into new and

Figure 3.2. Chacoan architecture: Pueblo Bonito (top), Chetro Ketl (bottom).

sometimes Frankensteinian arrangements with emphases and highlights suited more to the researcher's theoretical paradigm than to cultural realities. This situation has been a key part of anthropological interpretation since Malinowski's early programmatic statements: the anthropologist must take "the brute material of information" gathered in the field, "reduce" it to meaningful—that is, Western—analytical categories, and then "construct the picture of the big institution" (Malinowski 1922:3–4, 14, 84).

How have Malinowskian archaeologists constructed—and let us note Malinowski's telling choice to write in terms of "construction" rather than "reconstruction"—the fragments of Chacoan society? Clearly, there are many neo-evolutionary scholars who read Chaco as a fundamentally political phenomenon around which religion and economics were adjusted (Earle 2001; Lekson 1999; Sebastian 1992; Wilcox 1993). Others foreground the religious at the expense of the political; Renfrew (2001; see also Yoffee 2005), for instance, views Chaco as an essentially "egalitarian" phenomenon (that is, lacking centralized and overtly political leadership) in which pilgrims were drawn by their own religious beliefs to participate in the construction of a collective "Dream." "The Chaco region," he suggests, "functioned in terms of religious faith rather than under a centralized hierarchy of persons and an ideology of power" (Renfrew 2004:104). Still others begin their reassembly with the economic. Saitta offers a Marxist reading, arguing that Chaco's ceremonial architecture began as "a medium for building and celebrating communal relations of production" that, in the context of prolonged environmental stress, was transformed by ritual specialists into "a medium for exploiting labor and manipulating mass psychology in the interests of creating and sustaining tributary class relationships" (Saitta 1997:18). Here, the relations of economic production take center stage and religious practice is relegated to a means of support.

Many things Chacoan fascinate us, however, precisely because they resist political, economic, or religious categories. The famous "great houses" (see figure 3.2) with their elaborate multistory masonry, formal layout, and primarily nonresidential rooms, were more than mere congealed labor in the Marxist sense; they also congealed cosmology and ritual practice, allegiance and discipline, confounding simple classification as either shrines, storehouses, or palaces. Consider also the large timbers transported more than eighty kilometers to build the roofs of great houses, or the importation of pottery that was subsequently smashed on immense refuse piles, or the long-distance procurement of turquoise, macaws, and copper bells. Were these acts of piety, politics, or production?

This sort of question should be left unanswered. (Even checking "all of the above" has its problems.) Rather, we would do well to follow Stein and Lekson (1992) in thinking about Chaco more simply as a "big idea" in which much of the Pueblo world once held stock, an idea or set of ideas that necessitated certain ways of building, dancing, trading, traveling, leading, following, giving, taking, living, dying. We might alternately view Chaco as a "big road,"[1] to use a Puebloan metaphor, a line of flight along which the northern Southwest moved in greater or lesser unison. Regardless, to describe this idea or road as, say, 50 percent religious, 30 percent political, and 20 percent economic would muddle our understanding of it completely.

Talk of Chaco as a big idea sounds vague, but just as a whole vessel has formal characteristics that are more than the sum of its sherds, so do big ideas. Here, let me highlight three characteristics that have struck many scholars as particularly significant, not only for understanding Chaco in its heyday, but also for understanding the Pueblo reaction to Chaco following its decline.

First, its impressive regionalism. Estimates of Chaco's spatial reach vary, but all scholars agree that in the early twelfth century a large portion of the northern Southwest (perhaps sixty-five thousand square kilometers) was occupied by groups that signaled their participation in a common project through the construction of formal great houses, great kivas, and roads or processionals. "Luxury"—or, better, "powerful"—items such as turquoise, shells, macaws, parrots, cocoa, and copper bells clearly moved through this regional network, and research has even suggested that maize, a staple foodstuff, was regularly transported in bulk over many dozens of kilometers to support Chacoan centers (Benson et al. 2003). Such regionalism is the source of the bigness in Stein and Lekson's "big idea," and it indicates both a cultural hegemony and a level of long-distance influence that was very different than the balkanized patterns encountered by the Spanish in the sixteenth century.

Second, its extravagance. Chacoan lifestyles were only extravagant in a relative sense, of course; they never approached the gaudy displays of ancient Egyptian tombs or the sacrificial zeal of the Aztecs. Nevertheless, a clear excess is apparent in the hundreds of empty and seemingly unused rooms of the largest great houses, rooms whose walls were constructed of elaborately patterned masonry that was hidden beneath plaster and then roofed with unnecessary quantities of imported timbers. Chacoan roads were also over-engineered. Far larger than needed for foot travel, they maintained famously straight courses that ignored principles of least resistance. The mortuary record—particularly the lavish Bonito burials that included piles of turquoise and arrays of specially crafted objects—is more striking still, although I will set this record to the side for the moment. The main observation I want to highlight is that profligacy of this sort, like Chaco's regional aspect, was quite out of keeping with Pueblo patterns at the time of the Spanish conquest.

And finally, certain patterns of differentiation sharply distinguish the Chacoan era from other periods in Pueblo history. Recent Pueblo societies have certainly been divided into positions with various levels of power and moral worth, but it is a remarkable aspect of Pueblo life that these divisions have few material trappings. Dwellings, dress, diet, mortuary treatment, and the like have historically been relatively uniform, and strong social sanctions (witchcraft accusations and, in the past, executions) are earned by upstarts who attempt to grow their poppies taller than the rest. Difference in the Chacoan system, on the other hand, was institutionalized, highly materialized, and theatrically marked. The imposing, multistory great houses were home to a small segment of the population while most lived nearby in small pueblos, modestly constructed using expedient materials. There is much archaeological debate over whether the contrast between a great house and its surrounding hamlets really mirrored a contrast between great house leaders and their surrounding low-status followers. But even if priestly "public servants" occupied and maintained the great houses, theirs was still a far showier life—vis-à-vis their flock—than the Pueblo elders of recent centuries. Indeed, differentiation was evident at a regional level as well. Much has been made of the obvious centrality of Chaco, of the fact that the architectural and artifactual remains found along a mere fifteen kilometers of the arid canyon clearly distinguish it as *the* nexus of monument building, pilgrimage, and the movement of exotic goods. Chaco did indeed have a core whose occupants led a visibly elite and much more cosmopolitan life than the residents of distant "outliers" (the term used by Southwestern archaeologists to describe the somewhat smaller great houses located outside Chaco Canyon).

Death often presents the most sharply visible evidence of social difference, and many claims of stratification at Chaco have been based upon burial data. Osteological studies, for instance, have indicated that those interred in Pueblo Bonito were taller, lived longer, and dined better than their contemporaries in the canyon's small hamlets (Akins 2001:184). We also know that great house residents were buried with greater pomp. Sadly, a number of the great house burials in Chaco Canyon were plundered early on and are known to us only through hearsay. Pepper (1909:248) refers in passing to prior excavations at Pueblo Bonito and Peñasca Blanca in which "masses of turquoise ornaments have been found associated with bodies," and Vivian (cited in Akins and Schelberg 1984:91) learned that early excavations in Pueblo Bonito unearthed a man wearing a beaded turquoise headdress in the center of a room surrounded by thirteen women. The current non-excavation policy of Chaco Culture National Historical Park makes testing for additional burials of this sort impossible; others surely exist, however.

Most of our understanding of Chacoan mortuary differentiation comes from Pepper's (1909) excavation of the famous Room 33 burials at Pueblo Bonito (see Plog and Heitman 2010). Unlike the consistently austere burials at smaller sites throughout the Chaco world, those in Room 33 were accompanied by many thousands of exquisite objects fashioned out of imported turquoise, shell, and jet as well as a wide array of painted wood, ceramic, and textile artifacts. At least seventeen individuals were interred with these objects, two of whom (both tall adult males) held positions of special significance at the base of the complex below an unusual plank floor. The fifteen or so individuals later buried in the sandy fill above the plank floor were largely disarticulated—a consequence, in Pepper's interpretation, of extensive water damage to the upper room, although given the remarkable preservation of many highly perishable eight-hundred-year-old wood objects it seems much more likely that the disarticulation resulted from conscious cultural practices. The more extreme interpretation is that these were the victims of some form of retainer sacrifice, though such claims are difficult to evaluate.

The Room 33 burials tell us a great deal about continuity and discontinuity over the *longue durée* of Pueblo history. On one hand, the iconic repertoire in the grave goods (tadpoles, frogs, birds, etc.) as well as many of the artifactual forms (flutes, prayer sticks, burial mats, etc.) are quite similar to those in use today, eleven hundred years later. Pepper (1909:250) went so far as to suggest that the burials were associated with ancestors of the modern Hopi Flute societies. On the other hand, the burials are decidedly "non-Puebloan" in a variety of respects. Most jarring is that the bulk of the associated objects were ornamental and designed to be worn in showy display. Bracelets, pendants, beaded necklaces, and headpieces—such baubles would have only made sense within a material orientation toward status of the sort that modern Pueblo peoples meticulously avoid. It is also remarkable that the two men initially buried in the room appear to have been the focus of subsequent ritual attention. A hole cut into the plank floor was appropriately identified by Pepper as a likely sipapu, a portal to the underworld through which ancestral spirits were addressed. Contemporary Pueblo peoples still use sipapus in this way, but the spirits with whom they commune are only the deceased in a general sense. Never are they named or otherwise linked to specific community members who have passed on, which is to say there is no pattern of "ancestor worship," as traditionally defined. At Pueblo Bonito, in contrast, the corpses of the two turquoise-bedecked individuals appear to have been directly engaged, their bodies literally dominating the spirit world on the other side of the sipapu, their memory prompting the subsequent use of the room as a charnel house and shrine.

The mortuary complex just described may well be the most complicated in the American Southwest, but before considering its implications, let us consider a somewhat parallel case farther west, in the Sinaguan region at the margins of the Chacoan sphere, this time dating not to the start of the Chacoan sequence but to the end of Chaco's florescence. Ridge Ruin is a relatively modest multistory pueblo east of Flagstaff, but it boasts the remains of another individual of unquestionably high status. There, WPA archaeologists in the early 1940s encountered an early twelfth-century mortuary complex—often referred to as the "Magician's Burial"—constructed into the floor of a kiva and composed of an adult male adorned with more than six hundred finely crafted objects, many of which were fashioned out of exotic raw materials from hundreds of kilometers away (figure 3.3; see McGregor 1943). The "magician" appears to have been ancestral Hopi—at least, informants from Shungopovi, Mishongnovi, and Oraibi quickly identified some of the objects as known Hopi paraphernalia specifically used in "witchcraft" to build strength in warfare. All agreed the magician would have been a powerful leader of war and war ceremonies.

For anthropologists, the burial at Ridge Ruin has prompted additional questions about prestige and privilege: "So much fine material found with one man led to the immediate question of just what sort of man this individual must have been in life to have been deemed worthy of these rich offerings. It is now quite contradictory to general Pueblo concepts to encourage the acquisition of personal wealth" (McGregor 1943:271). At issue, of course, is whether the large amounts of turquoise and shell mosaics, carved wood, sculpted lac, beadwork, and ceramics interred with the magician really should be viewed as his personal wealth or whether they are better interpreted as clan property, badges perhaps of the man's public service and sacrifice. As McGregor (1943:296) suggested, perhaps he held an important priestly capacity and simply died without a sufficiently trained successor to carry on the rituals that accompanied the objects, prompting their burial as well. Perhaps all those exquisite objects represented the sanctified community rather than the aggrandizing individual. Perhaps we should therefore interpret the deposit as much more "religious" than "political."

Perhaps. But let us not lose sight of the fact that elaborate mortuary complexes—of which the Magician's Burial and the Bonito Room 33 interments are the best-known examples—effectively bookend the Chacoan period.[2] Despite extensive excavations at a number of very large post-Chacoan villages, no burials of comparable scale and opulence have been encountered, a temporal pattern that demands some sort of explanation. Neither must we lose sight of the fact that the material culture accompanying the magician included many items of bodily adornment specifically designed to mark his social position with high visual impact. These included a very large nose plug of turquoise and red argillite, shell ear pendants, turquoise earrings, a headdress composed of thousands of delicately shaped stone and shell beads, and a quantity of elaborate bracelets, pendants, and carved staffs or wands. In such finery, this individual—like the men in Pueblo Bonito's Room 33—would have cut the figure of a very tall poppy indeed.

The key point is that while certain priestly positions, ceremonies, and icons may have great temporal depth, the manner in which they were engaged and the sociology surrounding those engagements have clearly changed since Chacoan times. Today, the general asceticism of the Pueblo priest's appearance and lifestyle makes a strong "political" statement that his power, significant though it might be, is of a particular sort and can only be directed toward particular ends. In contrast, the fancy bodily accessories, great house architecture, and mortuary elaboration of Chaco-era priests simply *must* have sent a different message. Consider the reflections of Rina Swentzell, a member of Santa Clara Pueblo, after visiting Chaco Canyon:

> My response to the canyon was that some sensibility other than my Pueblo ancestors had worked on the Chaco great houses. There were the familiar elements such as the nansipu (the symbolic opening into the underworlds), kivas, plazas, and earth materials, but they were overlain by a strictness and precision of design and execution that was unfamiliar, not just to me but in other sites of the Southwest. It was clear that the purpose of these great villages was not to restate their oneness with the earth but to show the power and specialness of humans. For me, they represented a desire to control. (Swentzell 2004:50)

Continuity and discontinuity—familiar Pueblo elements, differently organized according to a strangely un-Puebloan glorification of power and control, strictness and precision.

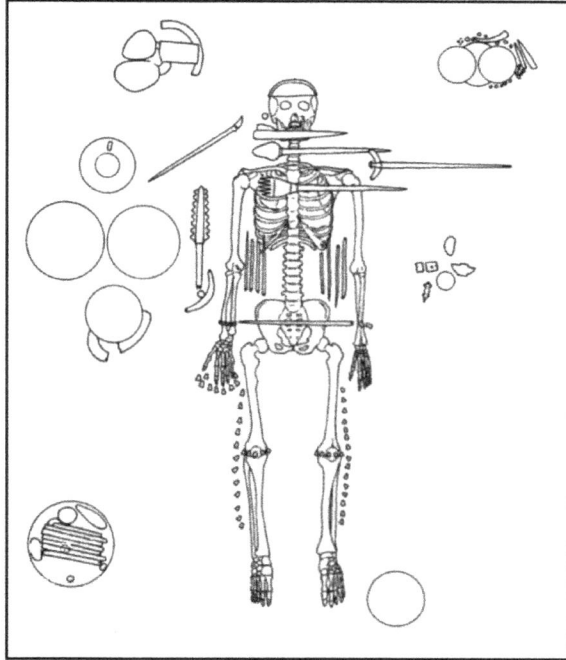

Figure 3.3. The Magician's Burial from Ridge Ruin, depicting some of the many valuable objects interred with an adult male (based on McGregor 1943).

What historical path led from the regional cultural hegemony, material extravagance, and marked social differentiation of Chaco to the autonomy, subtlety, and veiled social differentiation of the villages encountered by the Spanish? How did the Chacoan sensibility of the early twelfth century evolve into the very different Puebloan sensibility of the early twenty-first century? A number of archaeologists have asked these important questions (Fowles 2010a, 2012; Lekson 2009; Lekson and Cameron 1995; Ortman 2010; Ware and Blinman 2000). "Clearly the memory of what had happened in Chaco Canyon," writes Kantner (2006:44), "was both empowering and cautionary for new religious authorities as they emerged in the vacuum left by the disintegration of the Chaco world." Much more could be said about what had happened. Alongside the extravagances already noted, for example, Lekson (2002) has asked us to acknowledge that the Chacoans occasionally choreographed "spectacularly brutal" executions in which small residential groups were aggressively dismembered—in some cases, perhaps even cannibalized—as a means of terrorizing the masses. This is an especially sinister model, and I have elsewhere argued that it vastly oversimplifies the situation (Fowles forthcoming). Nevertheless, the pattern of periodic targeted violence seems clear and demands some sort of explanation. To what extent was such violence the fate of dissidents who opposed Chacoan orthodoxy?

Let us assume that there *was* something to oppose and struggle against, a rotten seed in Chaco's evolving gestalt that the population eventually left behind. The

Pueblos themselves frequently imply as much. Their historical narratives often reference a succession of past worlds (Chacoan and other) gone corrupt and abandoned in favor of newer worlds, truer center places. Corruption takes many forms in these stories: from general licentiousness, to ritual negligence, to the greed and arrogance of leaders, to outright witchcraft, the latter indicated as often as not by the presence of a decayed or putrid substance where a sacred object should be.

If indeed something was rotten in Chaco, if, as one Laguna Pueblo individual put it, Chacoan leaders with "enormous amounts of power...were causing changes that were never meant to happen" (quoted in Lekson 2006:104), then the populace may have seen the evidence in a prolonged drought following 1130 CE. Most archaeological models place great emphasis on this drought, arguing that it either weakened Chaco's economy, destroyed faith in the priestly leadership, or both. In any case, building in Chaco Canyon ended shortly thereafter, and it would be foolish to ignore the effects of climatic variability in a landscape where water can be scarce even in the best of years. The drought could not have helped matters. But environmental arguments, to put it bluntly, tend to be far too easy (a drought can be found either coinciding with or just preceding all historical events in the Southwest), and upon closer scrutiny many appear inconsistent (environmental arguments often fail to explain why earlier droughts did not also prompt comparable culture change). The more important point, as Lekson (2009) reminds us, is that Pueblo communities in the northern Southwest not only moved away from the harsh arid landscape of Chaco Canyon; they moved away from the excesses of leadership described above. New Chaco-style regional systems and patterns of authority were not re-created in the northern Southwest during the thirteenth century, indicating that the greatest problems stemmed not from drought per se, but from the evolution of Chacoan orthodoxy itself.

Big ideas can easily turn hegemonic and dreams nightmarish, and we know that significant sweeps of history have been defined by efforts to overcome the lingering weight of such nightmares. Let us remember that nearly five centuries after Martin Luther nailed his protest to the door of the Wittenberg Castle church, Western Europe continues to be broadly defined by a pronounced anti-clericalism born of Catholic excesses that are now largely a thing of the past (recent scandals in the church regarding sexual abuse notwithstanding). Perhaps the northern Southwest saw its own Reformation of sorts in Chaco's dissolution, its own Protestant response to the greatness of great houses and the leaders therein. Indeed, once we posit that twelfth-century Chacoans were steeped in a clericalism that would have made twelfth-century Catholics envious, we might also accept the possibility of a corresponding Pueblo anti-clericalism. With belief comes unbelief or counterbelief, with orthodoxy comes critique—these truths seem self-evident.

If it is possible to read Pueblo reorganization after Chaco as the collective rewriting of a big idea (or, at least, of the regionalism, material extravagance, and marked social differentiation that went hand in hand with the big idea), then we should expect to find earlier signs of dissent and dissatisfaction setting the stage. In the northern San Juan, the occasional executions described by Lekson (2002) may be the most archaeologically visible indexes of dissidence, tragic though the consequences apparently were. We should not, however, limit our consideration of this matter to the area of Chacoan hegemony, for social criticism often comes from the edges, voiced by those who, by choice or coercion, have fled to the margins.

Chaco's western margin, as we have seen, was home to the magician and perhaps others who drank from the same cup of clericalism as the priests buried in Pueblo Bonito. We encounter a very different pattern when we turn our attention eastward, however. Throughout the tenth, eleventh, and twelfth centuries, the well-watered valleys flanking the Rio Grande stood apart as a region of remarkable nonparticipation in the Chacoan system. This was a region with neither great houses nor great kivas. Its population, while significant, remained dispersed and decentralized. And there is no evidence that elitism was ever materialized through architectural, ornamental, or mortuary differentiation.

Archaeologists tend to shrug off such patterns as a simple indication of the Rio Grande valley's provincialism prior to the late thirteenth century when migrants from the northern San Juan finally arrived and transformed the region into a core area of Pueblo settlement. But the Rio Grande's non-Chaconess *should* surprise us. Chaco Canyon was the center of the Chacoan world, the location from which certain ideas emanated and toward which a variety of material goods traveled, and we can trace this center's influence two hundred kilometers to the north, west, and south (see figure 3.1). Major roads unfurl outward from Chaco Canyon in each of these directions toward outlying great house and great kiva communities. To the east, however, the pattern abruptly truncates after about fifty kilometers. Why?

It was not that the leaders in Chaco had no use for the Rio Grande region. Turquoise was an important material for building prestige, and the Cerrillos mines near Santa Fe were a major source. Large quantities of obsidian from the Jemez Mountains also appear in Chaco Canyon, indicating the importance of a second Rio Grande resource (Cameron and Sappington 1984). Hides and dried meat from the mountainous northern Rio Grande were probably also imported into the Chacoan sphere, although the isotopic studies that might demonstrate this linkage have not yet been undertaken. Nor was it the case that the Rio Grande valley lacked cultural links to its western neighbors. Ceramics produced in the Rio Grande were clearly part of a broad stylistic tradition that included much of the San Juan basin. A number of tenth-century sites in the northern Rio Grande contain Red Mesa black-on-white sherds imported from the west, and by the eleventh century, the dominant locally produced type, Kwahe'e black-on-white, employed forms and painted designs that differed little from the Gallup black-on-white tradition in the Chacoan core. (Early Rio Grande archaeologists went so far as to refer to Kwahe'e B/W as the "Chaco II" type.) At a broader level, the overall appearance of settlements in the northern Rio Grande—pithouses accompanied by modest blocks of surface rooms to the west or north in classic "unit pueblo" style—was similar to the small residential sites that surrounded Chacoan great houses. Chaco, in short, had vested interests in the Rio Grande valley as well as manifold cultural links. Why, we must again ask, did the Rio Grande remain outside the Chaco tradition? Why were there no great house communities in Taos?

Perhaps because Rio Grande populations wanted it that way. As I have argued elsewhere, superficial "absences" in the archaeological record are often "presences" in disguise (Fowles 2008, 2010b; Fowles and Heupel forthcoming). Here, for instance, we might reinterpret the absence of Chaconess as the presence of a kind of anti-Chaconess. In the absence of clericalism we might imagine the presence of anti-clericalism, and in the absence of great houses we might find evidence of a refuge from Chacoan orthodoxy.

To explore the implications of this change of perspective, I want to consider the case of the ancestral Northern Tiwas who lived in the northern Rio Grande a millennium ago. Archaeologists refer to this population collectively as the Valdez Phase (950–1200 CE), but in the discussion that follows I will build upon the oral history of Taos Pueblo and refer to them instead as the Winter People. The Winter People were not the bumpkins so many early archaeologists made them out to be. I suggest we envision them instead as cultural refugees, conscientious objectors who opted out of the Chacoan system and chose to build a simpler life in the northern Rio Grande. To anyone living in the Taos area today, the plausibility of this image should be immediately apparent: modern Taos, after all, is largely peopled by expatriates from San Francisco, Dallas, New York, and Chicago who have traded in high-tech urbanity for a more bohemian lifestyle in small desert homes built of mud and straw. Like the hippies who flocked to the area in the 1960s (though now with much more money), these recent Taos immigrants by and large view their new lives as a deliberate rejection of the capitalism, industrialization, consumerism, and class inequalities of the modern world. Moving to the desert, giving up television, raising chickens, not shopping at department stores—for a half century these have been local forms of protest.

Long before the hippies of the 1960s, there were the Winter People of the 1060s (or thereabouts)—Taos's *original* sixties counterculture. As I have documented elsewhere, the first Pueblo groups arrived in Taos in the late tenth century CE and expanded in the mid-eleventh century to establish a series of dispersed, seemingly egalitarian communities (Fowles 2010a). The arrival of the Winter People occurred in the wake of the initial spurt of great house construction to the west in Chaco Canyon, and their community swelled just as Chaco's regional influence was becoming entrenched. Below, I will suggest that these events in Chaco and Taos were closely related. Before that historical argument can be made, however—before the Winter People are reinterpreted as having been *anti*-Chaco rather than merely *non*-Chaco—we would do well to consider in greater detail who the Winter People were.

The Chacolessness of the Winter People

As with all matters worth the inquiry, the question of the Winter People's identity can be variously answered. To the members of Taos Pueblo, the Winter People were and are one of many ceremonial sodalities, their membership being closely linked to the Day Kiva (Stevenson 1906–1907:file 3.1).[3] To speak of the Winter People of the tenth or eleventh century, then, is to speak of the ancestors of a specific, living kiva group. In most pueblos, however, ancestors simultaneously occupy a mythic space, and in the Taos origin narrative we learn that the Winter People were specially sent by Kwathlowúna, the principal deity, to make the upper world solid and habitable for humans. They were also the first of the Taos ancestors to emerge into the upper, or present, world, occupying the northern portion of the Taos district as skilled hunters until they were attacked and overcome by the Summer People in an epic battle.

Archaeological characterizations of the Winter People are more detailed, if more staid. As in Northern Tiwa oral history, archaeology has revealed that Taos's earliest "pueblo," or post-archaic, occupants were primarily hunter-gatherers who practiced only limited agriculture and initially settled the northern portions of the region in the vicinity of the modern towns of Arroyo Hondo and Arroyo Seco (see figure 2.2). Pithouses first appeared in this area in the tenth century CE and were widespread by the eleventh century. To date, a dozen or so of these early pithouses have been excavated. The excavations have demonstrated that the homesteaders arrived with a developed ceramic technology that included both painted (Red Mesa black-on-white and Kwahe'e black-on-white) and unpainted (Taos Incised, Banded, and Plain) wares as well as an established architectural tradition (Fowles 2004:208–233). Significantly, no sites have been located that display a transitional development out of the previous archaic occupation. We must, therefore, view the Winter People as tenth-century immigrants, an observation that will become important shortly.

Existing chronometric and ceramic data suggest the population grew significantly during the mid-eleventh century, expanding south into what is known as the Rio Grande del Rancho drainage. The drainage incorporates roughly two hundred square kilometers and includes three major ecological zones: the sage-covered Taos Plateau to the north, the rugged Sangre de Cristo Mountains to the south, and a relatively wide valley that extends from the plateau south into the mountains (figure 3.4). The area is rich in game, wood, clay, chert, water, and, to a certain extent, arable land—all the resources needed for a strong "Neolithic" society. It is also an area for which we have good survey and excavation coverage. More than 150 settlements dating to the early Pueblo period—locally known as the Valdez Phase, roughly 1000–1200 CE—have been recorded, and of these, eighteen architectural sites or major site components have been excavated (Fowles 2004:234–261). Most include between one and four pithouses dug deep into the ground, each perhaps sheltering a family of up to five or six persons (figure 3.5). On the broad alluvial fans of the Taos

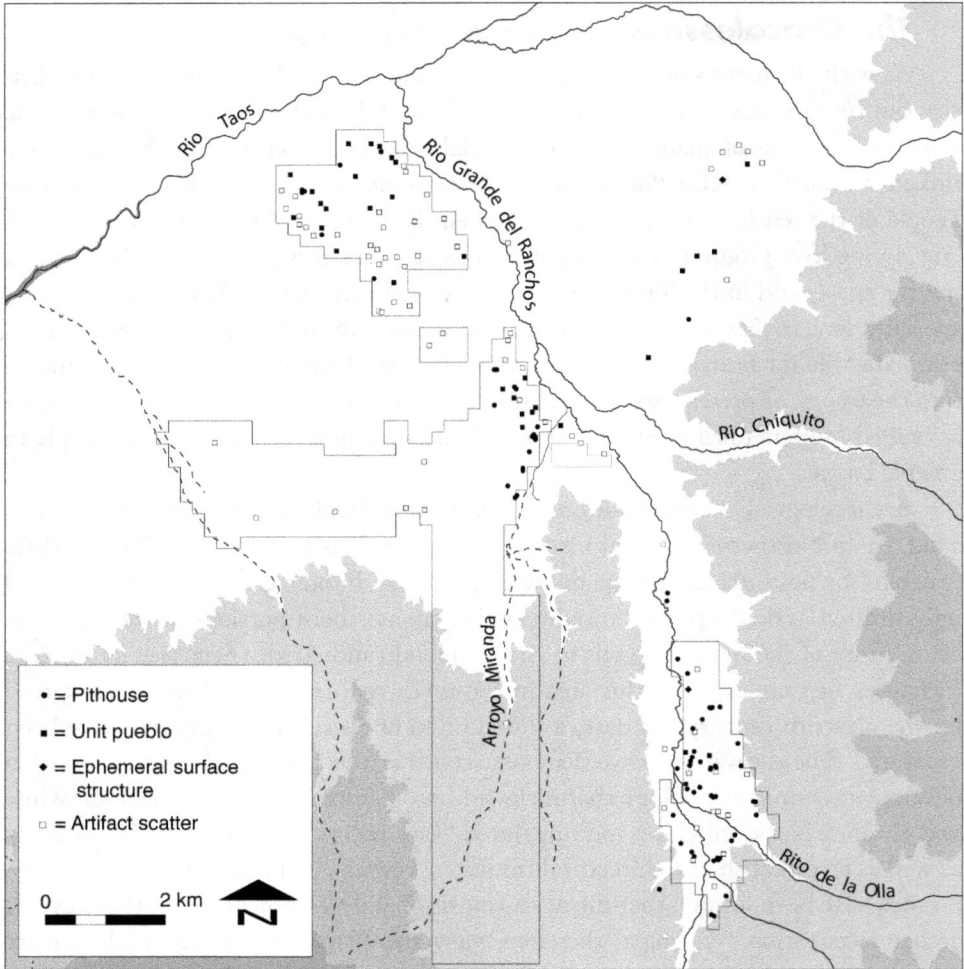

Figure 3.4. Distribution of all known Valdez Phase sites in the Rio Grande del Rancho drainage. Geometrically outlined areas indicate the extent of formal survey coverage (see Fowles 2004:appendix D).

Plateau, where the most productive agricultural land is found, pithouses were often accompanied by surface adobe structures with five to ten rooms. In the foothills and mountain zones, where there was less potential for agriculture and fewer storage needs, accompanying roomblocks tended to be much smaller and more ephemerally built. In both areas, early Pueblo sites mapped closely onto resources, and no hint of a site-size hierarchy or regional center is apparent. Mortuary patterns paint a similarly egalitarian picture. Young or old, male or female, the Winter People were interred with marked simplicity in unprepared pits, accompanied by neither grave goods nor bodily ornaments (Green 1976). Generally speaking, the material culture of this period was simple as well (figure 3.6), and long-distance imports were extremely rare.

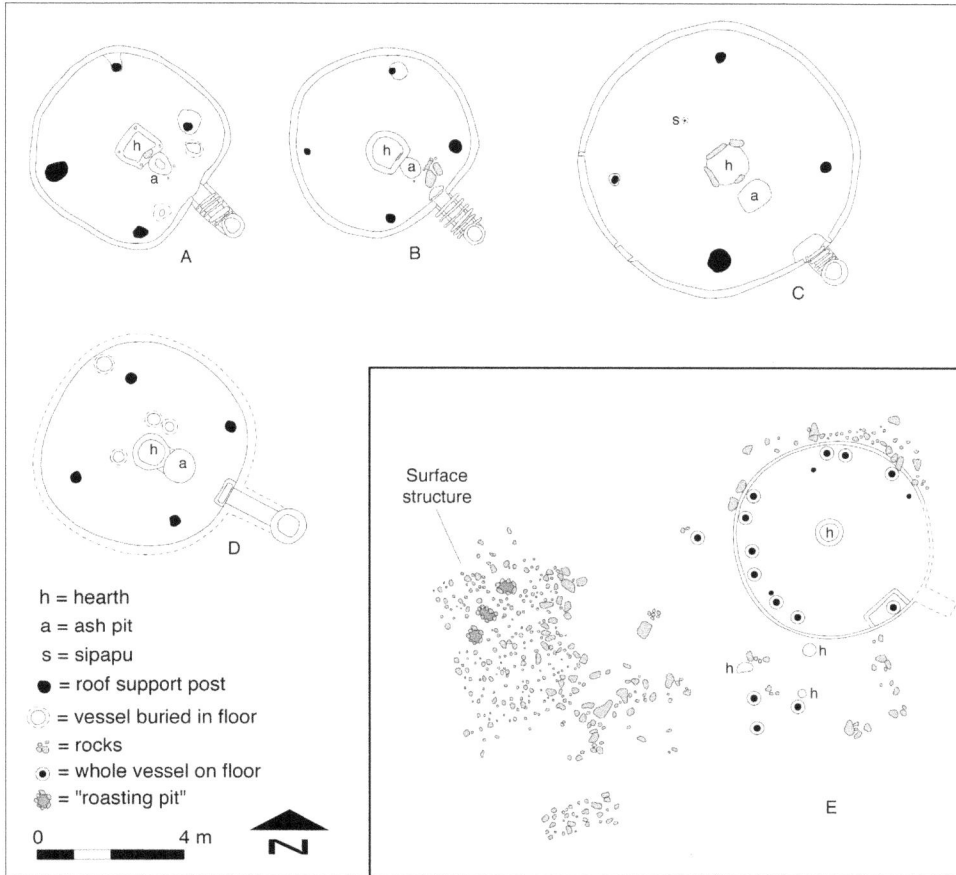

Figure 3.5. Plans of select Valdez Phase pithouses in the Rio Grande del Rancho drainage. A = Pithouse A at LA 102062; B = Pithouse B at LA 102062 (based on Green 1976); C = LA 133151 (based on Green 1976:13); D = LA 3643 (based on Peckham and Reed 1963); E = Cerrita Site (based on Woosley 1986:152).

Much more could be said about these settlements of the Winter People, but my concern is simply to underscore the obvious: nowhere in the Taos region, neither to the north or the south, on the plateau or in the mountains, was there anything even close to the extravagant great houses, great kivas, formal roads, and so on that were under construction in the San Juan basin to the west. This raises an important question: did the Winter People lack the manpower, the knowledge, the regional connections, or the desire to engage in Chacoan monumentalism, in Chacoan "complexity"?

Population modeling reveals that somewhere between 300 and 460 people probably dwelt along a fifteen-kilometer extent of the Rio Grande del Rancho drainage throughout most of the late eleventh and twelfth centuries (Fowles 2004:889–915), and all indications point to comparable populations immediately to the north and east. All told, 1,500 or more people may have lived east of the Rio Grande gorge on

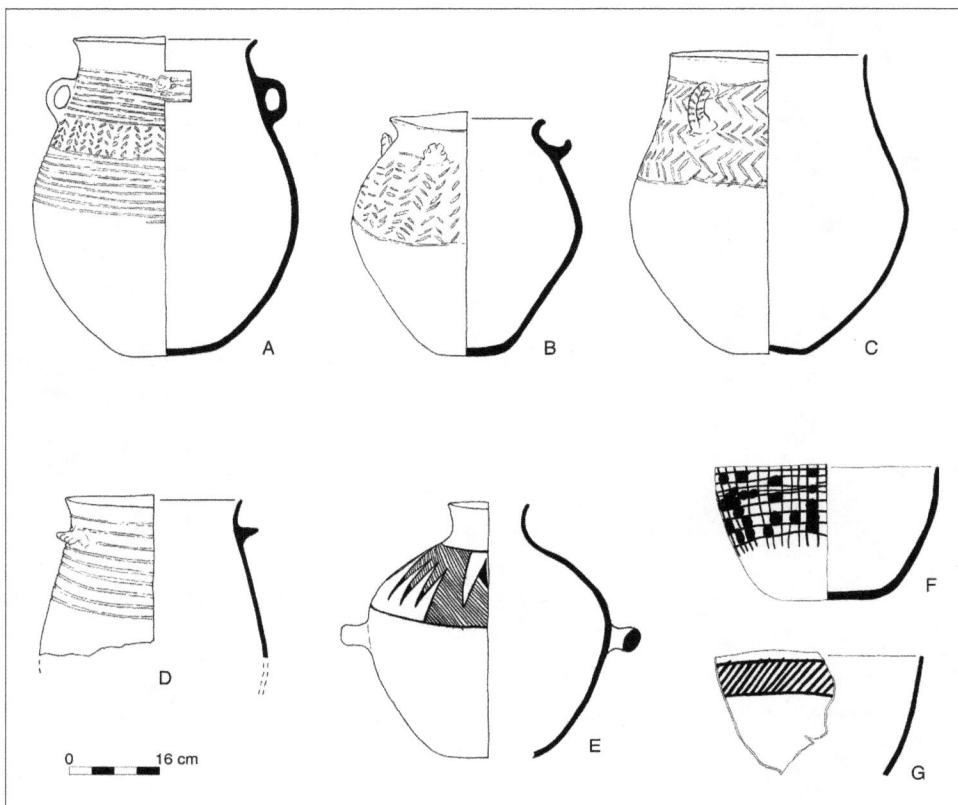

Figure 3.6. Examples of Valdez Phase ceramics. A, B = Taos Incised jars from the Cerrita Site; C, D = Taos Incised jars from LA 102062/TA20; E = Kwahe'e B/W (var. Taos) jar from T'aitöna; F = Kwahe'e B/W (var. Taos) bowl from LA 102063/TA32; G = Kwahe'e B/W (var. Taos) bowl from LA 102062/TA20.

the Taos Plateau and adjacent valleys—a significant population density for the time, and one that was larger, I suspect, than the populations accompanying most great house communities in the San Juan basin (see Mahoney 2000). It would be difficult, therefore, to argue that they lacked the demographic base to fund an "outlier" center, had they desired such a thing.

Perhaps the early Pueblo settlers of the Taos region simply lacked knowledge of things Chacoan. After all, many archaeologists have posited a Northern Tiwa origin in the east on the Great Plains, based in large part on the local tradition of incised pottery, which is without clear Puebloan precedents. But this explanation has never been very satisfying, for it ignores the sudden appearance of formal architecture and black-on-white pottery—notably, Red Mesa B/W—that goes hand in hand with the arrival of the Winter People and links them stylistically to Pueblo communities farther west. Moreover, the Plains origins hypothesis ignores Taos Pueblo's own historical account of the past. The Winter People, it is said, originally dwelt at "Pueblo

Colorado" (Stevenson 1906–1907:file 2:19) in the Piedra district of southwestern Colorado (Ellis and Brody 1964:326) before settling in the northern portion of the Taos region, where a number of ancestral sites exist that are still specifically discussed in Winter People narratives (Ellis 1974[1962]:48, 123).

I am inclined to trust indigenous historical knowledge of this sort. True, most Pueblos speak in mythological terms of a northern origin, as often as not "somewhere in Colorado," but Taos Pueblo has been quite specific about the role played by Chimney Rock—the dramatic geological formation that dominates the Piedra district—in the oral histories of the Winter, or Day, People (Eddy 1977:1). (Together with the neighboring Companion Rock, Chimney Rock continues to be an important, if geographically distant, shrine that symbolizes the presence of the Divine Twins; it even continues to be a pilgrimage destination for some at Taos Pueblo, who have traveled to bless the site.) Archaeological research in the Piedra district has demonstrated the plausibility of such a historical connection. This was an area with a very large late ninth- and early tenth-century pithouse occupation whose population dropped in the late tenth and early eleventh centuries (Eddy 1977; Parker 2004a:56), just as the pithouse occupation of the Taos district rapidly increased. Moreover, the material culture of the two regions displays certain striking similarities—for instance, the distinctive form of large unpainted storage vessels.[4] Craniometric studies have even suggested a relatively close biological relationship between twelfth-century populations in the northern San Juan and the Taos region (Schillaci et al. 2001).

These are important details, for as soon as we view the Winter People as emigrants from the Chimney Rock area, their potential entanglement with the Chacoan system becomes much more complicated. No longer can we accept the simple image of developmental isolation and provincialism posited by a former generation of Taos archaeologists. "There is nothing," wrote Woosley, "that documents any major breaks or significant change through the introduction of new cultural elements from outside the [Taos] District. Changing settlement distribution, increasing complexity in site organization, as well as alterations in material culture assemblages such as ceramics can all be easily interpreted in terms of a Taos District continuum of gradual cultural development within the local Anasazi sequence" (1986:161). The slow, deliberate evolution of a population from an archaic adaptation of hunting and gathering, through Pueblo farming and its intensification, to the development of large aggregated towns: a history of the world, writ small, from the Paleolithic to Childe's Neolithic revolution —this sort of in situ model was attractive to late twentieth-century archaeologists who viewed society as an evolutionary adaptation to local environmental conditions. How different the picture looks when we seriously investigate the migrations, creolizations, battles, alliances, and so on that fill indigenous histories! Consider the following sequence of regional contingencies that surround the Winter People's claim to Piedra origins.

In the late ninth century CE, a significant population resided in the Piedra district, a portion of whom, let us assume, were ancestors of the Winter People. Then,

Chaco Canyon emerged as a center of regional activity in the San Juan basin to the south, its prominence marked not only by the construction of a number of great houses, but also the large-scale importation of turquoise and the first legibly elite burials the northern Southwest had seen. The ripples sent out by these developments undoubtedly affected a significant portion of the northern Southwest, even if formal outlier centers had not yet been established. Indeed, violent waves appear to have been felt in the Navajo Reservoir area immediately south of the Piedra district, where stockaded villages, torched structures, and the occasional presence of disarticulated, burned, and even anthropophagous human remains all index the contested nature of the tenth-century landscape (Eddy 1966:370–371, 493; 1974:81)—initial growing pains, it seems, of the northern Southwest's first regional system.

I have already indicated that the population of the Piedra district peaked early and then rapidly declined over the course of the tenth century. At roughly 1000 CE, new types of surface architecture appeared that some archaeologists interpret as the establishment of immigrant communities (Lightfoot and Eddy 1993). Be that as it may, the relatively clear presence of Chacoan immigrants is evident by 1050 CE when Chacoan ceramic technologies were introduced into the area (Parker 2004b), and then more profoundly with the establishment in the 1070s of a great house, poised dramatically on the narrow ridge below Chimney Rock itself (Eddy 1977). With its core-and-veneer walls, fancy masonry, dualistic layout, and high formality, the Chimney Rock great house—the "Ultimate Outlier" (Malville 2004)—was a piece of Chaco Canyon orthodoxy transplanted far to the north, and it seems to have represented the maturation, rather than the initiation, of foreign influence in the area. It didn't last long. Fifty years on, as the centrality of Chaco Canyon faltered, the Chacoans of the Piedra district emigrated again, and the Chimney Rock great house stood empty in fading grandeur.

This was the history the Winter People left behind: a period of social turbulence at the edge of an expanding Chacoan world. The details of the Piedra-to-Taos migration remain archaeologically obscure, but the broad demographic outlines of the two regions articulate nicely. As populations fell in the Piedra district during the latter half of the tenth century, a culturally related Pueblo occupation was established in the Taos region. And when a direct Chacoan presence appeared in the mid-eleventh century, additional Pueblo families moved to Taos, contributing to the burgeoning population in the Rio Grande del Rancho drainage. To what extent, then, might we view the Winter People as refugees, dissidents who fled an expanding regional system just as many seventeenth-century Tewa families fled to the Hopi mesas to escape the Spanish presence along the Rio Grande? Or more provocatively: to what extent might we view the Winter People as a counterculture that opted out of Chacoan orthodoxy and so foreshadowed the 1960s migrants who flocked to the Taos communes as an overt rejection of the capitalist ideologies of urban America (Fowles 2010a)?

Perhaps it is part of the human condition that we are forever running away from ourselves, forever seeking to escape or overturn the worlds we have created. And perhaps it is part of the human tragedy that every exit strategy becomes, in the end (or, in this case, in chapter 4), an entrance into some new hegemonic order that must be opposed. But there is a more pressing point: if we are to adequately understand the Chacolessness of the Taos region—or, indeed, the Chacolessness of the entire Rio Grande valley—it would be foolish to rashly conclude that the local communities were simply "at the end of the line" (Peckham and Reed 1963:24), "really very much off the beaten track of Pueblo culture" (Fox 1967:10), characterized by a "notable conservatism and peripherality" (Herold 1968:39) or an overall "lag in cultural development" (Wetherington 1968:97), as did most early commentators on Taos prehistory.

Why assume that social complexity—Puebloan or otherwise—is necessarily desired? To do so is to follow the "would-have-if-they-could-have" paradigm that burdened so many early evolutionary studies in anthropology. Mobile hunter-gatherers, it was assumed, will always choose to settle down and become Neolithic when the opportunity presents itself; villages of farmers who can afford to do so will always embrace the chief who has risen to manage them; all societies with the golden carrot of statehood dangling before them will, inexorably, bite (or collapse trying). Clastres (1989; see also Graeber 2004) put such flawed logic to rest long ago, and his arguments need not be repeated. Suffice it to say that it is unlikely that all eleventh-century communities in the northern Southwest would-have-if-they-could-have become Chacoan. Many may have purposefully avoided such a fate, viewing social simplicity as more progressive, more enlightened, more *evolved* than complexity (Fowles 2010a).

Who were the Winter People, then? I suggest that many were refugees driven east by increasing Chacoan expansion into their traditional homeland. Far from being unaware of Chaco's regional influence (could any group in the northern Southwest have been so naive?), the Winter People may have been defined by their opposition to it.

Belief and Unbelief

Let me rephrase the last proposition. To claim that "Chaco" served as a contrast in this way is to imply that the tenth- and eleventh-century residents of the Taos region stood, more specifically, in opposition to Chacoan clericalism and orthodoxy—that is, to the structures of leadership and conformity that were exported (or extracted) from Chaco Canyon after the tenth century. And this possibility should prompt us to consider what such a culture of opposition might look like, sociologically, materially, and, in particular, "religiously."

Asked to identify an eleventh-century religion in the northern Southwest, most would place Chaco Canyon, Vatican-like, at its sacerdotal center. Archaeologists may build careers arguing over the degree to which Chaco organized economic redistribution or demanded political obedience, but no one has ever seriously suggested that it was an entirely irreligious phenomenon. Quite the contrary. Most models present Chaco as peopled with priests and steeped in religiosity, the key disputes being over the ends to which such religiosity was put. But if the Chaco phenomenon was, in some essential way, a "religious" movement—debatable though I think this assertion is (see chapter 7)—is it possible that the Winter People's opposition to Chaco simultaneously left them ambivalent about Pueblo "religion" itself? Is there a way in which Chacolessness could be interpreted as a form of reactionary "secularity" in the eleventh-century Southwest?

Existing data certainly suggest that the Chacoless occupants of the Taos region during the tenth, eleventh, and twelfth centuries were religiously unmusical when compared with their western neighbors. Copper bells, worked shell, jet, turquoise, painted wood, macaws—all the trimmings that presumably heightened the resonance of Chacoan choirs—were absent. As I have already noted, burial practices marking the transition between the world of the living and that of the dead were austere: grave goods were absent and flexed bodies were interred in simple shallow pits. There have never been grounds for identifying any individual within the Taos mortuary record as a shaman or priest.

Indeed, there is very little in the material culture of the Winter People that can easily be labeled "religious" at all. Nineteen Chaco-era pithouses and half again as many surface structures have been excavated and reported in the Taos region, and tens of thousands of objects have been collected. And still, the number of potentially ritual objects in this sample barely deserves mention: (1) a half dozen crudely painted or sculpted figurative images (birds, dogs, and, in one case, a horned toad) on pottery that may well have been simply decorative,[5] (2) a few vessels with unusual forms, such as double bowls, whose use is unknown, (3) twenty-four fragments of simple ceramic pipes that anticipate the cloud-blower pipes used in much historic Pueblo ritual practice, and (4) eleven sherds from miniature black-on-white vessels similar to those known to have had ceremonial uses in more recent times (figure 3.7; Fowles 2004:287–297).

Bear in mind that the ritual designation assigned to these objects is built upon ethnographic data recorded a millennium after the fact. And insofar as it is commonly assumed that the domestic pithouse evolved into the primarily "ritual" kiva over this same time period, there are certainly grounds to question whether something like the plain ceramic pipes of the eleventh century were considered as sacred as their more elaborate nineteenth-century counterparts. Time alone, as is well known, has its way of transforming the mundane into the magical, the ordinary into the extraordinary. Indeed, all the objects just mentioned were recovered from general refuse areas (none were cached or coated in red ocher, in other words), and there is no significant clustering of the plausibly ritual detritus such as would elevate the status of one settlement over any other. Archaeological context, then, does nothing to bolster the argument that these objects were considered special.

All of this is to say that the artifactual evidence for religiosity among the Winter People is slim. Perhaps it would be going too far to say they ignored the sacred altogether. But even if we accept (as I will, for the sake of argument) that most of

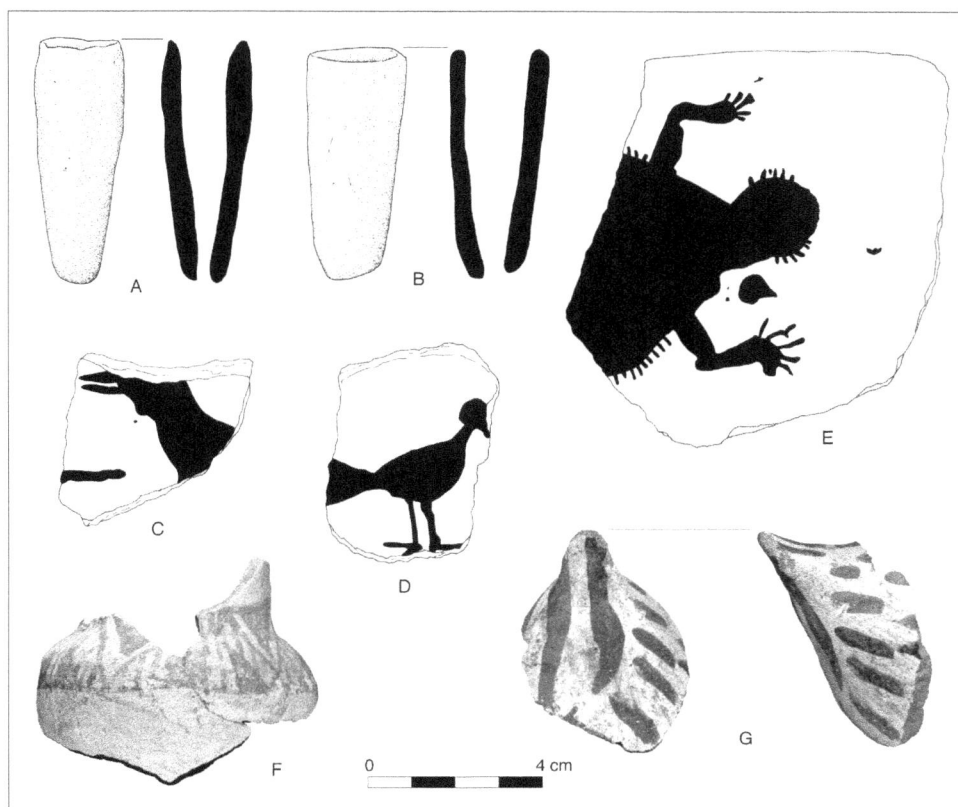

Figure 3.7. Potentially "religious" material culture from Valdez Phase sites in the Taos region. A, B = plain gray ceramic pipes from TA18; C = Kwahe'e B/W jar sherd from the Cerrita Site; D = base of a Kwahe'e B/W bowl from LA 3643 (based on Peckham and Reed 1963, fig. 10); E = Kwahe'e B/W bowl sherd from the Cerrita Site; F = partial Kwahe'e B/W miniature jar from LA 80504/TA26; G = "tail" sherd of a Kwahe'e B/W duck pot from the Cerrita Site.

the objects listed above had a vaguely ritual function, we are still left with the more significant observation that these ritual objects appear to have been highly democratized. Unlike the San Juan basin, where ceremonial objects were elaborate, crafted by specialists using imported materials, and very unevenly distributed, those of the Winter People were uniformly crude, made of easily obtainable local materials, and available to any household who chose to have them. Very un-Chacoan—which perhaps was the point.

Architectural evidence draws this contrast into starker relief still, for here too we find evidence of a "religious" life that was muted and highly democratic. It is not just that the Winter People chose to do without great houses and great kivas, the showy signs of asserted orthodoxy that gave Chaco its definition. The Winter People lacked specialized ritual structures altogether. Prior to the thirteenth century we have no evidence of anything in the Taos region that could be properly called a "kiva" in the traditional sense of a nondomestic space managed by a specific ritual group. True, the standard domiciles, or pithouses, of the Winter People did anticipate the form of later kivas, and in some cases these pithouses contained features that were probably related to prayer and connection with nonhuman forces. Sipapus—those small holes in the floor that symbolize the place of origin and provide a means of access to the ancestors in many modern Pueblo communities—have been identified in roughly half the pithouses in the Rio Grande del Rancho drainage, for instance (Adler 1993; Fowles 2004:268–286). For a feature of such subtlety and simplicity, however, the sipapu tends to be burdened with a tremendous interpretive weight—to the extent that some archaeologists take the presence of any hole-like discontinuity in the middle of the floor as evidence of a "sipapu" and, by extension, a specialized "kiva" as well (see Lekson 1988 for an extended critique of the kiva category).

The fact is that *every* pithouse in the Taos region prior to the thirteenth century was encircled by the mundane debris of everyday life. Every pithouse was used for diverse domestic functions; in other words, none were kivas in the contemporary sense. However, to deny that the Winter People built kivas does not at all require us to drag the sipapu down into the realm of the profane as well. I am perfectly willing to extend the core symbolism of the sipapu back a millennium (no less reasonable a move than the extension of Christian cross symbolism back a millennium) and to accept that the Winter People both possessed a basic cosmological vision involving an ancestral underworld and communed with this underworld in an architectural space. Again, the more interesting observation is that sipapus were common additions to residential life. Every nuclear or extended family appears to have had direct control over its symbolic place of emergence and direct access to the world of its ancestors with little or no mediation by ritual leaders beyond the immediate household.

Elsewhere, I have argued that the layout and orientation of Taos pithouses also held cosmological significance (Fowles 2004:268–286; see also Lakatos 2007). Pithouses were unerringly constructed with their ventilators toward the southeast (figure 3.8), a direction viewed as especially important among the contemporary Northern Tiwas. This is where Father Sun rises at winter solstice when he is weakest and in need of the greatest human ritual assistance, and the physical orientation of the household toward this direction probably went hand in hand with a moral orientation stressing respect for this most powerful of nonhuman beings. The lines of evidence supporting this interpretation are varied and would require more background than I have space to provide here. If correct, however, we are again led to the conclusion that every household had its own architectural means of communing with larger cosmic powers.

Classical evolutionists would undoubtedly look upon this state of affairs in eleventh- and twelfth-century Taos as a gratifyingly predictable starting point: surely it makes sense that such household-level religiosity was society's original condition before emergent theocrats began positioning themselves as the supra-household

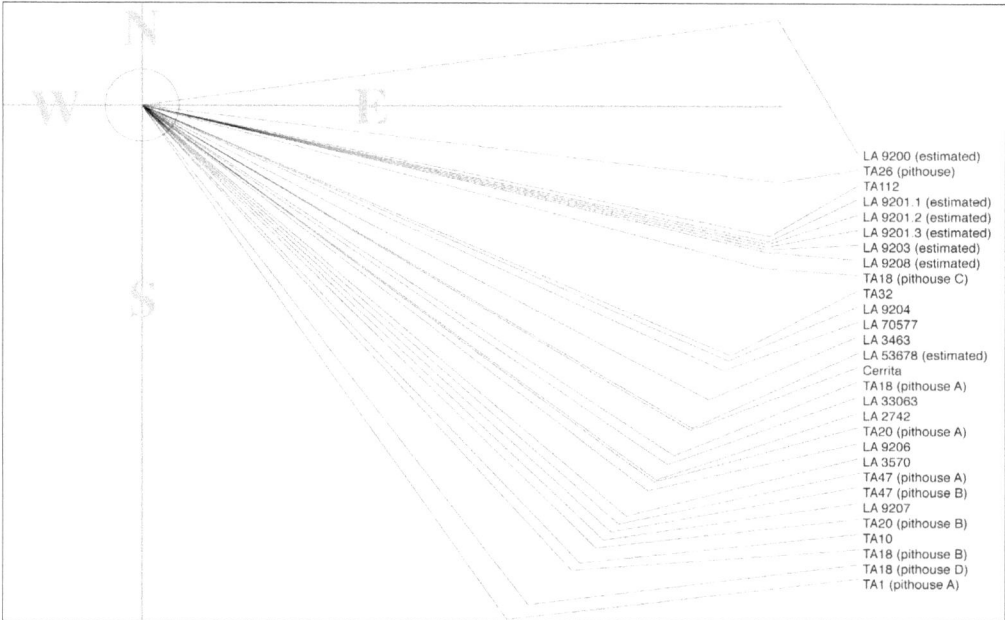

Figure 3.8. Orientations of all excavated Valdez Phase pithouses in the Taos region.

leaders of group ritual. Why complicate matters when the evolution of religious patterns in the region seems so straightforward? Is this not how social complexity evolved the world over, with aggrandizers exploiting the basic human belief in the gods to legitimize their own positions of earthly power? Couldn't the priestly patterns described in chapter 2 have evolved locally as household autonomy was increasingly breached, as belief was transformed into ideology, and as religion was enlisted in politics?

How easily the Protestant story line (see chapter 1) enters the picture. How quickly the idea of a "natural" or "true" religion—as a matter of private belief rather than political action—is reified. And how comfortably the Winter People become a model of primitive simplicity to be equated with proto-Neolithic societies the world over. But at what a cost! Note how such an evolutionary narrative demands that we assume the ancestral Northern Tiwas were characterized by a completely unrealistic parochialism, that we ignore the archaeological evidence of their historical connections to groups in the northern San Juan, and that we brush aside Taos Pueblo's own account of its ancestral migrations.

A different perspective is called for, something akin to that offered by Kenneth Sassaman (2001) in his discussion of traditions of resistance. For Sassaman, no group of people is or ever was an island, isolated from the currents of regional history in which it is set. All societies are partly defined by their oppositional stance to real or perceived social orders, be they in rival communities of the present or in their own social past. Pueblo oral historians are well aware of this reality, but indigenous scholars elsewhere in Native America also challenge us to reevaluate what counts as progress. In commenting on the long-term development of Iroquoian society as a rejection of Mississippian excesses, Seneca historian Barbara Mann writes:

> I suspect, therefore, that a much more encompassing political movement was afoot in the demise of…mound culture than western scholars realize, and that, if such collapses as that of the Cliff Dwellers of the desert southwest are figured into the mix, it seems to have been continent-wide. Socially, politically, economically, and religiously, Native America advanced significantly between the sixth and twelfth centuries, shunning spiritual terrorism, throwing off class-based hierarchy, turning away from war, organizing gift-based economies, and developing the rule of democratic law. The magnificence of mound culture might have died, but its old order was little missed. (Mann 2003:167–168; see also Trigger 1990)

Here is a worthy charge indeed. Where once anthropologists saw a series of societies who had traveled only a short distance in their inevitable advance toward the state (the Iroquois nations, of course, were Lewis Henry Morgan's classic example of the stunted evolutionary stage of barbarism), we now see communities of conscientious objectors, voluntary simplicity, and a historically contingent turn away from the state. The evolution of counterculture. A model for an anarchist anthropology (in the sense of Graeber 2004).

The effects of this position are significant, for it now becomes impossible to view societies on a scale from cold (traditional, primitive) to hot (modern, evolved). We are forced to acknowledge that the social world is forever hot; even those societies that appear unchanged through the ages—those allegedly locked in a domestic mode of production or a private mode of religious belief—have run mightily to stand still, to stand their ground. Asad (2003) has discussed this issue from an overtly postcolonial perspective. The West, he argues, has always judged the non-West by its willingness to *change* (that is, to develop, as in a "developing country"), and it has consistently denied that social efforts to resist change are viable expressions of human agency. As a result, opponents of Western-style modernity are cast as backward slaves to the past rather than as authors of the present, although this ignores the reality that fundamentalist, revivalist, or conservative movements always produce entirely novel social constructions. Even when their rhetoric is laced with promises of a return to a utopian past, they are always, first and foremost, defined by their oppositional stance, by what they are not—inexorably modern in their very rejection of modernity.

Would it have been so different in twelfth-century New Mexico? Replace the cultural hegemony of "modernity" with that of "Chaco" and the Winter People assume a structural position not dissimilar to the Amish or Mennonites: cultural critics who opted for geographic marginality and seemingly pre-Chacoan ways that were assertively simple. No churches, no formal priests, no clear material evidence of supra-household ceremonial organization of any kind: in comparison to their neighbors in the northern San Juan, they were indeed "plain people" (as the Amish are sometimes called). But plain by default or design?

The evidence supports the latter position. The more troublesome issue is how to interpret the paucity of evidence pointing to the religious life of the Winter People. Certain ceremonial activities may have failed to leave an archaeologically perceptible trace, but there must be a point at which one trusts the data one has. Again, we are prompted to ask: might the developing clericalism in the core Chacoan area have led those emigrating to the Rio Grande to push formal, centralized religion aside? To what extent had religion become a much more personal or individualized matter? To what extent had the emigrants lost (or run away from) faith altogether? Is there a sense in which the Winter People of the eleventh century could be described as secular?

"Secular" will prove too loaded a term for most. On one hand, there is little question that the Winter People held certain core cosmological notions that structured ritual practices, even if those ritual practices were a good deal subtler and more individualistic than we typically imagine for tribal societies. On the other hand, most students of secularism are unwilling to separate the concept from the historical particularities of Europe's religious wars, the philosophical and economic upheavals brought on by the discovery and conquest of the New World, capitalism's new emboldening of the autonomous subject, the rise of the nation-state, the effort to transcend (rather than reject) religion through new policies of religious tolerance, and so on. Which is to say, most regard secularity as a uniquely modern condition. But in so vigorously closing down any discussion of secularism as a general phenomenon—and by "general," I mean a phenomenon that may have structural or historical parallels in many different times and places—there is a real danger, for to do so is to claim, once and for all, that there is an unbridgeable chasm between the modern and the premodern, the very sort of great divide that plays into colonial ideologies, Enlightenment narratives of progress, and much else that should be approached with a highly critical attitude. Not to mention that there is nothing anthropological about research in which the core analytical category is so historically contingent that it cannot be translated into any other cultural context anywhere in the world prior to the fifteenth century. We have many histories of secularism, but despite recent efforts we still await the development of an anthropology of secularism.

I make no pretensions to undertaking this project myself. Rather, I have raised the question of premodern secularity principally to explore what it exposes about our use of "religion" as a cross-cultural category. Is talk of secular tribes any less absurd than talk of religious tribes? Why is the secular treated as a historically contingent phenomenon while religion is so easily treated as universal? Such questions are difficult to answer. They demand new ways of talking about the past, new methods of comparative study. I return to this issue in the final chapter. My immediate goals have been more modest, more regionally localized, and more archaeological. If we are to go looking for the so-called religiosity of the eleventh-century occupation of the Taos district by the Winter People, let us at least be on the lookout for both their devout beliefs *and* their devout unbeliefs. Let us struggle to read the archaeological record as evidence of both culture *and* counterculture, cognizant of the fact that no community is ever oblivious to the swarm of other communities that preceded it, surround it in its present, and loom as desirable or undesirable possibilities for the future.

If religion seems less clearly politicized in eleventh-century Taos than in Chaco Canyon, if it was less implicated in the negotiation of social power, if it was much more of a private affair, then we might assume that this was because the Winter People actively chose to constrain it in this way. Which is to say that they, no less than their more orthodox neighbors, were doing politics with religion. Or doing religion with politics. Or simply "doing," as I argue more precisely in the next chapter.

four
Doings

Almost everything we do is a religious act, from the time we get up to the time we go to sleep. How can the white man ever understand that?
—*Hopi informant, quoted in Courlander,* Hopi Voices

Doings. This is the wildly ambiguous term used in many Native American communities to talk about what I have uncomfortably referred to in the previous chapters as religious practice. Anglos, such as myself, who spend time poking around the peripheries of the Pueblos quickly learn that there are certain times of year when tribal members "have their doings" and that these are times to keep a respectful distance. Rarely does the outsider learn much about what doings entail beyond that they are clearly private affairs of palpable significance to the community and that they have the weight of indigenous tradition behind them. One could speculate as to the particulars: twentieth-century ethnography is full of statements describing secret Pueblo rituals, often in surprising detail. But even if one speculated correctly, even if one knew all the prayers and pilgrimages involved, there would still be something strangely impenetrable in the description of these practices as doings.

To be told of doings is to watch a curtain being drawn. There is a brief pause in the conversation, an inaccessibility, an uncertainty of how to respond—at least for the outsider who is no longer able to look in. "Doings" signals a problem of translation. When told that Taos Pueblo is having its doings, the tourist from New York or Chicago stumbles and thinks to himself: "Doing...what?" Or she finds herself struggling to clarify matters: "Now, is this to say that you're 'doing' your religious ceremonies, that you're 'doing' something sacred?" In Euro-American society, one never simply has doings; one is always doing *something*, and that something can always be classified as a discrete type of behavior (work from nine to five, family time in the evening, church on Sunday). *Doings*, in contrast, has a Heideggerian ring to it. It seems to zoom out from the typologies and classifications of our chopped-up practices to describe an ungraspable mode of being-in-the-world.

What is the difference between "doings" and "doing something religious"? The question could hardly be more central to this study. Some might say the difference is between the premodern (or nonmodern) and the modern. People who have their doings clearly do not live in the compartmentalized Western world with its strategies of purification. Doings exist in worlds where newspapers do not come with sections labeled "religion," "arts," "business," and "politics." When the ancient Egyptians engaged the gods, for instance, they were not practicing religion but rather *irt ht*—literally, "doing things" (Routledge 2008). "Doing things" has an even louder Heideggerian ring, particularly if we think of these "things" as gatherings in which the cosmos—the fourfold of earth and sky, humans and gods—is drawn together into a unity.

The Pueblos are like the ancient Egyptians in being nonmodern, but by virtue of their profound entanglement with the forces of modernity (colonialism, capitalism, tourism, anthropologization, and the like) they are, more accurately, anti-modern. Within the walls of Taos Pueblo, pride is taken in the absence of electricity and plumbing, in the residents' ability to drink directly—both literally and figuratively—from the river running through the village. And when the Pueblos talk about doings rather than religion, we seem to confront this same anti-modernist stance, the same quiet rejection of a Western project in which they hold little stock. They seem to be emphasizing, in parallel with Asad (1993), that religion is a historically contingent institution of the post-Reformation West, not a universal category that can be translated willy-nilly into a world of kivas and clans. Doings even sweep away the supposed universality of the sacred-profane division. Doings are not sacred in the sense that they oppose some other set of practices that are irreligious. Pueblo philosophy differentiates *the sacred from the sacred*, I have heard some native intellectuals insist, not the sacred from the profane. In this sense, it would be possible to still write an archaeology of the ancestral Pueblos using terms like "religion" and "sacred," providing we acknowledge that *everything* was probably more or less religious and that nothing was truly profane. But this path leads toward analytical sterility: to say that everything is at least vaguely religious is the same as saying nothing is. Worse still, by writing of Pueblo people as *Homo religiosis* we run the risk of reifying the popular perception that they are either Sahlins's "full-time servants of mumbo-jumbo" or that they dance through history on a sort of rarified spiritual plane.

Could we write an archaeology of Pueblo doings instead? Much depends on what exactly one means by "doings."

The Pueblos are (as the ancient Egyptians were) always doing things, and we must therefore establish why certain practices (and not all practices) can be specially described as doings. Rather than viewing doings as we would religion and assume they are opposed to some other set of practices in which nothing is doing, I suggest we view Pueblo doings as practices characterized by a heightened awareness of interconnectedness and the relations between things. This requires explanation. "Interconnectedness" is a fuzzy term, almost as fuzzy as doings, and it smacks of an uncritical New Age interpretation of American Indian spirituality and ecological harmony. But connectivity is a recurrent and conscious theme in much indigenous commentary (e.g., Cajete 2000; Lomawaima 2004; Swentzell 1985, 1990) and so deserves careful consideration. For some, the Pueblo vision of a world in which society, religion, economy, ecology, and so on explicitly occupy the same space, a vision that objects to any division between nature and culture is a far more accurate model of the world *as it really is.* We are all, argue Latour (2005), Haraway (2008), and their followers, residents in a world of networks in which humans are only influential by virtue of the hybrid forms they assume in relation to other nonhuman entities. "Premoderns" such as the Pueblos simply approach these networks in a far more forthright fashion. "While the moderns insure themselves by not thinking at all about the consequences of their innovations [that is, of their acts upon "nature"] for the social order, the premoderns—if we are to believe the anthropologists—dwell endlessly and obsessively on those connections between nature and culture" (Latour 1993:41).

Perhaps there is an element of truth to Latour's observation, but this image of an endlessly obsessive attention to interconnectedness obscures a key point. The Pueblos—and, no doubt, all other so-called premoderns—do not maintain, day in and day out, the same heightened consciousness of the networks that link nature and culture together into a single natureculture. Again, the incisive words of Vine Deloria: "The people did Indian dances. BUT THEY DIDN'T DO THEM ALL THE TIME." Some premodern individuals (those we tend to label priests or shamans) focus their attention on these networks more than others do, and some practices (those we tend to refer to as rituals or ceremonies) are more explicitly networked or webby than others. Indeed, it is precisely when an indigenous group acts socially to influence nature (for example, when they dance together to maintain the abundance of deer herds) or when they interpret natural events as commentaries on the state of society (for example, when a drought is interpreted as due to witchcraft) that we begin jotting down notes about "religion."

Anthropologists—grounded as we are in a broadly secular tradition—view such connections as necessarily illusory cultural beliefs, and we mark them as illusory by designating them as religious. The Pueblos may leave prayer-stick offerings to the katsina so that the rain will fall; they may build a check dam so the falling water will stay in the fields; and they may view both as strategies to make corn grow. But within anthropology we seem to have no choice but to wrench these practices apart, categorizing the former as ritual and the latter as agricultural technique.

This is where an archaeology of doings has something to offer. Doings are neither

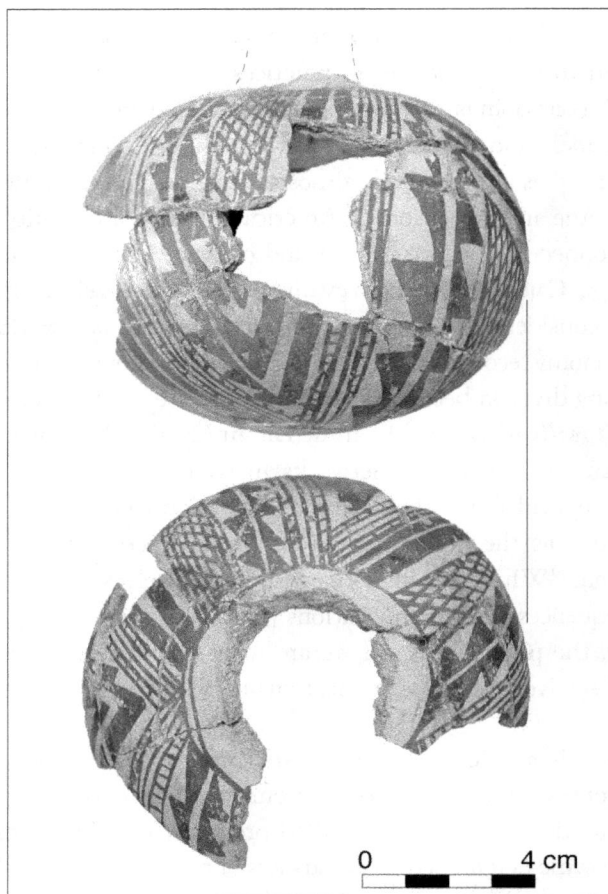

Figure 4.1. An imported miniature jar from an early thirteenth-century pit structure beneath Roomblock 2 at T'aitöna.

true nor false, neither sacred nor profane, and they are without the original sin that inevitably taints so-called religious behavior in the eyes of secular analysts. Doings are simultaneously social, economic, political, cosmological, technological, and so on, as are most human practices. They are not, in other words, a separate species of Pueblo behavior. But they *are* distinguished from other practices by the extent to which they mark and make explicit the mutual entanglement of people, things, and cosmos.

As an illustration of this point, consider a miniature jar (figure 4.1) unearthed at the ancestral Tiwa village of T'aitöna, a late thirteenth- and early fourteenth-century settlement. The jar is the sort of thing that Western anthropologists would refer to as a "sacred object" used in "religious" practices in a specialized "ritual structure," or kiva. We can describe the jar in many ways; in fact, a small piece of it was included in a compositional study (Fowles et al. 2007), permitting us to talk about its chemical and mineralogical characteristics at length. We can also describe the pottery techniques used to form, paint, polish, and fire the vessel, and we can describe the style of its decoration as being emblematic of one social tradition rather than another.

Miniature jars, such as the one in question, are known to have played key roles in Pueblo doings. At various springs, lakes, and rivers, they were filled with water, and this water was then transformed into powerful medicine used to influence the world (Jeançon 1923:72). Ethnographic reports describe the process in some detail. At Picurís Pueblo, for instance, miniature jars were still in use during the late twentieth century. In the springtime, members of the kiva societies would run to water sources located far away from the pueblo in each of the five cosmological directions (the four cardinals as well as "east again," or the important southeast direction of winter sunrises). There they would fill their jars and return to the round house in the village where water from all five directions was collected in a single large bowl to be used at a later date in agricultural preparations (Donald Brown, personal communication 2001; see also Brown 1973:144–145). Similar practices occurred at Taos Pueblo, where Stevenson (1906–1907:file 4.14) further reported that miniature jars were principally used to bring rain; pine twigs were dipped into them, and the water was sprinkled in a kiva toward the various directions to help the rain fall.

What is being performed here? Superficially, the miniature jars are implicated in religious rituals (insofar as they reference the cosmos and its forces), although such practices are clearly also economic (insofar as they are strategies to assist agriculture) and political (insofar as these strategies are uniquely controlled by particular kiva leaders rather than the village at large).

None of these terms are at all adequate. Miniature jars are used in *doings* that can be described more precisely as a kind of exegesis of worldly interconnections. When youths run with the vessels, they trace out networks that link the village to the five cosmic directions. When they return with water from these directions and pour them into a single bowl, they physically gather together the cosmos into a single point. And when this water is later sprinkled outward to the five cosmic directions, the interconnections are again underscored. Pueblo individuals are always linked to the rest of the world in all that they do, but doings seem to *emphasize* the linkages; they make them explicit, tangible, sensuous.

Indeed, the particular miniature jar being considered may have emphasized more than just spatial linkages. Compositional analyses demonstrated that the jar was not produced with local clays, and based upon stylistic evidence it appears the vessel was created hundreds of kilometers away in southwestern New Mexico.[1] The most plausible explanation of how it came to be recovered near Taos is that the jar was among the personal effects of an immigrant group for which it held special significance. (Such objects are treated as inalienable possessions in the pueblos today.) Use of the kiva jar, we might speculate, linked the immigrants to their ancestral home and to a specific history of population movements. As a durable index of the group's past, the jar would have gathered together not only the cosmos it traversed, but also the time it transcended.

The miniature jar, then, assumes a position not unlike the jug in Heidegger's celebrated essay "The Thing." The jug, for Heidegger, served as a useful means of exploring the distinction between, on one hand, the "objects" that stand before us as perceived, cognized, and heavily mediated representations and, on the other hand, the "things" that stand forth in their own unmediated reality and so remain hidden from us as perceiving subjects:

> As the self-supporting independence of something independent, the jug [as a thing in itself] differs from the object. An independent, self-supporting thing may become an object if we place it before us, whether in immediate perception or by bringing it to mind in a recollective re-presentation. However, the thingly character of the thing does not consist in its being a represented object. (Heidegger 2001:164–165)

What is the thingly character of the jug according to Heidegger? Not merely the material clay of the vessel's body but also the void it defines, the wine that fills the void, the gathering together of earth and sun and air to make the wine that fills the void, the outpouring of the wine back into the world, and on and on. The jug is what it is by virtue of the particular way it gathers together and articulates the cosmos.

So too with the Pueblo miniature jar, which gathers together both time (it is an inalienable possession that stands forth as a durable piece of the past in the present) and space (through its use, it becomes the point around which the world is assembled and out of which it is distributed again). "In the gift of the outpouring earth and sky, divinities and mortals [and let us add past and present] dwell *together all at once*" (Heidegger 2001:173). Pueblo doings and Heideggerian metaphysics are not so very different in this regard (see also Saile 1989). Both seem to seek a sense of what Heidegger (2001:175) referred to as "nearness," a sense of the world as interconnected and unified, a sense of every thing being filled by every other thing. Both offer philosophical treatises on the gathering power of things, be these things jugs or jars, masks or prayer sticks, boulders or lakes.

The comparison should only be taken so far. Heidegger was aiming merely for better philosophy. Pueblo doings are more ambitious; they aim for better worlds. They are undertaken not only to illuminate the ontology of things but also to act upon or influence those things. And this is the interesting point for anthropology, because the devil (that is, the question of power) resides in *how* the world is gathered. It resides in *how* groups of people come to be connected to one another, to water, to land, to corn, to macaws, to deer, to imported pottery, to houses, to the ancestors, to spirits, and to the practice of gathering the world itself. Pueblo doings articulate and institutionalize particular, cosmic configurations—this is how they act upon the state of affairs. Little surprise that they have been seedbeds of debate, contestation, and factionalism no less than they have been sources of group solidarity.

Such statements require elaboration and examples, both of which I offer below as we return to the pre-Columbian archaeology of the Taos region. But before doing so, let us briefly take stock of the broad trajectory of the argument thus far.

In chapter 1, I suggested that as the general relationship between modernity and religion is rethought, as we are increasingly told that the industrialized world might *not* be progressing toward an ever more rational state of secular irreligion, and as we are told instead that the world is heading toward a state of greater religiosity, it becomes incumbent upon archaeologists to critically reevaluate the old narratives of religion's evolutionary development. Rather than keeping the past at arm's length, on the sidelines of the present, we must acknowledge the interpenetration of origins and futures and ask how this new vision of the emerging postsecular world order remakes religion's early history as well. We must, that is, examine our models of hoary old religion with the same fresh critical eyes that contemporary scholars are using to examine radicalized Islam in the Middle East or the Christian Coalition in the United States.

In chapter 2, the groundwork was laid for taking religion seriously in the Pueblo world, one of anthropology's core examples of intense premodern religiosity. And in chapter 3, I argued that to take Pueblo religion seriously we must begin by not taking it for granted. Ancestral Pueblo religion, like all past religions, shifts its ground as soon as we also create analytical spaces for premodern *non*religiosity, tribal humanism, and primitive secularity—categories that seem illegitimate but that nevertheless help to expose the contingent nature of religion in the past no less than in the present.

Over the course of these arguments, however, the very phenomenon of interest—religion or, more specifically, Pueblo religion—grew ever more awkward insofar as we were repeatedly forced to describe it in terms that opposed it to something called politics or economics, terms that left it impotent and marginalized from the outset. "Look at how important religion is," we said. "Religion—even Neolithic religion—is *political*." This is to say that our method of enhancing religion's analytical position was merely to point to a shadowy image of political machination that we, in our anthropological diplopia, assumed lay just behind the ritual performance. Religion only became powerful when viewed as a tool wielded by a hidden political hand, when it became the signifier of the political signified.

Now we are ready to leave such double vision and spurious semiotics behind. Taking religion seriously, let us finally admit, means not only making space for its assertive nonexistence or for its politicization; it means putting to the side the search for a universal premodern religion altogether. In the American Southwest, it means seeking out the deep history of Pueblo doings and the complex world configurations they gather together.

Nonmodern Exegesis

I am well aware of the criticism that might be made of such an analysis: that the study of Pueblo doings easily slips right back into the old category of religion. There is a risk of this, to be sure. Neologisms do little on their own. Off what intellectual platform, then, might we leap to the new conceptual terrain of doings without falling straight back down into our original footprints? How can we avoid just talking about religion by another name?

It is easier to say where not to begin. Most of the existing theoretical orientations in archaeology offer little traction. Dyed-in-the-wool functionalists (and there are plenty still around in archaeology), for instance, cannot see doings in the present, let alone in the deep past; following Rappaport (1971:72), they tend to read tribal religion as a "functional alternative to political power," as a means of sanctifying practices that are of benefit to the group. Marxists are equally unsatisfying; their materialism typically leads them to see religion as a disguised means of achieving nonreligious ends. We can leave both functionalist and Marxist intellectual platforms to the side. Might structuralist or interpretive archaeologies offer a better alternative? No, they are too consumed with what things mean to appreciate what doings do. Phenomenologists, then? Within archaeology they tend to be too theory-bound to individual human perception to appreciate the sort of expansive web of connections that doings entail. None of these orientations gives us leverage. Perhaps if Bruno Latour came to excavate in New Mexico we would see doings in something approximating midday sunlight—that is, without any infrastructural shadows cast behind them—but this is unlikely to happen anytime soon.

What about something closer to a native footing, then? Pueblo doings, after all, are not just performed; they are *explained* or accounted for in the course of historical narratives that situate present practices in relation to past events. To a certain extent, the old anthropological notion of myth as a charter for ritual resonates for the Pueblos; upon reaching puberty, for example, a young woman might ceremonially grind corn for the community, re-creating the primeval acts of the Earth Mother at her own maturation (Fowles 2006). But there is much more to the Pueblo mode of historical explanation than charter myths. Oral histories frequently describe the process by which certain doings came to be owned by particular groups as well as how and why these doings came to be practiced in particular villages. Scratch the surface of simple statements that explain doings as attempts to keep the world in balance, and one finds a vast indigenous appreciation of historical contingency and of causal linkages between present and past.

This is nicely illustrated by another of the Taos doings. The Feather Kiva is said to have traditionally performed a ceremony during late summer involving the destruction of elaborate shields (Stevenson 1906–1907:files 2.9, 2.28). Unlike the animal-hide shields used in precolonial warfare, these were vegetable shields composed of five different types of plants that varied in their resistance to cold, the outermost plant being the most resistant and the innermost being the least so. Once constructed, the shields were given as offerings over a fire constructed in a large pit, in order that "the heat may rise over the world and make the earth warm that it may never be too cold for the abundant growth of vegetation" (Stevenson 1906–1907:file 2.9). Ostensibly, this ceremony was about keeping the world in balance, performed as it was to promote a fecund earth and perhaps more pointedly to ensure that Taos's crops were protected from damaging frosts, which can come as early as August. The shields, then, might be read as symbols of the Pueblos' labors to defend Mother Earth, and the heat of the fire might be read as a kind of sympathetic magic designed to influence, mimetically, the heat of Father Sun.

But let us go beneath the surface. The fact that the "Offering of the Plant Shields" was performed by the Feather Kiva is significant, because the peoples of this kiva (the Golden Warbler People, the Macaw People, and the Eagle People) are essentially equivalent to the membership of the Summer People (Pilaína), who figure prominently in Taos oral history (Stevenson 1906–1907:file 3.1). The Summer People originated, it is claimed, to the south, where they lived as agriculturalists with powerful "medicine"—which is to say they possessed certain objects and knowledge, bequeathed from the Creator, that enabled them to engage in particularly powerful doings.

With respect to our analysis of the plant shields, the key chapter in Taos oral history is the description of an epic battle in which the Summer People traveled north to conquer the Winter People, those early counterculture occupants of the Taos region discussed at length in the previous chapter. The details of this encounter will become increasingly important to the discussion, as will the idiom in which it is narrated. Hence, a lengthy excerpt:

> The father of the Summer People directed [his community] to make ready to…conquer the Winter People,[2] destroying their power. The Summer People prepared their shields of plants and put on their clothing of plants with wreaths of plants around their wrists and ankles. They started out for their conflict with the Winter People....
>
> On reaching the land of the Winter People, the associate to the father of the Summer People was sent to the Winter People whom he questioned. "What have you to say? Are you friends or enemies?" The representative of the Winter People replied, "We are not your friends." "It is well," said the man of the Summer People. "We will fight you."
>
> Then the associate of the Summer People returned to his people giving his father the result of his meeting with the Winter People. The father said, "It is well, I guess there are many of these people." The Winter People approached the Summer People, driving them back to where the others were who had turned back to engage in their negotiations. The Winter People almost blinded the Summer People with their ice and snow, and the cold was very great. At this point the Summer People got the better of the Winter People, driving them back some distance. And so the struggle continued, first one then the other side driving the others back. When the Summer People were forcing the Winter People back, their lightning arrows flew through the air making everything hot.
>
> Finally the Summer People succeeded in driving the Winter People not only to their village, but into their kiva. The Summer People now had possession of the village and they looked down into the kiva and sprinkled medicine through the

hatchway. Soon there was much water in the kiva for the medicine of the Summer People had caused the ice floor to melt, and the ice melted from the ladder leaving only the wood frame. This medicine caused the Winter People to sneeze and cough. *Then the Summer People threw their plant shields and clothing into the kiva* after which the Summer People descended into the kiva. They found the Winter People to be a fine and beautiful people after their ice clothing had disappeared. (Quoted in Stevenson 1906–1907:file 2.29, emphasis added)

There is a great deal going on here. On one level we are presented with a cosmo-logical tale of the changing seasons. Warmth seeks to conquer cold and bring back summer, a common theme in most non-equatorial cultures that suffer the physical challenges of a prolonged winter season. In this sense, the narrative adopts a mythic quality, each group commanding the forces of nature to battle the other. But it would be wrong to reduce the battle to mere myth. Indeed, the protagonists are simultaneously presented as the forebears of *real* social groups at contemporary Taos Pueblo. Long ago, it is claimed, the ancestors of the Feather Kiva peoples (a.k.a. the Summer People) actually *did* conquer the ancestors of the Day Kiva peoples (a.k.a. the Winter People).

When early twentieth-century members of the Feather Kiva—the "leading kiva," according to Stevenson's informant—engaged in their late summer doings with the plant shields, then, they were rehearsing a history of divine privilege, physi-cal conquest, and social domination. Yes, they were keeping the world in balance, but relations of power between human groups are part of the world, and just as sum-mer must repeatedly assert its supremacy over winter, so too must power relations be repeatedly performed and maintained. Control over nature is part and parcel of control over society—or as Latour might put it, the "Offering of the Plant Shields" reveals itself as doings that exerted influence over a single natureculture. Rhizome-like, the ceremony's shoots extend down into history and other worlds, outward into society and other peoples, upward to the sun and rain.

The narrative, let me emphasize, is both mythic and real. Despite a resurgence of attention to indigenous accounts of the past in the post-NAGPRA era, it remains the case that most Southwestern archaeologists are deeply suspicious of the historicity of oral history, and most take stories in which Summer People shoot lightning arrows as precisely that: stories, the product of a creative imagination. Here, too, the Western analyst in modernist style seeks to purify categories and separate history from myth, fact from fiction, as if this could be so easily done. I am less suspicious than most of indigenous knowledge and mytho-histories, and I am inclined to grant most oral accounts of the past a fundamental reality, even if it is a reality that outsiders may have difficulty reading or translating.

For those more persuaded by cold, hard (arti)facts drawn from the ground, how-ever, it is indeed the case that the battle implicitly referenced by the "Offering of the Plant Shields" ceremony and explicitly discussed in the Taos origin account accords well with the archaeological record of the late twelfth century. Excavations at the last settlements of the Winter People—that is, at terminal Valdez Phase pithouse sites (see chapter 3)—have demonstrated that a remarkably large number of individuals died violently. Bodies found on the floor and in the fill of late twelfth-century pithouses exhibit axe wounds, blunt force trauma, decapitation, and the like (Fowles 2004:353–372; Whitley 2009). It is an unsettling assemblage that points to a species of violence perpetrated across rather than within ethnic groups, a species of violence perpetrated by those who seem to have been able to look upon the Other as fundamentally different and, hence, violable.

The Taos origin narrative describes just such an ethnic encounter in the meeting of the Winter and Summer Peoples (note that the Winter People only became recognizable as fully human in the eyes of the Summer People once the plant shields had melted their outer layer of ice), and I read this as residual commentary on actual events that were under way at roughly 1200 CE. Indeed, broadly coterminous with the violence just noted, the Taos archaeological record exhibits both a population increase and relatively clear material culture changes, including abrupt shifts in unpainted ceramic styles, a shift in settlement patterns from dispersed pithouses to aggregated pueblos in lowland settings, and the practice of newly intensified agriculture. Elsewhere I have argued not only that this is the signature of a relatively punctuated period of immigration but that it also marks the arrival of the Summer People discussed in the Taos origin narrative. Indeed, the term "Summer People" may have been adopted to describe and socially situate the congeries of formerly Chacoan peoples (broadly conceived) who entered the northern Rio Grande some eight centuries ago (Fowles 2004:316–369; 2005). Woe unto the Winter People: they escaped Chacoan hegemony in the eleventh century only to find Chaco come to them at the end of the twelfth. This, at least, is the most compelling story line in light of both the oral historical and archaeological evidence.

I want to explore how we might understand the varied negotiations between immigrants and autochthons as a kind of doings. My aim is to counter the tendency among archaeologists to read such phenomena as political conflicts to which religion is applied, post facto, as a spiritual salve, as a way political animals lick their wounds once the battle is over. The remainder of this chapter, then, picks up the archaeological story of Taos where it was left in the previous chapter. Whereas unbelief and countercultural rejection of orthodoxy were the dominant themes in chapter 3, we will find that the construction of a new sort of religious discourse—or more precisely, a new architectonics of doings—now emerges as our foremost concern.

Violent Doings

Enter the thirteenth century—the turbulent 1200s, as Lipe (1995) has put it for the northern Southwest generally. This was a century that began uneasily in the Taos district with a clash between post-Chacoan immigrants and the relatively autochthonous pithouse dwellers discussed in chapter 3. Oversimplifying what was undoubtedly a complicated landscape of social identities, I have referred to the former as the Summer People and the latter as the Winter People in keeping with certain aspects of Taos oral history. My goal in doing so is not to impose an artificial tidiness on the archaeological record. Rather, it is to explore the degree to which the ancestral Tiwa undertook this work of tidying themselves, ultimately through the construction of a new village, T'aitöna, or "People House" (a.k.a. Pot Creek Pueblo, LA 260), which was organized around a system of pervasive dualities. North versus south, winter versus summer, hunting versus agriculture—these structural oppositions were inscribed into the very architectural plan of this new village, forming the lived reality and habitus of those who moved, cooked, slept, and prayed within its walls. By the end of the thirteenth century, in other words, the ancestral Tiwas appear to have presented themselves *to themselves* as a society divided into two groups. As analysts we might alternately view these groups as complementary or opposed; either way, they were connected and premised upon one another, and it is this issue of connectivity that demands our attention.

As the first large nucleated settlement in the Taos area, T'aitöna represents an important benchmark in the development of a legibly "Northern Tiwa" society, but the settlement must be understood in its historical position; indeed, I suggest the real action occurred in the century leading up to T'aitöna's establishment, a time period known locally as the terminal Valdez Phase (1150–1190 CE) and subsequent Pot Creek Phase (1190–1260 CE). Archaeologists have only expressed mild interest in this period; most have treated it as a preface to T'aitöna, a transitional time when settlements grew a bit larger and ceramics changed somewhat as a local population of dispersed hunters and part-time horticulturalists adopted more intensive agricultural strategies and expanded the scale of their households (e.g., Crown and Kohler 1994; Woosley 1986).

Archaeological methods frequently draw us toward the local: it is far tidier to study a developmental sequence fully contained within a clearly delimited study area, migrating communities being notoriously difficult to track from their material residues alone. When a local group responds to local exigencies in such a way that their material practices are noticeably altered, the local archaeologist with a local data set is well equipped to construct a comprehensive explanation linking local cause with local effect. Not so when changes in material practices are interwoven with the movement of groups into and out of the study area. In such cases both the authorship of and the underlying motivations behind social change can be difficult to ascertain. There are, in other words, methodological pulls that entice archaeologists into reading the material record in terms of geographically stable group identities.

Any serious analysis of the late twelfth and early thirteenth centuries in the northern Rio Grande, however, would have to work mighty hard to ignore the impacts of immigration. Stuart and Gauthier (1988[1981]:51) observe that both site and room counts suggest that "somewhere between AD 1150 and 1250 population increases by *tenfold* in a 600 square mile area" (emphasis added). This trend has been documented with particular clarity in the Santa Fe district (Crown et al. 1996; Dickson 1979) and the Pajarito Plateau district (Orcutt 1999a, 1999b) where large-scale surveys have greatly aided demographic reconstructions. My own surveys in the Taos district confirm that significant early thirteenth-century population increases were experienced even in this northeasternmost extension of the Rio Grande valley (Fowles 2004:appendix D). Were there any lingering doubts as to the reality of a major post-Chacoan influx from the northern San Juan into the Eastern Pueblo region, Scott Ortman's (2010) extraordinary synthesis of the relevant craniometric, linguistic, and archaeological data should put these to rest.

My goal here is not to rehearse the evidence for immigration but to interrogate its effects. The arrival of the Summer People in the Taos district left clear marks in the archaeological record. Some marks were mundane: the style of unpainted pottery abruptly shifted from jars with direct rims, conical bases, lugs, and incised decoration to jars with flaring rims, globular bases, handles, and "smeared indented corrugated" decoration (figures 4.2 and 4.3). A locally made variant of Santa Fe B/W was also introduced and with it a new technology of vegetable-based paint (see figure 4.4). Architectural and settlement patterns were also affected: the former pattern of dispersed pithouse settlements gave way to classic unit pueblos (figure 4.5), typically situated in clear settlement clusters or loosely defined villages with far expanded storage space adjacent to prime agricultural land (figure 4.6). These were the earliest sites at which excavations have recovered corn remains and ceramic jars with exterior charring, suggesting significant dietary changes.

But not all of immigration's effects can be checked off with an air of analytical detachment. Behind the cold numeric assessment of changing population densities or ceramic ratios hovers a much more spectral image, an image I first encountered on the cover of Ernestene Green's (1976) brief monograph documenting Southern Methodist University's early excavations of a number of Valdez Phase pithouses. On the cover is a photograph of a dwelling, a pithouse still filled with the objects of everyday life: a metate poised for corn grinding, storage jars broken but in their position of use, and so on. Among these workaday objects, however, sprawled ignobly on the floor, the excavators also found the bodies of the family that presumably once dwelt within: a thirty-five- to forty-year-old patriarch with evidence of blunt force trauma, cast onto the hearth while the fire was still burning (there was light charring on some of his bones); a thirty- to forty-year-old matriarch with multiple broken and partially disarticulated bones; a seventeen- to eighteen-year-old male with a crushed scapula, pelvis, and thoracic vertebra; a three- to six-year-old child with a broken neck, who was stuffed into the ventilator shaft. Rocks scattered about the bodies appear to have been thrown from above—a stoning that was responsible, undoubtedly, for many of the crushed bones. In short, we are presented with a picture, not of death, but of massacre and, it seems, abject defilement.

Pithouse D of LA 102064, as this context is known, is one of the very latest

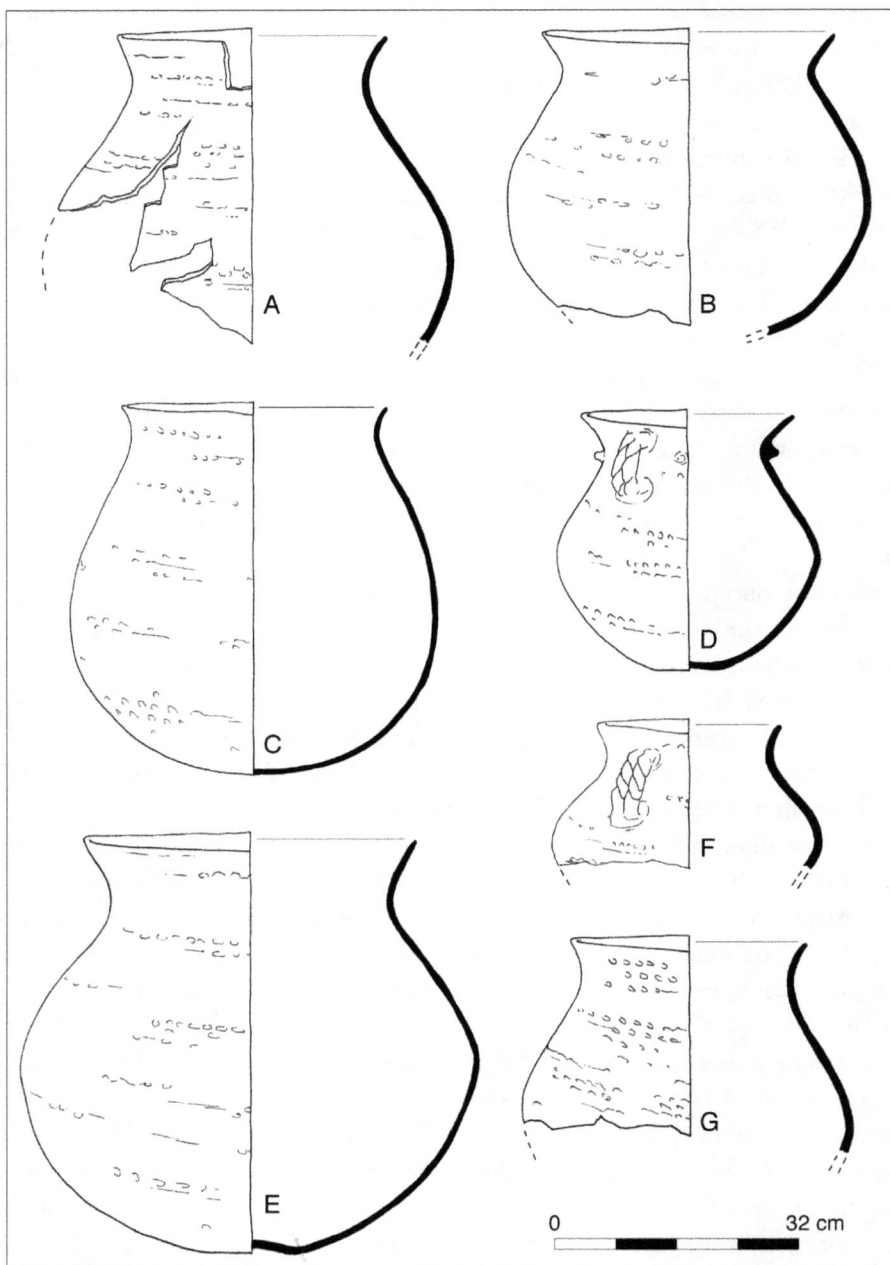

Figure 4.2. Examples of smeared indented corrugated vessels. A is from LA 80504/TA26; B–G are from T'aitöna.

of the classic Valdez Phase or Winter People dwellings, probably dating to right around 1200 CE (Fowles 2004:359). And it casts a dark shadow on the larger story of the Summer People's immigration, forcing us to acknowledge that the relationship

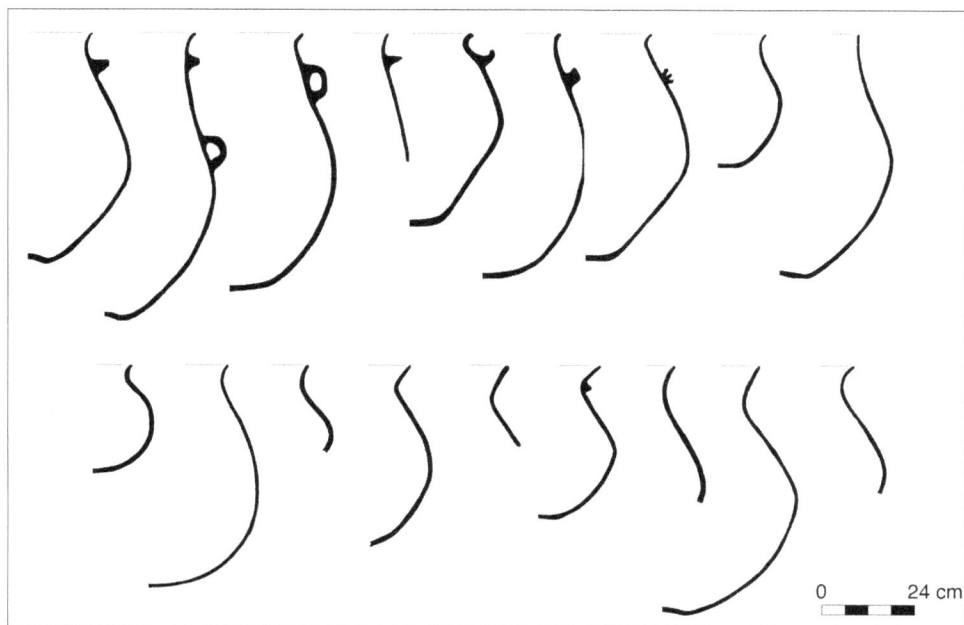

Figure 4.3. Vessel form comparison between Taos Incised (top) and smeared indented corrugated (bottom) vessels from the Rio Grande del Rancho drainage.

between immigrant and autochthon is almost never entirely peaceful. Indeed, the shadow grows darker when we critically evaluate the larger corpus of terminal Valdez Phase contexts, for it quickly becomes apparent that this act of violence was part of a much broader pattern.

A few miles to the south of LA 102064, a young adult male with a crushed skull had been tossed into late Valdez Phase deposits at TA10 (Fowles 2004:367). Six miles to the north, at another terminal Valdez site (LA 102068),[3] excavators unearthed nine more individuals, many of whom had been simultaneously interred and some of whose remains were described as "scattered" or "very scattered" (Green 1976:76–77). The latter included the decapitated cranium of a twenty-five- to thirty-five-year-old female and an eighteen- to forty-eight-year-old male who had died from two prominent axe wounds to the head and had been subsequently decapitated. And there are other examples; based on the existing excavations it would seem that roughly half of the Winter People who died at the close of the twelfth century died violently (for a more complete discussion, see Fowles 2004:353–372; Whitley 2009).

Let us return to the specific case of the family beaten and stoned to death in the pithouse at LA 102064. The proposition toward which I have been moving is that they suffered at the hands of post-Chacoan immigrants, at the hands of a relatively powerful group of the newly arrived whose linguistic and cultural differences from the Taos autochthons, the Winter People, may well have led them to view the latter as radically Other and, hence, especially violable. There are purely archaeological

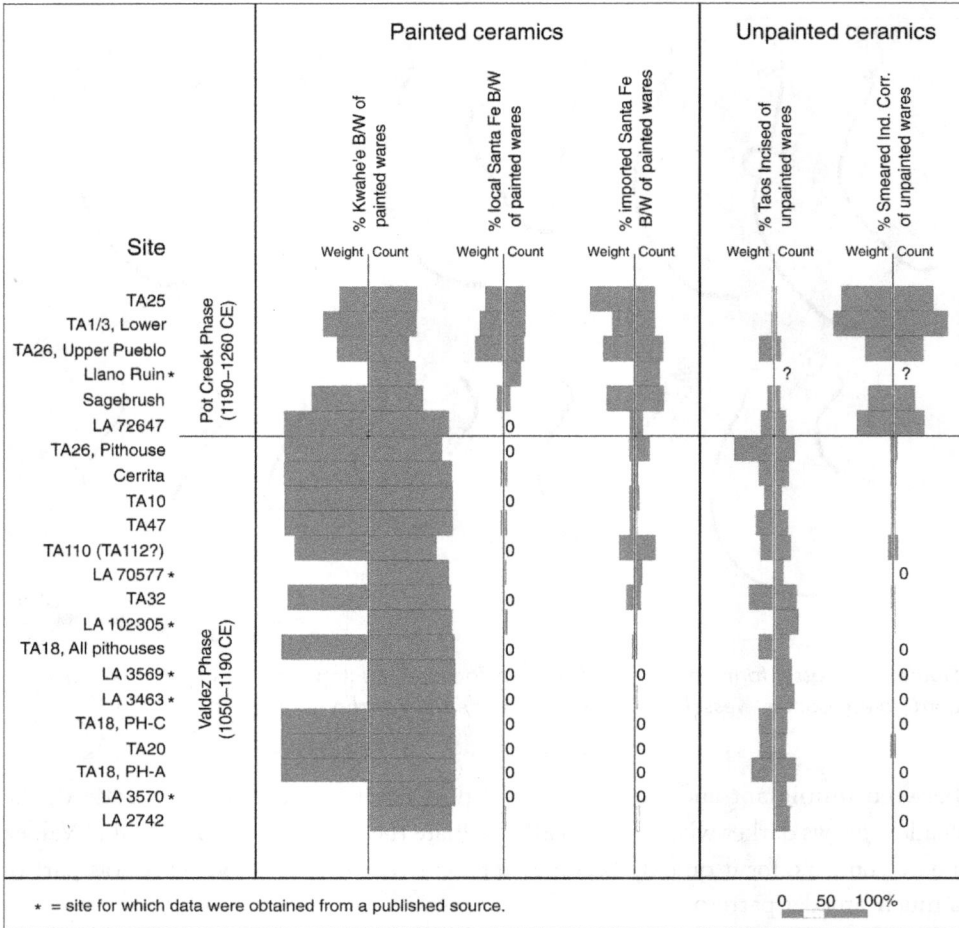

Figure 4.4. Changing ratios of major ceramic types during the Valdez and Pot Creek phases in the Rio Grande del Rancho drainage. (For details on the local ceramic seriation, see Fowles 2004:appendix D.)

grounds for drawing this conclusion when one bears in mind the larger currents of history in which this small settlement seems to have been caught up: the growth of Chacoan power in the eleventh and twelfth centuries; the demise of Chaco and the subsequent centers to the north followed by the dislocation of large populations during the thirteenth century; the relatively abrupt arrival in the Rio Grande valley of large numbers of migrants accustomed to a greater level of centralization and hierarchy. The family at LA 102064, in this sense, perished at the hands of history. Like sunlight through a magnifying glass, an era of regional instability narrowed into a momentary beam of searing, highly localized violence.

The case of LA 102064 can be explored from a second angle by looking to a narrative recorded by Elsie Clews Parsons at Taos Pueblo in the 1930s. "Race between Antelopes and Hawks" is a story about two groups of people, the "good people" and

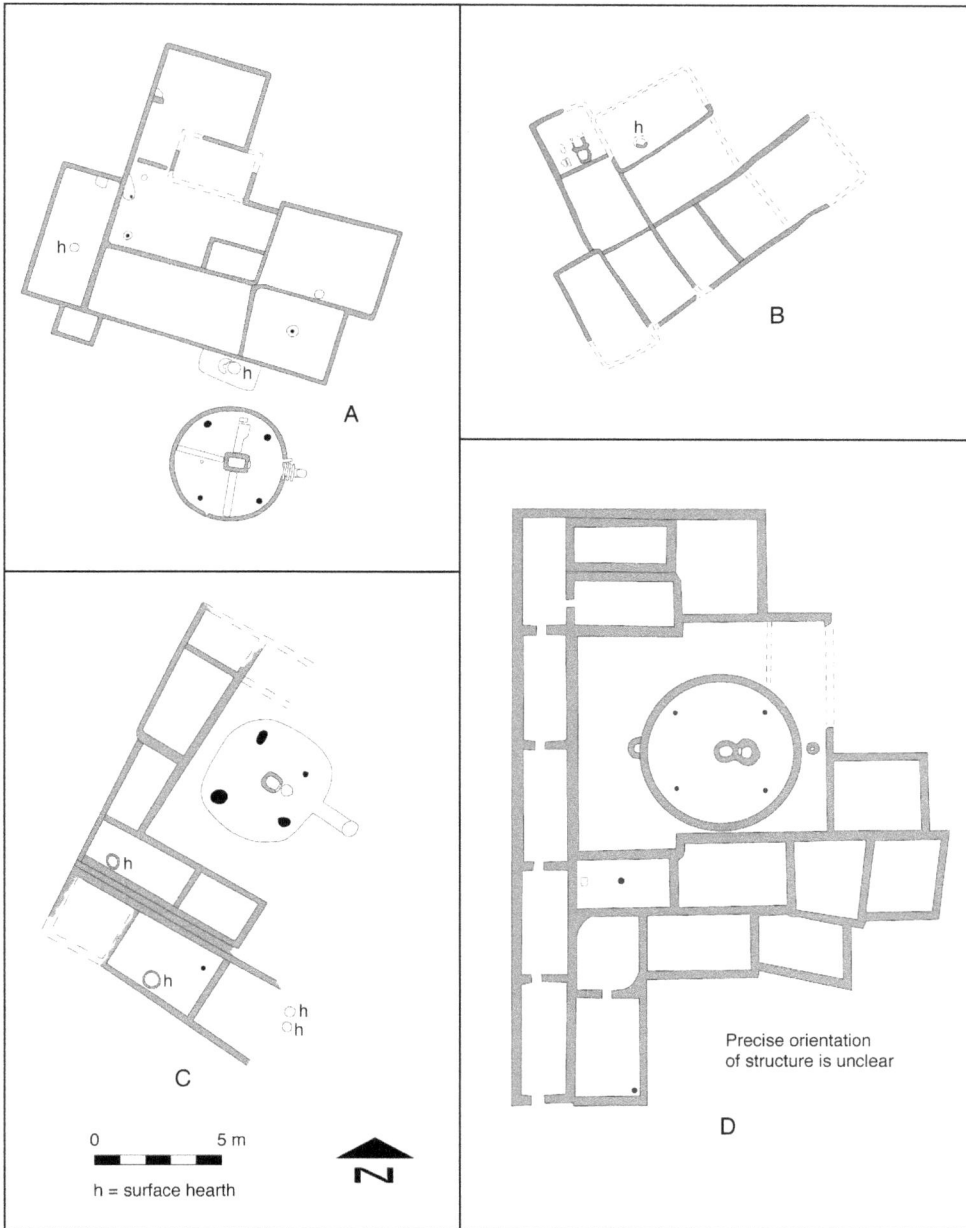

Figure 4.5. Early thirteenth-century (Pot Creek Phase) unit pueblos in the Rio Grande del Rancho drainage. A = LA 80504/TA26; B = Archuleta Site (LA 243/TA25); C = Sagebrush Pueblo; D = Llano Ruin (LA 1892).

a "band of witches," both of which allegedly once lived in the Taos district. The two groups, we are told at the start of the story, were at odds: "The good people never agreed to do things together {with the witches} because the witches were bad people.

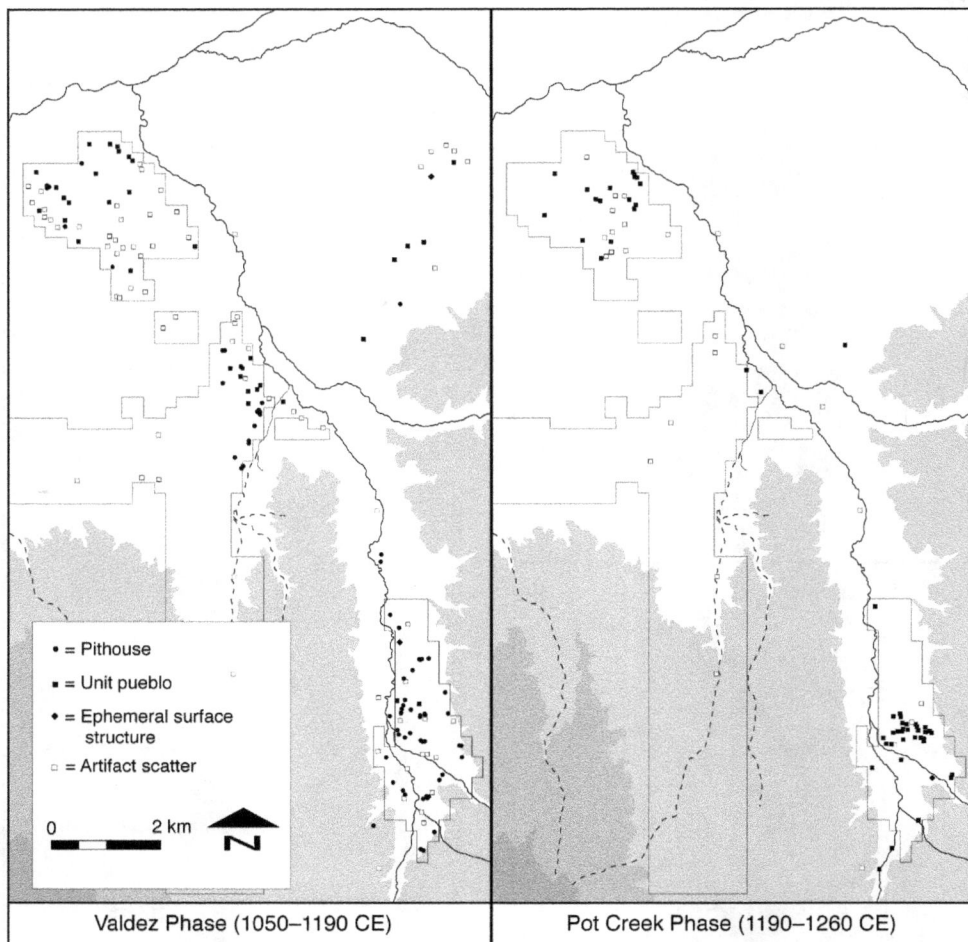

Figure 4.6. Comparison of Valdez Phase (1050–1190 CE) and Pot Creek Phase (1190–1260 CE) settlement patterns in the Rio Grande del Rancho drainage. Geometrically outlined areas indicate the extent of formal survey coverage (see Fowles 2004:appendix D.)

Whatever the good people did the bad people would destroy. They did not like each other" (quoted in Parsons 1996a[1940]:45). The animosity between the two groups having grown dangerously high, they agreed to resolve matters through a footrace, the winning group thereby earning the right to kill off the losing group and so to put a definite end to the conflict. The racers of the good people won (they were, after all, the "good" people), at which point "the good people began to club the witch people and kill them with their war clubs. So some of them ran into their pit [i.e., their pithouse], the good people followed them. So they shut up the hole, they threw in dirt and rocks" (46). I am not suggesting that this particular story was passed down specifically as an account of the massacre in the pithouse at LA 102064, eerie though the parallels may be. Rather, it serves to remind us that violence is never isolated but is forever entangled in complicated networks of beliefs that are ontological and cosmological as much as ethnic and political. One does not negotiate or seek compromise with witches, because they represent the antithesis of society; intrinsically, they are "bad" people rather than merely different people.[4]

Taos oral history repeatedly references an early period of polarization in which immigrants came into conflict with autochthons. I have already reviewed the narrative recorded by Stevenson in 1906 relating the story of the Summer People's conquest of the Winter People. Other scholars report similar tales at the pueblo:

> The Taos Indians have a tradition that they came from the north; that they found other Indians at this place [Taos] living also in a pueblo; that these they ejected after much fighting, and took and have continued to occupy their place. How long ago this was they cannot say, but it must have been a long time ago. The Indians driven away lived here in a pueblo, as the Taos Indians now do. (David J. Miller letter, quoted in Morgan 1965[1881]:166)

> Before the Taos people were living where they now are, other pueblo people lived in the valley. Traces of what are supposed to have been their houses may still be seen. While these people were living here, there came a big man, tall as a pine tree, and killed many of them. Those who were left went away. (Miller 1898:46–47)

> According to the story, the Winter People were living on the [b]anks of the Rio Grande at the time when the Summer People started for Taos and there was a serious encounter between them in which the Winter People were defeated. (Jeançon 1930:7–8)

We need these sorts of indigenous statements to read the crushed bones of the archaeological record as something other than a systemic response to population pressure, drought, or, worse yet, a "natural" Hobbesian state of "Warre." We are dealing here with history—profound history—with all its contingencies, momentums, and tragedies. But we are also dealing with a specific historical tradition in which cultural alterity and social deviance were repeatedly cast in the idiom of witchcraft (Darling 1998; Fowles forthcoming; Walker 1998). Were the inhabitants of LA 102064 stigmatized in this fashion? Did they die precisely because their aggressors looked upon them as a "band of witches"? Might accusations of witchcraft have been widespread during this "serious encounter...in which the Winter People were defeated"?

There is one additional site that poignantly speaks to these questions. The Cerrita Site is a small, terminal Valdez Phase pithouse settlement located a short distance southwest of LA 102064 (Fowles 2004:369–370; Woosley 1986). Its situation—atop a steep-sided ridge—could be interpreted as evidence of defensive concerns, as if its inhabitants knew times were uncertain. Such concerns would have been entirely reasonable; as at the other sites just considered, the final days of the Cerrita Site were marked by an unusually violent episode. In this case, an elderly woman was killed and dismembered. Her body was left on the floor in a state of partial articulation, but her head and upper neck and her right hand were found in the pithouse's ventilator (Whitley 2009:81). Decapitation was not uncommon, but the dismembered hand is unusual, and its placement beside the severed head in the ventilator suggests we are confronting something carefully premeditated, something that was more than an act of simple violence. But how to read such an act?

That it was the right hand suggests the killers may have been targeting the hand of action and manipulation. The hand icon was frequently presented in ancestral Northern Tiwa rock art as a locus of extrahuman power. Shamanic figures were depicted with dramatically oversized hands, for example; in other cases, hands appear with lightning bolts shooting from them (figure 4.7). In this sense, the presence of the hand alongside the head may be an indication of the Cerrita woman's extraordinary powers—dark and dangerous powers, perhaps, given the circumstances of her death. The most unusual aspect of this interment is that, alongside the head and hand, the excavators also found a nearly complete rattlesnake skeleton, an uncommon find indeed. The snake is particularly significant because it more directly suggests that we are looking at the assassination, dismemberment, and ritual placement of an accused witch. "Snake-women are witches," noted a Taos storyteller. "Indians must never marry snake-women. They are witches" (Espinosa 1936:125–126). And dismemberment was a key Pueblo strategy for dealing with witches (Darling 1998).

I have drawn the reader rather deeply into the Taos archaeological record, so let me take a moment to broaden the discussion. Was the killing of the old woman at Cerrita an act of politics or of religion? Clearly, such terms fail us. Insofar as we are correct in interpreting the violence as embedded in a much more widespread contest between two populations (the Winter People and the Summer People), the violence seems to have been "politically" motivated: locals and immigrants vying for regional control. Taos oral history (as well as the unusual nature of many of the terminal Valdez Phase deaths), however, direct us toward much more "religious" territory: a ritual struggle against witches. Of course, most archaeologists—firmly rooted in Western secularism—would simply conclude that we are dealing with a fundamental competition for power and resources that has been *legitimized* by a religious ideology. Strip away all the talk of snake women, lightning arrows, and magic medicine, and one will eventually arrive at a hardened core of individual competition, optimization, and biological strategy—where individuals talk religiously as a way of competing politically, as a way of acting economically, as a way of (in the end) reproducing biologically.

But identifying underlying motivations can be an impossible enterprise, ultimately devolving into speculation about what people *really* want despite what they say they want, about real rather than surface motivations. And this places into question, once again, just what we mean when we talk about "religion." Talal Asad asks: "Is motivated behavior that accounts for itself by religious discourse ipso facto religious

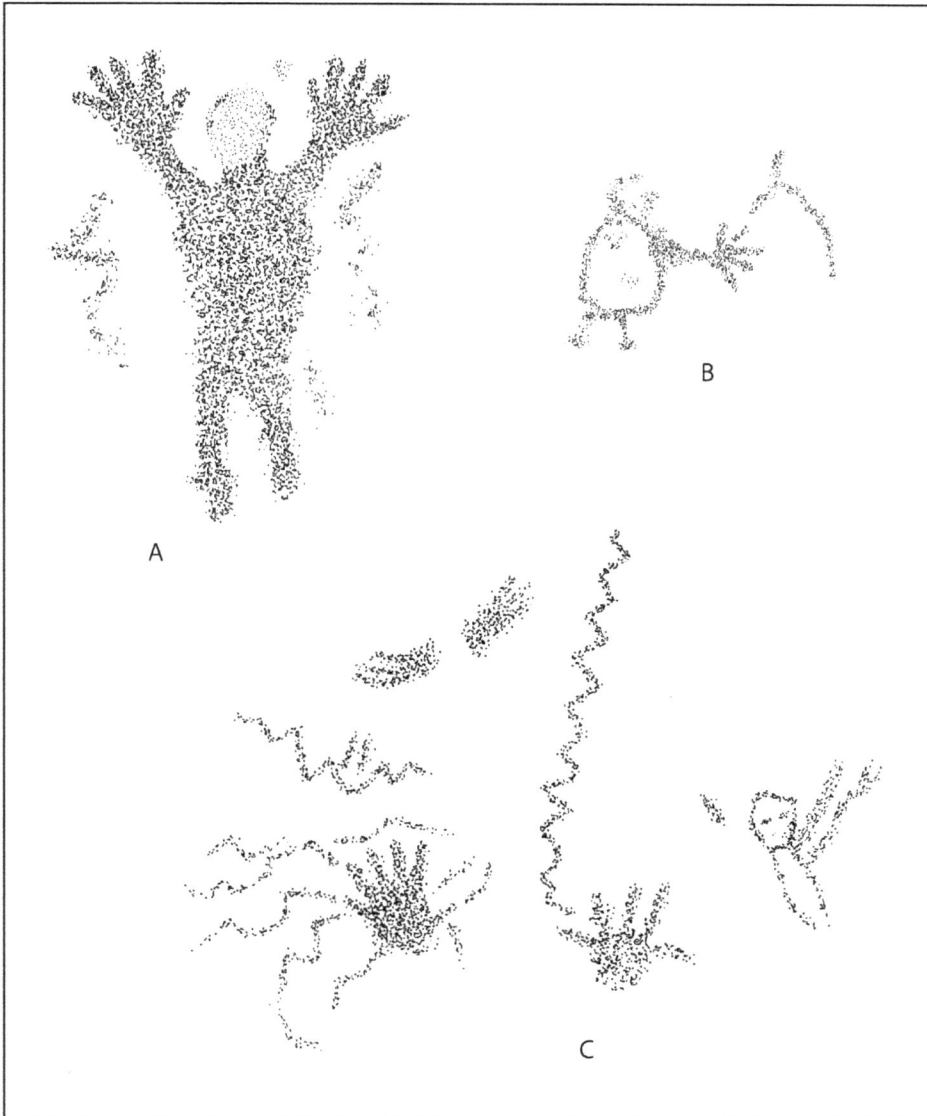

Figure 4.7. Pre-Columbian rock art from the Rio Grande gorge. A = Kissing Fish Site (2007-P288); B = Suazo Site (2007-P101); C = Houses of the Holy Site (2007-P213A).

or only when it does so *sincerely*? But insincerity may itself be a construction of religious language. Is it assumed that there is always an *unconscious* motive to a religious act, a motive that is therefore secular, as Freud and others have done? But that begs the question of how to distinguish between the religious and the secular" (2003:11). Or at least it *should* beg the question. Instead, explanatory reductionism pervades the archaeological literature, as it does so much of Western scholarship. How readily we assume that an explanation is only an explanation if it reveals some hidden set of underlying causes that renders superficial or naive whatever actors might say about their conditions and motivations. Explanation, in this sense, becomes an iconoclastic gesture of critiquing mere surfaces. Worldviews are separated from worlds as religious ideology is separated from political practice—the former always assuming the position of the explanandum and the latter the position of the explanans. All of this, of course, is premised upon the same anthropological diplopia that sees non-Western societies in terms of post-Reformation dichotomies. The dispositions and motivations of the ancestral Pueblos are dismembered then reassembled with a religious skin and a secular heart—both of which are merely transplants from the West.

We will never know the precise motivations that surrounded the death of the old woman at Cerrita, but we can say that it was neither an act of religion nor of politics. Was it, then, a kind of doings? Perhaps. Death—however it occurs—prompts most humans to dwell upon worldly connections. The deceased is released from corporality, left to travel and take up occupancy in other realms, which, for the Pueblos, are typically regarded as the lower worlds of the spirit ancestors. Death, then, begets cosmological reflection. The death of a witch, however, does more than this; it illuminates a particular morality, demarcating the legitimate from the illegitimate use of power. We must read the stoning of the family at LA 102064 similarly. Like the ceremonial throwing down of the plant shields discussed above, the throwing down of stones onto the bodies of the Winter People was a ritualized act of violence that can be read either as political (if we accept that it was born of a historical moment of ethnic conflict and competition) or as religious (if we accept that it would have been understood within a discourse of witchcraft that referenced sinister, unseen forces). What we must resist is the temptation to privilege one over the other, to treat the idiom of witchcraft as ideological justification for an underlying or more fundamental competition over resources and control between ethnic groups. And the only way to do away with such reductionism is to do away with the religion-politics divide itself. We are left, then, with a gathered world of practice and belief punctuated by doings, those periods of heightened concern with, and commentary upon, just *how* the world is to be gathered.

"We Will Have Summer and We Will Also Have Winter"

I have argued that the violence at the close of the twelfth century in the Taos district can be read as a particular species of doings born of the confrontation between two distinct but historically intertwined traditions. In one corner, the Winter People, the catchall denomination I have been using for the indigenous pithouse dwellers of the Taos district. In the other corner, the Summer People, the immigrant groups who entered the region as part of a much larger movement out of the northern San Juan during the late twelfth and thirteenth centuries (Fowles 2004:323–324). Viewed in terms of the greater sweep of Puebloan history, it was a confrontation between (1) a non-Chacoan or anti-Chacoan tradition composed of those who had purposefully removed themselves from the experiment in marked inequality developing farther west, and (2) a post-Chacoan tradition composed of those who had once been much more deeply entangled with the hierarchy and centralization of Chaco.

Undoubtedly, this emphasis on a clash of cultures obscures a great deal of variability in the identities of the Pueblo III period residents in Taos. Elsewhere, I have explored the archaeological evidence of immigration from the Trinidad district to the north, the Cimarron district to the east, and the Santa Fe district to the south (Fowles 2004:323–324). Some ancestral Northern Tiwas may have come from all of these regions. Indigenous accounts also point to a proliferation of named peoples—each with its own complicated migration history—even while foregrounding the conflict between two primary groupings (Bernardini and Fowles 2011). The easy critique of the history I have offered, then, is that it is merely a projection of the contemporary Northern Tiwa dual division onto a past that was considerably messier.

This sort of critique is misplaced, however. History is always complicated, but historical narratives are necessarily less so. As Jorge Luis Borges observed in the tragic story of Ireneo Funes, it would take an entire lifetime to recall the "real" history of another's life, and a thousand lifetimes to tell the complete story of a village. Memory is premised upon forgetting, and history, no less, is premised upon illuminating omission—upon abstraction, distillation, metonymy, and other tools for navigating through the dense foliage of lived details. Social identity, consequently, is born of these same techniques and is forever seeking a binary world of self versus Other, us versus them. Periods of migration tend to be crucibles in this regard as the cultural practices of immigrants are thrust into stark relief vis-à-vis the locals they encounter. At the close of the twelfth century in the northern Rio Grande, the polarizing moment must be envisioned in just this way: diverse and idiosyncratic though the post-Chacoan migrants may have been, they were all still "post-Chacoan" migrants seeking to position themselves in a new social landscape; and however diverse the locals may have been, they were still all forced to contend with foreigners just down the road, if not at their very doorstep, as appears to have been the case in Taos. The internal solidarity of groups is forged through social foils, through opposition, as Barth (1969) emphasized.

And yet, by the time the Spanish arrived three and a half centuries later, this opposition had been transformed into the building blocks of a legibly Northern Tiwa collectivity. Summer and Winter had become structurally interdependent elements of the moiety divisions within the Northern Tiwa village, rather than a basis for ethnic violence. How were stable relationships between immigrant and autochthon established, then? What sort of doings eventually made these interconnections possible? Again, let us take our cue from Taos oral history:

[Following the defeat of the Winter People,] the father of the Summer People lit his pipe, and after smoking it passed it to the father of the Winter People who said, "Thanks. I guess there will be no more ice." Then the father of the Summer People said, "It is well. Now you are my child. Now I have a good large family (referring to the Winter People)." All of the ice had by this time disappeared; only a little snow was to be seen on the mountains. The father of the Summer People continued addressing the Winter People, "Now we are as one family. If you desire, come to where I live. We will have summer and we will also have winter." (Quoted in Stevenson 1906–1907:file 2.29)

As we have seen, the version of Taos oral history recorded by Stevenson is a story about the changing of the seasons and in this sense is classically "mythic." But it is also a history of a people, and the passage just reviewed can also be read as a reference to real negotiations among Taos's varied ancestors. We might imagine a similar kiva scene taking place during the thirteenth century as the leaders of various ancestral Tiwa groups passed a pipe back and forth, discussed an end to the violence, and made plans to gather the people into "a good large family." Serious doings: the horizontal movement of the pipe tracing newly established social relations between former enemies, the vertical movement of the smoke tracing spiritual relations between human groups and the gods of the sky.

Perhaps this will strike readers as vague and speculative. What we can say with considerable empirical support, however, is that the earliest large village in the region does exhibit both a mixture of local and nonlocal material culture traditions *and* an elaborately marked system of dualism dividing the community into two physically distinct architectural groups. T'aitöna (a.k.a. Pot Creek Pueblo) is a large ancestral Tiwa settlement with roughly 320 ground-floor rooms and nearly as many upper-story rooms (figures 4.8 and 4.9). I suggest this is where Summer and Winter Peoples, immigrant and autochthon, came to dwell together, perhaps not in complete peace and harmony (as we will see shortly), but at least within a single organizational nexus that helped establish the broad contours of what came to be known as Northern Tiwa society.

T'aitöna has a deep archaeological pedigree, having been excavated by archaeologists from Southern Methodist University and other institutions for nearly fifty years (1957–2003). Indeed, it is among the most heavily studied sites in the American Southwest: more than a hundred domestic rooms, five kivas, three mealing rooms, midden areas, and extramural spaces have been excavated (Adler 2002; Crown 1991; Fowles 2004; Wetherington 1968; Woosley 1986); the chronology of the village's development from its establishment in the late 1250s until its abandonment in 1319 has been worked out in detail (Crown and Kohler 1994; Fowles 2004; Wetherington 1968); and the site's material culture has been studied (Fowles et al. 2007; Newman 1997; Whitley 2009). Archaeologists have now occupied the site almost as long as did the ancestral Tiwas.[5]

Unlike the settlements that preceded it, we know a great deal about the doings undertaken at T'aitöna during the late thirteenth and early fourteenth centuries, but I will reserve the bulk of that discussion for the next chapter. The more pressing need is to build a clearer picture of the actors involved and in particular to review

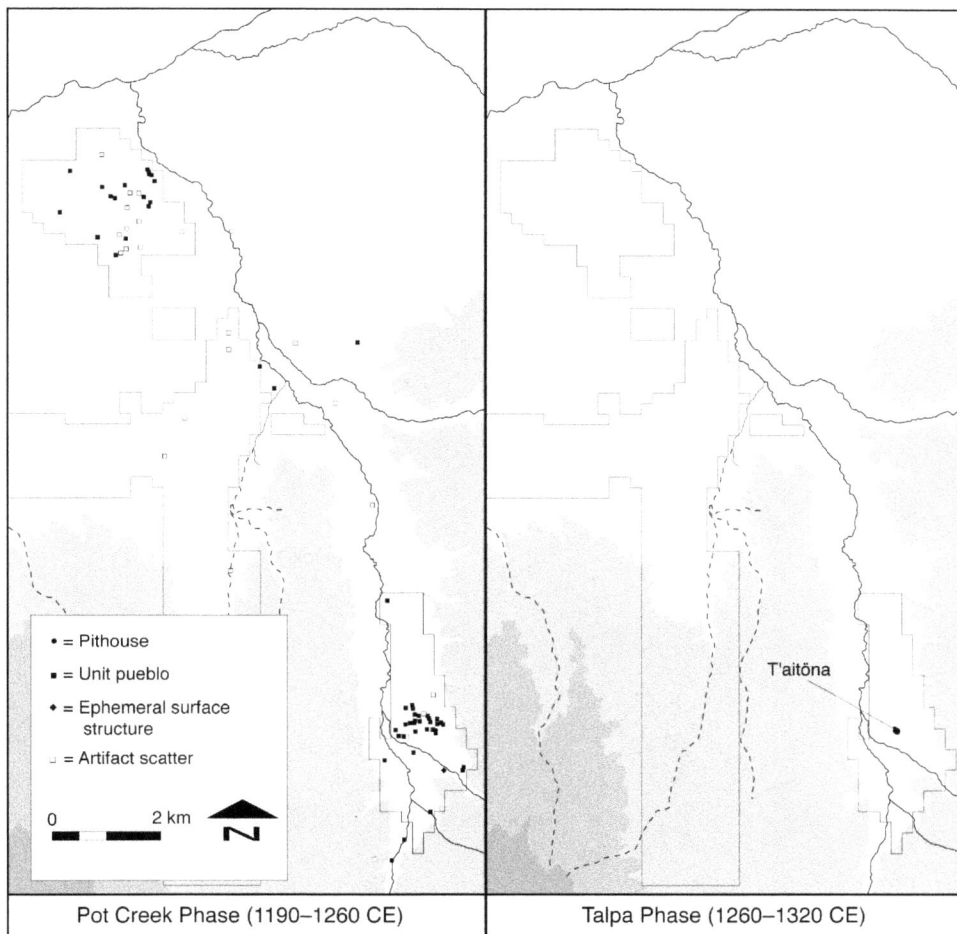

Figure 4.8. Comparison of Pot Creek Phase (1190–1260 CE) and Talpa Phase (1260–1320 CE) settlement patterns in the Rio Grande del Rancho drainage.

the ceramic and architectural evidence supporting the claim that T'aitöna was home to both immigrants and autochthons.

First, the ceramics: I have already suggested that the presence of a local variant of Santa Fe black-on-white (a.k.a. Talpa black-on-white) dating to the early thirteenth century is one line of evidence pointing to post-Chacoan immigration. Santa Fe black-on-white was primarily distinguished from the twelfth-century pottery of the region (alternately known as Kwahe'e black-on-white or Taos black-on-white) in that the latter was decorated with a mineral-based paint, while the former utilized a vegetable-based paint, resulting in a variety of modifications to the overall appearance of pots. Not only did the change in paint recipe alter the color and surface quality of the designs, but the tendency of vegetable-based paint to bleed appears to have encouraged a shift in the designs themselves: away from fine lines and the extensive

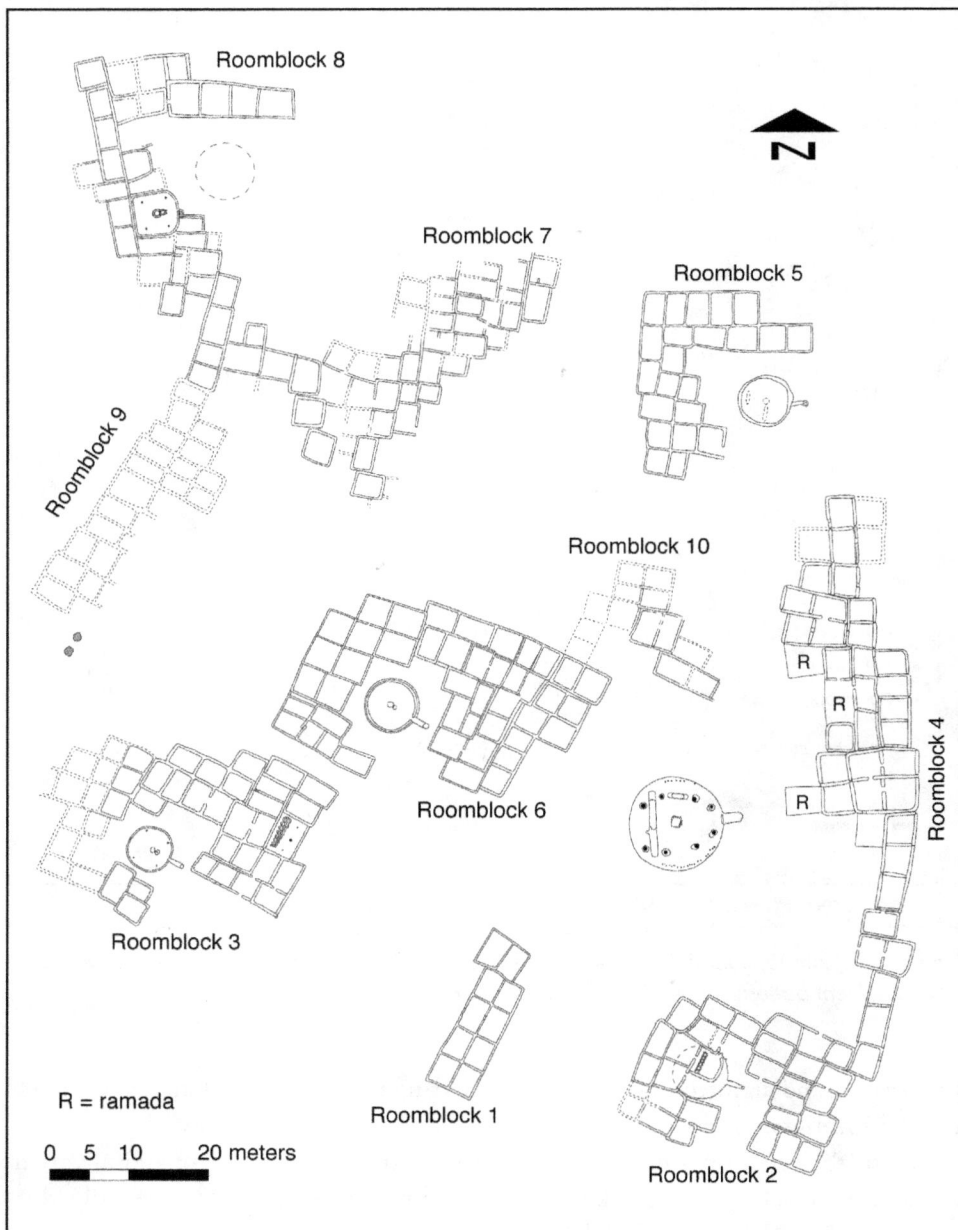

Figure 4.9. T'aitöna (a.k.a. Pot Creek Pueblo). Dashed lines indicate probable walls.

use of hachure, toward much less detailed designs emphasizing solid shapes and bold lines (figure 4.10). As I have learned from my own mediocre efforts to replicate pre-Columbian ceramic techniques, vegetable-based paint applied to local clay is also far more prone to burn off during firing, and it is likely that lower firing temperatures were adopted as a result, further altering the look and feel of vessels. All of this is

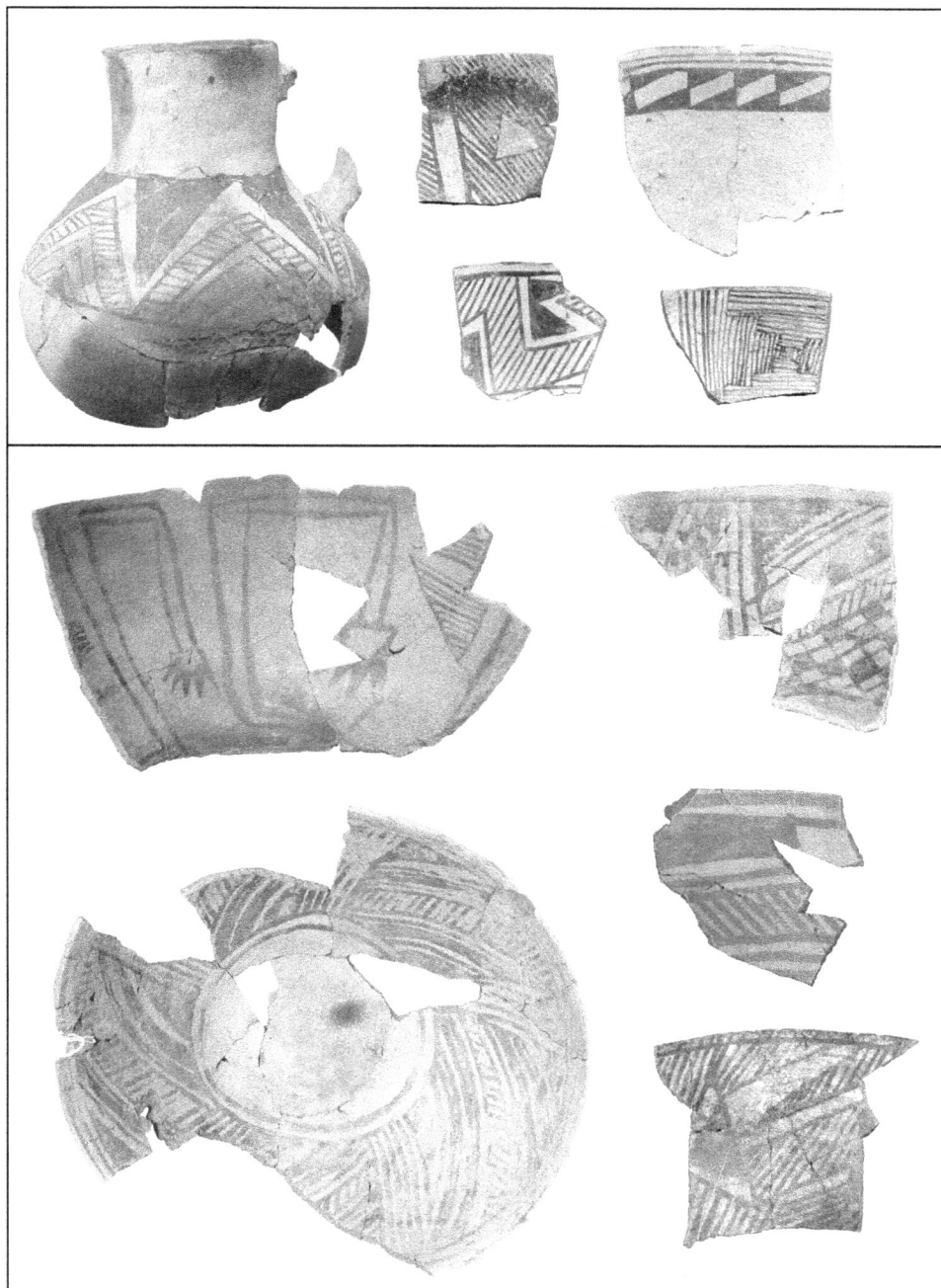

Figure 4.10. Comparison of Kwahe'e B/W (top) and Santa Fe B/W (bottom) pottery, all locally produced.

to say that the introduction of Santa Fe black-on-white involved changes in both ceramic technology and overall design aesthetics (Fowles et al. 2007).

It is noteworthy, then, that throughout the thirteenth century and well into the occupation of T'aitöna, the two black-on-white traditions existed side by side (see figure 4.4). Unpainted pottery shifted abruptly at the start of the century from incised to smeared indented corrugated (another likely indicator of immigration), but painted pottery—which may have held deeper links to cultural identity and so inspired greater conservatism—reveals significant overlap (Fowles 2004:847–888). This suggests the continued presence of two communities of potters born of different traditions. One might even speculate that the presence of two distinct paint recipes within the local ceramic tradition marked something more than just the perpetuation of inherited technological habits. As we have seen, the difference between the Summer People and Winter People at Taos Pueblo has historically played out in a symbolic contrast between plants and animals, farming and hunting. Thus in the "Offering of the Plant Shields" ceremony described above, it is essential that the shields of the Summer People (Feather Kiva) be fashioned out of layer upon layer of various gathered plants; this is what gives the shields their special potency and distinguishes them from the normal shields made of durable animal hides. So too might we imagine that the early pottery of the Summer People had to be painted with a vegetable-based paint for compelling cosmological reasons, despite the fact that this compromised the visual impact of the designs after firing. Potters from the Winter People community may not have wanted to shift to vegetable-based paints; even if they did, they might not have been permitted to do so. It is conceivable that pots did equal people in this case. Indeed, the very materiality of the paint in the two ceramic traditions may have been another means of redundantly inscribing the moiety division.

In contrast, the architectural techniques employed at T'aitöna present much greater evidence of cultural fusion and innovation, no doubt reflecting the far more collective production of built space. Long-standing local practices of coursed adobe construction continued (the unavailability of stone appropriate for building would have left little alternative in this respect). More notable, however, was the sudden introduction of multistory architecture into a tradition that had been uniformly single-story prior to T'aitöna's occupation. Extensive excavation at the site has demonstrated that, with the exception of a handful of early rooms, all cooking, sleeping, and other workaday activities in the domestic sphere took place upstairs in second or third stories. The lower rooms became relegated to storage alone.

I want to underscore the significance of this architectural shift toward verticality on two counts. First, it would have entailed an entirely new approach to ensuring structural integrity insofar as the erection and maintenance of multistory mud dwellings are no small matters. There is abundant evidence that the occupants of T'aitöna grappled with these very issues: double-thick walls became common, the footprint of roomblocks increased significantly, and an unusual technique of centerpost roof supports was developed (Wetherington 1968). Why go to such trouble when there was more than enough land for horizontal expansion of the settlement? We may assume that strong motivations were driving the move upward. Second, we must bear in mind the phenomenological effects of enclosed multistory architecture, which would have been quite different from the prior pattern of open, low-lying dwellings. Indeed, by the early fourteenth century, T'aitöna was a walled-in compound with a labyrinth of hidden rooms and an imposing two- to three-story external facade. To be inside the village was to be within the unyielding embrace of a fully constructed world where much of the surrounding landscape was hidden from view. To be outside the village was to be decidedly *outside*.

There can be little question that multistory architecture would have made T'aitöna a far more defensible settlement, and I have elsewhere argued that defense may have been an important concern (Fowles et al. 2007). But verticality and the sort of spatial massing of rooms exhibited at T'aitöna do much more than protect against enemies; they also transform a settlement into a theatrical and semiotically dense space. Consider the scene presented to a visitor arriving at the village for the first time. The principal approach would have been from the west. The visitor would have initially confronted a solid two- or three-story architectural mass, 110 meters long, with a single break in the middle where a restricted opening was flanked by two large boulders. Cupules and a grinding slick mark the boulders as shrines, and, together, they may have referenced the sacred landforms left behind in the Chimney Rock region (i.e., Chimney Rock and Companion Rock) as well as the pervasive pattern of dualism that organized the new village (see chapter 5). We might even speculate that the paired stones more specifically referenced the twin war gods who hold so prominent a position in Eastern Pueblo cosmology and are sometimes conceived of in petrified form.

The early fourteenth-century traveler would have passed between these war gods to enter the village proper. Once inside the village, an enclosed plaza would be seen off to the left, perhaps the day-to-day work area for one of the village's many kin groups. More likely, the traveler's attention would be drawn straight ahead, toward two impressive architectural complexes looming ten or more meters above him. Roomblocks 3 and 6 were the highest points of T'aitöna—even today, they rise out of the ground more like Near Eastern tells than Pueblo roomblocks—and the orientation of the village's western entrance suggests the visitor would have been guided to the main plaza via a narrow passage running between them. Let us further imagine that our traveler has come to T'aitöna to attend a dance, a public ceremony of the sort that has drawn outsiders to the pueblos for centuries and probably did so in late pre-Columbian times as well. In the main dance plaza, then, we are led to envision familiar images of the theatrical use of verticality in the modern pueblos: the priestly leaders perched atop the tallest house, calling out their directives to the populace; the *koshare*, or ritual clowns, rambling over the terraced architecture to delight onlookers; the rooftops filled with community members seeking a better view of the dance in progress. More important than the details—which must, perforce, involve a great deal of speculation—is the simple observation that T'aitöna would have offered a strange new architectonic experience for those who had grown up in the dispersed pithouses of the prior era.

Those with ancestral ties to the west would have read the scene somewhat differently. Multistory architecture, enclosed plazas, choreographed entrances, and the like were all well-established Chacoan innovations of the Pueblo II period, and while T'aitöna was not a great house in any direct sense, the spatiality and formal aesthetics of the village would no doubt have been contextualized within the longer-term genealogy of Chacoan (rather than indigenous Rio Grande) architecture. This point emerges with even greater clarity when we narrow our focus and consider the morphology of specific architectural components like T'aitöna's great kiva, which carried on a history of large-scale ceremonial architecture that began hundreds of years earlier in Chaco Canyon, or its D-shaped kiva (see chapter 5), which partook in a Pueblo III tradition that Bradley (1996) suggests was an explicit form of Chaco revivalism. Even the pairing of kivas and grinding rooms in the southern half of T'aitöna harks back to Chaco-era conventions in the northern San Juan (Fowles 2006; Mobley-Tanaka 1997; Ortman 1998). Such details point to more than the diffusion of ideas. As I have already argued, T'aitöna was a community born of direct ethnic confrontation, a place where immigrants met autochthons, where post-Chacoans met anti-Chacoans.

In fact, the very organizational solution settled upon by these groups as they sought a new nonviolent means of social interaction betrays a Chacoan influence. Consider again the somewhat cryptic statement of the father of the Summer People in the wake of the defeat of the Winter People: "come to where I live," he announces. "We will have summer and we will also have winter." Perhaps this statement was more than just a satisfying narrative resolution. Might we read it as a kind of political decree, as the establishment of an actual, on-the-ground moiety system in which immigrant (henceforth, Summer People) and autochthon (henceforth, Winter People) were formally placed in opposed but also complementary positions within a single community? Elsewhere, I have suggested precisely this, noting further that the key principle of organizational dualism, so prominent in the Eastern Pueblo world today, can be linked back to earlier patterns in the Chacoan heartland, where the formal division of sites into complementary halves was an architectural trademark (Fowles 2005). Rather than review that argument at length, I will use three images to make the broader point: first, the iconic image of early twelfth-century Pueblo Bonito; second, the plan of thirteenth-century Sand Canyon Pueblo in the Mesa Verde region, an area with close historical ties to Chaco; and finally, the plan of post-sixteenth-century Taos Pueblo (figure 4.11). Setting aside the shift of orientation toward the east at Taos, the similarities in the layouts of these three sites are striking. From the bisecting wall of Bonito, to the bisecting spring/arroyo of Sand Canyon, to the bisecting river of Taos, each of these D-shaped pueblos was designed according to a shared spatial logic.

This is not to say that dualism meant the same thing in thirteenth-century Taos as it did in eleventh-century Chaco Canyon. My claim is only that many of the structural elements of Northern Tiwa architecture (and society) have deep historical

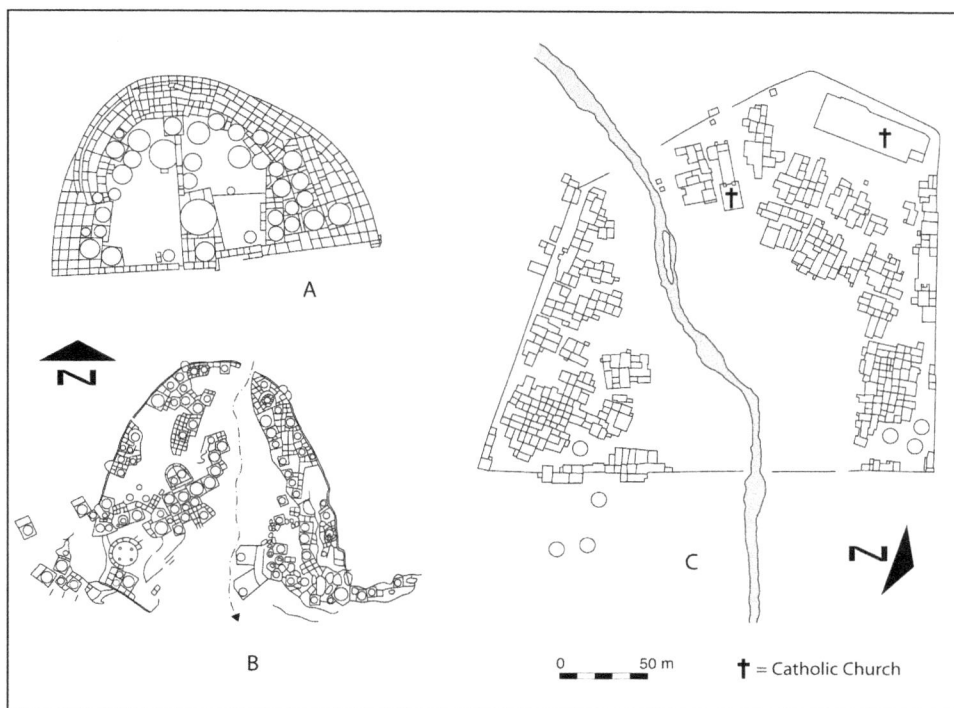

Figure 4.11. Comparison of Chacoan and post-Chacoan D-shaped village layouts. A = Pueblo Bonito; B = Sand Canyon Pueblo; C = modern Taos Pueblo.

roots that originate in the west. As yet, there is little consensus on how to understand Chacoan patterns of opposition and symmetry except that they comprised an elaborate cosmological system that was materialized at both site and regional scales (Fritz 1978; Heitman and Plog 2005; Vivian 1990:298–299). In the post-Chacoan world of the Rio Grande valley, we can say somewhat more, for there we know that dualism came to be woven into the very fabric of community life through the establishment of village-wide moiety systems, famously described by Alfonso Ortiz (1969) for the Tewas but also present among the Northern Tiwas (see chapter 2). Past scholarship has generally understood the rise of Rio Grande moieties from a functionalist perspective, the common claim being that they emerged as a natural adaptation to the new managerial demands of large Pueblo IV villages (Dozier 1970; Eggan 1950:315–317; Hawley 1950; Kantner 2004:173; Wittfogel and Goldfrank 1943). I read them instead as historical phenomena whose origins were contingent upon the vagaries of historical processes themselves. Begin with a profound symbolic commitment to dualism during the Pueblo II period (900–1150 CE), pass through the major population dislocations of the Pueblo III period (1150–1300 CE) that forced large numbers of post-Chacoans to join communities in the Rio Grande valley, and we are poised to see the emergence of ceremonial moieties at the start of the Pueblo

IV period (1300–1540 CE) as a means of reworking existing concepts to make sense of the experience of punctuated immigration and social polarization. This strikes me as an entirely plausible model.

What, then, of T'aitöna itself? Are there archaeological traces that would support such a model of emergent moiety organization? Indeed, there are. Forty years of excavation and tree-ring dating have provided a relatively clear understanding of the community's physical development from a series of spatially discrete roomblock and kiva groups in the latter half of the thirteenth century to the walled-in architectural complex of the early fourteenth century (Crown 1991; Crown and Kohler 1994; Fowles 2004). And one of the most significant discoveries of this research is that the initial roomblocks at the site are clearly divisible into two architectural groups (figure 4.12). In the northern half of the site, two essentially identical L-shaped roomblocks were erected. In the southern half, we encounter three U-shaped roomblocks—duplicates, again, of one another but quite morphologically distinct from those in the north.

The orientations of the two roomblock groups are noticeably different as well. The three southern roomblocks and their associated kivas all face southeast while the two northern roomblocks face due east—a pattern whose significance only emerges when rephrased in terms of orientations toward the rising sun. Solar observation for calendrical and spiritual purposes is a vital component of Pueblo doings throughout the Southwest, and much village and shrine architecture stands in explicit relation to the sun and its path across the sky. Given this cultural backdrop, it is surely no coincidence that the north and south roomblocks at T'aitöna were oriented toward the sunrise positions at equinox and winter solstice, respectively. As we saw in the previous chapter, all prior dwellings in the region were unerringly oriented toward the southeast (see figure 3.8); this is the direction of sunrise at the winter solstice, when the days are shortest and Father Sun is weakest (Fowles 2005; see also Lakatos 2007:55). To face the southeast would have been to orient one's attention toward Father Sun in his time of greatest need and to work on his behalf in the battle against winter. To direct one's thoughts and prayers in this direction was to work for worldly renewal, for the return of summer's warmth and fecundity. This is why the southeast was the most sacred of the Northern Tiwa directions.

The eastern orientation of the northern roomblocks was a notable divergence from long-standing tradition, then, and I argue it only makes sense if we imagine the establishment of a novel moiety system in which the leadership of doings was divided seasonally, following something like the historic Tewa model outlined by Ortiz (1969). To the Summer People, those of the south, went the ceremonial leadership of summer as well as the critical task of directing their prodigious ritual power toward the sun in its time of greatest need. The Summer People had emerged from the preceding period as victors, and if I am correct in associating them with the southern roomblocks at T'aitöna, then they also appear to have emerged as the more populous group, occupying the tallest and most visually striking portions of the village. It was they who faced southeast. Leadership for the remainder of the year—for

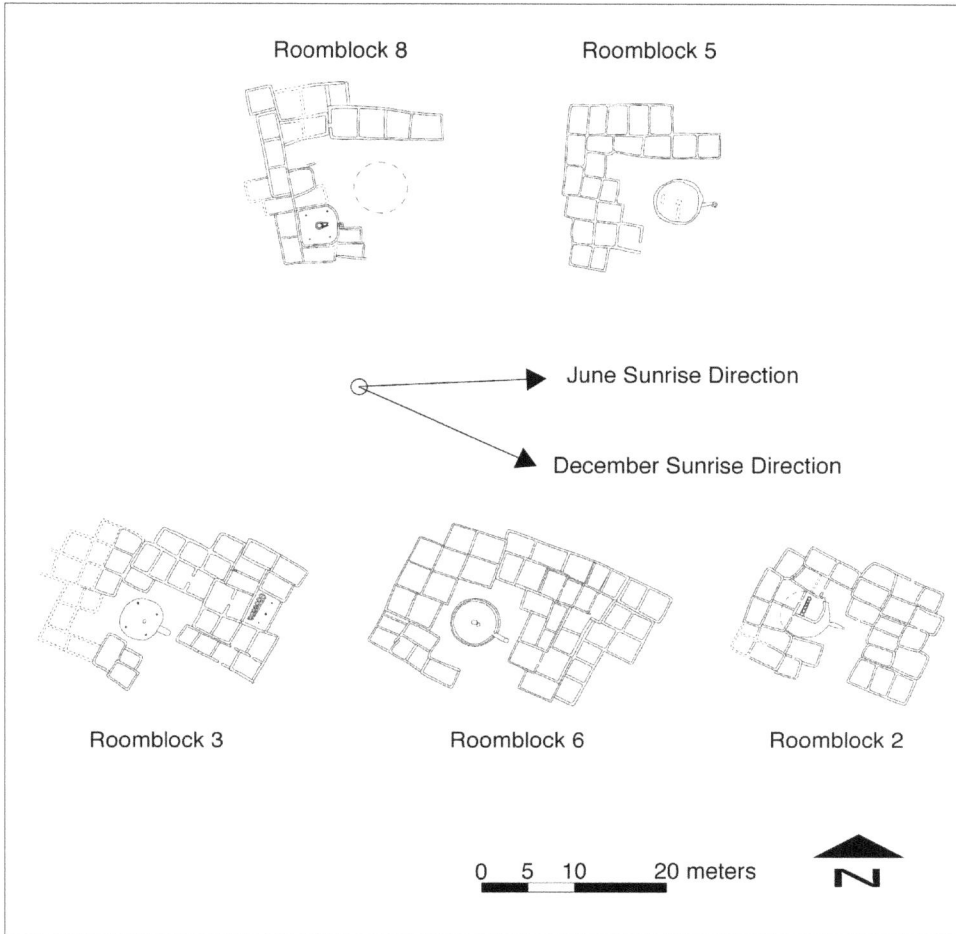

Figure 4.12. Comparison of northside and southside architectural units at T'aitöna.

the period of increasing cold between the summer and winter solstices—would have been left to the Winter People.

There is additional evidence supporting the north-south ceremonial division at T'aitöna. For instance, it is noteworthy that all of the village's formal mealing rooms—the specialized rooms used by groups of women to grind corn—were located in the southern roomblocks, which might lead us to conclude that, as among the contemporary Northern Tiwas, the south side of the village was the symbolic province of plants, agriculture, and the female (figure 4.13). *Unlike* the contemporary Northern Tiwas, however, such north-south symbolism also appears to have been expressed in the habitual practices of its occupants. In her analysis of the T'aitöna skeletal assemblage, Whitley (2009) made the striking discovery that women at the village fell into two distinctive labor groups as indicated by such markers as the degree of medial rotation of the tibia, humeral hypertrophy, and the like. In short, T'aitöna

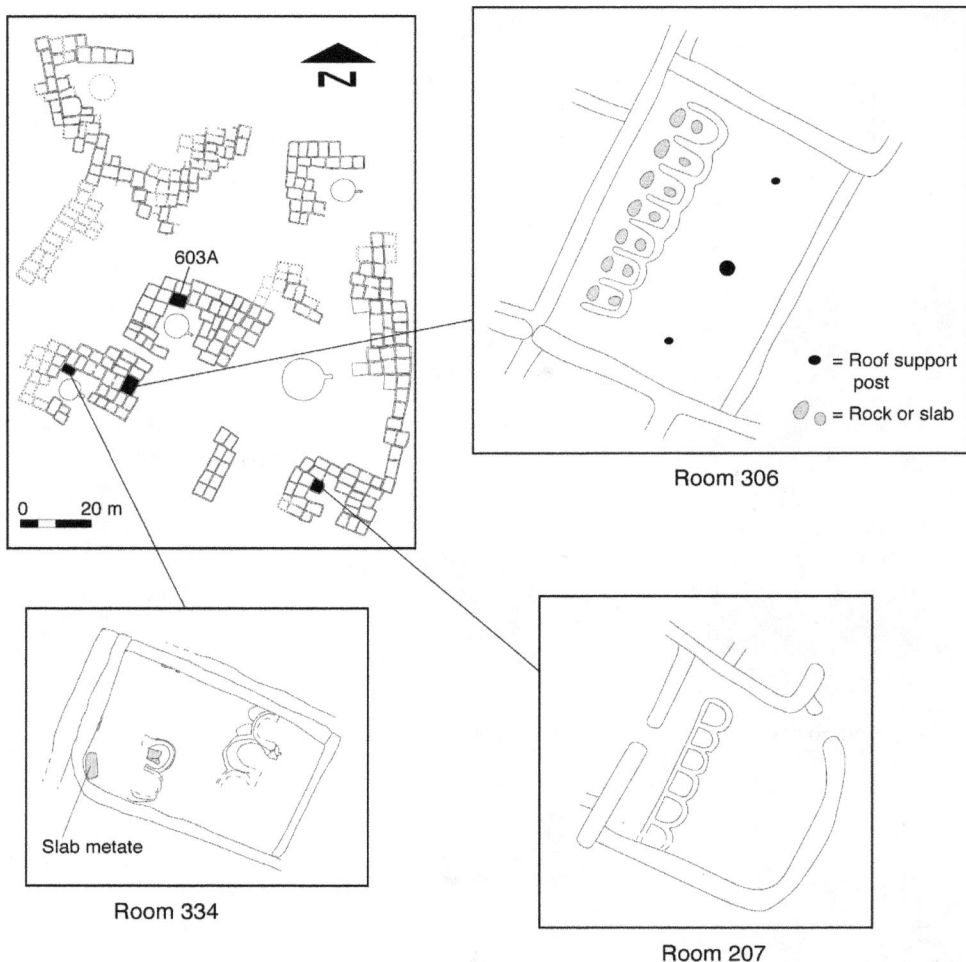

Figure 4.13. Mealing rooms at T'aitöna.

was composed of two populations of women, one whose bodies performed repetitive tasks that required great upper arm strength and another population whose mechanical tasks were more diverse or generalized. The most parsimonious explanation is that the former spent much of their time grinding corn, while the latter did not. One senses the bodily habitus that accompanied the moiety division for women, at least. I will have more to say about this material in the next chapter. The broader observation is that dualism was not merely a matter of living in the northern or southern half of the village; it was a founding principle dictating everything from how one engaged the spirits to how one prepared food.

Admittedly, I have just offered a highly speculative reconstruction of a village whose hearths went cold nearly seven centuries ago. They have, I hope, been reasoned speculations that align the archaeological and ethnographic evidence while offering a plausible account of Northern Tiwa community organization as a historically situated phenomenon. But even if you are among those who remain unconvinced by the model of emergent pre-Columbian moieties I have offered, you undoubtedly will have begun to sense that we are now, with the growth of T'aitöna, looking at a very different sort of "religiosity" than existed in the region previously. These were not the anti-Chacoans of old, committed as they were to a decentralized and nonhierarchical mode of spirituality that would have made the Mennonites proud. These were post-Chacoans in a tense and ethnically diverse postmigration landscape, building centralized communities in which coordinated doings played an important role. Ceremonial moieties that established and rehearsed the relationships between immigrant and autochthon—moieties that explicitly put each community member in her place—were but one part of a much more expansive world of village doings, as we will see in the next chapter.

five
On Effervescence and Sympathy

On October 17, 1259 CE, at two o'clock in the afternoon, the sun blackened in the skies over Taos. What is the significance of an eclipse, fleeting as it is and without any apparent long-term impacts on the physical world?

Let me offer a crudely methodological answer first. Along with comets, supernovas, and the like, eclipses tend to be of special significance to archaeologists because they are highly retrodictable phenomena (see Masse and Espenak 2006). With a fair degree of certainty we can imagine a scene 750 years ago when most Pueblo people in northern New Mexico and southern Colorado stopped what they were doing, gazed heavenward, and watched—undoubtedly with no little surprise—as daylight queerly faded. Astronomers are able to say when this scene would have taken place, and they are able to add that the celestial event in question would have been among the most dramatic solar eclipses of the last two millennia in the northern Southwest.[1] For a brief three and a half minutes (the duration of the 1259 CE eclipse) in Pueblo antiquity, we know precisely what was going on. And this, in itself, is quite moving.

An eclipse gains significance when we consider how it would have moved those watching it centuries ago. Late nineteenth-century scholars of premodern religion like Edward Tylor made much of seemingly unnatural natural events, arguing that therein lay the primitive urge to explain the unexplainable, to turn a blackened sun into a frightful deity, and to piece together the rudiments of religion itself. It is easy to roll our eyes at such theses, but we mustn't be so smugly dismissive as to forget that full solar eclipses can be remarkable phenomena—visually, but also socially. There is something innately powerful about events that synchronize mass experience, events of which everyone takes note. Perhaps we take this for granted in the age of mass media. All Americans watched their televisions in collective disbelief as the events of 9/11 unfolded. Tens of thousands stood amid the crowds in front of large outdoor screens to jointly witness the inauguration of Barack Obama; billions more simultaneously watched the broadcast. We each know where we were when these events took place, and by comparing notes we are led to reflect upon how each of us is part of various communities—local, national, and transnational. The social is brought into consciousness.

In premodern times, the experiential scale of most social phenomena would have been far more limited. Before radio, before television, how many events actually did draw together and synchronize the experiences of the masses beyond the level of the individual settlement? Very few, it would seem. Indeed, punctuated celestial phenomena may have been somewhat unique in this regard.[2] At least, it is difficult to think of many other events that were instantly visible to all members of a regional population. "Where were you when the sun disappeared?" Then, as today, these sorts of questions invite us to map out the social. Is it surprising, then, to learn that an eclipse marked the founding of the League of the Iroquois, one of Native America's most elaborate, formal, and consciously constructed systems of regional political interconnection? Eclipses were one of many "sky signs" used by the Iroquois to reckon the state of social affairs (Mann and Fields 1997), and any thorough semiotic analysis of such phenomena must duly note not just the indexical roles performed by sky signs in explicit Iroquois historiography, but also their implicit system of signification, for sky signs index the simultaneous unification of human contemplation. They index the birth of the audience on a mass scale.

Of course the eclipses of the modern world—impersonal alignments of lifeless, celestial masses bound by the laws of physics—are predictable as well as retrodictable. This leads most of us to regard them with little more than pleasurable excitement. For many past societies, however, the unpredictability of eclipses was more likely a source of at least passing bewilderment, if not consternation. The important question may not have been, "Where were you when?..." but rather "What is to be done about this? How should we respond?" In this sense, a better modern comparison might be with something like the tragic and unpredicted disintegration of the *Columbia* shuttle in the skies above Texas in 2003, which, in its own way, was a celestial event that suddenly synchronized the experience of millions.

I want to take this comparison seriously for a moment. Space shuttles, satellites, and airplanes have become matter-of-fact phenomena in American society, as much a part of the stratosphere as the sun, moon, and meteors. Until, that is, they break down and force us to reflect anew on the many people, technologies, funding institutions, and more that are responsible for keeping them in their paths across the sky.

Latour considers the *Columbia* shuttle incident to make precisely this point. Techno-logical breakdowns, he observes, are revealing moments that seem to have a special ability to transform taken-for-granted objects into profound matters of concern—"things" in the Heideggerian sense—around which whole social worlds are gathered:

> What else would you call this sudden transformation of a completely mastered, perfectly understood, quite forgotten by the media, taken-for-granted, matter-of-factual projectile into a sudden shower of debris falling on the United States, which thousands of people tried to salvage in the mud and rain and collect in a huge hall to serve as so many clues in a judicial scientific investigation? Here, suddenly, in a stroke, an object had become a thing, a matter of fact was considered as a matter of great concern. (Latour 2004:234–235)

His point is that when things are running smoothly, when the sun or the shuttle is moving across the sky as it should, we tend to treat them as given, as black boxes, as discrete objects that stand over and against us. We ignore, in other words, the vast array of relationships that link them to the rest of society. This is what the swarm of activity surrounding a breakdown exposes: that the *Columbia* shuttle only flew by virtue of an expansive network of technical, economic, nationalistic, and even spiri-tual relationships within American society at large.

It doesn't take much to imagine a solar eclipse as a kind of breakdown. Nor does it take much to imagine that such an event, in a less predictive age, might prompt serious reflection on how the sun is a matter of concern around which an extended community is gathered. This is especially true when we begin to explore the posi-tion of the sun in non-Western cosmologies such as that of the Northern Tiwas. Like all Pueblo groups, the Northern Tiwas have long been portrayed as engaging in a kind of "sun worship," a misleading and primitivist notion but one that does, at least, underscore the Copernican significance of the sun within local belief. Among those who learned this firsthand was Carl Jung who, while visiting Taos in 1925, had a brief conversation about "religion" with one of the pueblo's elders: "As I sat with Ochwiay Biano on the roof, the blazing sun rising higher and higher, he said, point-ing to the sun, 'Is not he who moves there our father? How can anyone say differ-ently: How can there be another god? Nothing can be without the sun.... The sun is God. Everyone can see that'" (Jung 1973[1961]:250–251).

Nothing can be without the sun, but the sun is nothing without the assistance of the human community. It is the relationship of mutual dependency that is sig-nificant. This, perhaps, is why Father Sun is referred to in genealogical terms and why he is the focus of so many Pueblo doings. Ceremonial relay races, for instance, are regularly performed at both Taos and Picurís and are expressly conceptualized as efforts to help the sun in its progression across the heavens. During the winter, when the sun is weakest and travels low in the sky, a great deal of human ritual is under-taken to bring back solar potency. As we have seen, this is why the southeast—the direction of sunrise at the winter solstice—is an especially sacred direction toward which prayers must be directed. "All the dances and feasts that the Taos Indians have are a sacrifice to the Sun," wrote one early ethnographer (Espinosa 1936:133). What happens, then, when the sun unexpectedly disappears? What happens when it breaks down?

Solar eclipses—and lunar ones, for Moon is important as well—have been serious matters of concern among the Northern Tiwas in recent times. Eclipses leave humans impure and vulnerable. They cause disease and disorder. The degree of threat posed by an eclipse is indicated by the fact that the members of Taos Pueblo respond with community-wide action. Nearly all other curing ceremonies at the pueblo are individualistic in nature, but after an eclipse there is always a purification or exorcising ceremony for the entire village (Parsons 1996b[1939]:934–935, 950–951). "When there is a solar eclipse" at Taos, Bandelier's (1984[1885–1888]:80) late nineteenth-century informants told him, the pueblo "must pray, fast, and dance, and race for five days." Society is consciously assembled.

Indigenous stories provide additional insight. Many dwell at length not just on Father Sun but quite specifically on solar eclipses. The following extract is from a longer Taos account of their history in which the narrator tells of a time long ago when the "old sun" grew frustrated with human impiety and refused to illuminate the heavens any longer:

> There was a great noise when the old sun descended upon Taos. All of the women cried. Both men and women were terrified and they threw out corn pollen and white fluffy eagle plumes, and begged that he would return to the heavens. After the descent of the sun there was just a little white light. The sun said, "I was working for you and you would not pay me. You failed in your duties. I will work no more for you." The sun remained but a short time in the pueblo then traveled over the north road and descended into the lake of Kwathlowúna near Sierra Blanca. He was followed for a distance by all of the people begging that he would continue to work for them, but he would not turn back. Just a little white light was emitted from the sun as he retreated. The people returned very sad to their village. From this time the people lived in utter darkness until the new sun was created. (Stevenson 1906–1907:file 2.22)

What were the sun's grievances in this story? That his presence had been taken for granted as a mere matter of fact. That he had been objectified by a people who failed to remember their interrelations, interdependencies, and reciprocal responsibilities. That the people had failed in their doings. "Let me show you how you have blackboxed me"—these, in effect, were Father Sun's irritated words as he snuffed out his light.

Back to October 17, 1259. I have suggested there are crudely methodological reasons for being interested in this date, for we can say with astronomical precision that the occupants of the Taos region would have all witnessed the same celestial spectacle at the same moment. Beyond this, we can also reasonably surmise that—given the significance of solar eclipses among the descendant communities at Taos and Picurís—there would have been a marked social response to the 1259 eclipse as well. Perhaps this response involved corn pollen and white fluffy eagle plumes. Perhaps it involved group purification. This is beyond our skills of reconstruction. What we do know is that 1259 stood at the tipping point of a major shift in local settlement patterns. As discussed in the previous chapter, the occupation of the Taos district prior to the 1250s was fragmented into a series of discrete nuclear- or extended-family compounds. By 1270, shortly after the eclipse, the Summer People and the Winter People had already converged in two or three large collective villages, T'aitöna among them.

Did the eclipse play a role in this process of village aggregation? Might the brief afternoon midnight in October have served as a punctuation mark at a critical juncture in the story of the Winter People and the Summer People discussed in chapter 4? Parsons learned that an eclipse "is viewed with apprehension" at Taos Pueblo; "it means that 'something is going to happen'" (1936:112). Certainly we know that something did happen during the thirteenth century on the heels of a major eclipse. The Northern Tiwas' ancestors constructed new architectonic worlds in which the relationships between people, spirits, and the cosmos at large came to be materially diagrammed and emphatically traced in far more explicit ways than had been the case previously. To what extent, then, must we regard T'aitöna as a post-eclipse settlement, no less than a postmigration or a post-Chacoan settlement?

In the present chapter and the next, I consider T'aitöna and its doings in greater detail, with particular attention to the sorts of models archaeologists and anthropologists have traditionally used to account for such phenomena. The models under consideration are not just matters of regional interest and I would argue that they are not just matters of archaeological interest either, for it is here that one sees with special clarity the modern secular narrative of "religion" busily at work. After all, T'aitöna and the other pueblos of the early fourteenth century represent local Southwestern examples of the consummation of the Neolithic revolution, the transition that—even more than the Industrial Revolution—laid the foundation for the modern age in the traditional origin story of the West.

A good deal has already been established about the internal structure of T'aitöna. In chapter 4 we saw that the village was architecturally divided into what appear to be north and south moieties, each with its own spatially discrete roomblocks and kivas—a pattern that finds many parallels in the organization of contemporary Taos Pueblo. I have also suggested that T'aitöna's settlement plan must be further read in terms of Northern Tiwa oral history as a place where formerly opposed peoples—now glossed by the terms Summer People and Winter People—resolved their differences, or at least where they transformed their differences into a social organization that worked well enough for a period of time.

Before turning to consider the doings that accompanied village growth during the late thirteenth and early fourteenth centuries, however, it will serve us well to briefly examine the matter of growth itself and the role of scalar arguments in traditional understandings of religion's evolution more broadly. Villages such as T'aitöna, although small by urban standards, would have been leviathans in contrast to the single-family settlements that locally preceded them, and it is this punctuated increase in size, as much as any changes in economic practices, that has come to define the Neolithic moment in evolutionary theory. Many archaeologists have looked to scalar evidence with almost obsessive interest, as if knowing the size and density of a population were itself an end goal of archaeological understanding. Why is this so? Why should it matter so deeply how many families lived in a village?

Magic Numbers

As with eclipses, there are crudely methodological explanations for the obsession with population scale. Simply put, scale tends to be regarded as important because it can be measured with comparative ease using archaeological data. One can count hearths, quantify architectural mass, and use standardized equations to produce population estimates; in extensively excavated cases, one can even tally bodies themselves. Thus are we encouraged to make much out of our rigorously reckoned numbers, searching out correlations between the sizes of settlements and various aspects of political, economic, and religious organization.

It would be wrong to be dismissive of this sort of research. Gregory Johnson (1982) in particular has provided archaeologists with a good deal of important food for thought, stimulating a highly influential body of research into the effects of group communication challenges, also known as "scalar stress." But I do want to register my frustration with the loose manner in which correlation is so frequently confused with causation, as if having documented a change in scale immediately authorizes researchers to treat this change as a causal stimulus for other, less quantifiable phenomena. A strange species of Malthusian argument results, one in which scale becomes a kind of agent or invisible hand that makes its own demands upon society. This is particularly true in orthodox discussions of social evolution within archaeology, where it is frequently argued, for instance, that overtly hierarchical leadership is needed once a decision-making community exceeds about 2,500 people, or that large ritual structures become necessary to integrate a population once it exceeds 250 people (e.g., Adler 1989; Bandy 2004; Kosse 1990, 1994, 1996; Lekson 1999:164). Rarely is it acknowledged that the causal arrow might just as well be reversed. Rarely is it seriously considered that aspiring leaders, prophets, or even new ideologies of human and cosmic order may have themselves been demanding larger communities. Rather, scale is presented to us as cause, while the actions of leaders and followers are relegated to effects.

The same problem exists when we look to the typical interpretation of correlations between population and the relative degree of "religiosity." Larger numbers of people require greater management or integration, and in egalitarian societies it is regularly assumed that this need is met by an increase in religious activity, true "politics" having not yet developed. (We are, after all, still in the infamous province of the so-called acephalous, or stateless, society.) Religion, in other words, serves as an "alternative to political power" (Rappaport 1971:72). This is a classically functionalist argument, grounded in early twentieth-century ethnology but finding its fullest expression in more recent archaeological studies of small-scale societies where the positive correlation between scale and religiosity is regarded as an empirically confirmed fact (e.g., E. C. Adams 1991; Adler and Wilshusen 1990; Bandy 2004; Bernardini 1996; Friesen 1999). Again, however, the issue of causal direction receives inadequate examination. Was intensified "religious" activity really just a response to population increase, or might it also have been a cause? To ask this question is to shift from a functionalist position toward something more akin to a Weberian understanding of the influential role of religious prophets in bringing about social transformations. It is to make room for a more complex world of causality in which religion is no longer merely superstructural and the actions of individuals are no longer reduced to background noise.

How easy it is to forget that numbers are merely signifiers and that communities of historically situated individuals are the real phenomena of interest. Indeed, when archaeologists talk about population scale as driving change, when we say that scale induces organizational stress, we often slip into a kind of quantitative fetishization in which our number signs become more real than their referents. In this sense, it is ironically appropriate that scalar discourse typically focuses upon a set of what are colloquially referred to as "magic numbers"—6, 25, 500, 2,500 10,000—that serve either as thresholds beyond which a given social order is increasingly threatened or as nodal points that have a kind of sociological gravity. Magic is the right word here, for these numbers are invoked as if they have a force all their own.

Magic numbers are magic because they do not care at all about the varied identities of the persons they signify. Six people are six people, no matter if we are dealing with six members of a single kin group or six unrelated people who speak two different languages, embody three different genders, and were raised in four different communities. This methodological erasure of social diversity is magical in the same way that capitalism is magical when it tells us that one coat has the same value as twenty yards of linen. Of course, those who conjure with numbers will readily admit that a notion like scalar stress is simply a generalized shorthand for a multitude of disputes between real people over lovers, farmland, bruised egos, and the like, just as exchange value is a shorthand for a multitude of past economic transactions and labor relations. Their argument, they will emphasize, is rather a statistical one in which the swirl of idiosyncrasies is less important than the broad, cumulative pattern. And isn't the identification of large-scale social patterns a core goal of anthropology? From Tylor's 1871 discussion in *Primitive Culture*: "There is found to be such regularity in the composition of societies of men, that we can drop individual differences out of sight, and thus can generalize on the arts and opinions of whole nations, just as, when looking down upon an army from a hill, we forget the individual soldier, whom, in fact, we can scarce distinguish in the mass, while we see each regiment as an organized body, spreading or concentrating, moving in advance or in retreat" (Tylor 1913[1871]:11). Setting aside the strangely militaristic model of society in Tylor's text, the logic here would seem to be basic to any science of society. The individual must eventually give way to the general. This is how knowledge is pursued.

But everything depends on perspective. It is no slight to those whose project is generalization (I count myself among them) to say that there is a fundamental difference between the analysis of a single army in abstract isolation and a messy battlefield filled with people mobilized in opposition to one another. Indeed, drop just one enemy combatant among Tylor's regimented ranks and the formerly organized body will suddenly look a good deal different. Or see how things look when we draw the circle of analysis around the battlefield itself, where opposed soldiers are "socially interacting" through hand-to-hand combat. An ethnography of the frontlines cannot generalize from these particularistic interactions to a single organized body, for this would pervert the situation completely. It must instead reverse its mode of analysis and explore how whole national and militaristic histories are mobilized to make specific actions explicable.

All of this bears directly upon our understanding of thirteenth-century events at T'aitöna, as we will see shortly. In keeping with trends in Southwestern archaeology generally, research during the 1990s strongly privileged scalar evidence in the interpretation of T'aitöna's social organization. Ritual structures in particular—and, by implication, the religious sodalities associated with them—were presented as a systemic adaption to the information-processing demands of a growing population (see Adler 1993; Bernardini 1996; Crown and Kohler 1994). This research sidelined the possibility that a village would have been composed not of a generalized set of cultural actors, but rather of Summer People and Winter People (and Water People, and Big Earring People, and so on), each with their own histories. It also sidelined the possibility that these histories involved competition and occasionally intense violence. Would it not affect the overall flow of information processing if some village members felt the lingering sting of defeat when negotiating with their decision-making equivalents? Would not communication rates be impacted by the likelihood that not everyone even spoke a common language? And yet, we are told that T'aitöna met archaeology's generic scalar expectations for autonomous village societies. Magic numbers are magic because they normalize histories as much as individuals.

To return to the question of why scale matters in the first place, I have suggested that population size tends to be archaeologically measurable and that this goes a long way toward explaining why it is so frequently drawn into debates surrounding prehistoric religion. Correlations between scale and religiosity (however defined) can be sought, and the former—allegedly, an independent variable—can be presented as the proximate cause of the latter. Nevertheless, there is a second reason for drawing scale and religion into a common discourse, a reason that has less to do with archaeo-logical methods than with the intellectual history of anthropology more generally. I am referring to the strong and lasting influence of Durkheim's notion of *effervescence*.

Durkheim is a key figure in the anthropology of religion, but he has a quieter presence in equivalent conversations among archaeologists, which is strange given that so much of Durkheim's writing speaks directly to major transitions in prehis-tory. This is particularly true of his understanding of religious effervescence as a consequence of population aggregation. Effervescence is, admittedly, a vague notion. Durkheim used it to reference a kind of social excitement—a "vivifying action" (1965[1915]:240)—that arises when individuals come together in large groups:

> The very fact of the concentration acts as an exceptionally powerful stimulant. When they are once come together, a sort of electricity is formed by their collecting which quickly transports them to an extraordinary degree of exaltation. Every sentiment expressed finds a place without resistance in all the minds, which are very open to out-side impressions; each re-echoes the others, and is re-echoed by the others. The initial impulse thus proceeds, growing as it goes, as an avalanche grows in its advance. (247)

It was this self-amplifying social experience that Durkheim looked to as an explana-tion of why, for instance, the Australian Aborigines developed such a vivid ceremo-nial life during their seasonal aggregations, and why the eighteenth-century French public joining together in revolution were incited to make a religion out of principles of liberty and reason.

At its heart, Durkheim's understanding of effervescence strongly privileges pop-ulation aggregation as a phenomenon that is itself generative of religious dispositions and spontaneous ritual acts, the latter of which seem to rise to the surface naturally like tiny bubbles in a glass of seltzer whenever people assemble. It is in this sense that Durkheim so clearly stands as a founding intellectual vis-à-vis modern archaeo-logical models of the evolution of religion (and Neolithic religion in particular), for both tend to bury the idiosyncratic motivations of individuals beneath, to use Dur-kheim's metaphor, the growing avalanche of collective interactions. But it is easy to oversimplify Durkheim's model when we fail to remember its intellectual context: the late nineteenth- and early twentieth-century struggle to promote the analytical significance of the social and to clear space for the young disciplines of sociology and anthropology. In his writings on religion, Durkheim was further motivated to coun-ter the positions of his predecessors in France and England who by and large regarded religion as a grand mistake or illusion that was, at best, a misguided science and, at worst, the product of a fully irrational mind. By fundamentally wedding religion to the social, Durkheim sought to save it from such secularist critics, a project that may have had much to do with Durkheim's Jewish cultural heritage and German ancestry. Indeed, the very notion of effervescence might well be read as an echo of an earlier counter-Enlightenment emphasis on the power of human passions.[3]

In contrast to the intellectualist positions of Tylor and Frazer, who saw religion as originating in naive philosophical inquiry into ontology and causality, Durkheim stressed the nondiscursive and experiential. In the midst of an assembly, he emphasized, the individual comes to transcend himself:

> [He] feels within him an abnormal over-supply of force which overflows and tries to burst out from him; sometimes he even has the feeling that he is dominated by a moral force which is greater than he and of which he is only the interpreter.... Now this exceptional increase of force is something very real; it comes to him from the very group which he addresses.... The passionate energies he arouses re-echo within him and quicken his vital tone. It is no longer a simple individual who speaks; it is a group incarnate and personified. (1965[1915]:241)

Reread this passage, please, if you are among those who draw from Durkheim's text the simple conclusion that religion is little more than an expression of social solidarity—that God is really just a projection of society, or that rituals lead us to sense that each part or individual contains some common kernel of the collective whole. Clearly, Durkheim saw more in religion than merely a force that binds the collective like a magnet drawing together iron filings. Ironically, the latter position seems closer to that of Hobbes (one of Durkheim's intellectual nemeses), particularly Hobbes's discussion of the godly power that alone kept the commonwealth in a state of collective awe, saving its members from regression into the primitive war of all against all. For Hobbes, power resided in the immortal God, filtered downward to his mortal representative, the sovereign king, and only then was legitimately distributed to the awestruck populace. We encounter something very different in Durkheim's discussion of effervescence. There, power bubbles upward, sui generis, from groups to individuals who come to experience the duality of their personhood—the sense in which they are simultaneously unique agents and also parts of a larger social whole—as an oversupply of force.

One cannot ignore the common critique of Durkheim's model: that collective effervescence is not only a vague concept but that it is also premised upon an unrealistic uniformity within the assembled group. In the case of T'aitöna, for instance, I have stressed that the various peoples who joined forces to construct the region's first aggregated village would have been anything but dronelike replicas of one another. In the previous chapter we saw that indigenous histories present the community as multiethnic and linguistically diverse and that archaeological research leads us to similar conclusions: indeed, the differences among women at the site even appear to have been etched into their bones. When I think upon these data, I have in mind one of T'aitöna's aged and arthritic women, born of immigrant parents, who spent a good deal of her life grinding corn and still probably spoke a foreign tongue in the home. What effervescent spark of likeness would she have shared with a local woman raised in a household of recently conquered foragers? To speak of mechanical solidarity in such a scenario would be absurd.

But this is not a damning critique, and it need not lead us to reject Durkheim out of hand. It merely calls for certain theoretical adjustments, notably that we decouple effervescence and mechanical solidarity as conceptual tools, the latter of which seems irreparably flawed. Suffice it to say that even in the most homogeneous of societies, likeness could never, on its own, give rise to a sense of transcendence, nor could it lead to an awareness of the unseen order of things. Indeed, likeness cannot even be said to foster commonality of purpose, insofar as those who aspire toward the same structural positions in society logically have the strongest reasons for competing with one another. What is the source of the vivifying power of assembled groups, then? Not likeness alone, but rather likeness in the face of difference or even likeness *by virtue* of difference. True transcendence is premised on a paradoxical realization that we are all, each of us, incommensurably distinct and yet, in spite of this, somehow connected and unified as parts of a greater whole, witnesses to a common world, offspring of a common mother or father, reliant upon the contrast between ourselves and others for our own self-understanding. All solidarity in this sense is organic (providing this term can also be decoupled from its traditional association with an economic division of labor).

Recast in this way, Durkheim's understanding of religion's wellspring moves closer to the interpretation of Pueblo doings developed in the previous chapter. Just as doings can be said to reference those periods of heightened reflection on the interconnectedness of society's parts, so too does effervescence reference those periods in which the distinction between individual and group partly collapses in upon itself in the minds of community members who have come to regard themselves as both discrete and radically extended throughout the social world. Let me emphasize again that awareness of interconnection or of radical extension, far from coming at the expense of an appreciation of individual difference, is in fact premised upon it. All individual identity exists only by virtue of difference and opposition as Barth (1969) emphasized for ethnicity and as Derrida (1982) emphasized for meaning more generally. Thus, even though we may be committed for practical purposes to the assumption that individuals, social groups, words, and things all have self-standing essences, there are nevertheless times when we are also led toward the realization that nothing, in the final analysis, really is self-standing, times when we begin to dimly sense that all "essences" inevitably fragment into an unanchored network of relations or oppositions. For Derrida, these may be analytical moments of deconstruction. For the Pueblos, we may speak more precisely of doings. Either way, these are effervescent instances when the network of rebounding oppositions is made the *focus* of conscious reflection and, by virtue of this, a source of power.

We are left, then, holding onto a more complicated notion of effervescence in which (1) an experience of aggregation or assembly (2) prompts a heightened encounter with social difference that (3) specifies, redefines, and transforms the worldly position of individual actors by placing each actor in a new or newly visible skein of relations, but that also (4) undermines the individuality of actors by drawing attention to the relations of interdependency that give form to both self and other, and that (5) suffuses the assembly with a pool of potential energy insofar as interdependency is the basis of all social power. To be aware of this process—to be engaged in the act of overtly tracing out the worldly relations that make all things what they are—is to be in the province of doings.

Needless to say, this is an awkward definition of effervescence and a convoluted translation of Durkheim's model into terms that suit my analysis of Pueblo history. One way to simplify matters is to let go of the core notions of difference and opposition, which hold an ingrained prominence in anthropological theory, and to replace them with notions of balance and complementarity, which occur far more regularly in Pueblo commentary on doings. The shift from difference to balance is more profound than it might at first seem, for here it is possible to trace a buried fault line that, with a little nudging, quickly wrenches apart to expose the great chasm allegedly separating the modern from the premodern (or, better, nonmodern). It is the liberal humanist subject—the autonomous individual agent of capitalism, democracy, and Darwinian selection—who must see the world coldly in terms of difference and opposition, self-interest and competition. To speak instead of *balance* is to forsake Western individualism and to acknowledge that difference is already a mode of connection and ecological interdependency. Another way of putting this is to say that "balance" functions as a mediating category, resolving and transcending the Durkheimian paradoxes of likeness in the face of difference and of independence in the face of interdependence.

This will become clearer as we return to Northern Tiwa history. With the rise of the aggregated Tiwa village in the thirteenth century, balance and complementarity became profound, pervasive, and strongly materialized themes: as north is to south, so winter is to summer, men to women, hunting to agriculture. We have already seen this in the physical organization of Taos Pueblo. Three kivas to the north balance three to the south; two northern middens balance two to the south; and two main architectural complexes—North House and South House—face one another on opposite sides of the Rio Pueblo, which, fulcrum-like, separates and joins together a world in equilibrium. We have also seen that this characteristic balancing act first emerged in the Northern Tiwa tradition some seven centuries ago at T'aitöna, where the Summer and Winter Peoples transcended their differences and constructed a village with a parallel north-south division, each half oriented toward its own share of village-wide ceremonial responsibilities, each premised upon and completing the other.

Below, I consider the issues of complementarity, balance, and connection at T'aitöna in closer detail; let me stress, however, that this discussion should not be misconstrued as providing evidence of how "religion" came to foster "social integration" as a means of accommodating mounting "scalar stress." To speak of a world in equilibrium, as I did a moment ago, is to begin to shift the focus from the messy realities of social history to the ideologies that are produced in the course of that history. But let us not forget that although ideologies are the children of history, they are not history itself. Indeed, whenever the social world is explicitly gathered together into one sort of configuration rather than another, there is inevitably reason for continued dispute and dissent, the fuel for future transformations. Pueblo doings, we must remember, specify systems of inter*dependency* that put each person and thing in its place, and this balance can feel very unbalanced depending upon one's assigned seat at the table. Moreover, Pueblo doings are orchestrated by priests who, in the context of the assembly, are emboldened to speak not as mere individuals who stand apart from the world but as nodal points or keystones of the community of humans and nonhumans at large—as the "group incarnate and personified," to borrow from Durkheim once again. This is why doings are heady, powerful, and potentially contentious, a point I explore in chapter 6.

In orthodox studies of the religious life of ancestral Pueblo settlements like T'aitöna, analysis typically begins and ends with the kiva, which is assumed to have been the focus of collective ceremonies. At Taos Pueblo, there are six active kivas, each cloaked in secrecy. Today, the kivas are primarily male spaces in which a range of activities occur: here is where powerful objects, or *walö*—literally, "medicine" (Parsons 1936:103)—are used in a variety of ceremonial practices, where initiates are trained in the ways and histories of particular kiva sodalities, where the spirits are addressed, and where matters of concern are discussed. Colonial and early ethnographic documents suggest that kivas once functioned as generalized men's houses as well, places where the unmarried might sleep and where visitors would be entertained. In the late nineteenth century, Victor Mindeleff made this point about Pueblo kivas generally: "none of these kivas are now preserved exclusively for religious purposes; they are places of social resort for the men, especially during the winter, when they occupy themselves with the arts common among them. The same kiva thus serves as a temple during a ritual feast, at other times as a council house for the discussion of public affairs. It is also used as a workshop by the industrious and as a lounging place by the idle" (Mindeleff 1989[1891]:130). Nevertheless, kivas are classically understood as primarily "religious"—as the Pueblo equivalent to a Christian church—even if many other, more mundane activities leak in.

My interests are in T'aitöna's doings, not its religion, and yet I will also begin my analysis in the kiva, raising the question of just how meaningful my shift in categories really is. Ultimately, the answer to this question must be permitted to unfold gradually as the evidence is drawn together. For the moment, suffice it to say that whereas the study of Pueblo religion typically begins and ends in the kiva, I am aiming for an analysis that expands outward to trace the connections that link the kiva with the cosmos at large. One of the problems with calling the kiva a "religious structure" (or a "specialized ritual structure," which in archaeological discourse amounts to the same thing) is that this leads us to draw an unacceptable boundary between it and other, nonreligious structures, cordoning off the kiva in the same way that so many Western theorists of religion have premised their arguments on the conceptual chasm between the sacred and the profane. This firewall approach to categorization and analysis is precisely the modernist brand of purification that we must struggle against if we are to understand nonmodern societies on something closer to indigenous terms.

Read as a locus of doings, the kiva is also more clearly situated in its historical context. For nearly a century, one of the driving debates in Southwestern archaeology has surrounded the nature of the so-called pithouse–to–kiva transition, the assumption being that at some point in Pueblo prehistory the pit structure architectural form was recoded, shifting from an all-purpose domestic residence (the "pithouse") to a specialized sanctum of male religious ritual (the "kiva"). The transition is generally understood to have gone hand in hand with the relocating of domestic tasks out of pit structures and into surface roomblocks. Nearly all parts of the northern Southwest underwent this process of residential relocation at some point; in the Taos region, as we have already seen, the arrival of the Summer People at the close of the twelfth century effectively initiated this process for the autochthonous population of Winter People. At a general level, however, we run into serious problems as soon as the pithouse–to–kiva transition is understood as a recasting of a formerly profane space into a newly sacred space, for then the analysis of the transition is reduced to a stultifying search for architectural markers of an emergent sacredness. Thus has the question "When is a kiva?" (Smith 1994) become an unfortunate staple of local archaeological debate. It is, of course, a distinctly secular question, one that assumes that religion always stands apart from nonreligion and so can be identified as such in the archaeological record. In contrast, the Pueblos seem not to have had a special name for these structures, "kiva" being a Western corruption of *ki'he*, the generic word for Hopi buildings (Scully 1972:9).

The problems with the essentialist division of lived space into ritual versus domestic or sacred versus profane realms have been widely acknowledged in Southwestern archaeology since the 1980s (Adler 1993; Lekson 1988). Nevertheless, the alternatives remain unsatisfying. Many archaeologists have simply responded by emphasizing that Pueblo spaces, more often than not, were multipurpose and housed a variety of religious and nonreligious practices. On the surface, this position seems reasonable enough, but a moment's reflection reveals not only that it does nothing to alter our analytical categories *as categories*, but also that it plays into the Western myth that primitive societies were characterized by the conflation of domains (religion, politics, kinship, economics, etc.) that modern society has come to properly disambiguate. As I have repeatedly stressed, our goal must be to explore new non-Western concepts rather than simply explore new mixtures of old analytical categories inherited from the last half millennium of European intellectual history.

Other Southwestern archaeologists have sought to confront archaeological categories more directly. Michael Adler (1989, 1993) has proposed, for instance, that we reconceive kivas as "social integrative facilities," a term that has the advantage of sidestepping—in spirit, at least—the traditional ritual-domestic dichotomy. From this perspective, it is taken as axiomatic that most, if not all, Pueblo architecture was multipurpose and that the struggle to sharply differentiate religious from non-religious practices in the archaeological record is a fool's errand. Still, the shift from "religious structures" to "social integrative facilities" in the discourse surrounding kivas introduces its own insidious brand of analytical purification, for now we have fallen back upon the familiar image of primitive or tribal religion as a fully apolitical sphere. Kivas, we are told, integrate communities by design and in practice, building solidarity and authorizing communal activity through invariant acts and utterances as an alternative to strong centralized leadership. And as integrative facilities, we are told, they naturally arise in response to increases in social scale: "As the size of communities increased [throughout Pueblo prehistory], we should expect both an increase in the number of smaller, generalized integrative facilities and the addition of larger, ritually specialized [integrative] facilities, the latter appearing when community populations surpassed 200 individuals" (Adler 1993:336). Magic numbers again. But the more important point is that as kivas become spaces of social integration, politics—as the domain of competition, debate, negotiation, and conflict—is pushed out the door. "I hold ritual to comprise a wide range of activity that *necessarily* integrates groups," writes Adler (1993:321–322, emphasis added), expressing a sentiment that is widely held in Southwestern archaeology. The appropriate response was composed by Edmund Leach more than a half century ago: "Ritual," he wrote (1964[1954]:277–278), "[is] a language of argument, not a chorus of harmony. If ritual is sometimes a mechanism of integration, one could as well argue that it is often a mechanism of disintegration."

Integration, in the end, is a red herring, particularly when it is linked to questions of religion. Sociocultural anthropologists have argued this point for generations: "In any given situation," wrote Kroeber and Kluckhohn (1952:159), "the proper question is not, Is integration perfect? but, What integration is there?" Who says, in other words, that society ever *does* hold together? Such questions bring us back, once again, to a key observation of the present chapter. Doings—in contrast to the classic functionalist understandings of tribal ritual—do not necessarily integrate society. As I have emphasized, they are instead a kind of exegesis on worldly interconnection in which claims are made about the order of things, claims that may sometimes be designed to end quarrels but that are nevertheless always open to dispute, rejection, or revision. Doings, in other words, are explicit efforts to both mirror and assert structure, but they themselves are not structure. They are, more accurately, a discourse *about* structure, which is why they are also a discourse *of* power.

Regarding the question of the pithouse–to–kiva transition, then, we should avoid turning it into something it was not. Kivas were not the birth of the sacred, nor were they the separation of house and temple. They marked instead an intensification of Pueblo doings as the conscious scale of the interconnected social world grew and as the stakes of precisely *how* the social world was to be interconnected were raised. Indeed, pit structure architecture probably always served as a focal point for residential groups, as places where families would gather together, particularly during the winter when the warmth of earthen insulation and the cessation of agricultural chores would have encouraged long hours of storytelling and explicit social reflection around a common hearth. In the effervescent waters of a diverse and densely aggregated village, these focal points persisted, although now they became nodes that gathered together larger networks, larger families. ("Now I have a good large family," said the father of the Summer People on the eve of large-scale village life in north-central New Mexico.) As a rough proxy, consider that during the early thirteenth century, the ratio of surface rooms to pit structures was roughly 1:10 in the Taos region, while at the end of the century at T'aitöna this ratio had jumped to about 1:50. The family had become a village and the father a village leader.

Let us turn to the fine print. In the remainder of this chapter, I attempt to write what might be called an ecology of Pueblo doings. This is not to say that I will be suddenly shifting gears to foreground biological systems nor that I will be looking at the environmental or subsistence implications of kiva rituals. Rather, my analysis will be ecological in a sense closer to that of Jane Bennett (2004) when she writes of an "ecology of matter." Ecology, from this perspective, is the study of how every thing is caught up in the flux of every other thing.

The Pipe

Take a thing like a pipe (figure 5.1). Pipes were and continue to be important components of kiva doings: "Among the Pueblo Indians smoking is a formality, beginning and ending every important ceremony.... Formal smoking is a recognized rite without which no ceremony would be regarded as complete and efficacious. As bearers of individual prayers, smoke clouds rise to mingle with clouds in the sky and thus bring rain" (Judd 1954:299). I have already noted, in the previous chapter, one mytho-historical example of the use of pipes in the kiva of the Winter People following their defeat at the hands of the Summer People. A pipe was lit, it was passed back and forth between the former enemies, new human relations were established, and the smoke rose to the sky as clouds, anchoring the horizontal bond between families via a vertical connection to the spirits above. Whether or not this particular event occurred in just this way, ample evidence testifies to the deep pre-Columbian significance of pipes—or "cloud blowers," as they are often described. Thus do they appear in old traditional narratives, as in the following excerpt from a Hopi song in which the kiva men are observed by Swallow Bird Boy, who serves as an intermediary connecting people with the katsina spirits above: "*Atkya tsootsonglalwa, tsoongoy naa'itnalalwa.* 'Down below they are smoking,' reports Swallow Bird Boy, 'passing the pipe from one to another'" (Sekaquaptewa and Washburn 2004:480). Thus also do cloud blowers appear in ancestral Pueblo murals, where priests are represented on kiva walls in the act of blowing forth stepped cloud icons (figure 5.2B).

At T'aitöna, ceramic pipes as artifacts provide our primary means of exploring smoking's role in kiva doings. Excavations at the site have recovered a hundred or so pipes and pipe fragments, nearly all of which conform to the straight tubular variety

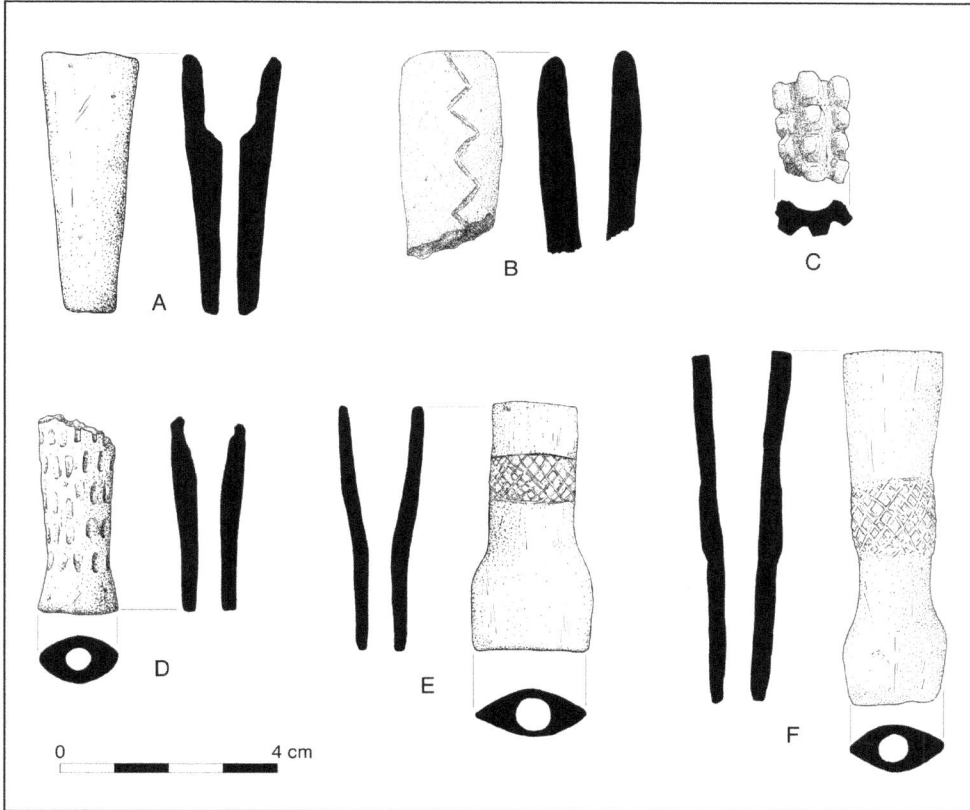

Figure 5.1. Ceramic pipes from T'aitöna. A = traditional, simple pipe; B = simple pipe with lightning motif; C = pipe with corncob texturing; D = pipe with flattened mouthpiece and punctate ticks; E, F = polished pipes with flattened mouthpieces and incised crosshatch bands.

that had been part of Pueblo assemblages in the region for more than two hundred years. Efforts to quantify the relative frequency of pipes have suggested that, compared with ancestral sites of the early thirteenth century, T'aitöna may have actually had a reduced ratio of pipes per occupant (Fowles 2004:figure 8.36). But this is not to say that their role was any less significant. In fact, it is at T'aitöna that we find the first material evidence of the elaboration and formalization of pipe construction, marking a newly explicit attention paid to their relationship with kiva doings generally.

The elaboration of pipe construction is apparent in two respects: first, in decoration and overall morphology. Earlier pipes in the region were simple tubes, decorated at most with a single incised line or small punctate ticks (figure 5.1A). At T'aitöna, these traditional pipes continued to be made, but they began to be replaced by more elaborate variants that would ultimately evolve into the cloud blowers of the ethnographic period. In some cases, a pipe would be textured along the shaft, effectively

Figure 5.2. Ancestral Pueblo mural details, Awatovi (based on Smith 1952).

turning the pipe into a stylized cob of corn. In other cases, a high polish and incised zigzags were added (figures 5.1B, C). Corn sustained the human community; zigzags, as lightning motifs, referenced the katsina spirits who brought the rain and sustained the corn (see Parsons 1936:115; Stevenson 1906–1907:file 2.35). Along with these new decorative elements, pipe form also began to change, notably including the first specimens with flattened mouthpieces (figures 5.1D, E, F). Simply put, the Northern Tiwas began to make fancier and more skillfully crafted pipes that directly referenced the beings upon which they were dependent.

But the most distinguishing characteristic of these new pipes is the clay out of which they were fashioned. Earlier pipes in the region, prior to the occupation of T'aitöna, were constructed using the same residual clays used to make jars and bowls. At some point around 1300 CE, however, the finest pipes came to be constructed using a distinctive dark brown, homogeneous, alluvial clay. This shift in the choice of clays is intriguing, particularly when we consider the explicit rules surrounding clay collection for pipe production at historic Taos Pueblo. Stevenson (1906–1907:file 4.14) learned that in their production of both pipes and kiva jars, men were required to use different clays than those used by women for the production of utilitarian jars and bowls. The latter used residual clays collected in the mountains, whereas the former had to be made using a blackish alluvial clay "collected from the banks of the Rio Lucero in the low pasture lands." The fact that it was mined near water—and not just any water, but in particular the Rio Lucero, which irrigated most of the pueblo's agricultural fields—was surely important. After all, the function of pipes was to produce the smoke clouds upon which prayers for rain and river water were sent to the heavens.

Once the clay had been drawn from the riverbank, it was specially treated in a manner appropriate to its future use in kiva doings. The details of this production process are revealing and deserve an extended extract from Stevenson's (1906–1907:file 4.14) notes:

As many men as wish to make pipes sit in a circle in the middle of the floor of the kiva. The clay is deposited on a grinding stone used only for this purpose, the stone resting on a buffalo hide. The clay is worked into a paste with water on this stone, the hand only being used. The father of the kiva sprinkles corn pollen and a powdered red blossom into the clay. The clay is worked to the proper texture by one man who, when the paste is ready, cuts it into strips giving one strip to each man who is to make a pipe.... The paste is constantly rubbed over the face and breast and under the arms during the working of it into the pipe form by order of Kwathlowúna [the Creator deity], to symbolize the growth of vegetation. "The water runs from the body into the earth as the rain falls from the heavens and waters the earth.".. .

[After an elaborate process of forming and drying the pipe,] the polishing then begins, and for this purpose a highly polished deer or buffalo leg bone is used. These bone polishers are very, very old. The pipe is rubbed over the forehead and breast and under the arms repeatedly during the polishing, no water being used during the process....

[Directly after firing,] it is immediately placed between beds of pulverized chamisa bark, where the pipe becomes a beautiful black, the high polish producing a fine pipe.... Should the father of the gens [i.e., of the "people" group] of any man having made a pipe care for it, his request is law; otherwise, the pipe belongs to the maker. There is no singing during the making of the pipe. The prayers are silent....

This class of fine pottery [produced with the special alluvial clay] is never made for other than religious purposes and only in the kiva. Kwathlowúna would be very angry if the people should make this paste.

Stevenson learned few details about the role played by the finished pipes, but ethnographic research at Picurís Pueblo sheds some light. As one Picurís informant told Donald Brown (1973:145): "They used to use [clay pipes] to pretend the clouds. Blow them and go to the water jug, pour that down in there so that form like a cloud. The smoke, blow it in, blow the smoke in around. 'Forming the cloud,' that's what they used to say."

How are we to understand, then, both the elaborate prescriptions surrounding production and the indigenous understanding of pipes as tools with which "to pretend the clouds"?

Pipes, like many other artifacts used in kiva doings, are magnetic or gravitational objects; they draw together into consciousness the interdependency of people, spirits, animals, plants, objects, earth, sky, and water. They are more than ecological; one might say they are eco-cosmological for they do nothing less than assemble the cosmos around a single point, bringing each part into explicit relation with the others. The materiality of the pipe emphasizes this. It is made, after all, of clay drawn specifically from the interface of river and earth to which is added corn from the fields and flower blossoms (referencing sustenance and fertility, respectively), as well as the flowing sweat of male laborers and the heat of the fire (referencing rain and the sun, respectively). Which is to say that an entire agricultural "economy" is micro-scopically present in the corporeal substance of this small "religious" object: corn, water, soil, sun, prayers, and the sweat of a human brow. Add tobacco and breath and the recipe is complete: clouds will then gather overhead.

All of this could be discussed in terms of the symbolism of the pipe, of course, and this is by far the most common approach taken in the archaeology of religion. But to reduce an object to a set of symbols is to deaden it; in their arbitrariness, sym-bols are the weakest of signs, meaningful only in the way that words are meaningful. This is why Alfred Gell (1998) placed such heavy emphasis on the *indexical* relations that link the objects of art and ritual to their referents. The index—which, for Gell, implicitly includes the icon—is the sign of causality and of action, a semiotic means of getting work done. In fact, there is a close affinity between Gell's understanding of the expanding web of indexical relations (what he refers to as the art nexus) and the model of Pueblo doings offered here, and I will admit to having been tempted, at an early stage in the writing of this chapter, to compose it as an overt continua-tion of Gell's project. In the end, however, Gell too often seduces us into accepting a coolly detached formalism in which enchantment emerges as a matter of equations and diagrams, and it would be unfortunate if this were our endpoint.

Ironically, it is Sir James Frazer, Gell's intellectual forebear, who charts the more interesting way forward. Frazer's ethnographic credentials were minimal to nonexis-tent, his orientation was fundamentally colonialist and primitivist, and yet his dis-cussion of the hidden sympathy between people and things, image and prototype, part and whole, has proven an essential point of reference in our understanding not only of nonmodern groups such as the Pueblos, but of modern Western societies as well. In his general treatment of "sympathetic magic," Frazer (1955[1911–1915]:12) famously defined two laws: a law of similarity ("homeopathic magic") in which like produces like, and a law of contact ("contagious magic") in which "things that have once been in contact with each other continue to act on each other at a distance." Of course, Frazer viewed these laws as the proto-scientific hocus-pocus of savages, and this goes a long way toward explaining why his work fell out of anthropological favor—for postcolonial scholars, Frazer's condescending primitivism made his ideas morally reprehensible. What has changed, then, to make Frazer relevant again? One could say that primitivity has quietly taken over social theory. A rising chorus now tells us that we have always been just as primitive as the so-called primitives, that the Enlightenment was a will-o'-the-wisp, that "we have never been modern." When Gell (1998) writes about object agency or when W. J. T. Mitchell (2005:26) advo-cates a critical idolatry, their underlying point is that sympathetic magic—far from being a "grand disastrous fallacy" (Frazer 1955[1911–1915]:22)—actually describes the world as it really is.

Here is not the place to argue for or against the ontological reality of Frazer's mag-ical laws. But I do want to argue that the basic notion of *sympathy* is important and useful, particularly in our effort to understand the Pueblo world. "Things act on each other at a distance through a secret sympathy," wrote Frazer (1955[1911–1915]:14), "the impulse being transmitted from one to the other by means of what we may conceive as a kind of invisible ether." There are two ways we can think about this sort of statement. On one hand, we can follow orthodox interpretations and focus upon the strategy of the magician or fetishist in which the law of sympathy is employed in an attempt to alter the course of events in the world in a cause-and-effect fashion similar to the way modern engineers employ the laws of thermodynamics. Thus we might say that the Northern Tiwas intended to directly influence agricultural success by fashioning pipes with actual particles of corn, soil, and irrigation water mixed in (i.e., contagious magic). And we might say they sought to directly influence rainfall when they produced flowing sweat that looks like rain or when they used their pipes to make smoke that "pretend[s] the clouds" (i.e., homeopathic magic). This sort of analysis could easily be expanded were we to explore the contagious contact between the pipe and animal bone, the placing of rainfall imagery on the pipe shaft, and so on, all of which can be portrayed as an effort to act upon nature from a distance.

The problem with such statements is that it is unlikely that any group of people—modern or nonmodern—ever believed in sympathetic magic to the extent that they thought their mimetic rituals were directly acting on the world in a law-like fashion. Here we could follow Mitchell (2005:10–11) in suspecting that *all* humans have a kind of double consciousness that permits them simultaneously to be both naive animists and hardheaded materialists; *all* humans have the ability both to believe deeply and, yet, to not really believe. But if the Pueblo actors who are the focus of this book were never foolish magicians in Frazer's sense, neither were they natural-born schizophrenics in Mitchell's. Consider how Pueblo people tend to talk about their doings. An act is performed—say, the prayerful smoking of a pipe, a pilgrimage to leave offerings at an ancestral site, or a village dance—and the subsequent world either prospers or it does not. Is the relationship between the human act and the subsequent state of the world really viewed as "causal"? Not in a technical or proto-scientific sense. Not in the sense of viewing pipes or prayer sticks as means of control that, in law-like fashion, have the power to force a change in the weather or to compel a return gift from the gods or the submission of hunted animals.

This is the problem with so many anthropological discussions of fetishism, animism, and idolatry in non-Western settings. There is no evidence at all that the Pueblos ever naively considered their doings to be premised upon cause-and-effect relationships. What one encounters instead is a more general philosophy of interdependency—a nonmodern cosmology, as Toulmin (1982) might put it—in which human doings and the cosmos are consistently read in light of one another. If good in the world prevails, then the doings must have been good; if bad prevails, the doings must have been bad. Not in the sense that some technical misstep was made, but in the sense that the actors involved must have been acting with a "bad heart," a condition that cannot be fully known in advance. Doings, in other words, are aggressively teleological and purposefully circular. The point is to underscore the degree to which everything in the world is bound up in a kind of mirror play. The point is that human and cosmic acts are always in balance, connected as if through an invisible ether, and that this fundamental truth must serve as the basis for one's system of morality. This is why the notion of *sympathy*[4] is so analytically useful, for to be sympathetic is to necessarily reflect the state of mind of other people and things. Because you are happy, I am happy. Because you feel pain, so do I. Sympathy is where ecology and morality meet, where one walks gently on the earth because the earth is the mother.

The Kiva That Holds the Pipe

Much more could be said about the Pueblo pipe as a sympathetic object, but let us move one step outward in our ecological analysis of T'aitöna's doings: from kiva artifact to the kiva itself. As I have already indicated, the Pueblo kiva tends to be viewed as a specialized religious structure, steeped in esoteric meanings. This is particularly true in discussions of Western Pueblo kivas in which the architecture directly models the cosmos at large. A small hole in the kiva's floor known as a sipapu gives material form to the place of origin and provides a means of accessing the ancestral spirits who reside below. The various levels or horizontal planes within the kiva further reference the four nested worlds through which the Pueblo people have traveled during their journey upward to the present, or fourth, world: from the sipapu, to the kiva floor, to the encircling bench, and finally up to the roof, the present surface of the earth. The details vary from pueblo to pueblo, but this under-standing of kiva-as-cosmos is pervasive. Among the Tewas, for instance, the cosmic significance of one's movement up the ladder while exiting the kiva through the roof is underscored by the presence of fifteen ladder rungs. Each rung, each step taken, parallels one of the fifteen stops made by the ancestral Tewas during their mythic migrations to their present abodes (Naranjo 2009). The bodily process of entering and exiting the structure, in other words, is a mimetic act that constructs a relation of sympathy between the contemporary Tewas and their ancestors.

Regarding the late thirteenth- and early fourteenth-century kivas at T'aitöna, I want to focus on a single structure, a rare surface kiva (Room 822) with certain notable differences when compared with the circular subterranean examples that are more common in the Northern Tiwa region. I do not suggest that this particular room can serve as a model for the other T'aitöna kivas, except in a general way. It is, however, a room I personally excavated, and it remains the only kiva at the site whose construction, use, and closure can be discussed in a rigorous fashion (see Fowles 2004:595–625; 2005).

Room 822 is an example of what Southwestern archaeologists, with character-istic flare, refer to as a "D-shaped kiva"—because it is shaped like a D (figure 5.3). The uninspired name, however, masks quite an interesting architectural pedigree: some scholars have suggested that these distinctive kivas were part of a widespread revitalization movement that explicitly referenced the earlier Chacoan system with

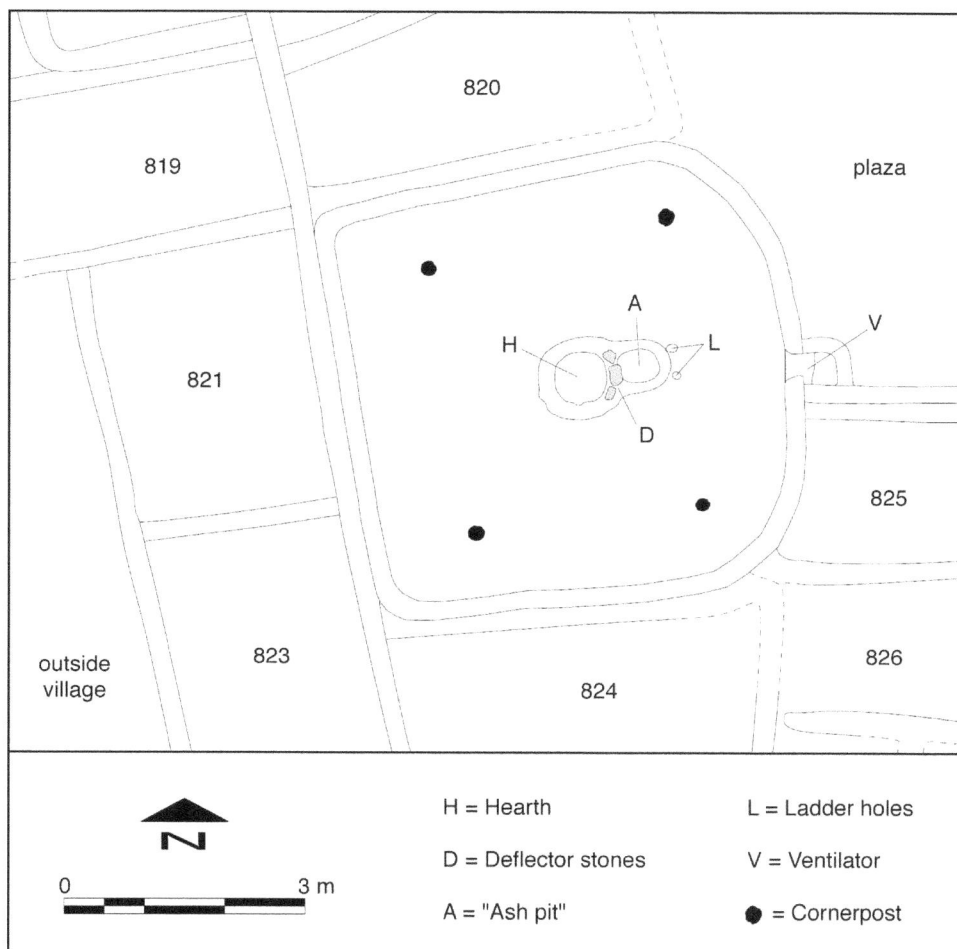

Figure 5.3. Room 822, a D-shaped kiva at T'aitöna.

its D-shaped great houses (Bradley 1996:244–247; Saitta 1997:26). It is a plausible argument; at least, in the Eastern Pueblo area, D-shaped kivas occur at many ancestral Tewa sites that are reasonably interpreted as having been built by immigrants from the northern San Juan who were heirs to Chaco's legacy. More prosaically, D-shaped kivas may simply represent a translation of the kiva from its traditionally circular subterranean form into a surface structure that necessarily abutted other surface rooms on at least one side.

Regardless, the most interesting aspects of Room 822 reside in its details, which, as in the case of the pipes just discussed, were premised upon a basic sympathetic logic. Our excavations revealed not only that the structure had been built with certain special features that distinguished it from other surface rooms at the site (in addition to its curved eastern wall and large size, it also exhibited four large corner posts, an oversized hearth, an accompanying ash pit, a small ventilator in the middle of the eastern wall, and an exterior "chimney" extending up from the ventilator opening), but also that the structure's features were built with an eye toward the doings that would occur therein. Consider the manner in which the floor was laid. Like most rooms at the site, Room 822's floor was of puddled adobe, roughly ten centimeters thick. Early ethnographic reports reveal that the adobe used for Pueblo floors was sometimes mixed with ash and/or animal blood to create a hard surface, and it is possible that this was the case in Room 822 although the compositional analyses that would be needed to confirm this have not been performed. We do know, however, that unlike most other Pueblo structures, the floor adobe of Room 822, while it was being prepared, was mixed with a great many squash seeds. This quickly became evident during subfloor excavations: as we began to remove the floor, we discovered that the large flat seeds acted as natural lines of fissure along which the adobe fragmented. Break open the floor and expose seeds, the stuff of sustenance and growth.

Why add squash seeds to the substance of a kiva floor? Again, we might talk about the symbolism of such an act. Squash imagery was frequently drawn upon when the Pueblos depicted fertility and femininity. Hopi maidens, having reached reproductive age, traditionally donned a "squash blossom" hairstyle as a means of signaling, it is assumed, their fertility. How deep into the past the connection between squash and female fertility extends is unclear, although kiva mural imagery from the late pre-Columbian period does include examples in which the equation of maiden and squash was made explicit (see figure 5.2A). In the case of Room 822, the builders used the seeds themselves (as well as, perhaps, other microscopic substances that have yet to be identified), and it takes little effort to imagine that they were added to the adobe in the same manner as when the kiva father sprinkled corn pollen and powdered red blossoms into the clay used to construct pipes.[5] Contagious magic again. Bits of the agricultural world appear to have been gathered together with earth and water to compose the very architectural substrate of doings.

The pattern continues as we turn our attention from the kiva floor to the central hearth built into it. I have already mentioned that Room 822's hearth was large; most notably, it was excessively deep. This is significant because had the feature merely been designed as a mundane container for a cooking or heating fire, we would expect it to have been similar to the standard local form with a small adobe rim bounding a shallow depression. Room 822's hearth, however, was constructed as a massive cylindrical pit, lined with adobe and extending sixty centimeters below the floor surface. Fires set in the bottom of this hearth pit would have been ineffective with respect to both oxygen flow and heat release, not to mention the logistical problems of tending an essentially subterranean flame. Again, we confront an excess, well beyond what we would consider merely functional, and we might speculate that the depth of the feature was therefore intended to establish it not just as a hearth, but also as a sipapu of sorts, a portal of entry to and communication with the underworld.

If Room 822's hearth was like a sipapu—if it connected its users with the ancestral spirits below—it was also like a cloud-blower pipe insofar as its smoke rose to the heavens, carrying human prayers to the spirits above. There are reasonable grounds for thinking the hearth may have been used in just this way. We have examined, for instance, the deep contents of the hearth fill, submitting half the ashy sediment to flotation techniques and macrobotanical analysis (Peacock et al. 2001), and, strikingly, we have found no evidence of cooking activity at all: nary a corn kernel nor a fragment of bone. In fact, the only inclusions not related to fuel use were a small assemblage of chipped stone flakes and three enigmatic clay objects (figure 5.4), the latter of which are semantically impenetrable but clearly the result of conscious purpose. Fires, then, were not set in the kiva to cook food, and this buttresses the notion that the rising clouds of smoke may themselves have been significant.

But we can go further, for as we have already seen, the Northern Tiwas invested much in the materiality of doings. For a pipe to be a pipe, it had to be made with alluvial clay mined from the contact zone between field and river. Something similar, it seems, was true of the fires built in Room 822. Analysis of wood charcoal from the fill revealed a heavy use of cottonwood (*Populus* spp.)[6] as the favored fuel, a significant fact because cottonwood is not a dominant wood in the vicinity of T'aitöna. Piñon, juniper, and Ponderosa pines are much more common, and past studies, not surprisingly, have indicated that juniper and Ponderosa (the heavy sap of piñon would have made it less desirable) were the standard wood fuels in pre-Columbian fires (Boyer et al. 1994:218–222; Moore et al. 1994:142–147). In addition to being relatively rare, cottonwood also burns quickly, releasing the lowest BTUs per cord of wood of any of the local species—quite an unfavorable feature both for cooking and for the efficient heating of a room. Why, then, was it used for kiva fires at T'aitöna? To answer this question we must look to cottonwood's most noteworthy characteristic: it grows at the edges of rivers and streams. Cottonwood is a *riverine* species; it emerges from direct contact with water and—like the alluvial clays used to make kiva pipes—was probably selected for precisely this sympathetic reason.

Cottonwood fuel may have been of additional importance because it burns cleanly to produce a pure white ash, the very sort of ash that comprised the lower two-thirds of the hearth's fill. At contemporary Taos and Picurís, white ash is regularly used to decorate the bodies of men during relay races, dances, and the annual pole climb, as well as, no doubt, a good many other practices within the kiva that are not open to outsiders such as myself. If white ash played a similar role in the doings at T'aitöna, it is possible that the deep hearth of Room 822 doubled as a storage chamber of sorts from which white ash could be drawn as needed. Used in this way, the substance would have had a special contagious charge: gathered as wood from the river, suffused with prayers in the kiva, transformed into smoke and ash in the fire, it was then redistributed via male bodies throughout the community once again.

The point I want to stress is that while our interpretation of certain archaeological details may be partial or faulty, there can be little doubt that the doings in Room 822 involved carefully orchestrated practices in which the linkages between people, things, and cosmos were of fundamental importance. Pueblo people are deeply philosophical in such matters. Indeed, when considering something as apparently mundane as firewood, I suspect that those affiliated with Room 822 not only had in mind the physical connection between cottonwood and water but also were drawing upon the sympathetic power of the cottony structures that are theatrically released by cottonwood trees each year—structures that float through the air like tiny clouds, carrying their seeds hither and yon. Like produces like. Trees that make cloud icons (cottony structures) become the fuel for fires that make cloud icons (smoke), which rise upward to establish a connection with the katsina who travel in the skies as cloud icons (clouds themselves). A homeopathic cascade of images.

With this in mind, it is worth adding one final note regarding the morphology of the Room 822 hearth: it was ringed by a thick adobe rim, and in the eastern portion of this rim, three stones had been embedded in an upright position, creating what is commonly referred to in the archaeological literature as a "deflector." The idea behind deflectors is that as fresh air entered the ventilator, it would be deflected by the upright stones (or another, comparable barrier), thus preventing gusts from disturbing the fire. Whether the stones in Room 822 served this function is less important to me than the following facts: (1) among the contemporary Northern Tiwas, these "deflectors" are referred to as "altars," (2) they typically take the form of large stepped pyramids, constructed in adobe, and (3) these stepped pyramids are expressly viewed as cloud icons (see Brown 1979:270; Parsons 1936:96–97). With this in mind, it is of considerable significance that the Room 822 deflector included a tall middle stone flanked by shorter stones on either side (figure 5.5), the visual result of which was a stepped pyramid—*another cloud icon*—and the earliest known example of such a deflector/altar in the Taos region.

By now I hope to have conveyed a sense of just what is involved when one claims, as I did in chapter 4, that T'aitöna was a ceremonial village, an effervescent place of significant doings. To live within the walls of such a village was not only to benefit from an economy of scale and to confront the new challenges of political decision making in a large population; it was to take part in spinning a new web of worldly connections between immigrants, autochthons, and the cosmos at large. That this was a profoundly conscious process is nowhere more clearly demonstrated than in the circumstances surrounding the formal closure of Room 822, perhaps only a decade or two after it was constructed. The structure was decommissioned during the middle of T'aitöna's occupation; we know this from the presence of trash deposited high in the structure's fill, and by the fact that a village shrine was later constructed atop these trash deposits. Excavation indicated that the main vigas of the roof had been intentionally pulled, collapsing the roof and effectively sealing off the interior space. The roof itself was found, unburned, not far above the floor. Its latillas, or secondary beams, had partially rotted, but the roof's overall structure (excepting the vigas) was in surprisingly good shape, suggesting it had been buried quickly and intentionally.

Beneath the decaying roof, lying upon the floor, was a remarkable gathering of

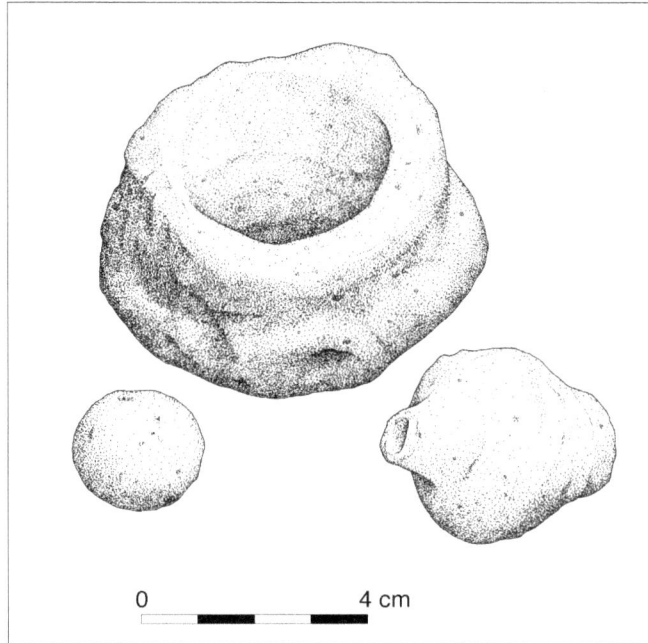

Figure 5.4. Clay objects from the hearth fill, Room 822, T'aitöna.

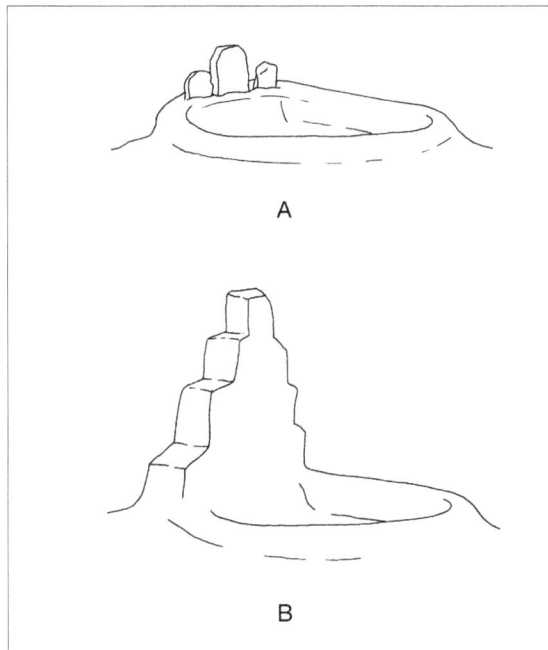

*Figure 5.5. Schematic representations of hearth deflectors (altars). A = Room 822, T'aitöna;
B = proto-historic kiva at Picurís (based on Brown 1979:270).*

things, all of which had been assembled into a kind of massive puzzle, a formal and semiotically dense mosaic that deserves extended consideration (figure 5.6). Here is a brief inventory of a few of the more notable finds:

- fragments of a woven yucca basket or mat
- burned pine boughs
- an intact ceramic jar overturned and covering corncobs and a piñon pinecone
- a pile of burned corncobs
- a fibrolite axe
- a portion of a digging stick
- four one-hand manos
- a bone awl
- the articulated lower front forelimb of an immature deer
- the antler of a mature deer
- a porcupine cranium and a few other isolated skeletal elements (plausibly from the same individual)
- a turkey cranium
- two bison third phalanges (probably the remains of a prepared bison hide)
- a five-month-old dog with a number of curiously missing skeletal elements
- a three-and-a-half-month-old dog (headless)[7]
- the fragmentary and largely disarticulated remains of two very young canids (both only weeks old)
- the headless remains of a one-and-a-half-year-old human infant, sheltered by two stone slabs

The inventory reads like the bizarre cast for a surrealist play. At first glance, it seems semantically impenetrable, haphazard even, except for the headless infant whose presence immediately forces us to humanize the assemblage and acknowledge not only that each object was placed on the kiva floor with intent, but also that each object bears its own life history, its own movement through the social world, and that what our excavation stumbled upon is less the tesserae of a mosaic than a weaving together of these histories or movements like the knots in a meshwork (see Ingold 2008). What we unearthed, in other words, is a set of object biographies out of which has been fashioned a genealogy, a network of spatiotemporal relations. At least, this is the interpretation I will offer.

To understand this assemblage, we will need to rely on three lines of evidence. First, we must attend to the spatial relations of the objects, each to the others, for every object indexes the intentioned human hand that was responsible for its particular position within the overall group. Second, we must explore the varied biographies of the objects, for each also indexes a different life of sorts, played out prior to the assembling of the objects on the kiva floor. This is as true for the stone and ceramic objects whose lives were geological and artifactual as it is for the animal remains whose lives were largely biological, or for the human infant whose brief life was

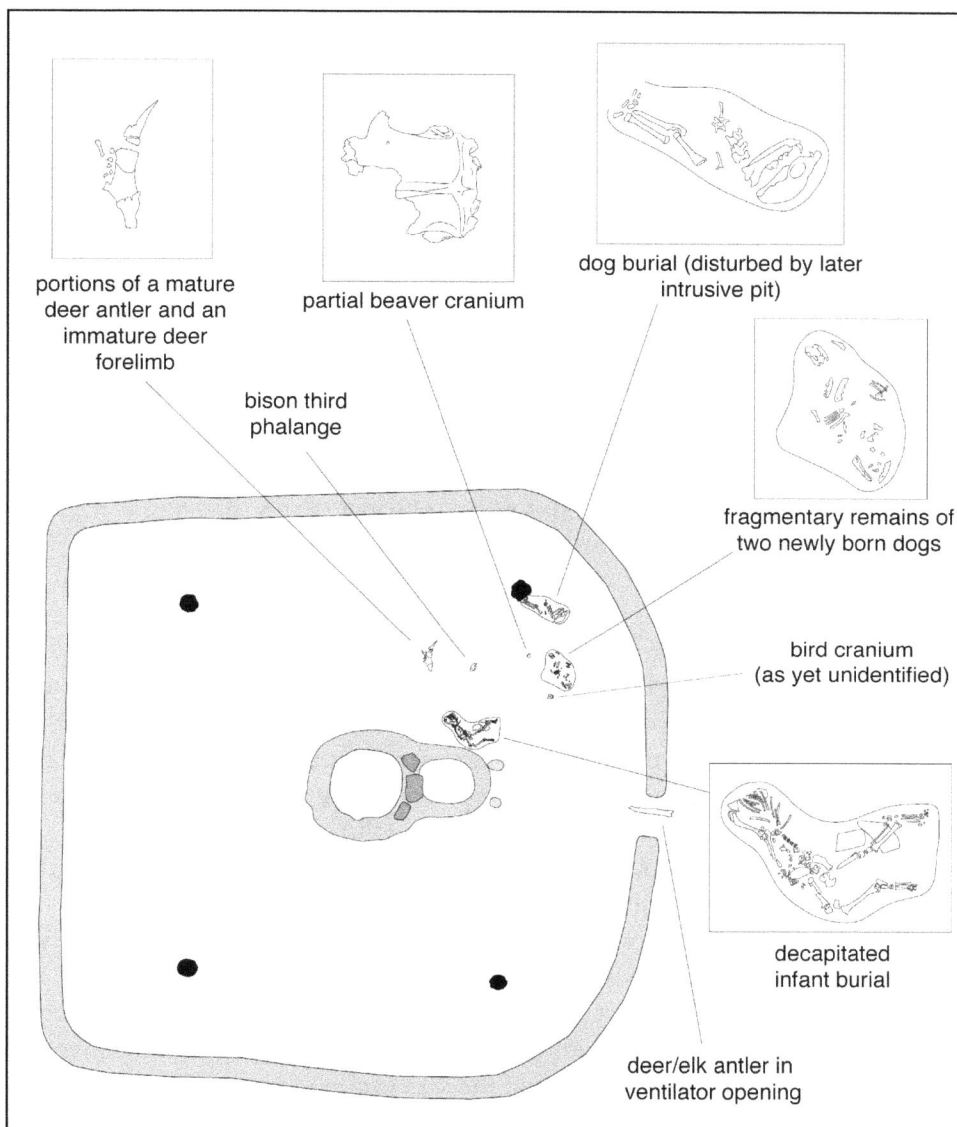

Figure 5.6. Room 822, principal floor objects in the northeast quadrant.

social. Third, we must, to the degree possible, learn from the descendant Northern Tiwa communities, drawing upon their more recent understandings of spatial relations and object biographies as guides for our own.

Let us begin with the kiva floor as a whole. Those who undertook the final doings in Room 822 had more than twenty square meters of floor space available to them. And yet, the artifacts just inventoried were all found in the eastern half of the room (figure 5.6). Indeed, few objects were encountered in direct contact with the floor to the west of the hearth, and those present—mostly isolated sherds—were generally small enough to be explained by unintentional depositional processes. In contrast, the floor area east of the hearth was clogged with objects. The first pattern we encounter, then, is a clear division of the kiva into east and west halves.

In prior chapters I have highlighted the significance of the north-south spatial division in the Northern Tiwa tradition, but east-west dualism is just as important. Each morning, the sun is born in the east, travels its road, and retires in the west, returning to the underworld where the ancestors dwell. Thus has the east come to be associated with birth and fertility and the west with death. Thus also has east come to be the focus of doings aimed at maintaining a fecund world. East, north, west, south, and "east again" (or "real east" or "in the middle"; see Trager and Trager 1970)—the ritual circuit begins and ends with the most precious direction, whether one is drawing out lines of cornmeal or running across the landscape to distant cardinal shrines. At contemporary Taos Pueblo, the east-west division could even be said to dictate the movement of tourists, though few visitors are conscious of this. Arriving at the western entrance, the tourist finds himself passing through a space that is palpably Western. Here he finds the Catholic church, the ticket booth, and the parking lots—icons, respectively, of the religious persecution, capitalism, and environmentally destructive technologies that European conquest has introduced. Colonialism, one might say, is kept in the west, the direction of death. In contrast, the eastern side of the pueblo is largely off-limits to tourists. East is the direction of the kivas, the rising sun, the mountains, Blue Lake (the place of emergence), and most of the tribe's doings. In fact, when electricity was introduced to the community during the mid-twentieth century, it was permitted in the western, southern, and northern portions of the village, but not in the eastern roomblocks (Brandt 1980:140). Electrical circuits, no less than ritual circuits or tourist circuits, must conform to Northern Tiwa cosmology.

This is not to say that, when looking at something like the east-west division in Room 822, we should impose a division between the sacred and the profane. Yes, the east is especially sacred, but so too is the west. (Again, the Pueblos distinguish between the sacred and the sacred, not the sacred and the profane.) Moreover, the absence of objects in the western half of the kiva can itself be regarded as an intentional construction just as the negative spaces of a painting are constructed no less than the positive spaces. The distribution of the floor objects in Room 822, then, could be said to delineate a cosmic balance of sorts, and it is this balance that has been emphatically composed:

West	:	East
Death	:	Birth/Rebirth
Absence	:	Presence

The greater interpretive challenge lies east of the hearth, for there we must contend with the great diversity of objects listed above, not least of which is the interred human infant. The infant was unexpectedly encountered while excavating the last level of the last unit in Room 822, and it was not our intention to disturb these or any other human remains at the site. Consequently, the infant's skeleton was exposed only to the point that it could be clearly identified as such,[8] after which it was reburied in place. Even this limited amount of excavation, though, was enough to indicate that the child was missing its head.

The infant's death and decapitation clearly must dominate our reading of the floor assemblage, as it must the closure of the kiva as a whole; the end of the infant and the end of the structure seem to be closely bound up with one another. Two obvious interpretations present themselves: either the infant's death prompted the closure of the kiva or the closure of the kiva prompted the infant's death. In the latter scenario, we are in the domain of "human sacrifice," and I am inclined to dismiss this interpretation as highly unlikely given the absence of references to such practices in Pueblo ethnography and mythology. Of course, there were killings in the Northern Tiwa past, and as I noted in chapter 4 there were periods when individuals were regularly decapitated as well; however, all existing evidence suggests that violence of this sort was directed outward, away from the residential group and toward one's opponents.

It is more likely, then, that the infant was killed and decapitated during a raid upon T'aitöna, the head having been taken to the attacker's village in a manner akin to the taking of scalps during more recent centuries. The infant's youth may have made it a target. "The younger the child the more valuable is the scalp," a Taos informant told Stevenson (1906–1907:file 1.20): "That of a child one day old is far more valuable than that of a child one month old. The scalp of a child who has ceased receiving nourishment from the mother is no more valuable than that of an adult. 'The young infant is new to the world as the world was new after the flood and the mother's nourishment helps the child as the new world helps vegetation, and our wish is to keep the world new.'" Similar understandings of the special sanctity of those who have not yet been fully weaned are found among the neighboring Tewas, who say that children younger than six or seven are "not yet *seh t'a*," not yet dry or hardened into a full human, still moist like the world prior to emergence (Ortiz 1969:16). Here, perhaps, one finds a rationale for the special procurement of infant body parts during raids. Additional supporting evidence is limited but suggestive: earlier excavations at T'aitöna encountered the burial of a twenty-two-year-old male—a man of warrior age, in other words—who had been interred with the mandibles of six children ages one through six (Whitley 2009:204). Isolated infant craniums have been reported from Pueblo IV sites in the nearby ancestral Tewa region as well (Fallon and Wening 1982:107–108).

If youthfulness explains why the Room 822 infant was killed, perhaps it also explains why the infant received the mortuary treatment it did. Children were traditionally accorded special burials throughout the pueblos, often interred beneath room floors or in rock fissures in such a way as to ensure the rebirth of their soul in the mother's womb during her next pregnancy. In the case of Room 822, it is reasonable to conclude that the death of this particular infant prompted the decommissioning of the kiva and its transformation into a tomb or, more accurately, a womb for the child's rebirth.

But even if this explanation is accepted, we are still no closer to understanding the strange assemblage of objects arranged on the floor around the infant. Are we to fall back upon archaeological convention and view them as mortuary offerings, as gifts to the child or supplies to assist in the process of rebirth? This would go against all that we know ethnographically about the Northern Tiwa tradition. Indeed, "offerings" (an awkward term with unwieldy baggage) are nearly absent in T'aitöna's mortuary record (Whitley 2009); certainly they have never been recorded in such quantity, let alone with a juvenile. Moreover, the diversity and specificity of the objects in question must be accounted for. Why offer porcupine and turkey skulls? Why an axe and a digging stick?

I have struggled with these questions, particularly as a parent with a child of my own, and I have repeatedly fallen back upon the likelihood that the untimely death of the child provoked, in some general way, a need to reassert the cosmic order of things. For those suffering such a loss, solace is to be found—to the extent it can be found at all—in the confirmation that death has not ruptured the world beyond repair, that it has not succeeded in ripping the cosmic order asunder. The objects assembled on the kiva floor, then, might be envisioned as an effort to map and repair that order. Again we see the law of sympathy: as the objects surrounding the physical corpse are brought into orderly relations, so too will the mourners be brought back into orderly relations. Each will again find its place. This, perhaps, is what it means to be *composed* in the face of death.

Truly, the objects on the floor were composed with great care—first, through the balance between east and west as we have seen, but second through a more elaborate balance between north and south. Draw a line through the middle of the eastern half of Room 822, from hearth to ventilator, and it quickly becomes clear that we are dealing with two quite different assemblages rather than one.

To the north of this line, we encounter flesh (figure 5.6): that of the human infant, that of the hunted animal, and that of the dogs which, as nonhuman members of human society, occupy a structural space somewhere between human and animal. First, the infant was placed on the floor just north of the ash pit; then its body was covered with stone slabs and afterward by a bison hide or robe that appears to have been draped overtop.[9] Northeast of the infant, the remains of two newborn dogs (apparently only a few weeks old) were placed on the floor in a small pile. Youth for youth. A slightly older dog was killed and interred as well. Death for death. Alongside the dogs were placed turkey and porcupine craniums. Heads for the headless. (At some later point, another dog was added to the assemblage; its head had also been removed.) Finally, a pile of hunted and butchered deer remains was placed to the northwest of the human infant: the articulated lower front forelimb of a young fawn and a large fragment of an antler (cranium) of a mature deer. Youth, death, and the head were again brought into conscious relation. The details and nuances escape us—I make no claim to having "cracked the meaning" of these objects—but it would be difficult to argue that the remains did not reference the human infant. It would also be difficult to argue that they did not reference animality or flesh at a more general level. Indeed, it is with this in mind that we are able to appreciate the significance of the last of the major objects included in this northern assemblage: a bone awl and a concentration of one-hand manos with wear patterns indicative of use in hide preparation.[10] The object biography of these tools would have involved repeated contact with animal skin, a powerful connection that was less symbolic than it was sensuous and contagious.

That is what was placed in the northeastern quadrant of the kiva: youth, animality, partible bodies, and the hunt (or something roughly along those lines). To the south, an entirely different—but entirely complementary—mosaic was assembled (figure 5.7). Rather than bone, flesh, and hide, quantities of plant remains were encountered. Immediately south of the ash pit, our excavations revealed a roughly one-meter-square area with remnant needles, twigs, and pinecone scales from lightly charred piñon pine boughs, positioned on the floor in such a way as to mirror the hide-covered infant burial to the north. Within the pine bough remains, fragments of yucca matting were found, as well as a fibrolite axe of the sort traditionally used by the Pueblos to chop wood and clear agricultural fields (see Fowles 2004:610–611). Nearby lay the charred and fused remains of a pile of corn along with the fire-hardened tip of a Gambel oak digging stick.[11] And at the southern edge of this cluster of items sat an intact ceramic cooking jar, overturned and sheltering two corncobs and a pinecone. The objects in the southeastern quadrant of the kiva, in short, were of two sorts: either they were plants (corn, piñon, yucca, oak) or they were agricultural artifacts regularly in contact with plants. The axe that repeatedly cut trees during field clearance, the digging stick that repeatedly broke soil for the seeds, the pot that repeatedly cooked corn—again we find an entire agricultural economy sympathetically gathered together in the kiva.

And still there are so many objects to consider! Is it not also significant that the entire assemblage in the eastern half of the kiva was covered with trash brought in from the middens—middens that the Pueblos today regard as "sacred" insofar as they are strewn with the discarded personal effects of ancestors who have now become spirits? And is it not significant that, following the collapse of the roof, special sorts of objects (notably, arrowheads) continued to be deposited in the decommissioned kiva, or that a stone shrine was eventually constructed high in the fill above the infant and dog burials (see Fowles 2004:622–623)? All of these details are important and cannot be summed up with the bland assessment that they were the strange symbolic practices of a "religious" or "ritualistic" people, as if identifying objects as religious or practices as rituals somehow explains them. The logic of T'aitöna's doings must be unearthed on its own terms by tracing out the web of sympathy that would have connected each artifact or archaeological trace with the larger world of the ancestral Northern Tiwas.

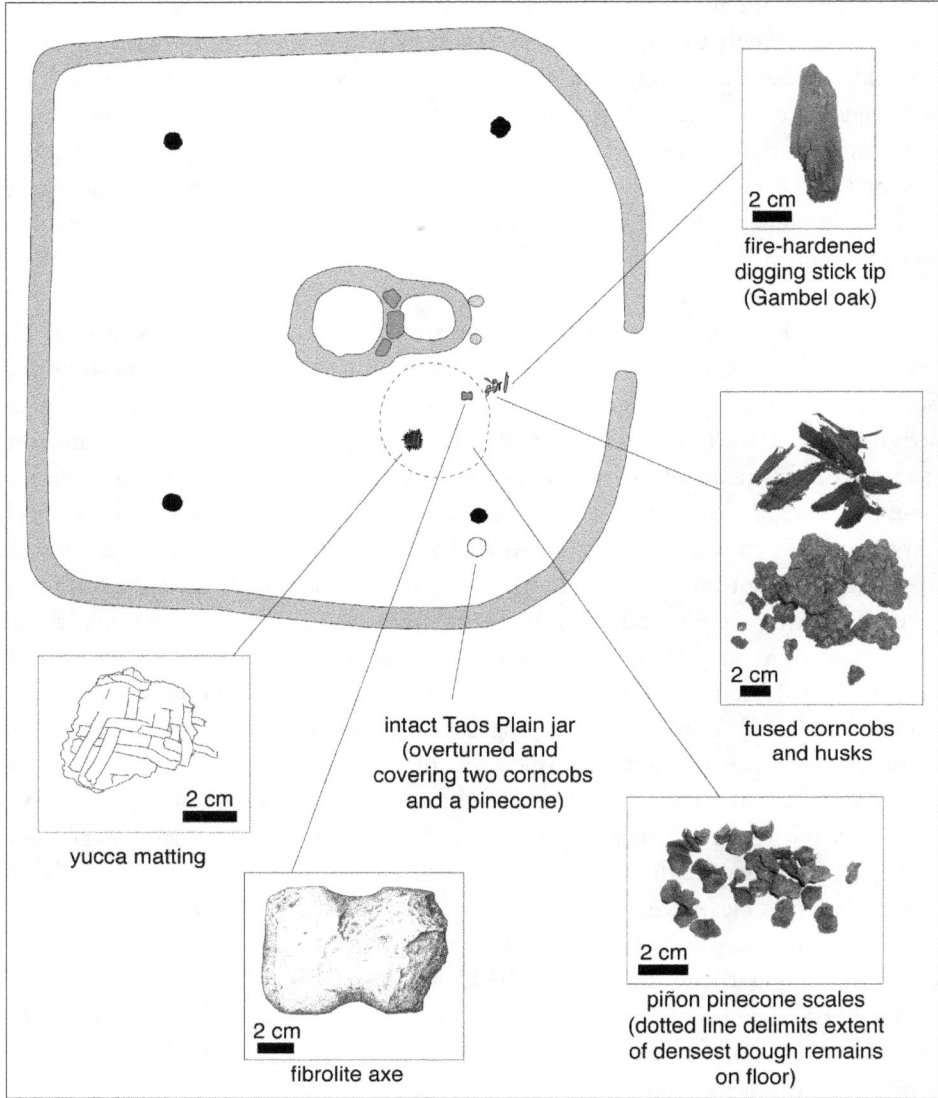

Figure 5.7. Room 822, principal floor objects in the southeast quadrant.

But I will draw this lengthy analysis to a close. I have suggested that the objects gathered together on the floor of the kiva mark a conscious reassertion of cosmic order in the face of a tragic death. That order was mapped out spatially with great care, first through a division of the kiva into east and west halves, and second through an emphatic north-south division that drew upon deeply embedded cultural models that by now should be familiar:

North	:	South
Hunting	:	Agriculture
Animal	:	Plant

The strong north-south patterning evident in the floor assemblage, in other words, is mimetically linked to the larger directional associations of the Northern Tiwa moiety system. As the cosmos is balanced by north and south, winter and summer, hunting and farming, let the kiva be similarly balanced. Or more poignantly, let those who have lost a child find a similar sort of balance in their lives. Let them not forget their place in the order of things.

The Village That Holds the Kiva

Pueblo objects assemble worlds, and so do Pueblo kivas. As we extend our ecological analysis one step further, it should be no surprise to learn that the village as a whole replicates, like an expanding fractal, the same vigilant attention to relation, balance, interdependency, and the effervescent process of assembly itself. We have already found this to be the case among the descendant community at Taos Pueblo, evident in such doings as the ceremonial relay races or plaza dances during which the entire village is gathered together. Other doings make this point even more strongly.

Consider the doings formerly held at Taos Pueblo in February, which were dedicated to the sun and moon as they struggle to overcome winter and warm the landscape. Stevenson's informant described the outlines of these doings in fascinating detail (Stevenson 1906–1907:file 2.12). At the center of the action were the human representatives of the sun and moon, individuals who were traditionally selected from among the Golden Warbler People (in the Feather Kiva of the southside moiety) and the Small Olivella Shell People (in the Day Kiva of the northside moiety), respectively, and who therefore embodied the balance not only between sun and moon but also between south and north. The doings began when the moon and sun met and bathed in Red Willow Creek just before sunset of the new moon. Together, they proceeded to the Feather Kiva, where they dressed in special attire and were greeted by the members of the Abalone Shell People (Big Earring Kiva) and the Golden Warbler People (Feather Kiva), both of whom spoke in turn. Moon and sun then traveled to the Water Kiva where, sitting on the north and south sides of the kiva, respectively, they sang. In the Water Kiva were assembled another group of representatives from both the north and south moieties: the Stone Knife People (Knife Kiva, north moiety), the Water People (Water Kiva, south moiety), and the Kwathlowúna People (Old Axe Kiva, south moiety). After the song, the pipe was passed between the groups. Moon and sun then retraced their steps back to the Feather Kiva, where there was more smoking as a pipe of the Macaw People (Feather Kiva) was circulated.

It was a moving ceremony, in the sense of being focused on movement (see Fowles 2011). As the representatives of the moon and sun processed from Feather Kiva to Water Kiva to Feather Kiva, they moved east and west, outside and inside the village compound in a manner that paralleled the runners in the relay races as well as the movements of the moon and sun across the sky. I assume this was intentional and that the logic behind the doings was, again, sympathetic: by demonstrating that they consciously reflected and therefore were homeopathically linked with the celestial powers, the villagers may well have been establishing the grounds upon which their own priestly labor was able to support and embolden that of the sun and moon, which work on behalf of the world at large. Again, this is not to say that the practitioners sought a relationship between human cause and "supernatural" effects that was predictive in a mechanical or formulaic fashion. They were not acting upon the world as a subject acts upon an object. The relationship was (and continues to be) one of trust between two agents who know and are sympathetic toward one another.

I suggest that this basic ontological stance is centuries old and would have characterized the community at T'aitöna, even if the details differed. Traditionally, the ecumenical relations between the various Northern Tiwa kivas, peoples, and ritual societies have been both elaborate and regularly materialized in practice, so much so that the entire village—including its architecture and spatial organization—became a locus of consciously orchestrated doings. This, we will see, was as true at T'aitöna in the past as it is at Taos Pueblo in the present.

In making this move, however, we have our work cut out for us. Once they leave the dark and hallowed interior of the Pueblo kiva, most archaeologists tend to think they have safely emerged into a more or less profane space, as if they, like the Pueblo ancestors, had climbed a ladder into an entirely new world. To make the kiva "sacred," in other words, Western scholarship is compelled to distinguish it from some other realm that is, by definition, "not sacred," and this feat is typically accomplished by looking to the Pueblo household as the contrasting locus of mundane, economic behavior. If the sacred must stand apart from the profane, then let the kiva stand apart from the household. Such is the oppositional thinking that too often governs the modernist perspective.

But this will not do if we are to come even remotely close to understanding T'aitöna from an indigenous perspective. One need only look at what, on the surface, would seem to be the most economic and profane of architectural spaces to discover just how inadequate this perspective is. The great majority of the rooms excavated at T'aitöna have been ground-story storage facilities, simple rooms with neither hearths nor any other indications of cooking, eating, or sleeping activities. Indeed, this is one of the great drawbacks of the site's archaeology: almost all interior dwelling spaces were in upper-story rooms that have, over time, fragmented, collapsed, and eroded beyond recognition. But the dozens of excavated ground-story storage rooms are not as disappointing as they might at first appear. Some have been found literally filled with burned corn, providing a wealth of potential information about this important companion species. More germane to the present discussion, however, is that nearly all have been found to contain a curious architectural feature: a centrally located post with an encircling basin.

The centerpost and basin complex at T'aitöna is unusual; it appeared suddenly and pervasively at T'aitöna in the late thirteenth century, and its only known parallels are at proto-historic Taos and Picurís, the two descendant Northern Tiwa communities (Dick et al. 1999; Ellis and Brody 1964). As such, it provides one of the clearest markers of Northern Tiwa identity during the late pre-Columbian and early colonial periods. Neither the post nor the basin can be explained as a bluntly functional solution to new architectural challenges presented by village life: centerposts were not structurally necessary to support pueblo roofs, and many of the "basins" were not basins at all, but were instead composed of low adobe rims with little to no storage potential (Fowles 2004:551–558). By now, however, it should be clear that there is nothing to be gained by falling back on the assessment that these seemingly impractical features were, therefore, "symbolic." Obviously the centerpost and basin complexes "meant something" to their Pueblo makers just like all objects "mean something" when humans find cause to reflect upon them. The more important question has to do with what the centerposts and basins, in practice, did. Toward what ends were they used?

Fifty years ago, excavators at the site learned from a Picurís potter that "her grandmother had seen such basins still in use, and that unshelled corn was stored in them, the cobs radiating in spoke-like fashion around the center-post." It was then argued that "the basins were originally used for the ceremonial storage of corn, perhaps from the first harvest of the season" (Wetherington 1968:30–31). Stevenson's notes from Taos Pueblo offer a more detailed picture of the ceremony that may have surrounded the placement of corn in center basins. Her description of a "Blessing of the Corn" ceremony, held in October after the village's corn had been husked, is particularly informative:

> Men and women of the village gather in the [Feather] kiva, each bearing several ears
> of corn tied together with corn-husk ribbons. The women carry their corn in baskets.
> The central ear of each cluster is a perfect ear. Five dark feathers from the back of
> the turkey and furnished by the Koyukän'na [Corn Mother Society] are attached to
> each perfect ear with cotton cord by the heads of the Koyukän'na and are regarded
> as gifts from them during the morning previous to the visit of the people to the kiva
> in the evening. The corn is deposited on the floor in the center of the kiva. The line
> of men offer[s] song prayers that the corn may be strong like the Mother Earth and
> Mother Corn to whom the corn is offered. After the prayers, the three heads of the
> Koyukän'na each blesses the corn and sprinkles it with medicine water made from the
> medicine of Koyukän'na. The vases which hold the water are of black pottery made in
> the kiva. The water is dipped from the vases with sprinklers of twigs of pinorial. The
> corn is afterwards placed at the base of the corn heap in the home as the "Mother"
> corn. (Stevenson 1906–1907:file 2.3)

I will refrain from another extended analysis of Pueblo kiva doings and their governing logic of sympathy, though clearly we are again confronted with a set of practices designed to make explicit and sensuous the connections between people and things. Suffice it to say that as "mother" corn from throughout the community was ceremoniously gathered together in the kiva and then redistributed to the households, relationships were traced as much between households and kivas as between people and their crops. Indeed, something of the kiva seems even to have been carried over into the household in this process: having been set up in its new residence in the basin and around the central post, the "mother" corn became the focus of her own gatherings as ordinary corn from the fields was collected and piled on top. Doings, in this sense, were distributed throughout the village along with corn as each storage room became connected to a kiva. I suspect the basins and centerposts underscored this.

We are now in a position to see how an archaeology of doings democratizes the sacred by doing away with the very category of the profane. Whereas the sacred and the profane define a state of *opposition* within Western ideology, the kiva and the household seem to define a state of *balance* within Pueblo thought. Doings draw the kiva and the household into a relationship of complementarity.

We are also in a position to see the tangible implications of this analytical shift vis-à-vis our understandings of gender relations. When the sacred is conceptually opposed to the profane, when religion is opposed to economics, or when prayer is opposed to production, we are led to construct false walls not only between kivas and households but also between men and women. Indeed, once an architectural space has been specially identified with female practices, its perceived sanctity, following archaeological orthodoxy, decreases. Thus pithouses are said to have become kivas when domestic activities ("women's work") were removed; and households are assumed to have been more or less profane partly because ethnographic research tells us they were under the control of Pueblo mothers.

This subtle act of analytical purification—in which sanctity/men and profanity/women are pulled apart into discrete domains—is particularly visible in the treatment of what are commonly referred to as "mealing rooms." Like many early fourteenth-century villages in the Southwest (see J. L. Adams 1993; Ortman 1998), T'aitöna contained a number of oversized surface rooms with rows of metates in formal bins used to grind corn in assembly-line fashion. Women performed this labor—the arthritic evidence in their bones makes this clear—and archaeologists have expended surprisingly little effort to interrogate these spaces further. The assumption, it seems, is that mealing rooms are comparatively easy to explain. Their economic rationality, we are told, is self-evident; their function, profane.

There are a few dissenting voices, however. Mobley-Tanaka (1997) points out that mealing rooms initially emerged in the northern Southwest during the Pueblo II and III periods as a complement to kivas in unit pueblo settlements, literally emerging side by side (see also Hegmon et al. 2000:72). In fact, early mealing rooms, like their kiva counterparts, were subterranean, raising the possibility that they partook of the same general connection with the underworld. Did the kiva and the mealing room *oppose* one another? Did they represent a separation of church and economy? Not at all, argues Mobley-Tanaka. Rather, she suggests, the locating of certain male and female activities in discrete architectural spaces may have been a means of underscoring gender balance and their mutual necessity to Pueblo ritual practice. This was why the two structures were initially paired and why mealing rooms were typically oriented so that the women faced the kiva while grinding corn (Mobley-Tanaka 1997:441). By Mobley-Tanaka's reckoning, however, this balance of gendered spaces was broken in the early twelfth century when subterranean mealing rooms disappeared and kivas continued to grow in elaboration. This was when men assumed control of Pueblo ritual life, she suggests, as women were increasingly relegated to positions in the home.

Evidence from T'aitöna reveals that Mobley-Tanaka's historical account may be incomplete, for there, in the early fourteenth century, the link between kivas and mealing rooms appears to have been reasserted. T'aitöna's mealing rooms were not subterranean, but they were large specialized structures in clear spatial association with the village's kivas (see figure 4.12). In Roomblocks 3 and 6, mealing rooms were directly adjacent to kivas. In Roomblock 2, a mealing room was actually constructed atop a former kiva. T'aitöna's architects, it seems, were consciously mapping out the relation between male and female, between the kiva and what was still referred to at Taos in the 1930s as a *koye* (mealing room; Parsons 1936:47).

But this balancing act between male-female and kiva-koye was not just mapped at the scale of the individual roomblock. As we move outward to consider the village as a whole, we find that the kiva-koye pairing was itself spatially patterned. Indeed, despite efforts to locate a mealing room in the northern roomblocks, none has been found, suggesting that the distribution of koyes was restricted to the southern half of the site. As we saw in the previous chapter, the south was also the residence of the Summer People moiety, immigrants from the west, where the mealing room tradition had its origin. All of this places us on familiar terrain. The distribution of koyes is one more replaying of the site's pervasive north-south dualism:

North	:	South
Winter	:	Summer
Hunting	:	Agriculture
Animal	:	Plant
Male	:	Female
Kiva	:	Koye

Koyes were loci of female doings that involved collective corn grinding. As such, they belonged in the south (see Fowles 2006).

The skeptic interjects: "But aren't we just talking about basic food preparation? Even if we accept that kivas are locations of 'doings,' how can one justify extending this status to mealing rooms? Doesn't this lead to an analytically impotent situation in which *everything* begins to be seen as doings?" Let me respond by making two points.

First, who is to say that food preparation—in this case, corn grinding—is any more basic than prayers or dances? Who is to say which of these practices is more fundamental to bodily nourishment? Or which is more deeply enmeshed in larger understandings of the cosmos? Indeed, upon what grounds can we say that an ear of corn is any less a "ceremonial object" than a kiva vessel or a katsina mask? Surely it is unacceptable to immediately locate corn grinding in the profane simply because it was a female practice.

Second, we must be careful to bear in mind the argument developed in the previous chapter. Doings, I suggested, are best understood as exegeses on worldly interconnection, as practices that draw the relatedness of things into consciousness. All things, all the time, are bound up in relations with all other things, of course. In itself, this observation is unenlightening; it is nothing more than a starting point, a basic axiom not only of Pueblo philosophy but also of much Western philosophy. Touch the world, attend to it with intellectual rigor, and one immediately feels the sticky web of interconnection expanding out in all directions. One finds this position articulated with special clarity in Bruno Latour's writings: in his vigorous critiques of reductionism (1988), in his deceptively simple observation that we dwell in a world in which "transcendence abounds" (1993), in his spirited plea that analysis therefore move outward through the web rather than inward toward an essence that, in the end, does not exist (2005).

But while a relational ontology may best describe the way of things *in the end* (that is, in the final analysis), it is certainly not the normal way of things *in practice* (that is, in the day-to-day perceptions of people). Whether or not stable, autonomous essences really exist, we have no choice but to act as though they do. Pragmatically, we cannot bear in mind the whole interconnected world each time we gather firewood, or swat a fly, or address friends on the street. We attend instead to the isolated or proximate effects rather than to the cascade of contingent realignments that occur with each of our actions. We regard other things as discrete self-standing essences so as to shield our ears from the deafening feedback that would result were we to acknowledge that one always acts upon all things all at once. Human perception inevitably involves the creation of "black boxes" (in the sense of Latour 1993), chunks of the world that have been carved out and essentialized so as to provide us with an illusion of control (see also Harman 2009). By filling the world with objects, we convince ourselves that we are subjects—regardless of the fact that few philosophers today would regard the subject-object divide as tenable in an ultimate or ontological sense.

I am interested in the Pueblo world as practiced by mindful actors. And in writing of Pueblo doings, therefore, my aim is to cast light on a kind of gradient of consciousness extending from the largely unreflective use of objects in workaday activities to the heightened meditations on the radical interpenetration of things that characterized certain special contexts—contexts often referred to by archaeologists as "religious." The question, then, is not whether something like corn grinding was a sacred or profane act, but rather: To what degree was it a conscious gathering? To what degree was it orchestrated as an overtly transcendent conceptual experience?

Here is what we know. Koyes, or mealing rooms, were designed to underscore the spatial logic of balanced dualism. From the scale of the structures, it is clear that women from multiple nuclear families must have labored in them simultaneously. Was this gathering of women purely an expedient activity then, undertaken whenever there was corn to grind and by whoever was available to do the grinding? Probably not. There are good reasons to think that collective female corn grinding was as highly choreographed as male doings in the kiva. Northern Tiwa mythology, for instance, contains a lengthy account of the month-long grinding rites undertaken by the Earth Mother when she reached puberty (Stevenson 1906–1907:file 2.7; see also files 2.13 and 3.42). Interestingly, these rites are said to have taken place in a specially prepared underground room—a lingering social memory, perhaps, of the Pueblo II mealing rooms discussed by Mobley-Tanaka. We also know that the puberty rites of the Earth Mother served as a charter myth for actual girls at Taos Pueblo. At first menstruation, a Taos maiden spent four days in the mealing room, observing various taboos and grinding the corn of anyone in the village who requested her assistance. Emerging from this period of grinding, "she assumes the woman's boots, and the style of her dress and headdress is changed" (Parsons 1936:47).

Our understanding of koye doings at T'aitöna is frustratingly limited. None were excavated with the rigor needed to reconstruct the range of practices undertaken within. Nevertheless, we can say that they were chambers where adolescent girls would periodically gather to perform extended periods of labor on behalf of the community as a whole. Here it seems, was where girls formally entered into womanhood. Not only would a cohort of girls have been made collectively manifest, but as families brought their corn and returned home with cornmeal ground on communal metates, the larger social networks of the village would have been mapped out as well. All the while, the girls would have been instructed in how their labor replicated that of the Earth Mother. All the while, they would have ground facing southeast (all grinding stations at T'aitöna were oriented this way), toward the winter solstice sunrise, the focus of prayful attention.

The Cosmos That Holds the Village

From the pipe to the kiva to the village, an expanding ecology of Pueblo doings is emerging that now must be permitted to seep beyond the architecture of T'aitöna, into the wider landscape, outward to the edges of the Northern Tiwa cosmos. Doings, needless to say, took place not just in kivas, koyes, and village plazas but also in agricultural fields, on the banks of lakes, and atop mountains. In recent centuries, members of Taos Pueblo have regularly visited a wide array of shrines within a roughly two-thousand-square-kilometer area surrounding the village (Fowles 2009), and while the overall logic of these shrines and their interrelations remains the private knowledge of the pueblo, it is clear they are regarded as parts of a coherent and balanced whole, similar to the shrine system so carefully outlined by Ortiz (1969) for the Tewas.

Of course, the systematic use of shrines to formally define cosmic boundaries has been part of the Pueblo tradition at least since the eleventh century, when Chacoan leaders orchestrated an impressive network of roads and other shrine features across much of the San Juan basin (Marshall 1997; Stein and Lekson 1992). Indeed, Chaco appears to have provided an early model for the later ceremonial landscapes constructed in the Rio Grande valley during the fourteenth century, when post-Chacoan migrants established or joined new communities in the east. This may help us to understand why the Pueblo IV ceremonial landscapes of the ancestral Tewas, Keres, and Northern Tiwas all developed in similar directions during the fourteenth century, each group drawing upon a common shrine lexicon (mountaintops, springs, lakes, caves, and a variety of constructed stone features) and a broadly similar shrine grammar (focused on dualism, balance, cardinality, and the definition of concentric ontological spheres with a village at the center) (Anschuetz 1998; Duwe 2011; Fowles 2009; Ortman 2010; Snead 2008; Snead and Preucel 1999). Regional differences exist, but the similarities are more striking. Increasingly it appears that the Rio Grande cosmologies documented in twentieth-century ethnography were constructed by post-Chacoan immigrants seeking to vigorously assert new center places after leaving former centers in the west behind them.

T'aitöna's shrine network was one of the earliest formal materializations of this new cosmological project in the northern Rio Grande. Surveys of the valley surrounding the village have led to the identification of dozens of shrine features ranging from isolated boulders dotted with small cupules or ground slicks to large circular enclosures of bermed earth and rocks, most of which appear to date to the late thirteenth or early fourteenth centuries. I have described these features in detail elsewhere, along with the methodological challenges involved in their study, and I will not review those discussions here (Fowles 2004, 2009). I will focus instead upon the special way that a subset of the T'aitöna shrines gathered together village and landscape into a larger villagescape. A "villagescape" is a cosmos that has been centered on a residential community, and we can use this term to transcend the traditional analytical opposition of village (culture) and landscape (nature) in much the same way that doings transcend the analytical opposition of religion and politics. Like doings, villagescapes are gathered wholes, and to study a villagescape is to explore just how these wholes are gathered together. At T'aitöna, shrines performed a critical role.

It should be abundantly clear from the discussion above that T'aitöna's occupants were attentive to dualisms—strikingly so. Just as the objects gathered together on the floor of Room 822 were divided into north and south assemblages, so too was the village divided into north and south moieties. One might read these as opposed halves, or even as political factions (as I did in an earlier work; see Fowles 2005); ideologically, however, it is more likely that the ancestral Tiwas understood them as reflections of one another. North is only north by virtue of south; summer would not legibly be summer without winter. Oppositions were transcended by the common relativity or relationality that gave each its identity. And doings, as we have seen, were a kind of mirror play that shone light on those transcendent relations.

T'aitöna's shrine network echoed this core preoccupation with dualisms. At the outskirts of the adobe roomblocks, for instance, were two primary shrine areas—one to the south and one to the west[12]—each composed of a large depression and a paired set of cupule and ground slick boulders (figure 5.8). There are differences between the two areas. The depression of the southern complex is much more substantial (twenty meters in diameter, one and a half meters deep) and would have involved substantial labor to construct. Previous excavators placed a small test pit in the center of the feature and dug a backhoe trench through the earthen berm bounding its southwestern side (Michael Adler, personal communication 1999) but were unable to determine whether the feature was an adobe-mining pit, an unroofed great kiva, or something else altogether. More recent research has located both cupule and ground slick features on boulders immediately southeast of the depression, as well as a rock alignment connecting the depression to the residential area (Fowles 2004:527–531). The latter find is especially significant, because small rock-bordered "roads" of this sort are known to have been important features guiding the movement of supplicants as they approached Pueblo shrines (Fowles 2011).

The western shrine complex differs primarily in the visibility of its features. As with its southern parallel, the western complex includes both cupule and ground slick boulders. However, the shrine boulders of the western complex are more prominently located, flanking the formal western entrance to the settlement like two stone lions. Most visitors to T'aitöna probably approached from the Rio Grande del Rancho to the west and so would have been guided into the community by passing between these two rock shrines. Thirty meters to the west is a large shallow depression. It is a much subtler feature than the deep depression of the southern shrine complex, which may be partly due to the accumulation of sediment washing in from the adobe roomblock just upslope. Regardless, another ground slick boulder was found fifteen meters south of the depression, suggesting that we are indeed looking at a spatial organization comparable to that of the southern shrine complex.

How should we understand such features? Ethnographic reports provide a few clues. Among the neighboring Tewas, women were said to peck cupules on special shrine boulders at sunrise "to attract the attention of the 'Sun god'" (Jeançon 1923:70; see also Jeançon 1911:96). Archaeological evidence from throughout the Pueblo world—such as the female figurine from Te'ewi into whose body a number of cupules had been ground (Wendorf 1953:83)—provide additional support for the general association between cupules and women (see also Fowles 2006:34; Hays-Gilpin 2000a, b). If cupules have broadly female associations, ground slicks seem to be associated with male practices. These features are poorly understood, but archaeological research has indicated they were probably first produced in agricultural contexts when men repeatedly sharpened axes in the process of clearing trees. Kurt Anschuetz and Richard Ford (Anschuetz 1998:339–340; Ford, personal communication 1997) have suggested that such axe sharpening in fields eventually developed into more overtly ceremonial acts, resulting in ground slick shrines.

While we can guess at the specific meanings of shrine features in isolation, the

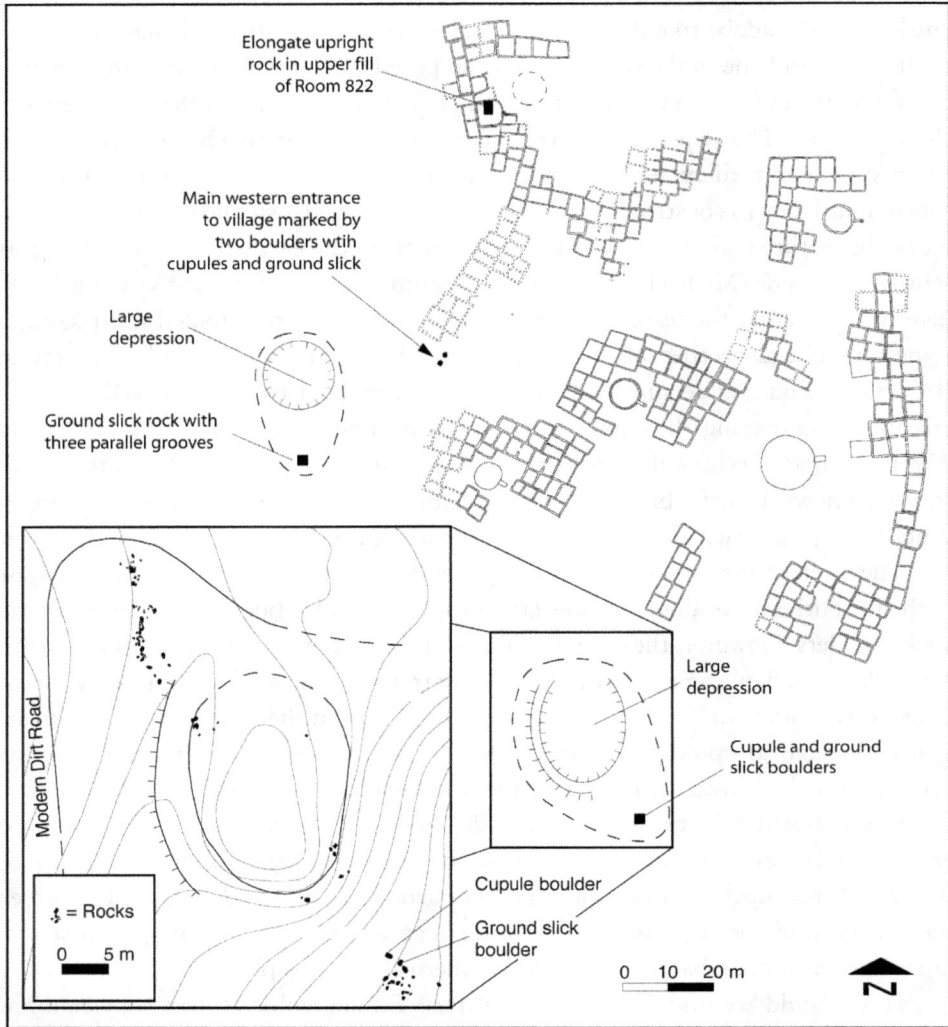

Figure 5.8. Shrine areas at the edges of T'aitöna.

more pressing question is why cupules and ground slicks were paired with each other within a larger set of paired shrine complexes at the edge of a settlement that was itself divided into paired north and south halves. Principles of dualism were clearly being emphatically materialized. More than this, though, I suspect that just as female koyes balanced male kivas in T'aitöna's architecture, female cupules may have balanced male ground slicks in the shrine complexes at the margins of the village. And this suggests that what we are looking at is indeed an extension of the village's spatial logic into the larger villagescape.

This interpretation becomes more secure as we expand our analysis to incorporate the archaeological remains within a five-hundred-meter radius around T'aitöna. This is a zone that contains an especially dense distribution of pre-Columbian features

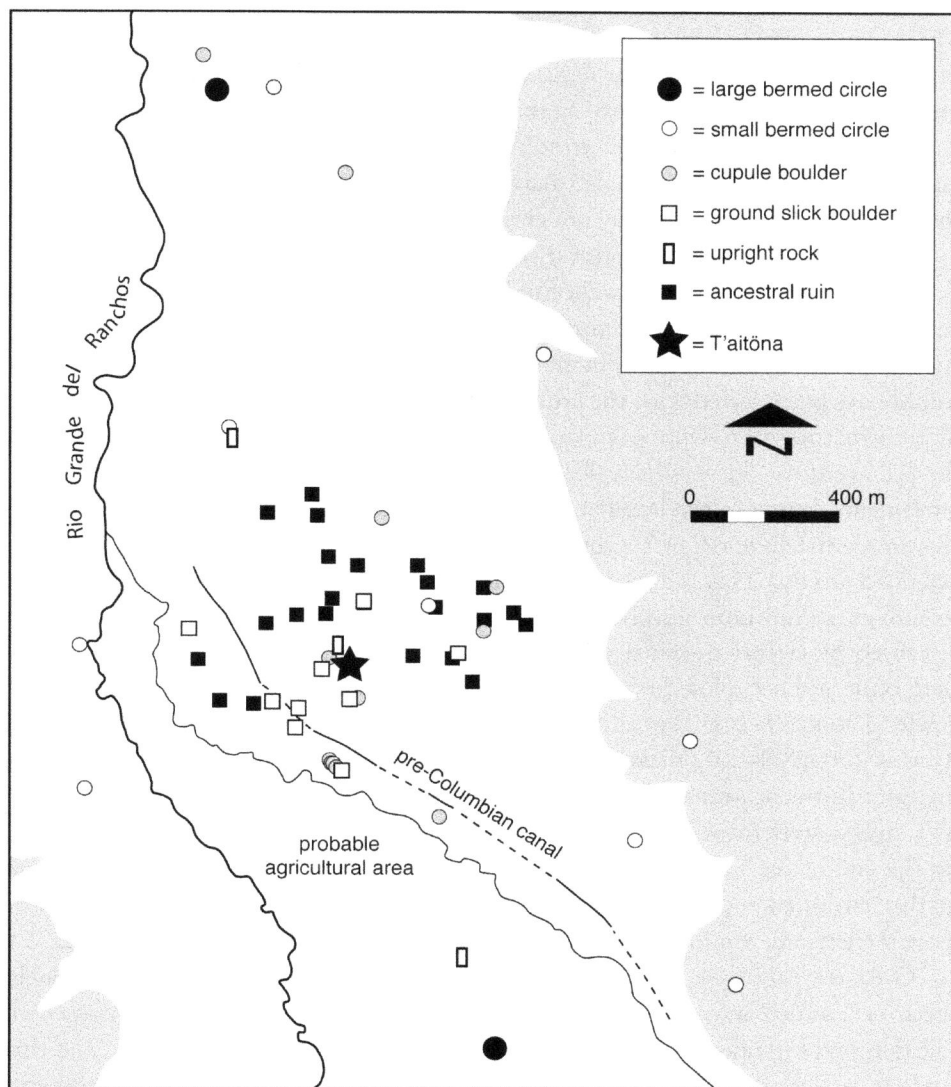

Figure 5.9. Shrine landscape surrounding T'aitöna.

and probably comprised the core space of T'aitöna's day-to-day activities (figure 5.9). Walking south from the village, for instance, one quickly enters into an important agricultural area through which ran a substantial irrigation canal, built by the occupants of T'aitöna in the late thirteenth century (see Fowles 2004:446–453). The canal tapped the Rito de la Olla roughly one kilometer upstream and would have fed cornfields on either side. It also would have been the nearest source of water for the community and so was probably the locus of many habitual practices. Crossing the canal, one soon arrives at the edge of a terrace overlooking the Rito de la Olla, roughly six or seven meters below. Here, T'aitöna's occupants no doubt took good advantage of one of the few riparian zones in the valley, an area filled with fish and small game but also important flora, such as the cottonwood trees used in the kiva fires of Room 822. This is not to say that the river was regarded as a natural resource per se. A number of cupule and grinding slick boulder shrines along the edge of the terrace reminds us that, as among many contemporary Pueblo people in the region, the Rito de la Olla was probably understood as a ceremonial road leading up into the mountains, where ancestral beings dwell.

In contrast, if one were to walk five hundred meters north of T'aitöna, one would pass through a very different semiotic terrain. Today, this area is a gradually sloping alluvial plain blanketed with piñon and juniper tree cover. In 1300 CE, however, it would have been dotted with the crumbling walls, rotting vigas, and partially filled-in pit structures of a dense population center built and occupied over the course of the prior century. Surveys have documented the presence of twenty-four unit pueblo settlements dating to the late Pot Creek Phase (1190–1260 CE) in the forty-hectare area immediately north of T'aitöna. (Each unit pueblo was probably occupied by an extended family.) This is a striking density of archaeological sites given both that it represents a minimum number of settlements (additional sites may well have been destroyed by twentieth-century logging in this area) and that all these settlements were built and occupied during a brief time span (no more than seven decades) (see Fowles 2004:239–241). Two unit pueblos within this cluster have been excavated (Fowles 2004:248–261; Vickery 1969), but we are still very far from understanding the early thirteenth-century occupation of this area, which would have been the valley's largest settlement cluster at the time—a dispersed village of impressive scale. By the end of the thirteenth century, this area had been vacated as the population further coalesced into T'aitöna. Nevertheless, the adobe walls of the two dozen or more settlements would have remained as crumbling reminders of earlier times.

Only recently have we begun to incorporate the swarm of ruins immediately north of T'aitöna into our understanding of the village as a spatial phenomenon. The dominant temporal orientation of archaeology is profoundly modernist, and this tends to lead us into thinking that spatial analysis should focus solely on "contemporaneous" sites. One must struggle not to conflate time periods, we tell ourselves— thus we implicitly treat the past as absent from the present. But there is nothing analytically rigorous about this approach, for it demands that we ignore the material fact that former settlements continue to be experienced as standing ruins long after their initial occupation is over. Worse yet, it demands that we ignore indigenous Pueblo temporalities in which the past is understood as residing alongside the present and in which former settlements are regarded as living places where the past is experienced and ancestral beings consulted. Pueblo ruins, in other words, become Pueblo shrines. They do not disappear from cognitive maps even if they are erased from the maps of archaeologists.

In practical terms, this means that the occupants of T'aitöna must have been acutely aware that their pueblo effectively divided the landscape into a southern agricultural zone where crops were grown and a northern zone of ruins where the ancestors dwelt. Again, in the early fourteenth century this would have been a self-evident pattern. And my suggestion is that it would have been understood as a natural extension of the north-south dualism diagrammed repeatedly within the village itself. Recall that the objects placed on Room 822's floor were divided into paired assemblages: to the north, a deceased child lay beneath a bison-hide covering; to the south, a cluster of corn and agricultural implements were covered by pine boughs. Expand the scale of this patterning from a few square meters to a square kilometer, place T'aitöna in the structural position of the central hearth, and we discover that the larger landscape replicated the same spatial pattern: agriculture to the south, the deceased to the north. We might go even further and conclude that the north-south dualism provided a model for spatializing time itself. North is to south as past is to present: each balances and gives definition to the other. Such deep ontological models, I suspect, governed the final decision of where precisely to locate the nucleated village within the larger Rio Grande del Rancho valley that surrounded it.

For the skeptic, let me make two additional points. First, there can be no denying that deep meditation on spatial patterning is characteristic of the Pueblo tradition. Ethnographically this is well known, and there is no reason to think it was any different in the late pre-Columbian period. Second, both of the descendant Northern Tiwa communities, Taos and Picurís, continue to regard ruins in a manner similar to that just outlined. A few hundred meters northeast of contemporary Taos Pueblo, for instance, are the adobe mounds of their ancestral Pueblo IV village, commonly referred to as "Cornfield Taos" (Ellis and Brody 1964). And a hundred meters north of Picurís Pueblo are the ruins of "Old Picurís," in which the last vestiges of the community's Pueblo IV architecture are still standing. At both pueblos, then, a modern village is paired with the remains of an ancestral village just to the north or northeast. And in both cases, the ruins are regarded as an integral part of the community, just as the past is an integral part of the present. This basic pattern, I suggest, is at least as old as the fourteenth century, and one might even trace its ancestry, in modified form, back to the twelfth century, when certain Chacoan roads ceremonially linked present settlements with past great houses.

Viewed in isolation from its surrounding landscape, then, the Northern Tiwa village is incomplete. In the Pueblo tradition, nothing can be cut out of its larger network of relations without being perverted irrevocably, and shrines—be they cupule boulders or ancestral ruins—would have made this lesson abundantly clear. "Rather than build walls, people built shrines," observes James Snead (2008:110) in discussing the Tewas, the Northern Tiwas' cultural relatives to the south. Walls separate; shrines gather together—a critical difference. And yet, Snead's point is that we must appreciate the manner in which shrines transformed the Pueblo landscape into an extension of the village (that is, into a villagescape); walls may have given way to shrines as one moved outward from the core of the village, but this is not to say that space became any less bounded, any less constructed.

Let us move still farther from T'aitöna. Eight hundred meters to the south one encounters a large elongate stone that was set upright into the ground long ago at the valley's edge, just outside what would have been an important pre-Columbian agricultural area. A second upright stone is found 650 meters to the north of the village center, just beyond the cluster of early thirteenth-century ruins. These stones represent a distinctive type of shrine found throughout the Rio Grande valley. Elsie Clews Parsons (1974[1929]:238–247) recorded the active use of such features in the Tewa area during the 1920s; shortly thereafter, an anonymous artist from Isleta Pueblo provided her with a watercolor image depicting an effectively identical feature among the Southern Tiwas (Goldfrank 1962:painting 139). Among both the Tewas and Southern Tiwas, such isolated stone shrines index the presence of particular spiritual beings; it is for this reason that the stone depicted by the Isleta artist was addressed as "Stone Old Lady." Tewa stones are similarly personified, such as Awe Kwiyoh (Spider Woman) and Nu Enu (Ash Youth), both of which are located at the outskirts of Ohkay Owingeh Pueblo (Ortiz 1969:20). We have a limited understanding of how such shrines figure into Pueblo doings beyond the fact that prayer feathers and other offerings are periodically deposited there (Parsons 1974[1929]:238–241); however, Alfonso Ortiz's (1969) research has made it abundantly clear that they are consciously regarded as points of articulation within the larger cosmic order.

Elongate upright stone shrines were never common in the Taos region. Beyond the two noted above—one north, one south, and both roughly equidistant from T'aitöna—I know of only one other local example, and this from the upper fill of Room 822, the D-shaped kiva already discussed. The Room 822 shrine stone had been pecked all over its surface and roughly shaped prior to being set upright in the northern half of the kiva fill at some point well after the structure's closure. Near its base were two projectile points and a piece of red ocher (Fowles 2004:542). As the surrounding adobe rooms weathered and collapsed following the abandonment of T'aitöna, the stone eventually came to be buried just beneath the modern ground surface (figure 5.10).

Viewed collectively, the three upright stone shrines further reveal the deep interpenetration of village and landscape. At the valley's edges, the north and south shrines replicated and extended T'aitöna's balanced dualism one step farther in space. In doing so, they would have simultaneously underscored the centrality of the village, placing it at the heart of a carefully delineated cosmos. In mirror-like fashion, the elongate upright stone shrine in the village would have reflected those in the surrounding landscape, gathering them together into a whole. Again, this is why one must speak in terms of integrated Pueblo villagescapes, rather than of an opposition between village and landscape.

The north-south dualism we have been tracing is nearly at its archaeologically perceptible limits, but one final group of shrines deserves our attention. These are the "large bermed circle" shrines, an inelegant name to describe circular open spaces, 7–10 meters in diameter, surrounded by a rock or earthern berm. Like the elongate upright rocks, only two of these features are known from T'aitöna's valley, one 1.5

Figure 5.10. Elongate upright rock shrines. Upper fill, Room 822, T'aitöna (top); EPS-8, 0.8 kilometer south of T'aitöna (bottom).

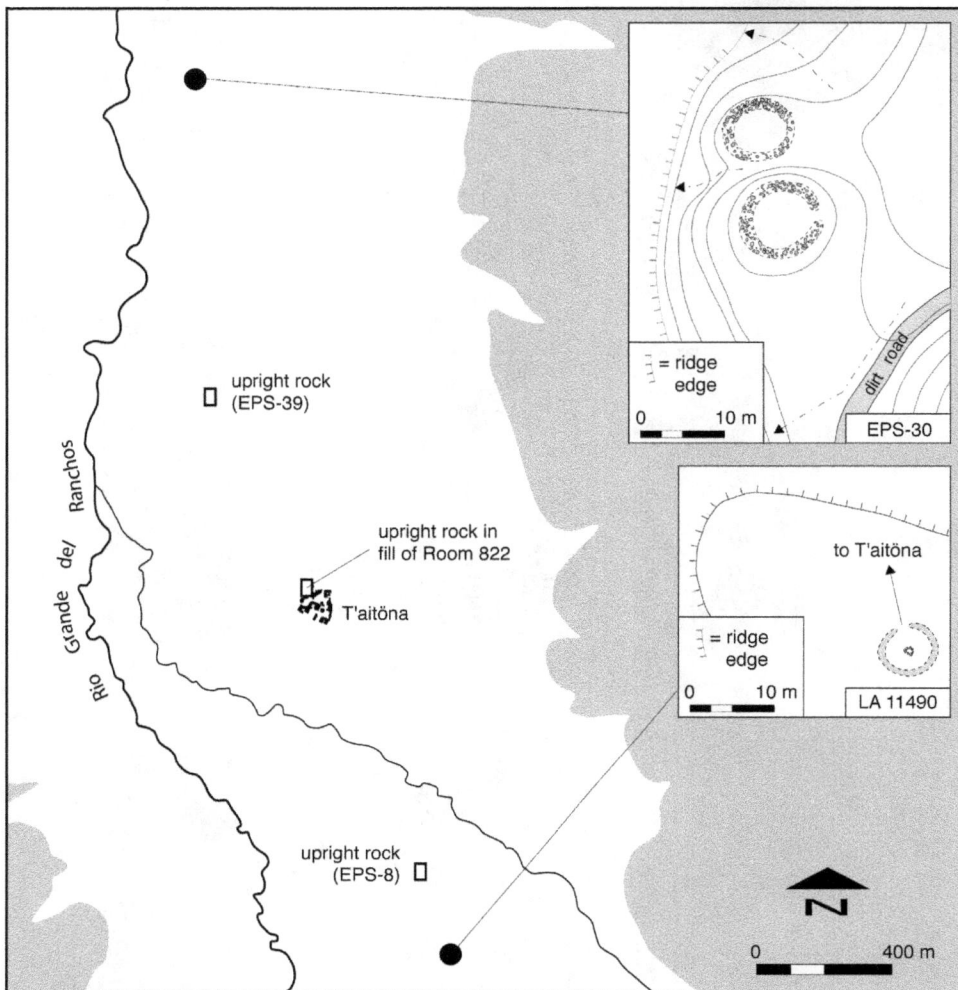

Figure 5.11. Paired shrines around T'aitöna.

kilometers north-northwest of the village center and a second 1.1 kilometers to the south-southeast (figure 5.11). Both are situated atop relatively flat ridges that jut out into the valley and so have commanding views.

Of the two, the southern (LA 11490) is more modest. It consists of a shallow depression surrounded by a low earthen berm. Three aspects of the feature suggest it was used as a shrine in pre-Columbian times. First, its location conforms closely to known patterns from the neighboring Tewa region, where "flat-topped hills" in the cardinal directions vis-à-vis the home village were regarded as key shrine locations, occupied by the *Towa é* spirits "who stand watch over the Tewa world" (Ortiz 1969:19). LA 11490 is situated in such a context. Second, a small circle of stones in the center of the depression echoes those found by Wendorf (1953:53) in the middle of shrines at the Pueblo IV Tewa site of Te'ewi.[13] Third, the surrounding berm contains a gap in its northern side, facing T'aitöna, and in this way broadly conforms to the logic of Tewa shrines, which Ortiz (1969:141n6) notes were designed to gather together worldly blessings and redirect them back toward the home village.

The northern example is more dramatic. It consists of two adjacent circle shrines, both nine to ten meters in diameter and nicely defined by one-and-a-half-meter-high rock and earth berms. A cupule boulder is nearby, and the area surrounding the bermed circles contains a moderate scatter of ceramic and chipped stone debris. Collectively, these features mark what must have been an important shrine complex during the occupation of T'aitöna, similar perhaps to the "earth navel" or "world quarter" shrines found elsewhere in the northern Rio Grande (see Fowles 2004:522–527). There is much to consider here from a cosmological perspective, but for the moment let me simply emphasize that the rebounding pattern of north-south dualism has now seeped beyond the valley and out into the hills. A northern ridge-top shrine balances a southern ridge-top shrine; the spatial logic seems inescapable. Indeed, the more prominent shrine of this pair even internally mirrors the broader pattern, its dual circles facing one another as north faces south and winter faces summer.

I doubt the pattern stops here, merely a kilometer or two distant from the home community. Contemporary Pueblo villagescapes are all-encompassing, and so one might reasonably guess that the residents of T'aitöna drew upon the core principle of north-south dualism to conceptually order the cosmos in its entirety. Perhaps there are additional shrine features, as yet undiscovered, that materially extended this pattern farther in space. Perhaps faraway geological formations (e.g., mountains, canyons, lakes) or places named in myth (e.g., Chipapunta, Taos Pueblo's place of emergence far to the north; Parsons 1936:112) were employed to define the outer cosmic layers of the villagescape. At present, we are unable to say. But the archaeological record is sufficient to demonstrate that T'aitöna stood at the heart of a consciously and redundantly diagrammed network.

It is difficult to know how the members of T'aitöna experienced this network. Doings, I have suggested, were an indigenous mode of perception that was at once sensuous and intellectual. To send young boys running out toward the cardinal directions to retrieve water from distant lakes and springs—water that was then conjoined at the village in a single vessel—is to perceive a world order, if not also to bring that order into being. So too is the act of traveling outward to leave prayer feathers at cardinally positioned stone shrines. Such acts implicitly acknowledged a sympathetic principle that served as connective tissue for the Pueblo cosmos. Water gathered together from the cosmic edges contagiously established linkages between what went on in the kiva and what went on in the world at large. In some cases, the ceramic vessel that held the water in the kiva was itself mimetically linked to the cosmos. Certain bowls used in kiva doings, for instance, have terraced pyramid motifs extending upward from the rim on four sides, and as Rina Swentzell (1990) beautifully demonstrates, the bowl encircled by terraced pyramid motifs indexes the kiva encircled by its walls, the plaza encircled by its roomblocks, all the way outward to the cosmos encircled by its four cardinal mountains. Each nested layer of the villagescape mirrors the others and so is connected to them. By assuming the form of these cosmic layers, the bowl—as an icon—already gathers them together.

Within Pueblo discourse, the sympathetic connections between people and things are concrete. Repeated references are made to the presence of actual underground passages, roads, or rivers materially connecting kivas, villages, shrines, mountains, springs, and other critical nodes in the cosmos. At Taos, Stevenson (1906–1907:file 3.31) learned that there was "direct under-ground communication between the home of Kwathlowúna [the Creator deity] at Sierra Blanca [the place of emergence], and the lake of the cloud people [katsina] and departed. In fact," she noted, "all sacred waters are connected by underground roads" (see also Parsons 1936:109). This subterranean network was sometimes even said to link Taos with other villages, such as Pecos Pueblo, far to the south (Satterthwaite 1945:388).

The basic idea of underground connections appears to be universal among the Pueblos (e.g., see Bunzel 1992[1932]:487), but the Northern Tiwa tradition is one of the few that actually gave this idea a tangible architectural expression. Extensive excavations of Pueblo IV and early colonial deposits have revealed that kivas at Picurís Pueblo were regularly constructed with hidden but formally built channels beneath the floor, radiating out from the central hearth toward the cardinal directions. "The Picuries refer to these channels as 'spirit channels,'" noted Dick et al. (1999:68). "One community member said that spirit messages are sent through the channels." Spirit channels, then, were like Chacoan roads or shrine pathways: they formalized the movement toward or away from key cosmological loci (Fowles 2011). But they were unlike these other roads and pathways in that spirit channels were unseen, a buried network, invisible but very real. Could there be a better model of the secret sympathy that connects all people and things?

Subterranean roads or rivers or spirit channels—at times, this core idea is also indigenously conceptualized as a root system. At Zuni, notes Barbara Tedlock (1983:94), "red willow is chosen for both winter and summer solstice prayersticks because its roots are connected to a common root stock. By analogy, the making of willow prayersticks connects all Zunis together into the common root stock of Zuni society." As with the homeopathic use of cottonwood—the cottony structures of which sympathetically establish links to clouds, spirits, and rainfall—the characteristically vast root systems of red willow trees have made them a key species used in Pueblo doings. As each human community is a node in an expanding network of relations lying just below the surface, so too is the red willow tree. Is it any wonder that the indigenous name for Taos Pueblo is the home of the Red Willow People?

This is the ecology of Pueblo doings. The prayer stick, by virtue of its substance, is contagiously linked to the red willow tree. The willow tree, by virtue of its hidden root system, is homeopathically linked to human society. And all people and things are sympathetically linked to the cosmos at large. To render this graphically, we can do no better than David Saile's (1990; see also Swentzell 1990) interpretation of the

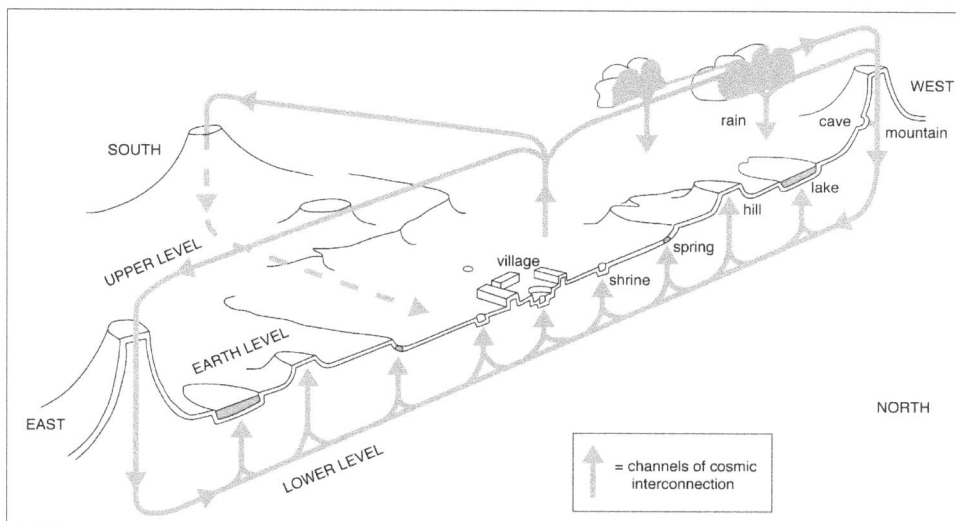

Figure 5.12. Saile's (1990) depiction of the Pueblo cosmos, based on Ortiz (1969) (adapted from Saile 1990:60 and Anschuetz 2007:135). Shrines, peaks, lakes, kivas, and other nodes on the landscape are presented as points of access to the upper and lower worlds where all things are connected.

Tewa villagescape, in which the flow of communication and energy is made explicit (figure 5.12). There is nothing mystical or obscure or supernatural about the worldly connections depicted in this model. As we have seen, the connective tissue is material and adheres closely to a sympathetic logic. Perhaps more important, we have seen that these connections do not simply exist on their own. The scientific cosmology of the modern West presents us with a world governed by natural laws that stand outside society and function regardless of human action. Gravity will always make trees fall in the forest, whether we are involved or not. In contrast, the laws governing Pueblo cosmology are as social as they are natural; the world is organized and maintained through human labor, through doings.

Effervescent Power

Let me now draw this lengthy chapter to a close. Effervescence is an old and tattered Durkheimian concept, but I have attempted to breathe a bit of life into it. I have argued that effervescence has special relevance to our discussion of T'aitöna given that we seek to understand a historical moment when the intensity of daily interpersonal interactions and the elaboration of Pueblo doings both dramatically increased. Scalar increases of this sort surely would have had organizational repercussions, but I have argued that this tells us little on its own. Effervescence is not a cause, not a hammer against the knee, not a source of something else. It is an animate and self-amplifying phenomenon that can be nurtured, domesticated, and grown like a vast field of corn to sustain a population. This was what the doings at T'aitöna accomplished: they domesticated effervescence and put it to work. But this is only a temporary answer that immediately raises a new question: in whose service was the effervescent act of assembly put to work?

Effervescence is a useful concept because it provides us with a language of power and force that resists separation—either analytically or historically—into discrete religious and political components. As I emphasize further in the next chapter, effervescence is the means by which power comes to individuals from the assembled group. This power might be described as "religious" insofar as it is premised upon the transcendence of the individual, but it is also "political" insofar as it leads some individuals not only to reflect but also to represent the collectivity, in both the semiotic and strategic senses of representation. To the extent that it concerns the sacred, then, effervescence is also fundamentally a matter of authority and the psychological underpinnings of leaders. It is a way of thinking about how certain individuals may convince themselves that they are transcendent, that they themselves embody the relations between people and things. One might even say that it is a way of thinking about what Weber called charisma, but with the important difference that this charisma is now reckoned as a kind of collective feedback rather than as an individual possession.

I suspect that the intellectuals of early village societies throughout the world would have found Durkheim's arguments compelling, much more so than contemporary scholars do. Indeed, effervescence is cheapened in the twenty-first century. It is no longer merely the immense crowds of the modern city that propel us from stimulation to overstimulation to numbness. Today, the Internet encourages a life of radical visibility and promises that one's words and images will reverberate on the screens of a million viewers, an unprecedented and self-amplifying hall of digital mirrors. The vivifying action of society when assembled in groups now makes every peon a prophet. Such is the heady charismatic nature of online personhood.

My point is that as we turn our attention toward earlier, pre-industrial moments in human history, we should not take for granted the generative nature of increases in social intensity and spatial density. The big, architectonic, structured village-scapes—such as T'aitöna—that emerged throughout the world as part of the Neolithic revolution were profoundly new media, quivering networks that brought into being radically new extensions of the self. Then as now, these media became, in some important sense, their own message. But here we must take care not to fall back into neo-functionalist analyses where scalar increase is simplistically presented as a cause of ramped-up decision-making stress, which, in turn, causes new managerial hierarchies. This is what systems may do when they are modeled in computer programs, but flesh-and-blood people, unlike numbers, have Dionysian as well as Apollonian aspects. Power inheres within the affective experience of human assembly itself. Emboldened persons assert themselves whether or not they serve the interests of the assemblies that are, in part, their makers. And as an effervescent social force takes hold of individuals, individuals sense the possibility of taking hold of society. These claims are taken up in the next chapter.

s i x
Katsina and Other Matters of Concern

In the weeks after 9/11, American flags were flown across the United States as the collective experience of catastrophe prompted a new mode of effervescent nationalism. Like cut flowers at a funeral home, bunches of flags cluttered airports, fire stations, government buildings, and other public spaces. They suffused private spaces as well, spontaneously appearing outside businesses, at the entrances to townhouses, on car bumpers, on lapels. However much these flags stood as a basic expression of solidarity, they also materialized an eerie sense of urgency, as if a new Passover ritual had hastily arisen in which American families sought exemption from the terrorist plague by marking their thresholds with stars and stripes.

Flags mean different things to different people. I was spending the year at the Fort Burgwin Research Center just south of Taos when the planes hit, and I watched the towers come down with a group of locals huddled around a television in the bar of the Sagebrush Inn. A sun-baked man with missing teeth sat next to me. He was loudly offering his own analysis: that the attack had been orchestrated by the US government to establish a violent rationale for a new era of American fascism and imperialism. Others in the bar quietly nodded. I don't know how many actually agreed with him (Taos is not far from the Los Alamos National Laboratory so conspiracy theories and a deep cynicism about the government are widespread among locals), but it really didn't matter. For the moment, we were a common audience, overwhelmed by the images flickering across a common television.

Two weeks later I was sitting on the ground in the dusty plaza of Taos Pueblo amid a larger audience, now mostly tourists. Members of the pueblo stood at the edges, overseeing things with their characteristically placid yet vigilant gaze. In the middle of the plaza was a massive, forty-foot-tall Ponderosa pole, specially harvested and prepared by the war captains in the mountain forests behind the village. September 30 is San Geronimo Feast Day at the pueblo, which begins with a footrace just after dawn and climaxes in the late afternoon when ceremonial clowns—members of the Black Eyes Society, or Chiffonana—scramble down off the North House and perform a ludicrous hunting burlesque with miniature bows and arrows. The clowns track an imaginary sheep, following its prints around and around the pole before discovering their quarry hanging high overhead, bundled together with various products of the harvest. Then comes the serious business of climbing the pole to retrieve the goods.

The burlesque and pole climb of the Black Eyes are remarkable doings with a complex significance that is lost on most visitors. The pole is an ancient icon throughout native North America, used to mark the axis mundi that connects the lower and upper worlds. "There, the sky and earth are held together by the vertical axis, which goes from the above to the below"—to borrow from Rina Swentzell's (1990:24) more general discussion of Pueblo cosmology. At Taos, the pole is expressly erected in the village's middle place (Parsons 1936:85; see also Brown 1973:162–164), the center of the world. As such, it partakes in a form of vertical iconography that extends back not only to the late thirteenth-century centerposts at T'aitöna but also to the eleventh-century Ponderosa tree that was nourished and maintained in the middle of Pueblo Bonito's plaza in Chaco Canyon. Presumably, all these poles, posts, and trees of the middle place collectively reference Pueblo stories about the ancestors' emergence from their prior home below the earth's surface, a migration frequently discussed as having been accomplished by climbing a tree that afforded passage to the upper world through a hole in the sky (e.g., Nequatewa 1967:18–23).

Taos oral history suggests that members of the Black Eyes Society have been called upon repeatedly to make this cosmic journey upward. It was they who were sent by Kwathlowúna, the Creator, to ascend to the upper world to "hunt" (i.e., find) the beautiful maiden who later became the Earth Mother (Stevenson 1906–1907:file 2.31). And it was they who first ascended to the present world to test the hardness of the earth following the Great Flood (Parsons 1996b[1939]:938; Stevenson 1906–1907:file 2.18). Even in death, it is the members of the Black Eyes who ultimately ascend to the heavens to become the stars of the Milky Way (Stevenson 1906–1907:file 2.31). The Black Eyes, then, are intermediaries, travelers between the lower and upper worlds, and from this we may conclude that the pole is their means of mediation, a ceremonial road or path within the larger cosmos.

All this dense foliage of meaning is necessary to appreciate what happened during the 2001 San Geronimo pole climb, the first Pueblo doings of the post-9/11 world. Most of the events that day—as far as I and the other tourists could tell—proceeded in typical fashion. The Black Eyes clowns descended from their perches atop the roomblocks, albeit with greater solemnity than usual. They tracked their quarry. And they eventually climbed the pole to retrieve the foodstuffs, all following tradition. Once the pole had been ascended, however, there was a striking deviation, for the clown who made it to the top then removed an American flag from his black-and-white costume and quietly waved it over the crowd who sat, hushed and transfixed, in a circle far below. For a brief moment, the pueblo's axis mundi was transformed into an international flagpole as the Taos nation formally expressed its solidarity with the American nation in the face of the recent tragedy. My wife and I were not the only onlookers who found ourselves overcome by tears for reasons we had difficulty expressing at the time.

Here is how I have come to think about the affective power of that moment, at least from the perspective of an anthropology student bearing witness. If the Black Eyes are cosmic intermediaries and the pole is a road upward and forward, then it is difficult not to vaguely sense that during the 2001 pole climb, we—natives and Anglos alike—were being presented with indigenous commentary on our collective emergence into a new historical era, a new world (a fifth world, perhaps),[1] one that has sadly come to be characterized by fundamentalism, militarism, and an unwinnable war on/of terror. At the pole climb, however, we were still unaware of all that was to come. We only understood that the ground had shifted, and we received the flag with a strange and ironic sense of international and interethnic solidarity.

This sense of solidarity was all the more profound and emotionally charged given that the scene was framed by a native community whose ancestors had been violently attacked not so very long ago in the name of the same flag. A stone's throw to the west of the pole climb stood the crumbling ruins of the old San Geronimo de Taos Church, a symbol in both its construction and its final destruction of the complicated relationship between colonial violence and Catholic salvation. The church was originally built in 1619 to convince the Pueblos that bloody conquest was, in fact, an act of Catholic love. Destroyed during the Pueblo Revolt of 1680, it was later rebuilt and stood until February 3, 1847, when it became the stage for the last military assault on a pueblo, undertaken in retribution for the assassination of Charles Bent, the first American governor of New Mexico, who had been scalped and killed by a group of Pueblo and Hispano rebels two weeks earlier. During the assault, more than a hundred Pueblo men, women, and children took refuge in the church; nearly all perished as sustained gun and cannon fire from the US military reduced the adobe structure to ruin. Ever since, the church has been preserved in its fallen state as a monument to native martyrdom and a politicized reminder of colonial violence. When the American flag was waved above the village during the pole climb ceremony, then, it marked an especially complicated and noble act of patriotism.

Let me linger on the 1847 massacre for a moment, for there we find a bleak parable regarding the modernist separation of religion and politics and its introduction into the Pueblo world. There can be little doubt that those holed up in the church—most of whom appear to have been innocent bystanders—were seeking refuge. Which is to say that they naively assumed that the church was truly a sanctuary, a place set apart from the battlefield. Indeed, running to the house of God when bullets are flying over your head only makes sense if you really believe that your aggressors really believe in some sort of separation of church and state. It only makes sense if you think your aggressors will keep their profane acts of militarism out of the sacred space of the Lord. This, after all, is supposed to be the foundation of the European notion of sanctity, in which holiness and inviolability are conjoined. And hadn't the Americans publicly asserted in a formal 1846 speech—just a few months before—that while political control of the region had recently shifted into US hands, the religious life of New Mexicans would not be affected?

Modernity has always been wildly hypocritical in such situations. The first Spanish colonists who settled in the Pueblo world at the close of the sixteenth century did so as proto-moderns. They came with two forms of leadership: the politico-military organization led by Juan de Oñate ("the last conquistador") and the religious organization led by men of the cloth. Despite their entwined agendas, the two were presented to the Pueblos as discrete forms of leadership: one focused on Pueblo bodies, the other on Pueblo souls; one focused on temporal matters, the other on spiritual matters; one focused on the kingdom of Spain, the other on the kingdom of heaven. The nuances may have been lost in translation, but the division would have been plainly evident to the Pueblos from the men's costumes alone: the conquistador in his shining metal breastplate and helmet with a sword at his side could hardly have stood in greater contrast to the ascetic Franciscan priest in his simple habit, unadorned but for a wooden cross. And to a certain extent, church and state did stand in opposition to one another: the seventeenth century was marked by jealous struggles between governors and Franciscans to control the fate of the Pueblo villages. But these struggles only served to underscore the heightened miscegenation of religion and politics in the modern era. As Latour (1993) has argued, it is the ideology of purification, paradoxically, that makes this possible. Priests become all the more political when they claim their interests are purely spiritual, focused only on saving souls. And politicians sound all the more religious when they assert their worldly power. Viewed from a Pueblo vantage point, then, the conquistador-priest must have appeared as a strange hybrid of colonialism, a polycephalous hydra with two heads that quarreled with one another but that were nevertheless attached to the same European body.

When the US Army entered the region in 1846, the hydra sprouted more heads. Now, American Protestants, with their strong anti-Catholic biases, could attack the Pueblos either for their indigenous "pagan" practices *or* for their Catholic iconophilia, which was widely regarded by the Protestant establishment as nearly as bad. In short, the quarrels within European Christianity made it impossible for the Pueblos to find refuge anywhere. Certainly, there was no refuge to be found in a Catholic church built by the ousted Hispano leaders of New Mexico. The men, women, and children of Taos Pueblo learned this blunt lesson soon enough.

What, then, did the American flag at the 2001 Taos pole climb mean? Needless to say, its meaning was neither stable nor singular, and it certainly could not be reduced to simple patriotism. The flag was too heavy for that. Conquistadors, cannons, tourists, terrorists, Black Eyes, a bullet-ridden church, Native American sovereignty, 9/11, prophecy, the cosmos—all these and more seemed implicated in the flag's sudden appearance at the height of the pole-climb ceremony. This was its affective power, at least for those of us who read the flag with this specific set of contradictory indexical extensions in mind. But if we leave aside the question of meaning and focus instead on what flag waving was intended to accomplish, we come closer to understanding the event as a component of Pueblo doings. Indeed, a sympathetic logic prevailed: by mimetically participating in the widespread display of nationalist iconography, the Black Eyes, like so many other Americans, were not just passively reflecting the world around them. They were intervening to alter the state of affairs. The United States was given a kind of tensile strength as radical Otherness was at once heightened and transcended. Half nude, with their bodies striped in ash and charcoal, the Black Eyes clowns are the very image of alterity—both within Pueblo society, where they embody chaos and disorder, and in the eyes of Anglo tourists, who all too often view the clowns as a kind of vestigial primitivity of the colonized. The American flag did nothing to suppress this heightened difference, but it did transcend it by emphatically underscoring interconnection, shared relations, and a state of sympathy. And this, as I argued in the previous chapter, is an effervescent experience, the very stuff of doings.

Whereas the goal of the previous chapter was to highlight the expanding logics of ancestral Pueblo doings, the goal of the present chapter is to consider how and why these doings were internally contested. This is a critical shift. Read in isolation, the previous chapter might easily be accused of slipping back into the very sort of secular functionalism critiqued at the start of this book. After all, the bulk of the analysis was designed to show how Pueblo doings traced and retraced the relations between people and things. And isn't this familiar territory? Isn't this just further evidence of the way in which religion fostered social integration in small-scale societies that lacked strong political leaders in possession of true individual agency? Not at all. As I have emphasized, we must be careful to distinguish models of worldly interconnection from the willingness of individuals to submit to the particular networks of relations that doings bring into being. In other words, if doings gather together and articulate whole worlds, they inevitably draw fire from those who prefer to live in rather different sorts of worlds and who prefer to relate to the people and things around them in different sorts of ways.

The American flag is a case in point. While some native individuals and communities may regard displaying the flag as both an act of patriotism (overt support for the United States and especially the many Native American veterans who have fought on its behalf) and an act of native sovereignty (insofar as it marks an *international* show of support), others find the flag icon fundamentally problematic—at best a reification of colonial relations, at worst a deep denial of a history of genocide in which so many Native American ancestors were indiscriminately slaughtered. In an e-mail response to queries by Catherine Corman, for instance, Matthew Tafoya of the Navajo Nation suggested, "Indians who fly American flags are 'brainwashed' and 'not thinking for themselves.'" "Indians do not join the U.S. military," Tafoya suggested, "because they are 'flag-waving patriots.' With unemployment on Native American reservations hovering between 60 and 70 percent...the military is the only sure way to get a paycheck" (Corman 2004). Tafoya's alternative response to 9/11 was to fight icon with icon. Rather than rallying behind the flag of the colonizers, he designed the now-famous T-shirt picturing nineteenth-century Apache warriors framed by the words "Homeland Security: Fighting Terrorism Since 1492" (figure 6.1).[2] Worn widely in both native and non-native circles, the T-shirt is a kind of anti-flag, and it gathers together a very different web of history, geopolitics, patriotism, and post-colonial critique. Michael Elliot provides a superb analysis:

> The language of the T-Shirt...echoes expressions of post-9/11 U.S. patriotism so closely that it allows the wearer to participate in that national patriotism—to be outraged at the U.S. history of colonization while still supporting contemporary efforts to protect the United States from terrorism. The shirt echoes, in other words, the contradictions of Means's calls for U.S. national unity and tribal sovereignty—and it does so through an act of historical reference in triplicate: calling to mind the initial arrival of Europeans in the Americas that began in the late fifteenth century, the late nineteenth-century resistance to United States territorial consolidation, and of course the attack on the United States in the early twenty-first century with its attendant calls for national unity. It is entirely unclear which of these historical moments should take precedence and govern the interpretation of the others, and the irony of the juxtaposition of slogan and image is that these historical events are not represented in a recognizable pattern of linear causation that would clarify the relationships among them. (Elliott 2006:1001)

The T-shirt inverts the flag's temporality. When American flags were displayed by native individuals following 9/11, the message conveyed was that American Indians were willing to put the colonial violence of the past *behind them* during America's time of need in the present. The message of the T-shirt, in contrast, is that contemporary problems can only be meaningfully dealt with if the past stands *before us* as an acknowledged part of the present and future.

As archaeologists, our challenge is to explore how certain pre-Columbian things—no less than the flags and T-shirts of today—periodically became matters of deep concern. We have seen how Pueblo doings asserted particular configurations of the world. How, then, were these configurations challenged, opposed, and reconceived? How did competing networks—competing understandings of the cosmos—rub up against one another as doings gave rise to counter-doings? Asking such

Figure 6.1. "Homeland Security" T-shirt. Courtesy of West Wind World.

questions forces us to pay special attention to the dissonance between, on one hand, the cosmic unity so often asserted in doings and, on the other, the social-disunity doings sometimes bred.

A good example of this is found in the themes of gender balance and complementarity that seem to have been promoted in the doings at early fourteenth-century T'aitöna. As south balanced north and agriculture balanced hunting, so did koyes balance kivas and women balance men—a key observation of the previous chapter. But it would be naive to conclude that T'aitöna was therefore an enlightened space of fully equitable gender relations. The discourse of equality is always more complicated than this, frequently harboring structural inequalities that can be pronounced in daily practice. All Pueblo communities, for instance, emphasize the nonhierarchical equivalency of women and men, and yet there are aspects of this balance that are quite unbalanced. It is not just that the doings in which gender symmetry is asserted are almost entirely orchestrated by men. At a basic level, the very ontology of Pueblo personhood uses balance to inscribe imbalance. Consider that, at Taos, women are referred to as "our mother" while the male priests are referred to as "our father our mother" (Parsons 1936:36), or that, among the Tewas, initiations were designed to "bring the girls to womanhood and the boys to *manhood and womanhood*" (Ortiz 1969:42, emphasis added; see also Babcock 1988:373; Fowles 2006). When confronted with such patterns, are we to conclude that we have struck upon another expression of gender symmetry within the category of maleness, or are we to point instead to the asymmetry between the singularity of women and the apparent dual personhood of men? When we learn that there are both male katsina and female katsina at Zuni, should we focus on this spiritual balance, or should we point to the fact that it is still the men who impersonate both in ceremonial dramas (Tedlock 1983:98)?

My point is that doings leave ample room for disagreement. Indeed, doings would hardly be worth doing if they did not assert a contestable agenda of some sort. Again, the question of power lies in precisely how the world is gathered together. It lies in the particular relations that are established. It lies in exactly how people and things are to be balanced. So let us put the stale notion of "ritual as social integration" behind us and move on to the far more challenging matter of how we are to locate agenda, dissent, and debate in the archaeological record. How are we to see doings as a discourse of power at pre-Columbian T'aitöna?

I intend to examine this in two ways. First, I will briefly return to the matter of scale, but now with an eye toward how *decreases* in overall community size—a neglected subject—can be read as evidence of emigration and how emigration, in turn, can be read as evidence of dissension. Second, I will explore certain doings at T'aitöna that fall outside the more or less "invariant sequences of formal acts and utterances," regarded by Rappaport (1999:24) and most archaeologists as the sine qua non of religious ritual. Many of T'aitöna's doings were fleeting, discontinued shortly after their introduction, and I will argue that in grappling with the brevity or even the non-occurrence of these doings, we learn much about the broader negotiations in the community at large.

Those Who Walk Away

The matter of population scale is again critical, both as an on-the-ground reality for past communities and because attempts to model changing population numbers reveal a great deal about our interpretive biases in the present. Much of the previous chapter challenged the manner in which archaeologists draw causal connections between scalar increase and social transformation, and those arguments need not be rehearsed. We can build upon that discussion, however, by noting that whereas population *increase* has been explicitly theorized within archaeology, population *decrease* has received comparatively little attention.

How are we to understand this disparity? Why has scalar stress come to be treated as a systemic condition that uniquely occurs when communities swell in size, as if the loss of significant numbers of people somehow necessarily reduces the overall level of stress? Is it not self-evident that too few can be just as stressful as too many, particularly when we humanize our numbers and acknowledge that certain individuals often hold irreplaceable knowledge and abilities? Why, in the end, should we be more interested in growth than decline?

Archaeology's nearly singular attention to scalar growth has Malthusian foundations. Increase, by definition, is naturalized, and reductions in scale tend to be regarded as abnormalities or deviations from the norm. During the twentieth century, this bias became institutionalized in a tradition of evolutionary thought that narrowly sought to explain the movement of political formations from small to large, simple to complex. Movements in the opposite direction were occasionally acknowledged, particularly when archaeologists grappled with the ruins of large ancient population centers in regions that subsequently were characterized by smaller and less centralized systems. But reductions in scale were almost always stigmatized as "collapses" or "failures"—devolutionary falls from the true and proper course of civilization's progress. Like a capitalist's ledger slipping from black to red, reductions in scale were to be pitied. Consequently, decrease has only rarely been viewed as the result of deliberate acts.

This intellectual background is essential to understanding a long-held archaeological misconception in the ancestral Northern Tiwa region. Taos archaeology, like that of so many other parts of the American Southwest, has been driven by investigation into the emergence of sizable aggregated settlements, which are widely regarded as marking the consummation of the Neolithic revolution and a major evolutionary advance. Thus the village of T'aitöna has received a half century of excavation, while smaller hamlets both have seen less work and have been fitted into an overarching narrative of growth that climaxed in the large communities encountered by the Spanish. This is understandable. Generally speaking, the local sequence certainly has progressed from isolated hunter-gatherer camps, to dispersed pithouse residences, to clustered small pueblos, to large autonomous villages. And as I suggested in the previous chapter, this process of assembly into densely packed aggregates must be regarded as a social phenomenon full of power and cosmic reverberations. The problem, however, is that past research has assumed that this progressive increase in population *density* was directly paralleled by an increase in community *scale*.

Patricia Crown and colleagues (1996), in fact, went so far as to construct a population graph that depicted a steady increase in community scale over the course of village aggregation in the Taos area. Their graph was intended only as an initial guess, derived from neither existing survey data nor explicit modeling of pre-aggregation population levels. I subsequently looked into this issue in greater detail, drawing together the results of past surveys in the Rio Grande del Rancho drainage (the major drainage in which T'aitöna is located), seriating the ceramics found at each site, and developing predictive models for the presence of unknown sites on land that is either inaccessible or disturbed by modern construction. The details are described elsewhere (Fowles 2004:appendix D). Here, let me simply stress that the results were surprising and led to a very different population reconstruction.

Indeed, once different settlement sizes, site life spans, and phase durations are all taken into consideration, two conclusions become clear. First, the largest population in the Rio Grande del Rancho drainage was probably not at fourteenth-century T'aitöna but earlier, at the beginning of the thirteenth century. The population increase during this period appears to have resulted from the arrival of a new wave

Table 6.1.
Population Estimates for the Rio Grande del Rancho Drainage, 1050–1320 CE

	Low estimate (families of 4)	Medium estimate (families of 5)	High estimate (families of 6)
Dispersed pithouse settlements (Valdez Phase, 1050–1190 CE)	310	387	464
Clustered small pueblos (Pot Creek Phase, 1190–1260 CE)	467	583	700
Aggregated village (Talpa Phase, 1260–1320 CE	352	440	528

Source: Fowles 2004:915.

of immigrants from the west—the Summer People, as discussed in chapter 4—who quickly established a relatively dense cluster of more than twenty-four unit pueblos[3] in a forty-hectare area just north of what would later become the site of T'aitöna (see figure 4.8). The second conclusion, related to the first, is that when the settlements of the drainage eventually did coalesce further into a single fortified village during the late thirteenth century, the overall population notably *decreased* (table 6.1). Put bluntly, the final and most marked phase of aggregation was characterized by an overall *reduction* in community scale.

These data are important in part because they complicate the simple gathering-of-the-clans narrative that has traditionally governed archaeological interpretations of aggregation in the Taos region and elsewhere. Too often we assume that newly established villages would have had a self-evident allure, a centripetal gravity that would have drawn in all those scattered families who previously languished in isolation, quietly longing for a proper Neolithic life. Perhaps there was a "bright lights, big city" appeal to villages in some respects, but we should not blind ourselves to the likelihood that many early aggregated settlements also had a decidedly centrifugal aspect. Recall the Taos origin story and the words of the father of the Summer People, announcing the coming of aggregation in the wake of the conquest of the Winter People: "Now we are as one family. If you desire, come to where I live. We will have summer and we will also have winter." Let us focus on the phrase "if you desire" and ask whether a new village like T'aitöna would have been regarded as desirable and, if so, by whom.

Surely the descendants of the Winter People conquered a generation prior might have had legitimate reservations. Others might as well. After all, any labor-saving benefits accrued from group living would have already been present prior to the establishment of T'aitöna. The early thirteenth-century unit pueblos, or extended-family households, of the Rio Grande del Rancho valley were all situated within easy yelling distance of one another. Children could have been jointly watched. Neighbors could have been quickly called upon to help with communal tasks. Why, then, vacate this semi-aggregated cluster of pueblos to live on top of one another in a single architectonic complex with rigidly specified orientations and centralized facilities? Defensive concerns must always be considered, but as I have already emphasized, the move to T'aitöna was also a profound and highly conscious cosmological project that reassembled the social realm and each individual's position within it. Which is to say that T'aitöna marked the emergence of a new world order orchestrated by a set of individuals who were newly giving orders. And I take it as axiomatic that every new set of orders sooner or later is challenged by those who are unwilling to obey by those who prefer to live in a different sort of cosmos with a different distribution of power and authority.

This is why the evidence of population decline during the shift to aggregated village life is so significant. It points to the likelihood that many did oppose the social restructuring that was under way at T'aitöna. Indeed, when population trajectories are rigorously quantified in other parts of the northern Rio Grande, similar patterns are found—for instance, on the Pajarito Plateau where residential aggregation also occurred during a period of overall population decline (Orcutt 1999b; Ruscavage-Barz 1999). It takes little effort to imagine the stories of those who packed their belongings and moved out. The colonial history of the Southwest is full of comparable examples in which Pueblo families threw off the yoke of Spanish oppression by voting with their feet. Some residents of Taos Pueblo, for instance, sought to escape their new masters during the mid-seventeenth century by traveling eastward into modern-day Kansas to join the Apaches. Members of Picurís Pueblo did the same in 1696. Both tribes were forcibly rounded up by the Spanish and eventually returned to their villages. In other cases, the physical move away from undesirable social contexts led to more permanent relocations. Many members of the modern Navajo Nation are said to be the descendants of dissidents who left Hopi and Zuni generations ago. The emigration of both individuals and groups is a deep-seated Pueblo strategy of managing disagreement.

T'aitöna may have been a dense, centralized village, but it also appears to have housed a somewhat smaller total population than the earlier dispersed communities in the region, and this scalar reduction should raise basic questions regarding public discord, dissidence, and why some early occupants of the region sought alternative lifestyles elsewhere. The challenge taken up in the remainder of this chapter, then, is to sift through the archaeological record with these issues squarely at the forefront. My goal is to unearth not only evidence of new institutions, organizations, and practices but also the opposition these innovations would have engendered. What might have prompted some families to walk away? What might have led those who stayed to disagree? And how might such disagreements have figured in the speedy dismantling of the community at T'aitöna after a mere three generations?

To address these questions, I will focus on an unlikely subject: the Northern Tiwa katsina tradition, which is unlikely precisely because, according to archaeological orthodoxy, the Northern Tiwas never had a katsina tradition. As we will see, however, the historical engagement with the katsina spirits at T'aitöna and at later Northern Tiwa settlements was much more complicated than previous anthropologists have acknowledged. I will argue paradoxically that the very non-presence of katsina icons in the region can be read as evidence of how important and widely contested the katsina were, not unlike the way flags and T-shirts are contested in the region today.

Katsina as Matters of Concern

At the start of the fourteenth century, the Pueblo world was undergoing important changes. Long-distance migrations left much of the northern Southwest vacant, and most ancestral Pueblo families were actively converging on a shrinking number of geographic zones, notably the Rio Grande valley, the Hopi mesas, and the Zuni district. Within these densely populated areas, large autonomous villages were rapidly becoming the only viable residential options, as individuals sought both new economies of scale and new defensive strategies emphasizing strength in numbers. Accompanying these developments were new schemes for charting the relationships between people, things, and spirits. Moieties, clans, kiva groups, medicine societies, war societies, and more were all implicated in these new relationships, but archaeologists have traditionally given special attention to the institutions and practices that developed around humans' engagement with a set of nonhuman beings known as the katsina. Many, in fact, have elevated katsina institutions and practices to the status of a separate "cult" or "religion," and this, in itself, is quite striking insofar as no one to my knowledge has ever suggested the presence of a medicine cult or a moiety religion among the ancestral Pueblos. The "katsina religion," then, has a special categorical status that deserves critical examination.

In contemporary Pueblo thought, the katsina are powerful agents who confer blessings and serve as intermediaries between humans and the higher gods. They are widely known, superficially at least, to outsiders because the katsina occasionally make public appearances, dancing in their ornate masks as part of elaborate doings that were once the target of violent Catholic reforms but that are now embraced as marketable icons in the Southwestern tourist industry (figure 6.2). During the twentieth century, many katsina dances at Hopi and Zuni were open to non-native visitors. Few remain open today, and most travelers now encounter katsina solely in the form of doll-like replicas on the shelves of Arizona truckstops, tucked between pink coyotes, plastic bow-and-arrow sets, and other "gen-u-ine Indian souvenirs" made in China. Regardless, in the eyes of both scholars and tourists, the katsina have emerged as the dominant outward look of Pueblo religion.

Katsina bring outsiders to the pueblos, but from a native perspective they are more significant as the bringers of rain and ecological prosperity. At a conceptual level, they are so closely linked with rainfall that the words used to refer to katsina

Figure 6.2. "Rain Katcinas at Walpi" (from Fewkes 1922:492-1, pl. 1).

are the same as those used to refer to clouds, cloud people, and storm clouds (Anderson 1951:1066–1070). This is not to say they are entirely benevolent. The power to bring rain is inseparable from the power to withhold it, and control over the world's fertility is always accompanied by the implicit threat of wreaking environmental havoc when they are displeased. To the extent that katsina are regarded as clouds, they are also regarded as lightning—with all the destructive potential this implies. Not surprisingly, a strong case has been made for a symbolic association between katsina and warfare, particularly during late pre-Columbian times (Plog and Solometo 1997; Schaafsma 2000). The katsina, in short, are complex, multivalent, and at times capricious beings with the ability both to bring life and to take it away.

From an iconographic perspective, the most distinctive characteristic of the katsina is that they are *masked* beings, and most scholars have accepted the mask as a signature element of the tradition as a whole (notably, Adams 1991). Indeed, it is only by tracking the presence of mask icons that archaeologists have been able to make compelling claims about the origin and spread of the katsina tradition prior to the colonial period. During the fourteenth century, in the context of significant demographic reorganization, mask iconography began to appear throughout the Southwest in a variety of media (rock art, murals, painted ceramics), marking for most scholars the beginning of a true "religious" movement. Whether these early mask icons should be interpreted as evidence that actual ceremonial masks were in regular use before the arrival of the Spanish is unclear. Be that as it may, physical masks fashioned out of leather, paint, fibers, seeds, and a variety of other materials have been central to katsina doings since at least the early colonial period. While the katsina serve as intermediaries connecting humans with the high gods, masks negotiate the boundaries between humans and the katsina. When a mask is donned, the wearer becomes a medium for that katsina; the katsina is present. The archaeological focus on the mask icon, then, makes good sense.

The mask also helps us see why the katsina, like many of the other so-called religious phenomena we have looked at, are better understood as Pueblo doings, for we encounter the same characteristically elaborate meditation on the interconnectedness of things. Indeed, as material objects, katsina masks gather together whole worlds no less than do the pipes and kiva floor assemblages discussed in chapter 5. Once again, substance matters, building worldly connections sympathetically. Just as the clay used in the construction of a pipe was moistened with human sweat at Taos, for instance, the paint for a Hopi katsina mask was necessarily moistened with human saliva that had been specially produced by chewing watermelon seeds. Seeds are the stuff of regeneration and growth, and through sensuous contact transmitted via saliva, masks became linked to these ecological processes. In some cases, seeds were literally brought into the mask, as when the katsina's eyes were constructed of deer hide sewn around a mass of seeds (Kennard 1938:9). Cotton was also sometimes placed in the katsina's eyes, further linking the mask both to the agricultural landscape and, mimetically, to the cottony nimbostratus clouds that bring water to the fields. Again, the connection between katsina and clouds—at once conceptual and material—is especially profound. At Hopi, the katsina are said to travel as clouds from the San Francisco peaks down to the mesas on which the contemporary villages are perched, before continuing their descent into the Grand Canyon where they pass through the sipapuni into the underworld. Like vapor trails left behind by jet airplanes, the katsina's movements inscribe paths of communication onto the cosmos, outlining relationships between mountain, mesa, and canyon, between sky and earth, and between the upper world of humans and the lower world of spirits.

A similar focus on connective pathways surrounds the treatment of katsina masks within the village. During Shalako ceremonies at Zuni, for instance, roads of cornmeal are laid out before the masks to materialize the routes of the spirits' approach and departure (Tedlock 1983). As we have seen, the interconnectedness of the world is not taken for granted in Pueblo doings; it is given explicit material form.

Networks are literally drawn upon the ground. This is what distinguishes doings from everyday practice.

But the networks that katsina masks bring into focus are not beyond debate. On one level, access to masks asserts a particular set of democratic social relationships. At Hopi, for instance, all adult village members have the right to participate in katsina dances and to possess their own katsina masks. In this sense, masking reinforces nonhierarchical human connections within the community, and this stands in contradiction to the many non-katsina doings that are secretive, tightly controlled, and designed to reproduce hierarchical relations between particular clans and households (Bernardini and Fowles 2011). On another level, however, katsina masks trace their own hierarchies. Common dance masks, for instance, are distinguished from the much more carefully guarded masks of the *mon*, or priest, katsina, which possess special powers and are owned by particular Hopi and Zuni clans (Cole 1989:314–315). And even if dance masks establish democratic relations among the men of a given community, they simultaneously distinguish initiated adults from the not-yet-initiated youths, as well as the initiated men from uninitiable women in the case of those villages where women are excluded from katsina doings. There are always two sides to a mask: an inside inhabited by those who know certain secrets and an outside inhabited by those who either do not know or must pretend they do not know.

Over the past century the katsina mask has come to stand for another, very different set of relations between Pueblo communities and Western tourists through the production and sale of masked katsina dolls. Here, too, the katsina have emerged as a contested matter of concern for many Pueblo people who oppose the commodification of their cultural property and the Western appropriation of native icons. As Leigh Kuwanwisiwma (2001) observes, the repeated Hopi calls to prohibit the sale of masked katsina dolls conflict with the economic realities of many native artisans who are financially dependent on the tourist trade. Interestingly, the one instance when the Hopi tribal council did reach consensus and intervened to prohibit the sale of katsina dolls was when a native artist began to carve dolls with removable masks (Kuwanwisiwma 2001:18). Mask removal is central to katsina society initiations—it is an emotionally charged moment of ceremonial unveiling that is constitutive of a new social status for katsina society neophytes—and the idea that non-Pueblo people would be able to playfully participate in this initiatory act was perceived as so severe an affront that it justified a formal iconographic prohibition.

Capitalism may have added new wrinkles to human-object relationships in the Pueblo world, but it is difficult to believe that something as significant as a katsina mask would not have engendered pre-Columbian debates as well, particularly during the late thirteenth and fourteenth centuries when villages across the Southwest had to decide whether and how to adopt mask iconography and the tangle of new social relationships that it brought into being. Of course, the deep legacy of functionalist analysis often gets in the way; many Southwestern archaeologists still implicitly assume that "religious rituals" in premodern tribal societies necessarily promoted social integration and so would have been essentially beyond debate. Thus, when evidence of katsina doings is found, it is generally assumed that all the icons, practices, and organizational structures involved would have been naturally welcomed into the local community with open arms. In contrast, when katsina doings are found to be absent, the local community tends to be regarded as regrettably marginal, as suffering from a lack of cultural elements that would have otherwise benefited them. Lekson and Cameron, for instance, have suggested that thirteenth-century communities in the Mesa Verde region were denied access to katsina ceremonialism by their far northerly location, and they contend that it was this cultural isolation that ultimately led Mesa Verde villages to fail. "Aggregation at Mesa Verde," they write, "failed in part because it lacked social mechanisms, such as kachina ceremonialism, that allowed aggregation to succeed elsewhere, and immigration out of the Mesa Verde area was one result" (Lekson and Cameron 1995:193).

This bears directly on our understanding of T'aitöna and its doings, insofar as scholars have always agreed that the most significant exceptions to the otherwise pan-Pueblo distribution of the katsina tradition at the time of Spanish contact were the two Northern Tiwa–speaking villages, Taos and Picurís. Twentieth-century ethnographers reported that evidence of the katsina "all but disappears" among the Northern Tiwas, "since there is here little objective observance of the cult, and only the rudimentary conceptual background" (Anderson 1955:404–405). Both Taos and Picurís were reported as lacking masked dances, katsina societies, and formal katsina initiations (Parsons 1936, 1939, 1996b[1939]), an observation that was bolstered and given temporal depth by ethnohistoric studies. Drawing upon mid-seventeenth-century Spanish documents, Schaafsma and Schaafsma (1974:543) concluded that the Northern Tiwas were the *only* Pueblo group among whom katsina doings were not strongly present in early historic times, and the presumed absence of mask iconography in the Taos archaeological record seemed to solidify that this was also the case well into pre-Columbian times. The alleged katsinalessness of the Northern Tiwas has thus received widespread consensus (e.g., Adams 1991; Hays 1994; McGuire 1995; Schaafsma 1994; Schaafsma and Schaafsma 1974).

How are we to understand such a phenomenon? Archaeologists, it would seem, are poorly equipped to query the meaning of absences like the lack of katsina masks in the Taos region. By disciplinary mandate, we are methodological materialists, committed to the study of things, as many have emphasized. Indeed, whatever one may think of the manifestos of those who now assert that "archaeology is THE discipline of things" (Shanks 2010, emphasis in original) or that archaeologists are "the most dedicated students of things" (Olsen 2010:2), it is nevertheless the case that our dedication to present things has gone hand in hand with a pervasive blindness to the significance and impact of that which was not present (Fowles 2008, 2010b; Fowles and Heupel forthcoming). Give us an assemblage of ceramic vessels painted with masked figures and we will have much to say. Take such objects away, leave us with an absence to grapple with, and we are at a loss. Confronted with the katsinalessness of the Northern Tiwas—confronted, that is, with the absence of mask icons in rock art, ceramics, and murals as well as the absence of masked dances historically—we tend to shrug our shoulders and dismiss the question with the tautological conclusion that the katsina tradition simply never "spread" (the language used is inevitably diffusionist) into the northeastern corner of the Pueblo world. The absence is not interrogated further. At most, it is chalked up to the ignorance, disinterest, or developmental lag of a local community that was "really very much off the beaten track of Pueblo culture," as Fox (1967:10) once described the Northern Tiwas.[4]

Needless to say, this will not do. Doings become matters of concern precisely because they can disappear, precisely because they can be lost, forgotten, rejected, or fundamentally transformed into other sorts of doings. Thus, we should give equal analytical weight to both the presence and the absence of doings, and this requires that we start with different premises. First, we must follow Lekson's (2009) wise entreaty that Southwestern archaeology push aside the presumed parochialism of ancestral Pueblo communities and instead build from the assumption that "everyone knew everything," or at least that major regional exchange centers like Taos and Picurís would have surely known something about the katsina doings being performed by their trade partners a short distance away. Second, we must accept from the start that absences—no less than presences—can be the product of intentional design and active human construction. That is, if the Northern Tiwas did not make masks, we must allow the possibility that their nonproduction was as much an act of agency as their neighbors' production of masks.

The Missing Masks

The question of the Northern Tiwas' relationship to katsina doings is even more complicated than I have let on. Ethnographic evidence does suggest that the absence of masks and masked dances has been a dominant pattern at Taos and Picurís in recent centuries, but this is not to say that the Northern Tiwas lack conceptions of the katsina as powerful agents. Both Parsons's and Stevenson's early twentieth-century research at Taos Pueblo reveal a deep belief in, and reverence for, the katsina that is little appreciated by those who summarily conclude that the "cult" was absent. As elsewhere in the Pueblo world, the Northern Tiwa pueblos regarded the katsina as rainmaking spirits.[5] While Stevenson's informants at Taos Pueblo were explicit about their recognition of a supreme being known as Kwathlowúna, the katsina were presented as critical intermediaries who carried out the orders of Kwathlowúna, particularly in climatological matters. In this proximate sense, the Taos katsina were the beings "from whom all good things come" (Ellis 1974[1962]:141; Parsons 1936:109). Of course, evidence also exists that the katsina's power elicited, at times, a certain amount of human trepidation. "When Kwathlowúna knows that the people in this world are neglecting their duties to the gods he instructs...[the katsina] to punish the people by showering hail upon their land and so cut the vegetation to pieces" (Stevenson 1906–1907:file 2.6).

In her discussion of the Taos katsina, Parsons (1936:109–110) concluded that they were "*not* the dead; that is, not the ordinary dead," but on this subject she was unable to learn much at all.[6] In contrast, Stevenson's (1906–1907:file 2.6) earlier notes indicated a much deeper conceptual tie between deceased community members and the katsina, which was related to the moiety division between north and south, winter and summer:

> The deceased Taos people become, after death, the rain makers, except the Winter People who send the snows and cold rains.... The hail is secured by the Ice [or Winter] People[7] from their great snow fields above the heavens. The Ice People of this world become the snow makers. The Summer People have nothing to do with making snow or hail, and have nothing whatever to do with the great snow fields.... The Summer People of this world sing songs both for summer and winter, and likewise the Winter People sing songs for winter and summer. (Stevenson 1906–1907: file 2.6)

It appears, then, that the moiety system of the living was replicated among the dead—that is, among the katsina. Indeed, there are some grounds for thinking that the deceased leaders of the winter, or northside, moiety became "winter katsina," bringers of snow and hail, while those of the summer, or southside, moiety became "summer katsina," bringers of rain. We know, for instance, that two named groups at Taos Pueblo appear to have been responsible for the organization of doings vis-à-vis the two types of katsina. The first and more prominent of the two groups was the Water People, a leading sodality within the southside moiety with known ties to katsina-related symbols (Parsons 1936:115). A second group, the Big Hail People, also appears to have had strong katsina connections. In contrast to the Water People, the Big Hail People were led by members of the northside moiety, and the group's principal responsibilities centered on the prayers for winter snow held during the forty days beginning at the end of November (Parsons 1996b[1939]:934), as well as prayers for avoiding hailstorms in the spring (Stevenson 1906–1907:file 3.1). They did so by appealing to the "hail people of the heavens," which appears to be a Northern Tiwa katsina variant that was woven into the moiety division between north and south, winter (hail/snow) and summer (water).

I should emphasize that, as anthropologists, we remain largely ignorant of the indigenous conception of the Northern Tiwa cosmos as we do of most Northern Tiwa doings. Unlike the Hopi, Zuni, Acoma, and Tewa pueblos, Taos Pueblo has always presented a unified front in vigorous opposition to the ethnographic gaze, successfully protecting its esoteric knowledge to an impressive degree, and it would be absurd for any outsider to assert authoritative knowledge of the Northern Tiwas in this respect. My goal is modest: merely to acknowledge that local katsina conceptions do indeed exist and appear to be quite deeply felt. Certain details might be added, perhaps. The Taos katsina seem to be connected to an array of specific doings—from personal offerings of prayer feathers in agricultural fields to enlist the katsina's support in bringing rain (Stevenson 1906–1907:file 2.4), to more group-oriented practices, such as when village members collectively gave cornmeal, corn pollen, and turkey feathers to the katsina at the completion of the yearly irrigation ditch cleaning (Parsons 1936:95). Even the annual pilgrimage to Blue Lake was undertaken, according to Parsons's (1936:100) informant, "to worship gods called *łachina* (*łatsina*), the ones that send all what they get." These details, however, merely gesture toward a hidden depth of katsina conceptions that appropriately remain off-limits to outsiders.

Regardless, with whatever confidence we can say that the Northern Tiwa katsina—as worldly agents and the subjects of doings—were *present*, we can say with equal confidence that the Northern Tiwa katsina—as masked, impersonated, and highly materialized images—were conspicuously *absent*. Since at least the seventeenth century, the Northern Tiwas appear to have held back from participation in the more visible and dramatic aspects of katsina doings as performed at other pueblos. There is no local tradition of mask production, mask maintenance, or katsina impersonation through mask wearing. Even in the case of those Northern Tiwa dances that were "about" the katsina, such as the Turtle Dance at Taos (Parsons 1936:109) or the Basket Dance at Picurís (Parsons 1939:219), ethnographers have never witnessed masks being worn, and there is no evidence that katsina impersonation was ever the explicit goal of the dancers. Moreover, there was little differentiation of Northern Tiwa katsina beyond seasonal and gender lines. Absent was the vast multiplicity of named and visually distinct katsina personalities found at Hopi and Zuni (Parsons 1936:109–110).

Whether this situation was always the case in the past is unclear. In 1907 one native informant from another Rio Grande pueblo told Stevenson:

> I visited *Topoliyakwi* (Taos) when I was a young man.... I saw the *Topoliyakwi* dance in masks much like the *Muluktakia*—blue green faces. They danced in line as we do. There were twenty-five or thirty dancers. The bodies [unclear word] were nude except [for] kilts of beautiful white deer skins held on with [unclear word] and belts. The lower part[s] of their legs were painted white. The upper limits of bodies were painted red. They wore moccasins. They wore moccasins colored red. I remained at Taos three days going on the fourth to Picuris. I saw the masked dance one night. They did not dance in plaza but in *kinisi*.[8] They danced only in the night. (Stevenson 1906–1907:file 1.22)

This statement was made by an outsider recalling long past visits to Taos and Picurís, so we should approach it skeptically. However, some twenty-five years later, Parsons was also told by a native of Taos that the Black Eyes People previously owned two masks made of buffalo hides with flat faces and erect horns. One of these masks had been lost generations earlier. "The other mask," she was told, "is no longer worn, at least publicly. It is considered exceedingly precious. These masks were kept in the mountains in charge of the Water People" (Parsons 1936:76). A similar situation was reported at Picurís.

If we accept the testimony of Parsons's informant, the Northern Tiwa masks were not only precious, but also dangerous objects that were secluded far away from the community and only displayed on rare occasions. New masks were not made. When asked if katsina images were ever used more generally, Parsons's informant only offered the vague comment that "[d]uring the rain calling ceremonies, on the wall of an inner room of his house, a man might chalk a *Ła'tsina*" (1936:110). Presumably, this ephemeral image was erased soon thereafter. Such scattered comments suggest that katsina images, what few the Northern Tiwas had, were things to be hidden away in the mountains, secreted in back rooms, or obscured by a veil of darkness.

How are we to understand such ethnographic evidence, scattered though it is? How are we to interpret the presence of katsina conceptions among the Northern Tiwas and yet the absence of certain key doings—notably, masked dances—that elsewhere lay at the heart of the tradition? How did this pattern come about?

Parsons, the only ethnographer to give serious consideration to such questions, offered two possibilities. The first was that what katsina belief did exist at Taos was a late introduction, presumably during the colonial period, that was adopted to handle the initiation of boys when the traditional war organization broke down. The relative youth of the local katsina tradition, then, could explain its supposed lack of complexity. "The other hypothesis for the meagerness of the kachina cult at Taos," the one Parsons found more compelling, was that it represented "the original cult which came to be highly developed in the western pueblos but remained unchanged at Taos" (Parsons 1936:115). Here, the suggestion was that Taos preserved a primitive or primordial version of the katsina tradition characterized by early pan-Pueblo conceptions that never evolved into the full "cult" with its emphasis on the impersonation of masked beings. Following this line of reasoning, the Northern Tiwas might be viewed as evolutionarily equivalent to, say, Zuni communities at about 1200 CE, at least as far as katsina doings were concerned.

Historical matters of this sort have never been the ethnographer's strong suit. History rarely flows smoothly toward the present, and developmental trajectories cannot be altogether retrodicted from their outcomes. Of course, archaeologists, for their part, are often guilty of simplifying the past to conform to their deep-seated assumptions about how events should unfold. But to the extent that their accounts are empirically bound up in material remains, there is always the possibility that the archaeologist's historical assumptions, no matter how seemingly self-evident, will be dislodged and challenged.

Just such a challenge came in the 1960s when a single sherd bearing a katsina mask image was unearthed at T'aitöna (figure 6.3C). The sherd is significant for four reasons. First, the image is extraordinarily clear; with its goggle eyes and upturned horn it easily fits into the iconographic repertoire of contemporary katsina masks at Hopi and Zuni (Schaafsma 1994:69). Second, it is surprisingly early. As Hays

(1994:57) observes, "it is the only kachina depiction on Rio Grande pottery that clearly dates earlier than AD 1320" (but see below), and so this single specimen establishes that many iconic elements of the katsina tradition were in place by the start of the fourteenth century. Third, there is no question that the sherd was produced using local Taos clays; it was not, in other words, created elsewhere and then imported into the Northern Tiwa area.[9] Fourth, this means that one of the earliest and clearest examples of katsina mask imagery known in the Southwest was painted on a bowl in the very region that the katsina tradition, according to ethnographic orthodoxy, never reached. Such is the power of the single sherd, for it alone renders both of Parsons's ethnographically based theories implausible. The Northern Tiwas' encounter with the katsina was neither late nor rudimentary, and this raises a new possibility: rather than a consequence of geographic isolation or developmental slowness, perhaps the absence of explicit mask iconography in more recent times resulted from an active prohibition or rejection of such images in the past.

I have explored this possibility further through extended study of the local ceramic and rock art imagery, consulting thousands of pre-Columbian sherds housed at the Fort Burgwin Research Center (Fowles 2004:847–888) and hundreds of rock art panels as part of an ongoing survey of the Rio Grande gorge just to the west of Taos. The results of this research measurably expand our understanding of the early katsina iconography of the Northern Tiwas. To begin with, I have located three additional sherds decorated with what appear to be katsina mask icons, all produced using local clays. The earliest depicts a blackened visage with a toothy mouth and feather-like extensions on the top of the head, characteristics that solidly situate the image within the broader katsina iconographic tradition (figure 6.3A). Surprisingly, it was found on the surface of a late eleventh- or twelfth-century pueblo (TA69) a short distance north of T'aitöna, making it one of the earliest known katsina masks in the Southwest. The two other locally produced sherds are more ambiguous. One sherd discovered during excavations at LA 102073 (TA25, Archuleta Site), an early thirteenth-century pueblo near T'aitöna (Fowles 2004:374–380), appears to depict a blackened visage with hair or feather extensions but lacking a mouth (figure 6.3B). The icon was painted just below the rim of a bowl and was accompanied on its left by a zigzag line, a probable lightning motif that strengthens the icon's association with the katsina tradition. The remaining example was excavated from the upper levels at T'aitöna and so can be chronologically placed somewhere between CE 1260 and 1320 (figure 6.3D). The paint is faint, as is common for the local pottery of the time, and the icon is only partially present. Nevertheless, a circular mask with two pupil-less goggle eyes and feather-like extensions from the top of the head appear to be present.

While sherds can be positioned chronologically but often present us with partial imagery, the situation is reversed with rock art, which typically offers rich iconographic detail but only ambiguous temporal indications. Rock art has been produced in the ancestral Northern Tiwa region for many millennia, almost exclusively on the basalt boulders that are exposed in great abundance along the Rio Grande and its

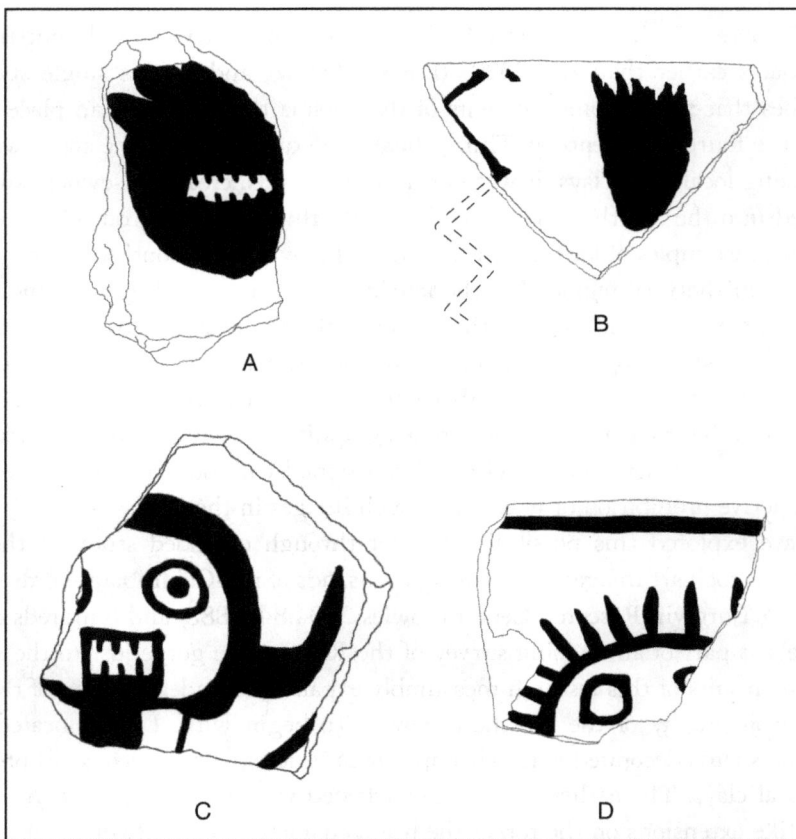

Figure 6.3. Katsina or katsina-like sherds from the Rio Grande del Rancho drainage.
A = Kwahe'e B/W (var. Taos), TA69; B = Santa Fe B/W (var. Taos), LA 80504; C, D =
Santa Fe B/W (var. Taos), T'aitöna.

tributaries. As such, it cannot be linked directly with T'aitöna or any other ancestral
Northern Tiwa settlements, all of which are located a short distance to the east where
the immediately occurring rocks (primarily sandstone, quartzite, and granite) were
poorly suited for rock art production. Nevertheless, it is significant that twenty katsina mask petroglyphs have been located at sites that are well within the traditional
territory of Taos Pueblo (figures 6.4 and 6.5).

A number of the katsina masks in the Taos rock art tradition have parallels
among the masks painted on local black-on-white bowls at T'aitöna. Again, we
see upturned horns, feather-like extensions from the top of the head, the presence
of both blackened and unblackened faces, and the association of masks with zigzag or lightning glyphs. Some of the rock art images, on the other hand, do not
have ceramic parallels but display similarities with katsina icons among the Western Pueblos. Unfortunately, it is impossible to say exactly when these images were
produced. Most, however, have a moderate degree of patina development over their

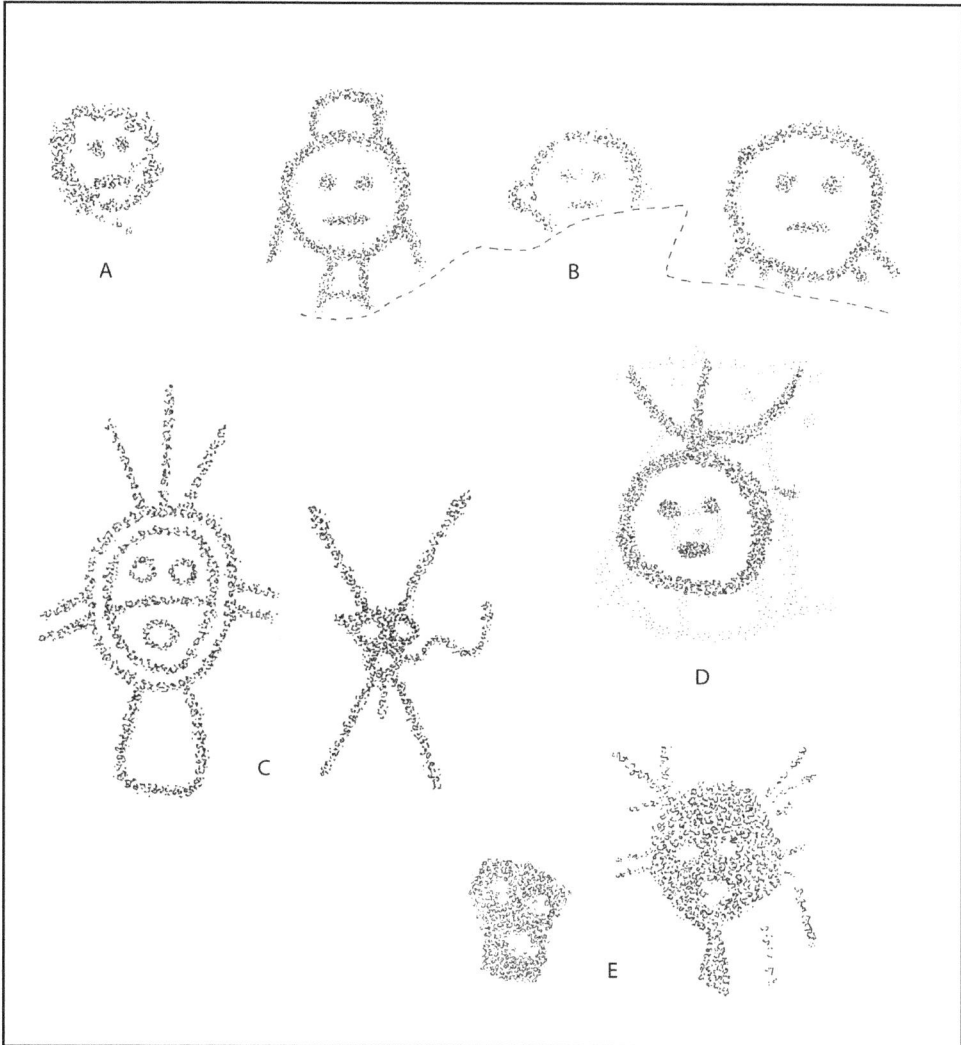

Figure 6.4. Katsina petroglyphs in the Rio Grande gorge, near Taos. A = 2008-8; B = 2010-95; C = 2008-442; D = 2009-6T; E = 2009-127.

pecked icons, indicating a certain antiquity. In the case of one panel (figure 6.4B), the mask icons not only displayed a moderate degree of repatination but also were partially buried beneath a natural accumulation of sediment, implying that they are older than most other Pueblo glyphs in the region.

Did the ancestral Northern Tiwas produce these images? In discussing the matter with colleagues, I have heard a number of regional specialists argue that Tewas or other foreign individuals must have pecked the glyphs while traveling in the Taos area. Surely it was not the Northern Tiwas, they say. However, this is only a reasonable position if one has already accepted the alleged katsinalessness of the

Figure 6.5. Katsina petroglyphs in the Rio Grande gorge, near Taos. A = 2009-6E; B = 2009-6R; C = 2009-6A; D = 2009-6N; E = 2009-6H.

Northern Tiwas as given, and this is the assumption that I am placing in question. Indeed, insofar as these images are both located solidly within Taos Pueblo's traditional territory and display parallels to images painted on early local pottery at T'aitöna, the most plausible affiliation would seem to be with the ancestral Northern Tiwas themselves.

Once this connection is made, additional evidence begins to fall in line. All the katsina rock art panels in figures 6.4 and 6.5, for instance, are located in the Rio Grande gorge, a deep and secluded rift valley fifteen kilometers west of modern Taos Pueblo (figure 6.6). The Rio Grande gorge receives little commentary in Northern

Figure 6.6. The Rio Grande gorge drops away from the Taos Plateau. Tres Orejas, a ceremonially important mountain for Taos Pueblo, is visible in the distance to the northwest.

Tiwa ethnography, but we do know it was used as a location for the doings of the Lightning People, a sodality at Taos Pueblo with ties to the katsina (Ellis 1974[1962]). More important, the very seclusion of the Rio Grande gorge may have made it one of the few appropriate locations for such images in the same way that Taos's actual masks, in recent decades, have been stored well away from the village in the mountains to the east. We are left with the impression, then, not of a Pueblo community lacking knowledge or understanding of katsina masks, but of a community that has chosen to keep these powerful, and perhaps dangerous, images at arm's length.

The Northern Tiwas' relationship to katsina doings—and to katsina images in particular—is much more complicated than previously thought. Whereas anthropologists working in the area once assumed that knowledge of masked beings was both inchoate and a comparatively late arrival, we are now forced to acknowledge that the Northern Tiwas may have authored some of the earliest and clearest images of katsina anywhere in the Southwest. Moreover, we have found evidence that a distinctive logic seems to underlie these images. In contrast to other pueblos, where the rights to produce katsina masks are universal and the display of masks in katsina dances is public and highly visible, the Northern Tiwas' masks are kept hidden, relegated to inaccessible portions of the landscape and to back rooms.

How are we to situate this new evidence within the broader developmental trajectory of the Northern Tiwas? How are we to understand the specificities of their (dis)engagement with the katsina as a historical phenomenon? Below, I will suggest that the alleged absence of katsina doings reported by twentieth-century ethnographers is better understood as the *presence* of a formal prohibition on katsina depiction that originally arose at the start of the fourteenth century as the leadership of T'aitöna and other Northern Tiwa communities debated—significantly, on the heels of a major period of migration and demographic realignment—which doings were acceptable and which were not. As we saw in the previous chapter, T'aitöna's founding involved the construction of an entire cosmos, complete with an entirely new configuration of agents, structures, and powers. The katsina, I suspect, were part of this cosmos from early on, but their relationships with humans, and especially the question of how those relationships were to be materially mediated, were matters of concern that had to be worked out over time.

Toward a History of Katsina Prohibitions

To build this argument, we need more evidence than a handful of fragmentary sherds and poorly dated rock art panels. If these were the only evidential traces of the Northern Tiwa katsina, skeptics might still dismiss them as anomalies or as the result of a brief, early contact with a tradition that never took hold locally. That is, there would still be those who would reduce the subsequent lack of katsina doings to a mere absence, whereas my goal is to demonstrate that the absence was assertive and strongly marked.

In this respect, it is significant that while only a few sherds provide direct evidence of mask imagery at T'aitöna, they are part of a larger assemblage of material remains that Southwestern archaeologists have come to associate with katsina doings. With its large, bounded plazas, for instance, the village layout of T'aitöna was very much in keeping with fourteenth-century architectural trends in the Western Pueblo area that many have linked to a growing popularity of katsina dances (e.g., Adams 1991). Today, Taos Pueblo has but a single katsina dance, the Turtle Dance, which is unmasked and is thus regularly used as additional evidence of the rudimentary and piecemeal nature of the Northern Tiwas' participation in the katsina tradition. Inquiring into the origin of the Turtle Dance, Parsons received a variety of answers:

> [One informant said,] "Long ago they got it from a southern pueblo; but perhaps they did not get all of it," i.e., the ritual. How long ago did Taos get the Turtle dance from San Juan? I asked a townsman. "We did not get it from San Juan; we have always had it," he answered characteristically and later he remarked that his grandmother had not liked the Turtle dance because it reminded her of the massacre by the American soldiers (in 1847); they were dancing Turtle dance at that time. Camouflage, perhaps; for another man said definitely that the Turtle dance was "given to Taos when the Laguna people went to Isleta," which was some time after 1847; in fact in 1880....

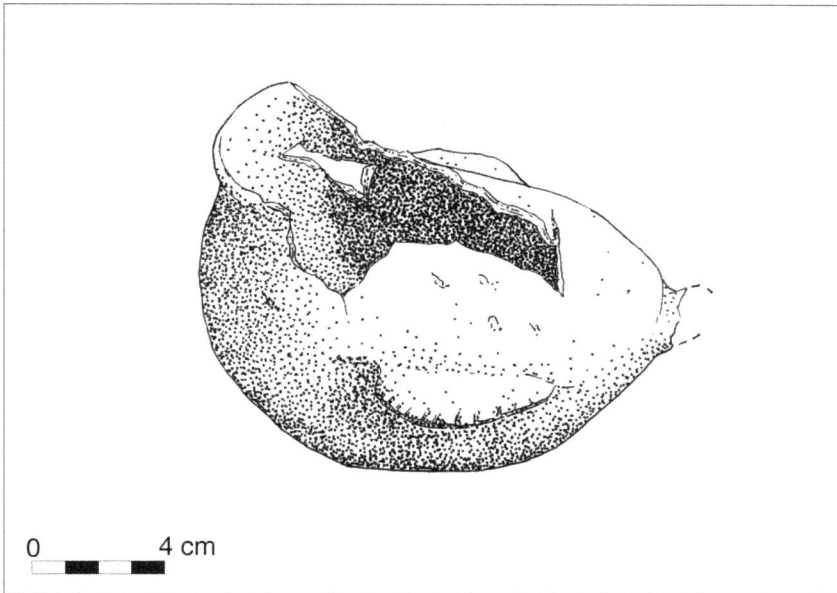

Figure 6.7. Bird effigy vessel (unpainted), T'aitöna.

The reference indicates that the Turtle dance came through Isleta rather than through San Juan. Indeed it may have come through the Isletan who married into Taos about that time. (Parsons 1936:91)

Parsons was inclined to believe the informant who suggested a late nineteenth-century importation of the Turtle Dance, because his answer best fit her general model of the shallow time depth of Northern Tiwa katsina doings. Archaeological remains suggest, however, that the dance may have a far deeper history. Excavations during the 1960s recovered a small piece of worked turtle carapace from T'aitöna (Wetherington 1968:65). The fragment clearly displays evidence of having been drilled in three or more locations, and the most plausible interpretation is that it came from a turtle shell rattle, an object that is both strongly associated with katsina dancers throughout the Pueblo world (Kennard 1938:9; Parsons 1996a[1940]:384) and traditionally worn on the ankles of Turtle Dancers at Taos (Parsons 1936:107). Was the Turtle Dance performed in the large, newly enclosed plazas at T'aitöna at the start of the fourteenth century? Perhaps. If so, did it originate as a *masked* katsina dance? This remains a possibility as well. The important point is that the available evidence suggests that katsina-related dances were present among the Northern Tiwas at least as early as elsewhere in the Pueblo world.

Other archaeological finds at T'aitöna lend further support to this interpretation. Three locally produced bird effigy vessels have been recovered from the site (figure 6.7). Frequently referred to as "shoe," "boot," or "duck" pots, such artifacts have been linked to the spread of katsina doings in the Western Pueblo region, where they also appear during the fourteenth century (Adams 1991:79, 154). Like clouds, birds are sometimes viewed as avatars of the katsina, for example among the Zuni, who claim that the katsina travel between the land of the living and the land of the ancestors as ducks (Bunzel 1992[1932]:517). T'aitöna's residents may have held similar conceptions. One partial effigy vessel found at the site was even painted with zigzag motifs—an effort, perhaps, to enhance the potency of the vessel by simultaneously indexing two of the katsina's material forms: lightning and bird.[10]

The elaboration of smoking pipes at T'aitöna (discussed in the previous chapter) adds further support to the antiquity of Northern Tiwa katsina doings. Smoking was clearly part of both katsina and non-katsina doings throughout the Pueblo world, but some specimens found at the site were decorated with lightning motifs (figure 5.1B), and all pipes would have been used "to pretend the clouds" (Picurís informant in Brown 1973:145). In short, the katsina, broadly conceived, appear to have been present among the Northern Tiwas from very early on, not just as mask icons on ceramic bowls and in rock art panels, but also as dancers in plazas, as clouds blown from pipes, as birds, as lightning. There was no developmental lag. At the start of the fourteenth century, T'aitöna might even be said to have been at the vanguard of katsina doings. Some elements may have been indigenous; others were surely introduced by the migrants who streamed into the northern Rio Grande during the prior century; still others may have been invented anew as the village grew.

At 1300 CE, then, the Northern Tiwas were poised to become a center for katsina doings no less than the Hopis or Zunis. They chose a different path, however—a path with muted katsina doings and a marked ambivalence toward masks. During the fourteenth century, as their neighbors to the south and west began indulging in the creation of explicit mask icons in a variety of media (kiva murals, rock art, ceramics, dance masks), the Northern Tiwas became especially unwilling to do so. Instead, they increasingly chose to gesture toward the katsina obliquely, through veiled or abstract references. This becomes evident initially during the occupation of T'aitöna itself, where the last known example of a mask motif on a locally produced ceramic was accompanied by an abrupt increase in the use of cloud (terraced pyramid) and especially lightning (zigzag)[11] icons (Fowles 2004:649), both of which would have indexed the katsina without explicitly materializing the mask. Again, the katsina travel as clouds and exert their agency, in part, as lightning. At Taos, the *ła'tsina* are referred to as both "Cloud Boys" and "Lightning People" (Stevenson 1906–1907:files 2.31 and 2.35; Parsons 1936:115). The cloud and lightning images provided an extra layer of mediation, an iconographic cover or shield that hid the mask, which presumably hid, in turn, an underlying katsina visage of some sort—which, even if *it* were ever exposed, could be nothing other than another mask, another mediating layer, for the katsina are ultimately a kind of pathway of communication or route of access toward higher powers. Indeed, there is a basic paradox bound up in the notion of the katsina as "masked spirits" that we begin to dimly sense when, for instance, the Zunis speak of their dance masks as being entered by spirits who are *already masked* (see Bunzel 1992[1932]:520) or when katsina society neophytes watch their elders unmask (Talayesva 1942:84), revealing an underlying humanity that somehow enhances the power and reality of the impersonated katsina insofar as it displaces the nonhuman agents into a deeper realm, one step farther away. There are complicated issues of representation and mimesis at play here (cf. Latour 2002; Taussig 1998). For the moment, I will simply suggest that the Northern Tiwas' decision to depict clouds and lightning rather than masks during the fourteenth and later centuries might be regarded as broadly comparable to the early Muslims' decision to depict holy texts rather than anthropomorphic images of God. In each case, we are prompted to consider how representational choices emerged out of a discourse that simultaneously reckoned one's relationships with the spirits and with other humans.

We have already seen a number of examples of cloud and lightning icons at T'aitöna, such as the hearth deflector stones in the Room 822 kiva, which had been erected in the shape of a stepped pyramid (see chapter 5) and anticipated the cloud altars in later kivas at Taos and Picurís. In another case, a lightning design had been incised into the adobe rim of Roomblock 3's kiva hearth; this also marked the beginning of a local tradition that would continue into the colonial period's kiva hearth complexes (Fowles 2004:604) and culminate in the temporary kiva altars at Taos that depicted lightning arrows standing upright, as if personified (Parsons 1936:105). To sit in the kiva, engaged in doings, around a hearth or beside an altar that bore such images would surely have been a form of communion or connection with the katsina—even, and perhaps especially, in the absence of the mask.

Ceramics provide especially robust evidence of the shift toward cloud and lightning iconography. Such icons were rare prior to T'aitöna, but by the end of the site's occupation they were present on a range of ceramic forms (figure 6.8). Lightning motifs, in particular, came to be closely associated with a special new type of bowl. "Kiva bowls," as I will call them, were small vessels with distinctive flaring rims decorated with a zigzag line (figure 6.9). One hundred rim sherds from such bowls have been recovered during excavations at T'aitöna, all but one of which was produced using local clays (Fowles 2004:647–648). We do not know how this special class of pottery was used, though the vessels are similar to the Northern Tewas' "prayer meal bowls" produced during the subsequent Pueblo IV period. Presumably, they were implicated in doings alongside miniature jars, gathering together cornmeal or some other substance just as the jars gathered together water from the various worldly directions. The inclusion of lightning icons suggests the katsina were involved in this gathering as well.

Of course, T'aitöna was hardly unique in its use of cloud and lightning motifs. Villages throughout the Pueblo world employed similar iconography in a variety of media during the fourteenth and later centuries, and much of this iconography was probably also associated with regional equivalents of the katsina. What is distinctive in the Northern Tiwa region, however, is that these motifs appear to have entirely replaced katsina mask images at the very moment when explicit masks

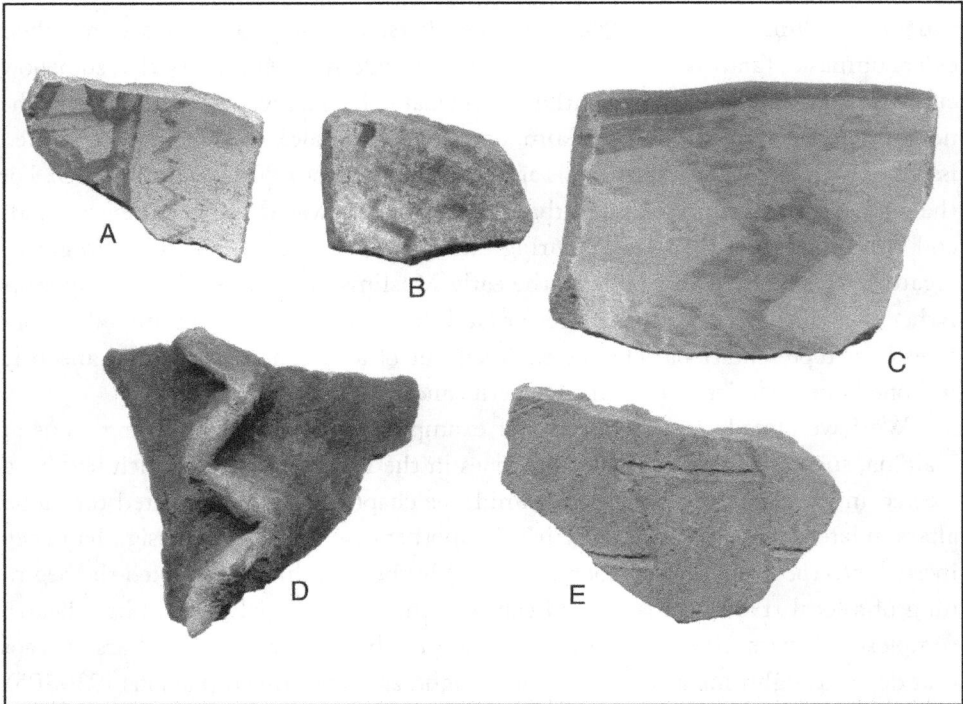

Figure 6.8. Lightning motifs on T'aitöna pottery. A, B, C = Santa Fe B/W (var. Taos) bowls; D = rare unpainted appliqué sherd; E = Taos Incised sherd found in association with late thirteenth-century deposits.

were proliferating elsewhere. This is most clearly seen following the abandonment of T'aitöna in 1320 CE when, according to local oral histories, its members fell into dispute and departed, some to Taos Pueblo, some to Picurís, and some, no doubt, to more-distant locations. Archaeological evidence for the post-1320 history of the Northern Tiwas is biased toward Picurís Pueblo, where Herbert Dick undertook extensive excavations during the 1960s (Dick et al. 1999), but all indications point to the likelihood that similar developments were under way at Taos Pueblo, a day's travel to the north.

Following the abandonment of T'aitöna, the Northern Tiwas produced no new katsina mask images that can be dated with confidence. Of the thousands of sherds excavated at Picurís, none portrayed explicit masks. Local rock art does occasionally include masks, but when exactly these were produced is anybody's guess, and as I have already suggested it is significant that such rock art was kept well away from the village. What few actual masks they possessed seem to have been kept at a safe distance as well, and it is unknown whether these masks were brought by immigrants or locally produced. Either way, there can be little doubt that the katsina mask went into hiding among the Northern Tiwas during late pre-Columbian times.

And yet, as lightning, clouds, and, increasingly, birds, the katsina remained very

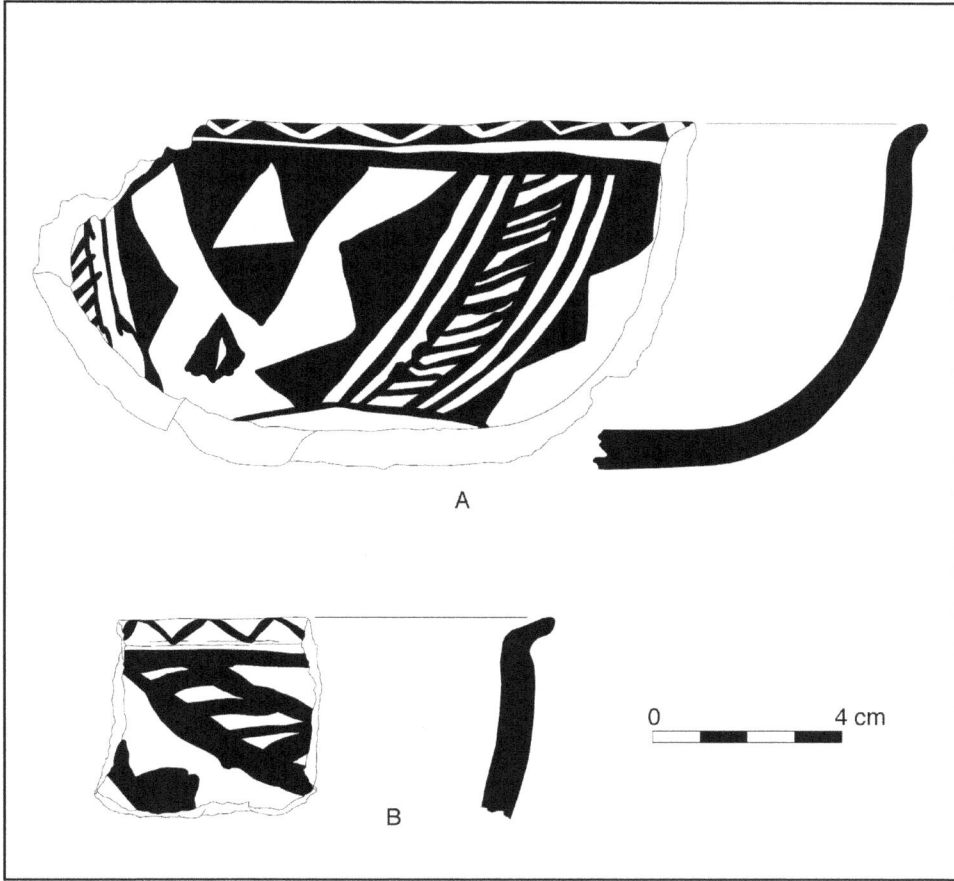

Figure 6.9. Santa Fe B/W (var. Taos) kiva bowls from T'aitöna.

present indeed. And evidence from Picurís suggests that these icons grew more elaborate. The cloud-blower pipe, which at T'aitöna had been little more than a simple ceramic tube with an occasional zigzag or other design, now became a true work of art, sculpted with multiple terraced cloud icons that mimetically reinforced the clouds of smoke produced during its use. Miniature jars at Picurís also bore clouds, frequently with accompanying lightning arrows (Wolfman and Dick 1999). In one striking case, a miniature jar was painted with a procession of terraced cloud icons rising up from the lower edge of the design field, along with two crocodile-like mouths extending down from the upper edge of the design field (figure 6.10). The latter detail is important, for the only other Pueblo context in which such elongated, toothed mouths have been documented is in masking, where they distinguish particular katsina (e.g., the Na'tashka katsina at Hopi [Kennard 1938:plate XI] or the "Black Cloud chief" katsina at Ohkay Owingeh [Parsons 1974[1929]:120]). This tells us two things: first, that the late pre-Columbian community at Picurís was well aware of specific katsina personalities, and second, that they were only willing to

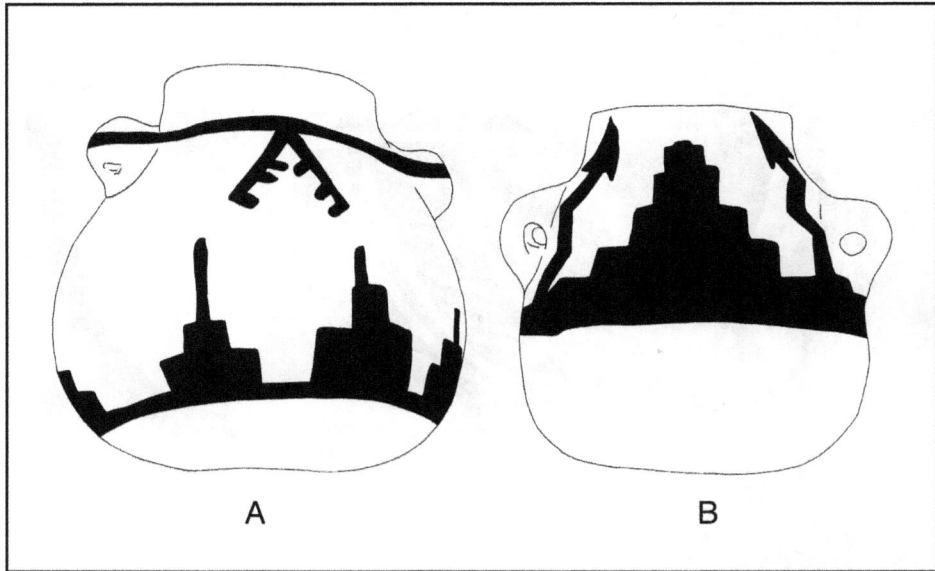

Figure 6.10. Miniature jars from a Pueblo IV cache at Picurís Pueblo (based on Wolfman and Dick 1999:111).

depict these katsina in a veiled or partial form. Thus was the toothed mouth used in isolation to subtly index the masked spirits flying overhead in the same way that a single hand descending from the sky is sometimes used to depict the otherwise undepictable form of God-as-father in Christian iconography.

This same representational logic—in which a part substitutes for a whole or an avatar indexes an agent without visibly exposing it—was used in the production of Northern Tiwa kiva murals. In keeping with trends throughout the Southwest, the community at Picurís Pueblo began to elaborately illustrate the inner walls of their subterranean kivas after about 1350 CE. Taos Pueblo probably followed suit, but at present the only evidence comes from twenty-two kivas excavated by Dick (Dick et al. 1999) at Picurís. Many of these kivas contained murals that provide an especially detailed window onto iconographic developments in the Northern Tiwa region during late pre-Columbian and early colonial times (figure 6.11).

Considered alongside comparable kiva murals in the Hopi, Zuni, and Keresan regions (cf. Smith 1952), the most noteworthy aspect of the Picurís murals is their exclusive use of non-anthropomorphic icons. While other Pueblo communities regularly depicted masked katsina as well as a variety of human forms, the Picurís kiva artists limited their iconographic repertoire to naturalistic motifs that built connections to the katsina without directly depicting them. This is not to say that the Picurís murals were in any way impoverished or rudimentary. On the contrary, Picurís artists invested their energies in detailed elaborations of elements that tended to be much simpler at pueblos where anthropomorphic beings were depicted. In fact, after analyzing kiva murals across the Southwest, Helen Crotty (1999) concluded

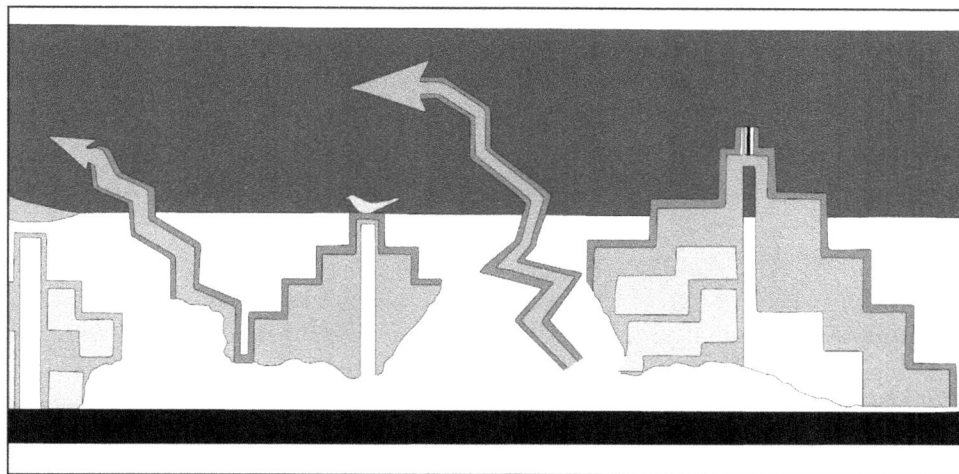

Figure 6.11. Kiva murals at Picurís Pueblo. Kiva C (top); Kiva B (bottom) (redrawn from Crotty 1999:162, 164).

that the Picurís cloud motifs were the only ones exhibiting deliberately asymmetrical patterns and internal decoration. Picurís lightning bolt motifs are similarly distinctive with thick, often multicolored shafts. Other pueblos depicted cloud and lightning motifs as well, of course, but typically in a far simpler style and often as a mere backdrop for some anthropomorphic scene. At Picurís, in contrast, clouds and lightning took center stage. Indeed, the only other prominent motifs in the Picurís murals are rainbows and birds, both of which probably also had katsina associations. Crotty notes that the "bird-atop-a-terraced-pyramid icons" in particular may have represented "something analogous to the Zuni concept of birds of various species as spokesmen of the lightning makers" (1999:182). "Lightning makers," as we have seen, is but another name for the katsina.

In the end, however, it is the presence of small goggle eyes on a number of the cloud icons that solidifies the link between the Picurís murals and the katsina (figure 6.11, *bottom*). In the Pueblo tradition, goggle eyes of this sort are solely reserved for the katsina and are critical to the enlivening theatricality of the mask. As Gell has beautifully argued, to regard an image that is regarding you back is to necessarily leap into an animistic mode. "The pupils of any eye are never 'things,'" he writes, "but always *holes*, orifices, giving access to the hidden interior within which 'mind' resides" (1998:147). "Eyes are, of all body orifices, those which signify 'interiority' (i.e., the possession of mind and intentionality) most immediately" (135–136). Here we begin to appreciate the inner logic of the mask, the technologies of representation that made the secret sentience of the katsina compelling. But the more immediate observation I want to emphasize is that these were the same eyes that had stared out of the much earlier katsina mask sherd at T'aitöna (cf. figures 6.3C and 6.11, *bottom*). Two centuries later in the murals at Picurís, the eyes still performed; they still made the katsina manifest as powerful agents staring down the audience gathered before them in the kiva; and they still opened routes of connection and communication with higher powers. The critical difference was that, by the time of Spanish conquest, the Northern Tiwas had, as it were, masked the mask. Clouds, lightning, birds, and rainbows had been adopted as added layers of mediation, and a single part (the eyes) was again left to stand for the hidden whole (the mask).

Let me offer one final set of images to help build the case for a Northern Tiwa movement away from explicit katsina depiction during late pre-Columbian times. As we have already seen, a number of mask images have been found in the rock art of the Rio Grande gorge, immediately west of Taos. While poorly dated, most of these images display a moderate degree of repatination, indicating that they were produced at some point after the large corpus of heavily repatinated Archaic rock art panels but before the equally large corpus of lightly repatinated later Pueblo panels in the region. This is the case, for instance, with the most elaborate of the katsina panels in the Rio Grande gorge: panel 2008-P442 at LA 75747, which includes two masks, serpentine wavy lines, a scorpion or spider, zigzag or lightning lines, and a few additional glyphs (figure 6.12). The iconography is clearly pre-Columbian, and the degree of repatination suggests it is significantly so. As such, it provides a useful comparison with a second panel in the Rio Grande gorge, which is also remarkable for its iconographic complexity but which lacks masks altogether. The site LA 166891 (2009-P170) is near Arroyo Hondo and includes a large panel constructed using a variety of technologies, probably by a number of individuals at different times (figure 6.13). Here, I am primarily interested in the central portion of the panel, which exhibits light repatination, was pecked with a combination of metal and stone tools, and therefore can be dated with confidence to the colonial period. As at LA 75747, the panel at LA 166891 contains a central glyph of parallel wavy lines running across its center, zigzag or lightning motifs extending upward, and a variety of surrounding icons. They are structurally similar in this respect. As the more recent of the two,

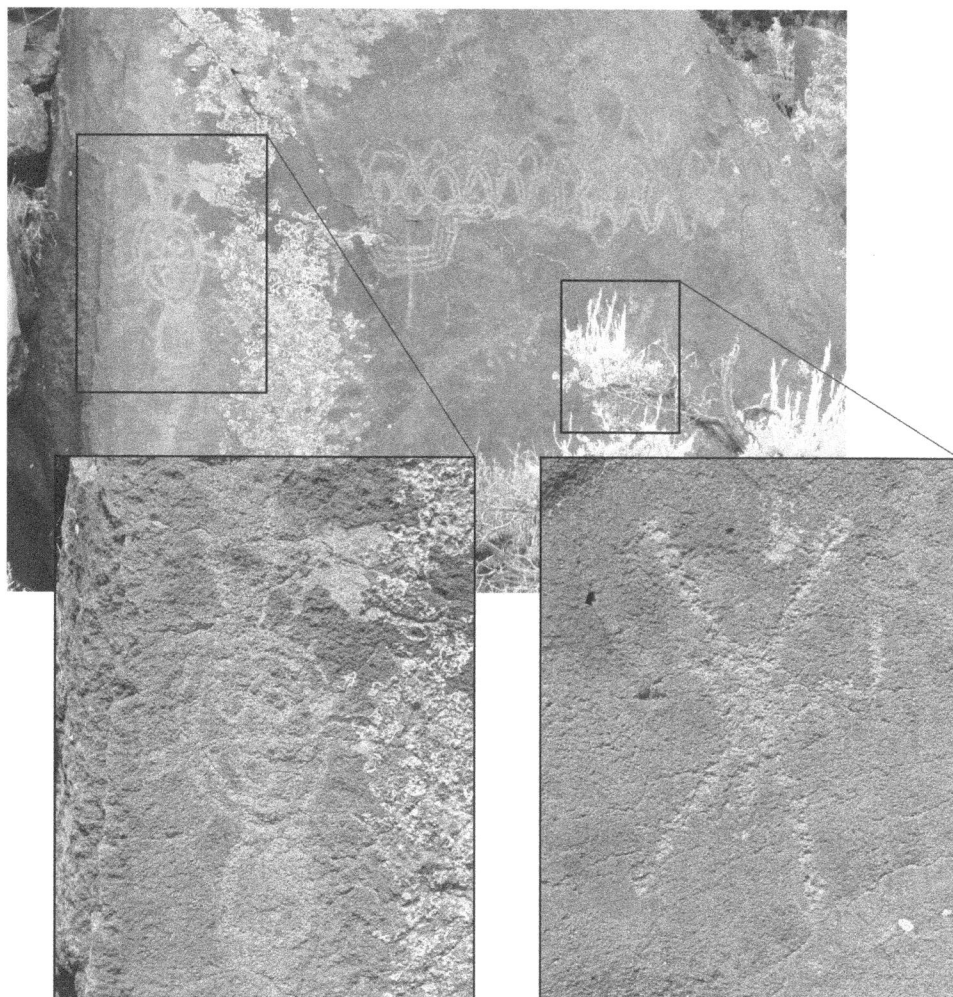

Figure 6.12. Panel 2008-P442 with katsina masks, wavy lines, a spider, and other glyphs at LA 75747 in the Rio Grande gorge.

however, LA 166891 clearly bears the mark of greater organization, probably modeled on the post-1350 CE kiva mural tradition; the central portion of the panel even uses natural cracks in the rock to divide the iconography into upper and lower bands in the same way that kiva murals at Picurís were divided into upper and lower bands through the use of color. It is tempting to read particular meanings into the strange and varied icons appearing in the two panels. I will refrain from doing so, except to observe that while katsina masks were prominent in the early panel, a centrally positioned terraced cloud motif (asymmetrically rendered with internal divisions as in the Picurís kiva murals) was inserted into the heart of the later panel. Broadly speaking, both seem to be "about" the katsina. By the time the later panel was pecked, however, the rules governing how to figure the spirits had changed.

Figure 6.13. Panel 2009-P170 at LA 166891, Rio Grande gorge.

This change, I suggest, involved the establishment of a Northern Tiwa prohibition on certain forms of katsina depiction during the fourteenth century. The katsina did not go away—again, to quote one Taos informant, they remained the beings "from whom all good things come" (quoted in Ellis 1974[1962]:141)—and an abundance of cloud and lightning icons testified to their presence. But the mask itself was no longer permitted. Its absence, marked as an absence, had become an intentional, highly evolved, and defining characteristic of the Northern Tiwa world. Ironically, it was precisely this historical development that led so many ethnographers, ethnohistorians, and archaeologists to mistakenly conclude that the Northern Tiwas were backward nonparticipants in an otherwise pan-Pueblo katsina tradition. In Parsons's estimation, Taos and Picurís seemed "fully prepared for mask usage and the more elaborate part of the kachina cult." "Yet," she added with the tone of a disappointed parent confronting a stubborn child, "there is a very notable resistance" (Parsons 1939:1093). My suggestion is that we remove the stigma from such observations and accept that this very notable resistance was a deliberate phenomenon with a history that deserves our analytical attention.

Iconographic prohibitions have probably always been part of the human experience. This is not something Southwestern scholarship has previously considered, and as I have argued elsewhere, it is a subject that archaeologists are poorly suited to study (Fowles 2008; Fowles and Heupel forthcoming). However, no society is ever completely permissive with respect to image production; there are always restrictions, ranging from "mere" rules of decorum to strict taboos that would be dangerous to transgress. The relative formality of something like the Northern Tiwa prohibition on katsina masks—once we have identified it as such—may be difficult to assess; indeed, the nature of such prohibitions may well have changed over time, as explicit bans graded into taken-for-granted customs or vice versa. Moreover, much of the ethnographic commentary needed to support such investigations is probably impoverished, insofar as subjects that are too dangerous to be depicted visually may also be too dangerous to be discussed with a pushy anthropologist taking notes.

But there are moments when the dangerous power of forbidden images bubbles into the open—flashpoints often clothed in the rhetoric of iconoclasm. Such a moment arose in New Mexico during the late 1930s when Elsie Clews Parsons convinced a financially strapped member of Isleta to paint and sell her a series of images of his community's secret doings. "I don't want any soul to know as long as I live that I have drawn these pictures," wrote the anonymous artist in a letter. "I have no way of making a living, no farm.… If I had some way to get help in this world I would never have done this. I expect to get good help" (quoted in Goldfrank 1962:1). The paintings were published posthumously in the 1960s, and they included, among many other highly sensitive subjects, a number of katsina depictions. This is how the larger Isletan community responded when the images were made public: "The representation of Kachinas in drawings is taboo," they told ethnographer Byron Harvey (1963:487). The paintings "would have been burned if the [priestly] organization had been able to get hold of them." Harvey notes that "the depth of the native objection to Kachina representations is shown by an informant's comment: 'They could have shot the one that did this. They'd probably burn it if they saw it.'" Isleta is a Southern Tiwa–speaking pueblo, and it shares with its Northern Tiwa–speaking relatives a number of historical experiences. Like Taos and Picurís, Isleta has autochthonous roots in the Rio Grande valley and was forced to reinvent itself as western immigrants from the northern San Juan arrived in large numbers during the late thirteenth and fourteenth centuries. Little surprise, perhaps, that Isleta provides the most compelling twentieth-century comparison for the sort of iconographic prohibitions involved in the Northern Tiwa movement away from the mask during pre-Columbian times.

The Undoing of Doings

Might there have been similar iconoclastic flashpoints during the early fourteenth-century occupation of T'aitöna? One approach to this question is to draw upon Taos oral history with its rich accounts of the arrival of various clans or kiva groups. Consider the story of the ancestral Water People, immigrants who are said to have swum into the region as fish from the south to settle among the Winter and Summer People. In a version recorded by Stevenson (1906–1907:file 2.19), the Water People are discovered in the Rio Grande del Rancho by a young woman who was washing food bits out of a jar:

The particles of food that had adhered to the vessel floated on the water and quantities of fish hastened to eat the crumbs. The woman left her jar at the riverbank and hastened home and told her father that she had seen many people in the river. "I do not know what people they are," said the woman. The father sent his daughter for another man and that man, on his arrival, inquired of the woman's father, "What do you wish of me?" The father replied, "I wish you to go to the river and see what people are there." Then not only this man but many of the people hurried to the river to learn something of the strangers. They saw many fish and the old men said, "Why these are the *Ba tai'na* [or Water] People." They knew [them] for they were in the underworld when the *Ba tai'na* People were sent to the Rio Grande.[12]

The directors of the Summer People ordered that a stalk of green corn with many roots be brought. The corn stalk was deposited in the river and the Water People gathered promptly about the green corn stalk. The mouths of the fish people caught [on] the many roots below the surface of the water. The directors of the Summer People were pleased and cried, "It is well, we guess all of the Water People will come." While the mouths of the fish clung to the roots of the corn…the stalk was hurriedly and carefully removed from the water onto the shore….[13] The Summer People threw much medicine water from large vases over the fish and covered them with *pachowen'na* (vine which runs on the ground and [has] many leaves). And soon this cover began moving and it gradually raised. When the cover was finally removed, men, women, and children were found sitting beneath the vine. Then the Water People thanked the Summer People for they had not known where to find the earth.

Considered within the larger corpus of Taos oral histories, the story of the Water People's incorporation into Northern Tiwa society seems to follow on the heels of the Summer People's conquest of the Winter People (see chapter 4), and it is plausible that this scene took place on the banks of the Rio Grande del Rancho adjacent to T'aitöna itself. Regardless, the powerful medicine of the Summer People again prevailed. As the Winter People were transformed from ice into flesh, the Water People were transformed from piscine into anthropomorphic form. Both were initiatory acts in which cultural alterity was overcome by making humans out of nonhumans. And in both cases, the doings involved not only established social relations between formerly unrelated groups; they placed the Summer People in a privileged position with respect to that new network of relations (here, mimetically represented by the vine with many leaves).

This story is especially relevant to our broader consideration of the development of Northern Tiwa prohibitions, because of all the Taos kiva groups the Water People have the deepest connections to katsina doings. It is they who traditionally lead the pueblo's unmasked katsina dance, the Turtle Dance. Indeed, it might even have been the ancestors of the Water People who brought the fragment of the turtle shell rattle, discussed above, to T'aitöna seven centuries ago. Moreover, the Water People's links to the katsina are implicitly established in Taos oral history, for as Parsons (1936:115) observes, the account of their arrival merges a sequence of migrations with "the well known Pueblo myth of the children who became fish and then kachina." As such, the story of the Water People might be read as the story of the introduction of new forms of katsina doings, prompting us to consider how such doings would have been received and, perhaps, contested. Might the arrival of the Water People have disrupted the already uneasy balance of power between the Summer and Winter Peoples at T'aitöna (discussed in chapter 4)? Might their conceptions of the appropriate means of depicting or not depicting the katsina have come into conflict with local customs? Might katsina doings involving masks have threatened to undermine or rewrite one group's relations with the others? Needless to say, we know neither the roles of the various actors involved nor the complicated negotiations that may have resulted. Nor can we be sure that the ancestral Water People were even resident at T'aitöna, although I suspect they were. Little matter. All available evidence converges on the conclusion that T'aitöna was composed of multiple groups with quite different histories, languages, and traditions, and it is enough to conclude, first, that worldviews and worldly priorities would have occasionally clashed in such a context; second, that the katsina would have been implicated; and third, that formal prohibitions on certain forms of katsina doings could have been one consequence.

These conclusions become even more plausible when we consider, by way of comparison, one of the more recent clashes over doings at Taos Pueblo—namely, the highly contentious situation that surrounded the development of a local branch of the peyote church during the first half of the twentieth century. Peyote was introduced to the community in 1907 through contacts with the Cheyennes and other Oklahoma tribes, and it quickly gained a following among a small group of young Taos men. Superficially, peyote ceremonies seem innocent enough. They were held to bring rain, protect the village from witches, and heal the sick. In the eyes of their practitioners, peyote ceremonies supplemented rather than competed with Catholic rituals and the traditional kiva-based doings of the pueblo. As one of the peyote church's leaders, Gerónimo Gómez, put it in 1936, peyote was "our own simple way of believing in God so that we shall be better men to mankind" (quoted in Stewart 1987:204). The leadership of the pueblo did not see it that way at all, however, and it was not long before kiva priests openly clashed with the Peyote Boys. Peyote "does not belong to us," its opponents argued. "It is not *the work given to us*. It will stop the rain. Something will happen" (Parsons 1936:66–67, emphasis in original). Indeed, something did happen. Many Peyote Boys were fined and stripped of their positions in the kiva hierarchy, a few were whipped, and the governor ordered raids on peyote meetings and the confiscation of participants' blankets, shawls, and other ceremonial paraphernalia (Stewart 1987:202–208).

Passions have since cooled. The peyote church survived and continues to remain active at the edges of Taos society. And yet, the controversy surrounding its introduction highlights how much is at stake when doings seek to map out new worldly relationships. There were many reasons behind the efforts to ban peyote ceremonies at Taos, of course, including the opposition of the Catholic Church. Significantly, however, the initial and most vigorous opposition came from the traditional kiva leadership of the pueblo itself—not because the stated goals of the Peyote Boys necessarily conflicted with their own (the well-being and fertility of the world was, after all, a shared concern) but because the practices involved in achieving these goals challenged established understandings of how society and cosmos were organized. Rather than receiving their spiritual education from the lulina, or old men, of the kivas, the Peyote Boys had begun to follow the teachings of outsiders from Oklahoma. Moreover, their use of psychedelics placed the Peyote Boys in vividly direct relationships with the powerful rain-bringing agents, circumventing the tendency of both Catholicism and the traditional kiva doings to embed each individual's access to the cosmos within the local social hierarchy. These seem to have been some of the motivating factors behind the pueblo's efforts to institute a ban on peyote use.

Katsina masks may have been similarly controversial during pre-Columbian times. Like peyote ceremonies introduced from Oklahoma at the start of the twentieth century, masking practices brought in by the Water People or some other group of immigrants may have been matters of deep concern at the start of the fourteenth century. "It is not *the work given to us*. It will stop the rain. Something will happen." Claims such as these, meetings held to discuss accusations, perhaps even raids on doings and public whippings for perceived transgressions—who is to say that such things did not take place at T'aitöna?

In the end, we must acknowledge that the comings and goings of a great many groups with a great many doings all contributed to the evolving cultural tradition I have awkwardly glossed as "Northern Tiwa," and the prohibition of the mask was surely but one chapter in a complex history of negotiations over competing practices. In this respect, it is telling that in moving away from T'aitöna, the Northern Tiwas abandoned not just explicit mask icons but also a range of other material forms, including D-shaped kivas, floor sipapus, foot drums, ash pits, and cupule shrines, all of which were present at T'aitöna but appear to have been discontinued following the move to Picurís and Taos. None of these things were "religious" objects used in invariant "rituals" that necessarily enhanced social integration by focusing collective attention on a supernatural realm or that were premised on faith, belief, and slavish devotion to inherited concepts. All these things were implicated in Pueblo doings; which is to say that they were matters of concern in which contestable assertions were made regarding how the world is or should be organized. As such, their power and force become most acutely visible at the very moment they are opposed, altered, or even eliminated.

This is especially true of the final case I will consider, T'aitöna's great kiva (figure 6.14), which was still in the midst of construction when the village was abandoned in 1319 CE or shortly thereafter. Like the D-shaped kiva discussed in chapter 5, the great kiva was an architectural form introduced into the Northern Tiwa tradition

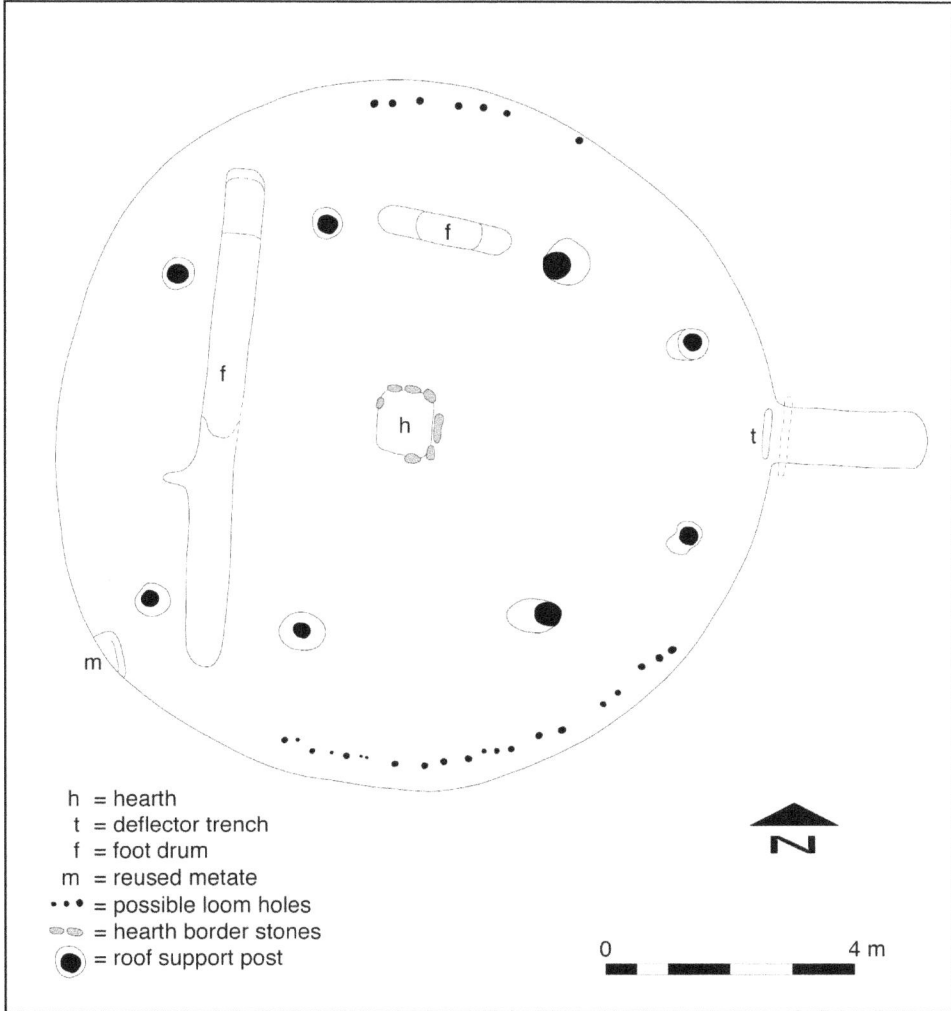

Figure 6.14. T'aitöna's unfinished great kiva (based on Wetherington 1968).

very briefly, so briefly that it was never actually used as a stage for doings at all. When T'aitöna's great kiva was unearthed in the 1960s, the excavators discovered that the hearth had never been fired and the floor and roof were incomplete (Wetherington 1968:40). Subsequent tree-ring studies demonstrated that the kiva's structural timbers were among the very last wood harvested at the site, confirming that the process of building was interrupted by the site's abandonment (Crown 1991:305). Because such structures had no precedent in the Northern Tiwa region, Crown and Kohler (1994:114) suggested, quite reasonably, that immigrants were responsible for the aborted introduction of the great kiva. Regardless, it was both the first and the last of its kind; in Northern Tiwa society, the great kiva tradition ended before it began.

Only a few hints of its intended use remain. Unlike the five small kivas, each of which was nested in its own private roomblock, T'aitöna's great kiva was being built in a communal location at the center of the site's largest plaza in the southern half of the village. As a material presence it would have dominated the plaza, its semi-subterranean walls extending upward perhaps two meters above the ground surface to interrupt and break apart an otherwise open space. The scale of the architecture suggests it was designed to serve a large assembly—perhaps the southern moiety, perhaps the village as a whole. The only other suggestion of the builders' intentions are two lines of small holes in the kiva's floor—one along the north wall, one along the south wall—that are best interpreted as loom supports. Paired sets of looms were relatively common kiva features during the fourteenth and later centuries, and it is generally assumed that male members of the kiva would have used such looms to produce cotton textiles, which were worn for warmth but also as essential costumes for many doings (see Mills 2000, 2008:244–245; Peckham 1979; Webster 1997). It is especially surprising, however, to find loom support holes at T'aitöna. From fragmentary ethnographic evidence we know that the local community at least occasionally received raw cotton through contacts with Zunis (Stevenson 1906–1907:file 2.25), but the high elevation and short growing season of the Taos region could never have supported cotton agriculture itself. Moreover, there are no indications of an indigenous weaving tradition, nor were loom supports found in any of the twelve pre-Columbian and early colonial kivas excavated at Picurís (Dick et al. 1999). This makes T'aitöna's great kiva that much more anomalous, strengthening the suggestion that it was designed not just by immigrants but by immigrants from a region where cotton was grown and weaving played a role in kiva doings.

Cotton is sympathetically linked to clouds, and clouds to katsina. This is why certain katsina masks among the Western Pueblos are made out of cotton and why many masks incorporate bundles of raw cotton, cotton cordage, or cottonseeds tucked behind protruding eyes, ears, or other decorative elements (Stevenson 1915:92, cited in Huckell 1993). It is why the face of the deceased is covered with a "mask" of cotton at Hopi, signaling an individual's transition into the ancestral world of the katsina (Talayesva 1942:313; Huckell 1993). And it is why cotton textiles are described as "woven expressions of place, prayer, and cosmos [that] transform and engage Pueblo people in relationships with the world around them" (Williams et al. 2007:22). As Lucy Williams learned from her colleagues Isabel Gonazales of Jémez and Shawn Tafoya of Pojoaque and Santa Clara:

> Pueblo people speak of their textiles as clothes of the spirits. With its roots in the
> earth and stalk and pods in the sky, the cotton plant links earth and sky together.
> Pueblo textiles are best understood as devoted acts of prayer for rain and well-being.
> Pueblo garments actively wrap the wearer in signs that communicate connections to
> the Pueblo world. In so doing, cloth directly engages, strengthens, and shapes the
> wearer's very being, his or her thoughts and actions. (Williams et al. 2007:23)

For a traditional Pueblo individual to work with cotton on a loom in his kiva, then, is to be consciously engaged with what Tim Ingold calls the "meshwork" of the world:

> The meshwork consists not of interconnected points but of interwoven lines. Every line is a relation, but the relation is not *between* one thing and another—between, say, an artefact here and a person there, or between one person or artefact and another. Rather, the relation is a line *along* which materials flow, mix and mutate. Persons and things, then, are formed in the meshwork as knots or bundles of such relations. It is not, then, that things are entangled in relations; rather every thing is itself an entanglement, and it is thus linked to other things by way of the flows of materials that make it up. (Ingold 2007:35)

Ingold writes in an ontological mode about the world-as-it-is. Pueblo people weave in an ontological mode about the world-as-it-was-as-it-is-and-as-it-is-hoped-to-be.

My point is that there is nothing simple or matter-of-fact about Pueblo weaving, nor would there have been anything simple about the loom support holes in the unfinished great kiva at T'aitöna. And this opens up interpretive space to ask why the Northern Tiwa tradition of cotton textile production ended before it began. Was it aborted due to its connections to other katsina doings that were undergoing reform? Perhaps some feared it would alter interpueblo relations, making T'aitöna dependent on distant communities for access to cotton. Others may have worried about the local repercussions as indigenous nonweavers were placed in positions of dependency vis-à-vis a group of immigrant weavers. Still others may have simply said: "It is not *the work given to us*. It will stop the rain. Something will happen." Regardless, the great kiva and its intended doings would have been community-wide matters of concern, particularly in light of all the new questions of leadership, labor, inclusion, and exclusion that would have swarmed around an undertaking of such scale.

Ultimately, the decision to terminate work on the great kiva must also be placed in the context of the abandonment of the village as a whole, for these events essentially occurred at the same time. T'aitöna's abandonment is curious. Not only was the great kiva left incomplete; other major investments in construction had also just been made (see Crown 1991), and a great many first-story storage rooms were left filled waist-high with corn. The image is of a community that had intended to stay longer. Nevertheless, in 1319 or 1320 CE, construction halted, households were cleared of their pots and other intact artifacts, the metates were pulled from their grinding bins, "offerings" were placed in some kivas, several portions of the village were formally burned, and the Rio Grande del Rancho valley was left vacant by native peoples for good. Why?

Other archaeologists have commented on T'aitöna's abandonment and its relationship to the unfinished great kiva. Using Johnson's (1982) scalar stress model as their starting point, Crown and Kohler (1994) suggest that the village had simply outgrown its existing decision-making structures. As the local population increased during the early fourteenth century, they argue, a threshold was crossed demanding a higher level of social integration, and the great kiva was adopted as a "ritual" strategy to meet this integrative need. Too little, too late:

> Construction of the [great] kiva and enclosing of the plaza area occurred in association with contemporaneous population growth and thus may reflect more direct and immediate responses to population change. Both of these architectural changes are viewed as reflecting the need for greater social integration and a reorganization of the decision-making structure at the site.... The abandonment of [T'aitöna] within a decade of the population increase there may indicate that the restructuring of interaction [i.e., the enclosing of the large plaza] with the incorporation of more community integrative structures [i.e., the great kiva] was *not successful*. (Crown and Kohler 1994:114, emphasis added)

A similar scalar stress model of T'aitöna's final days is offered by Bernardini, who also reads the great kiva as evidence of the community's efforts to grapple with an increase in organizational stress resulting from the incorporation of new families: "The construction of the large kiva may represent the reaction of the pueblo's inhabitants to the high levels of scalar stress being generated...in the decision-making system of the pueblo. The fact that the kiva was never completed and the site was abandoned soon afterwards suggests that this attempt was *unsuccessful*" (1996:22, emphasis added). Like Crown and Kohler's, Bernardini's account rests on three assumptions: (1) that the population at T'aitöna had increased beyond a critical threshold; (2) that there was no existing leadership structure to deal with the increasing number of decision-making units; and (3) that the great kiva was a last-ditch effort to ritually integrate the community, an effort that proved unsuccessful. The first two assumptions are largely empirical matters that have been undermined by more recent research. As we have seen, the evidence now suggests that at the time of T'aitöna's abandonment the local population was notably reduced compared with its thirteenth-century peak. Moreover, we know that by 1300 CE the village was well organized into an elaborate system of moieties and kiva groups—just the sort of decision-making hierarchy that is known to have structured far larger communities during the early colonial period.

The third assumption is more revealing insofar as it draws attention to the wide interpretive chasm separating orthodox archaeological analyses of religious ritual and the analysis of Pueblo doings offered here. Needless to say, to conclude that something like a great kiva was unsuccessful is to make a claim about the underlying intentions of the actors involved. In this case, Crown, Kohler, and Bernardini seem to conflate the goals of the system with the goals of the individual. In an intellectual tradition where ritual structures have repeatedly been referred to as "socially integrative architecture" by definition (see Lipe and Hegmon 1989), this comes as little surprise. Indeed, the analysis of T'aitöna's great kiva closely follows a script that has been in circulation at least since the early 1980s. Compare Graves et al.'s conclusions regarding a great kiva built at the end of the occupation of Grasshopper Pueblo in east-central Arizona:

> On the basis of a cross-cultural survey, Naroll…proposed, "when settlements contain more than about 500 people they must have authoritative officials and if they contain over a thousand some kind of specialized organization or corps of officials to perform police functions.… the larger the organization the greater the proportion of control officials needed." We suspect the population size of Grasshopper attained, if not exceeded, 500 persons, and certainly the region of interdependent communities contained many more than a thousand persons, yet there is no evidence of hierarchical regulatory control. The conversion of Plaza III to a Great Kiva late in the occupation of the Pueblo may reflect an attempt, albeit an unsuccessful one, to create a pan-community integrating mechanism. (1982:117)

One finds here the same strange willingness to read a great kiva's premature demise as evidence of an unsuccessful effort to use religion to integrate a community. The ancestral Pueblo people, it seems, were not just functionalists, but failed functionalists.

Southwestern archaeology is moving away from such explanations. Rallying around terms like "agency," "practice," and "structuration," many now seek to reread Pueblo religious ritual as a species of competition between differently positioned individuals (e.g., McGuire and Saitta 1996; Mills, ed. 2000; Plog 1995; Potter and Perry 2000; Saitta 1999; Schachner 2001; Van Dyke 2007). These are welcome trends, but they are not without their own drawbacks. In making its critiques of functionalism, such work tends to become all the more invested in a modernist division of society, where a religious superstructure stands apart from a political or economic infrastructure. Thus have so-called religious phenomena—great kivas, in particular—come to be treated as matters of competition only insofar as they have repercussions elsewhere, in a distinctly political or economic sphere. Agency is evaluated, in other words, by the degree to which control over ritual becomes a means of control over land tenure, agricultural labor, trade, craft production, or some other infrastructural phenomenon. Take McGuire and Saitta's (1996) influential analysis of the relationship between "religion" and the "material conditions" of Pueblo life, in which they conclude that it was the dynamic interplay between these two spheres that led to the development of the Pueblos' distinctive form of "complex communal society." And what is this thing called religion that somehow stands apart from a community's material conditions? According to McGuire and Saitta (1996:211), "pueblo religion is…esoteric." Others concur. Writing in a similar vein, Perry (2009:90) emphasizes that religious ritual involves "*nonmaterial* resources." And Van Dyke (2007:30, emphasis added) voices the common conclusion that Pueblo ritual leaders controlled "knowledge and…ceremonies *rather than*…disparate distributions of material wealth." Esoteric, nonmaterial, a question of ceremonial knowledge rather than tangible wealth. Ironically, such analyses are only able to argue that Pueblo religion is related to things that matter insofar as they begin with the premise that Pueblo religion is not, in and of itself, a thing that matters (in the sense of being *about* matter).

Western archaeologists, following Marx, may see religion as a misty realm, but Pueblo doings are emphatically part of the sensuous world. There is nothing immaterial about corn, cotton, clouds, pipes, pots, painted images, and turtle shells. They are all material conditions, all means of production no less than are irrigation canals or hunting territories. As we have seen, seeds were physically planted at T'aitöna, both in the flooring adobe of kivas and in agricultural fields. Which of these acts is superstructure and which is base? Which is ideology and which labor? Such categories are irrelevant. As I suggested in chapter 2, modern analyses tend to be premised upon a deep-seated anthropological diplopia in which singular phenomena are refracted and doubly perceived, in which Pueblo doings are broken apart into religious means and political or economic ends, into explanandum and explanans. Diplopia is a form of insidious analytical reductionism and can be easily diagnosed whenever we encounter terms like "legitimize" or "justify," whenever we find Pueblo doings being discussed as avenues or pathways toward something else.

What, then, of T'aitöna's unfinished great kiva? If neither an unsuccessful attempt to solve a prior decision-making crisis nor a veiled ideological effort to justify power inequalities in another realm, then what? I suggest we read it as we would the American flag at the pole climb ceremony in 2001: as a component of resonant doings that were at once commentary upon and an intervention into a contested state of affairs. The kiva marked an attempt to bring T'aitöna's world into orbit around a new center place with new gravities and relational logics. Might not these attempted innovations have prompted a disagreement so severe that it led to the abandonment of the entire village? Here is how one local story recounts the pre-Columbian fissioning of the ancestral Northern Tiwas into two separate communities at Taos and Picurís: "But all of a sudden a disagreement resulted between the various Fathers of the village, the many clan leaders. It was an extreme uprising of personal jealousies and reflection among the…clan leaders. The Cacique, the master supervisor of all ceremonies, failed to make [an] amicable settlement" (Picurís informant, as quoted in Brown 1973:106). The proximate reasons for the dispute are unknown. Perhaps it involved a great kiva, perhaps katsina masks. Regardless, T'aitöna was no longer an amicable settlement, and after 1320 CE the Northern Tiwa cosmos had two opposed centers of gravity: Taos to the north, Picurís to the south. Transformed into a border zone halfway between, T'aitöna's landscape would not be permanently settled again until the US military established a fort beside the village's melted adobe walls in 1852.

seven
Separation of Church and Kiva

"What religion is practiced at Taos Pueblo?" The tribe's website answers its rhetorical question this way: "The Pueblo Indians are about 90% Catholic. Catholicism is practiced along with the ancient Indian religious rites, which are an important part of Taos Pueblo life. The Pueblo religion is very complex; however, there is no conflict with the Catholic church, as evidenced by the prominent presence of both church and kiva in the village." Similar statements are presented by tribal tour guides, who sometimes note that while roughly 90 percent of the community is Catholic, 100 percent are members of the traditional Pueblo religion. Catholic religion is a matter of choice. Pueblo religion is a matter of being Pueblo.

It has never been easy to explain this situation to outsiders. Catholicism is a monotheistic religion that, according to its founding texts, eliminates the possibility of sharing souls with other, non-Catholic religions—particularly with non-Abrahamic religions. There is not supposed to be any such thing as a Catholic pagan. And this would seem to create categorical problems when dealing with Pueblo individuals, most of whom are located in precisely this paradoxical position. How is there no conflict in practicing Catholicism alongside the native practices that Catholicism has historically been so intent on stamping out?

Western analyses of the Pueblos' heterodox religiosity gravitate toward one of three interpretations. Some have concluded that the Pueblos must simply be insincere

Catholics. During a visit to Ohkay Owingeh Pueblo in 1881, the army captain and amateur ethnologist John G. Bourke assessed what he considered to be the general failure of Spanish missionization: "Unable to practice their ancient rites in public, the Pueblos [clung] to them in secret, and [clung] to them all the more tenaciously because the double halo of danger and mystery now surrounded them. The Pueblos became hypocrites, they never became Catholics" (Bloom 1936:262). His conclusion, then, was that native communities adopted Catholicism merely as a veneer to appease Spanish colonial powers, a strategy designed to protect rather than reform traditional ceremonies. Bourke himself was a devout Catholic, but his argument became especially popular among late nineteenth- and early twentieth-century Protestant leaders, who built their case for intervention in Pueblo affairs on a dual critique of the failures of Catholic missionization and the persistence of indigenous paganism.

The Franciscan priests and Catholic schoolteachers whose careers were invested in the missionary project saw things differently. While frequently lamenting the survival of certain pagan practices, they typically defended their efforts by observing that Catholicism must everywhere adapt to its congregation. The Pueblos, they claimed, were not insincere in their faith; they had simply developed a distinctive means of integrating Christian practice with local custom. Writing of Santo Domingo Pueblo in 1916, Father Jerome Hesse (1916:30) emphasized that "the inhabitants of this Pueblo are Catholic, and wish to be Catholic, but according to their own fashion." Needless to say, much depended on how one interpreted the phrase "according to their own fashion." One might just as easily speak of the Catholicization of Pueblo religion as the Puebloization of Catholicism. Either way, examples of cross-fertilization are readily found. Many Pueblo ceremonies have been calendrically aligned with the saint days; Catholic churches are painted with murals of corn, clouds, and other Pueblo imagery; certain biblical events and personages have been incorporated into native mythology; the list could be expanded (see Ellis 1954).

Despite this evidence, anthropologists have generally been unconvinced by both the Protestant critique of the Pueblos as superficial Christians and the Franciscan defense that they are good Catholics whose faith is simply expressed in a local idiom. Since the 1950s, the dominant anthropological position has been that the Pueblos[1] dealt with missionization by truly accepting Catholicism but also by keeping this aspect of their religious lives cordoned off from traditional kiva doings, to which the Pueblos are clearly still committed. Edward Spicer (1954, 1962) referred to this strategy as "compartmentalization," and he argued that it effectively permitted Pueblo individuals to participate in two discrete religions at once. Edward Dozier, an anthropologist and Santa Clara Pueblo native, concurred, emphasizing that Catholic religious practices had been

> grafted on as a coexisting system which is essentially distinct from the native sys-
> tem, but the purposes and objectives of both systems of cultural and social practices
> appear to be the same. Thus, while the explicit features of the two religious systems

are separate, the Indians regard both systems as serving the same fundamental ends. Rites of both are performed for favorable weather, rain, snow, stilling wind, abundance of crops, animals, children, cure of disease, and longevity—in short, for the attainment of all good things in life for the individual as well as for humanity. (Dozier 1958:442)

These purported ends may sound far more Puebloan than Catholic; at least, rites for rain, animals, and "stilling wind" are a far cry from the orthodox Catholic focus on sin, salvation, and securing a future spot in heaven. That said, the basic idea of compartmentalization—the notion that Pueblo communities have successfully partitioned their religious lives so as to accommodate two very different spiritual traditions—has served as an important rejoinder to those placing undue emphasis on hybridization or, as Ellis (1954) put it, cultural "amalgamation." Certain iconographic and mythological elements may have moved back and forth, but the dominant historical pattern is one of careful boundary maintenance, we are told. Church and kiva occupy distinct architectural spaces. They have fully separate leadership structures, dress codes, proscriptions, and prescriptions. Even the languages spoken in church (Spanish and English) stand apart from those spoken in the kiva (Tiwa, in the case of Taos Pueblo, and other archaic native languages).

There are, then, three dominant interpretations of Catholicism among the Pueblos: insincere, hybrid, and compartmentalized. The problem is that each builds from the same questionable assumption that the issue at hand is the interplay between comparable phenomena occupying the same social space. Each assumes that Catholicism and Pueblo doings equally fall into the category of "religion" and so have no choice but to compete, mix, or somehow be firewalled from one another. All three interpretations thus elide the important structural differences that unfold from Taos Pueblo's claim that tribal participation in traditional doings is complete (100 percent), while participation in Catholicism is just very common (90 percent). Nor do they address the manner in which governance at Taos Pueblo is inseparable from the kiva hierarchy, while Catholicism is kept separate as a nongovernmental affair. Consider the following statement by a Taos individual in the 1960s:

When you're important in the kiva it's because you're a good citizen; anyone that's a good citizen is the right kind of person to have as an officer, so people like that get elected to office and they belong on the council. The only way you can tell who the right people are is by the things they do, and people like that usually do the right thing because every day they know what is right. The kiva people don't think the peyote boys [i.e., members of the Native American Church] know the right way, so if you're peyote or Baptist and don't go to the kiva you can't get high up in office, but if you're peyote or Baptist and still go to the kiva, then that's OK. You can be governor or war captain. Star Road was an important man in the peyote group—he knew more than anyone else here about how to do things in the ceremonies—but he was in

the kiva too, and people could see that he knew the Taos ways, because he knew how
to talk in the kiva. So he was elected governor and was on the council. (Quoted in
Smith 1967:75)

At Taos, one can choose to be Catholic, Baptist, or a member of the Native American
Church; presumably, one could even enroll in the Church of Scientology. These are
largely individual matters. But kiva participation is different. The rights of full citi-
zenship, especially the ability to have a say in tribal decision-making, derive from an
individual's participation in and compliance with the kivas. The powers and authority of the tribal government—itself a product of Spanish colonial efforts to turn the
Pueblos into orderly political subjects—are not self-standing. Whereas government
may protect religion in secular American society, Pueblo "religion" governs the government at Taos. Sovereignty comes from kivas, not courthouses.

Indeed, Pueblo Catholicism and Pueblo doings are "religions" in such structurally divergent senses that we risk tripping into a category mistake when we discuss
the relationship between the two. Needless to say, Pueblo Catholicism is legibly religious. It fits comfortably within modernist understandings of religion as a collection
of beliefs and practices organized into a church that stands apart from the state—or,
in this case, from the tribal government—and is composed of members whose faith
is ultimately a matter of personal choice. Moreover, like other religions in modern
secular society, Pueblo Catholicism exists among a religious plurality alongside other
competing and more or less equal alternatives.

Pueblo doings are altogether different. They simply *are* the wider social framework within which Christian and non-Christian religions are tolerated. Doings
appear to be the warp and weft of Pueblo society, not one patch among many within
some more-encompassing institutional patchwork. They are less a matter of individual choice than of obligation and duty, a necessary consequence of having been born
in a particular landscape and a particular community. In this sense, doings perhaps
come closer to what Bellah (1967), following Durkheim, called civil religion. The
Universalist reverend William J. Robbins observed in 1941 that the Pueblo individual "talks much about rain...as others may talk about liberty and democracy" (33). I
take this to mean that Pueblo notions of rain, like Euro-American notions of democracy, refer to a general understanding of the order of things, to a totalizing network
of relationships between parts, to a necessity as well as a set of civic responsibilities.
As another Taos informant put it in response to anthropological inquiries into his
tribe's governmental organization, "What you call our self form of government, it's
all based on a religious ground" (quoted in Brandt 1980:140).

Such statements have led some anthropologists to describe the Pueblos as theocratic, inviting comparisons with state-level societies in which religious leaders wield
hegemonic political power. But the notion of "Pueblo theocracy" clouds the issue
immeasurably. Not only does it fully elide the matter of Catholicism's cohabitation
with Pueblo doings during the colonial period, but it also erects an analytical divide
between religion and politics that is, as I have repeatedly argued, entirely untenable

for the precolonial period. Unlike democracies in which politicians arbitrate politics and religion restricts itself to matters of religious power, theocracies have always been defined as dangerously hybrid formations in which religion is said to overstep its natural limits and priests are understood to double as politicians. Put bluntly, the term "theocracy" is always used accusatorily within modernist scholarship to signal the miscegenation of categories that can and must be separated, like two boxers awkwardly clinching in the ring before the referee has intervened to pull them apart. Whether used in reference to the pueblos or the papacy, "theocracy" is always an implicit form of Protestant critique.

Consider the relatively recent comments of one of the few sociocultural anthropologists with ongoing research interests in the Southwest. In his analysis of the evolution of leadership among the Western Pueblos during the colonial period, Triloki Pandey documents what he takes to be the unraveling of "Hopi and Zuni theocracies" as native communities experienced a "gradual separation of politics from religion after contact with Spanish and Anglo-American civilization" (1994:335). The process intensified, Pandey suggests, during the 1930s as the Indian Reorganization Act put new pressures on Pueblo governance to stand apart from the older religious system. "If the processes of secularization and democratization, which are well underway, succeed in Zuni," writes Pandey, "perhaps the secular leaders might become emancipated from priestly sources of legitimation" (334).

Pueblo society clearly has been forced to conform to Western principles of governance in many respects. And there is no question that, today, one can trace a boundary between secular and priestly leadership, even if the connections between these two categories of leadership continue to run deep. But Pandey's analysis implies a great deal more than this, for he asks us to believe that traditional or precolonial Pueblo society *already possessed* the Western division between religion and politics insofar as these categories are said to have been confused or conflated. To claim, in other words, that "the Hopis [traditionally] make no sharp distinction between religious and political domains" (Pandey 1994:330) is not the same as claiming that prior to the colonial era, the Hopis simply did not have religious and political domains at all. Nor is the claim that "in both the Zuni and Hopi theocracies, church and state were coalesced" (333) the same as saying that post-Reformation understandings of church and state are quite irrelevant to the pre-Columbian world of Pueblo doings. The former commits what Henare and colleagues (2007:20), following Marilyn Strathern, call the "negative gesture of hybridity" in which alterity is denied and non-Western cultures are reduced to mixed-up composites of Western categories that modernity has allegedly come to purify.

All of this implies that if contemporary Pueblo doings are increasingly perceived as a religion, distinct from but comparable to Catholicism in key respects, this is not because doings have been stripped of their political trappings, leaving behind a residual set of (now purified) rituals and supernatural beliefs. Pueblo doings could only become a "religion" through a basic transformation, by becoming something other than what they were. This transformation may have begun at Taos and neighboring pueblos, but it is far from complete and may, in fact, be reversing.

I have two objectives in this concluding chapter. First, I want to push the disambiguation of religion and doings one step further by examining in greater detail the evolving process of cultural translation from the early colonial era to the present. How have Pueblo doings come to be viewed as Pueblo "religion" within both Euro-American and native discourses? Which actors spearheaded this translation, and what were their motivations? What stakes were and are involved in the claim that the Pueblos have a religion? Second, I want to revisit and respond to the central challenges raised in chapter 1. Having cleared space for a nonsecular category of pre-Columbian doings, how does this category now contribute to, pull apart, or otherwise stand in tension with the master narrative of secularization? It will not do to simply respond with the observation that the Pueblos belong to *Pueblo* history and are unrelated to Euro-American history prior to the colonial encounter. Nor can we dismiss the matter by making the obvious point that the Pueblos do not represent an early stage in the development of Western civilization. The problem with such statements is not that they are wrong but that they are far too easy, drawing us away from a serious consideration of how every study of the non-West becomes a study of the West and its historical consciousness. Below, I follow Vine Deloria in suggesting that this is partly due to the strong Christian imprint on Western thought, according to which identity comes to be principally reckoned in historical or temporal rather than spatial terms. Be that as it may, the study of Pueblo doings inevitably leads to broader questions regarding where secular Western society thinks it has been, where it is, and where it hopes to go.

How Pueblo Doings Became Pueblo Religion

I will begin with the question of how Pueblo doings have come to be seen as Pueblo religion both by Westerners and, more curiously, within Pueblo society itself. I have already noted that tribal members do not always use the term "religion" to describe their dances, pilgrimages, initiations, or kiva practices. Informally, "doings" is often used instead, and I have suggested that there is something important and revealing in the commonness of this term. Nevertheless, when official statements are made, for instance on a tribal website or in a court of law, there is a marked tendency for the Pueblos to assert their deep religiosity. How has this situation arisen? If Pueblo languages have no native term for "religion," how have tribal members become so comfortable using religious discourse to describe their doings?

These questions open onto a complicated colonial history. Indeed, the very idea that religion, properly so-called, existed anywhere in the New World was hardly a foregone conclusion during the sixteenth and seventeenth centuries. Broadly speaking, two competing claims prevailed in the wake of the initial European invasions: either the American Indians were said to be blank slates lacking religion altogether, or they were portrayed as having a false religion, typically described as idolatry, paganism, fetishism, or devil worship. The former claim typically preceded a petition for royal investments in missionary and educational projects; the latter was more often drawn upon to explain the necessity of violent measures against the natives. At times, the two were combined into a left-right punch that rationalized conquest itself. Columbus inaugurated this strategy in his contrasting portrayals of the innocently irreligious Arawaks who allegedly lived in fear of the cannibalistic and irredeemably devilish Caribs. Such polarized images of New World societies performed extensive ideological labor: Christianizing the innocent natives received greater moral sanction when coupled with the battle against devils, and all such efforts became more economically viable once one group of New World inhabitants was shown to be beyond salvation and therefore legitimately enslaved in the fight to defend a second group of innocent natives.

To a degree, this ideological contrast was reproduced when the Spanish colonizers entered the Pueblo world: sometimes the Pueblos were portrayed as blank slates, open and receptive to biblical teachings; other times they were portrayed as tragically shackled to the pagan rituals of a false religion that must be violently stamped out. The dominant means by which the Spanish made the Pueblos legible, however, was through a comparison with Muslims, specifically the Moorish occupants of Iberia who had recently been ousted from Europe in an explicitly religious crusade. As Anouar Majid (2009) observes, the image of the vanquished Moor came to be widely used by Europeans during the early modern period as a means of placing colonized subjects, and minorities generally, in the enemy position within an imagined struggle to defend Western civilization. The Moor was a cultural/religious/military foil that gave shape and definition to a growing European self-consciousness. Significantly, this foil was imported to America as more than just a collective European memory; in New Mexico, the Moor was present in the flesh at the inauguration of the colonial era. It is one of history's great ironies that the first "European" to make contact with the Pueblos, in 1539, was a Moroccan slave, Esteban Dorantes, sent ahead to the Zuni pueblo of Hawikuh to prepare for the arrival of Fray Marcos de Niza's expedition. ("The first white man we ever met," say the Pueblos, "was a black man.") Dorantes had been born Muslim and presumably was forced to convert to Christianity as part of his enslavement. As if his religious position were not complicated enough, he also allegedly played the part of heathen god during his travels throughout the New World, using a gourd rattle to put supernatural fear in the hearts of the supposedly credulous natives. Whether any Native Americans ever treated Dorantes as a god as some reports claim, the Zuni were having none of it, and Dorantes was killed shortly after shaking his rattle and making his demands.

The conceptual equations of Pueblo with Muslim, paganism with Islam, and New World conquest with Iberian reconquest were persistent themes during the early colonial period. The first military foray into the Pueblo region following Dorantes's death, for instance, was prompted by a Spanish desire to find the fabled Seven Cities of Cibola, a mythical location derived from a European legend about seven bishops who had fled across the Atlantic to protect their riches from Muslims during the Moorish invasion of Iberia in the eighth century. The bishops were said to have established seven fabulously wealthy cities, and Coronado hoped to reclaim the wealth of those cities for Spain when he entered New Mexico in 1540. Needless to say, he did not find cities of gold. Instead, Coronado found quasi-Muslims living in a quasi-Moorish world. Through the eyes of the conquistador, "the trees of New Mexico were 'like those of Castile.'... Kivas were 'mosques,' dark-skinned Indians were 'Turks,' their bows and arrows 'Turkish bows,' and their wives 'Moorish women,'" notes Ramon Gutiérrez (1991:44). Such references helped repackage the invasion of sovereign Native American nations as a noble campaign in defense of God and country. Making Moors out of Pueblos was probably also an important means of steeling the resolve of the heavily outnumbered Spaniards on the battlefield. While waging war on the Pueblo "rebels," the conquistadors allegedly cried out the name of Santiago, also known as St. James the Moorslayer, whose holy strategy of protecting Catholics in Europe involved beheading Muslims (Sweet and Larson 1994:72). After the battle, the Spanish celebrated their success by performing a *moros y cristianos*, dramatizing the reconquest of Iberia (Harris 2000:161–169).

On its own, being called a Moor would have meant nothing to sixteenth-century native communities. Certainly, being accused of having a false rather than a true religion would have had no local referent. Nevertheless, an indigenous understanding of "religion" as a real, on-the-ground category would have speedily arisen as the Pueblos painfully learned that certain of their practices were being singled out as targets of Spanish iconoclastic reforms. Planting corn and performing katsina dances may have been two closely related practices from an indigenous perspective, but to the Spanish they were entirely separate matters: the former was a means of economic production, hence encouraged; the latter was an idolatrous practice of a false religion that must be eliminated. If the Pueblos came to see themselves as having an indigenous religion during the early colonial period, it was not a "religion" defined by spirits, the supernatural, or belief in an unseen order. Rather, "Pueblo religion" would have been initially perceived as the set of native practices that Franciscans attacked and Pueblo communities struggled to defend. As Wilfred Cantwell Smith (1978[1962]) observed, "religion as a systematic entity, as it emerged in the seventeenth and eighteenth centuries, is a concept of polemics and apologetics." This was probably even truer in the New World than the Old.

The same negative logic of stigmatization was still at work centuries later when New Mexico was recolonized by the United States. In 1883, for instance, the overwhelmingly Protestant Bureau of Indian Affairs initiated its own iconoclastic reforms by passing laws known as the Indian Religious Crimes Code (Irwin 1997). Indian dances and other so-called pagan ceremonies once again acquired definition through criminalization, though now this categorical labor was undertaken less by the disciplinary whip of the missionary than by the threat of formal imprisonment and the restriction of government rations. Such policies did much more than merely act upon an existing category of native life. They participated in the ongoing *creation* of Pueblo religion as an embattled cultural space with a palpable, legal reality for indigenous communities.

The most persistent colonial assessment, then, was that the Pueblos possessed a "false religion" (comparable to Islam), and this was driven into native self-consciousness from early on. A second colonial assessment also emerged, however, particularly following the Pueblo Revolt period, as the Spanish sought to make new compromises with native leaders. In her superb study, *We Have a Religion* (2009), Tisa Wenger highlights the extent to which Franciscan missionaries and Pueblo communities along the Rio Grande negotiated an implicit agreement whereby the natives were able to continue their traditional doings while simultaneously embracing Catholicism. For eighteenth-century Franciscans, this was an entirely pragmatic move designed not only to appease the Pueblos but also to counter critics who could now be told that the non-Catholic practices of the natives were relatively harmless regional "customs" rather than expressions of an unreformed and dangerous heathenism: "Frustrated by the practical difficulties of enforcing the laws against Indian 'idolatry,' Franciscans throughout New Spain began to define indigenous practices as *costumbres*. 'Customs' did not necessarily conflict with the Catholic 'religion,' and even when seen as problematic, these were legally classified as venial rather than mortal sins, with less serious repercussions" (Wenger 2009:28). The Pueblos, for their part, generally complied both by attending mass and by reducing the public visibility of doings like masked dances, which by now were well known to invite violent repercussions from the missionaries.

In the late nineteenth century this arrangement was unsettled when American Protestants began to compete with the Catholic Church for control over Pueblo education. The Catholic Church had grown accustomed to defending itself with the argument that Catholicism simply *was* the religion of the Pueblos and, as such, deserved protection, encouragement, and ongoing financial support. Protestants generally found this argument unconvincing. Whereas the Franciscans were willing to view Pueblo doings as mere customs, Protestant leaders sniffed a persistent paganism and accused the Catholic Church of having failed to Christianize the natives. At a deeper level, however, American Protestants were at least as interested in the critique of Catholicism as of Pueblo doings, both of which they viewed as anachronistic holdovers that impeded the development of a progressive secular society. Under Spanish colonialism, Catholics accused the Pueblos of being like Muslims. Under American colonialism, Protestants accused the Pueblos of being like Catholics.

Things came to a head after the First World War when new legislation—notably the Bursum Bill and resuscitated efforts by Protestant leaders to outlaw Pueblo dances—was initiated to further limit native sovereignty, land holdings, and traditions. Wenger's careful analysis of this period brilliantly reveals the manner in which modern conceptions of Pueblo customs as a true indigenous "religion" were constructed in response to this legislation by a new alliance of native leaders and sympathetic Euro-American intellectuals who, for various reasons, sought to defend Pueblo society against forced assimilation. Catholic leaders had once been successful in arguing that the Pueblos' faith in Catholicism (and the missionary efforts that supported it) deserved protection under the First Amendment, but this new alliance now used the American discourse of religious freedom to claim, first, that the Pueblos' own indigenous religion was as valid and deserving of legal safeguards as any other, and second, that Pueblo religion naturally extended into matters of land ownership and political sovereignty, which therefore deserved certain protections as well.

Euro-American anthropologists and artists figured prominently in the effort. By the 1920s, both groups had their own investment in the preservation of indigenous cultures, and as the most frequently studied, painted, and written-about groups in Native America, the Pueblos held an especially important position. By this time, whole art colonies and departments of anthropology had arisen around the study of Indians as Indians. Not surprisingly, additional support came from the New Mexico tourist industry, which increasingly depended on the exoticism of Pueblo ceremonies as a major cultural attraction and income-generating resource.

But not all the advocacy during this period can be written off as a crude matter of Euro-American self-interest. Disenchanted by the war and the industrialization of Western secular society, many intellectuals defended native claims on deeper philosophical grounds, presenting Pueblo religion as an especially authentic spirituality from which the West had much to learn. Writing from just outside Taos Pueblo, for example, D. H. Lawrence mused ruefully about the Indians, who "keep burning an eternal fire, the sacred fire of the old dark religion." "Let us try," he wrote, "to adjust ourselves again to the Indian outlook.... For it is a new era we have to cross into. And our own electric light won't show us over the gulf. We have to feel our way by the dark thread of the old vision. Before it lapses, let us take it up" (Lawrence 1982:17). Similar statements were made by John Collier, a key political ally of the Pueblos. Wenger notes that Collier celebrated Pueblo traditions

> as an "old magical, pagan religion" distinct from and perhaps even superior to Christianity. "Superficially, most of [the Pueblos] are Roman Catholic," Collier wrote in the *Survey Graphic*, "but all of them are fundamentally pagan—an active, institutional paganism with ritual and creed exceedingly rich, dramatic and romantic." Collier believed that in both spiritual vibrancy and ethical results this Indian paganism surpassed even the much-touted heights of the Quakers.... If the Indians were "admittedly weaker" in material development, "on the human and spiritual side" Collier found them more impressive than anything the "White Man's civilization" had produced. "They are groups of men and women rich in beauty, rooted in an inconceivably rich social inheritance, and, after generations of complicated persecution, still faithful to their way of the spirit—a way which might lead us white men far if we wished or were constituted to travel it." (Wenger 2009:118)

Needless to say, this is the same myth of eternal return that has long structured modernist thought (see chapter 1). Collier and his colleagues, in other words, did not contest the primitivity of the Pueblos' "old pagan religion." Rather, they argued that the primitive could provide a model for the future. In fact, Collier went so far as to compare the Pueblos with the classical civilization of ancient Greece (Wenger 2009:119–120), which since the Enlightenment had served as an inspiration for modernist, anti-papal reforms in Europe.

Collier's likening of Pueblo religion to Quakerism is of special interest, however, insofar as it could be interpreted as part of a broader effort to present the Pueblos not just as members of a true religion but also, and more specifically, as *true Protestants*. Indeed, with its combination of conservatism and high public visibility, Taos Pueblo came to exemplify this image of "Pueblo Protestantism" in the eyes of many Euro-American commentators. In the 1930s, for instance, anthropologist Ruth Underhill argued that Taos was best understood through a comparison with the seventeenth- and eighteenth-century Puritans who sought a society of pure and moral simplicity in contrast to the clericalism and religious hierarchy of Europe:

> One cannot help noticing the likeness of [Taos Pueblo] to other religious settlements of history.... Taos might in some respects be old Salem, settled by people with one belief, people who feel that their dress, their speech, even their food, are an expression of that belief and must not be changed.... Taos is run like one of the early Puritan hamlets where it was the joy and pride of the villagers to work together at their housebuilding, their harvesting, their quilting, to have the same beliefs and the same dress and to penalize anyone who deviated. Such comparison may sound strange... but Taos, like the Massachusetts Bay colony, is proud of its rigid principles and plain farming manners, a stickler for the white sheet and the moccasin even as the Pilgrims were for the drab coat and tall hat; demanding that all shall go to church (only in this case we read kiva) and that none shall marry out of meeting. (Underhill 1938:152–153)

In addition to bolstering the claim that the Pueblos had a legitimate religion, such comparisons carved out a place for indigenous communities like Taos in the larger nationalist origin story. Thus did Native Americans come to be presented as First Americans.[2]

The effects of the campaign to simultaneously identify and defend Pueblo religion were complicated. Most Pueblos fully embraced the deeply American discourse of religious freedom as a strategic means of fending off attacks on native practices. Centuries of abuse by missionaries and Christian educators had, by and large, come to an end, and many found it increasingly useful to draw upon overtly religious discourse as a means of securing greater levels of tribal self-determination generally, insofar as meddling with tribal policies could now be recast as interference with tribal religion. "The conduct of the government of our Pueblo is a part of our religion," argued the Santa Clara tribal council in 1924, "and we know that if we are citizens of the U.S. then we are guaranteed freedom in our religious customs and observations" (quoted in Wenger 2009:228).

Such arguments resulted in tangible gains—culminating in Taos Pueblo's great success in regaining control of the Blue Lake watershed in 1970—but there were significant costs as well. Having convinced the US government that they possessed a religion in the modern sense of the term, the Pueblos were quickly forced to confront the restrictions and limitations of the category. As Wenger (2009:184) observes, the discourse of religious freedom now became available to dissenting individuals within Pueblo society who sought to exempt themselves from tribal "religious" obligations and to participate in tribal governance without the traditional sanction of the kiva organization. Moreover, because religion in modern secular society is understood as a matter of personal choice, Pueblo leaders also lost the right to discipline those in their communities who *opted* to give up the old ways and become Christians or members of another non-Pueblo faith. Factional disputes between so-called progressives and conservatives intensified as a result. Taos Pueblo experienced these repercussions firsthand when the peyote church began to grow popular in the community during the 1920s and 1930s. As a foreign and highly individualistic religion imported from Oklahoma by young men working outside the kiva system, the peyote church was opposed by many kiva leaders. But the kiva leaders now found themselves without the legal authority to ban such intrusive "religious" practices. In fact, when they tried to directly intervene in the peyote ceremonies, Collier, who was then the commissioner of Indian affairs, insisted that Taos must accept peyote ceremonies in its midst as a matter of religious tolerance (Wenger 2009:240). In short, the same argument used to defend Pueblo religion within American society suddenly was deployed in defense of non-Pueblo religions within Pueblo society. This irony has reached even greater heights during the past half century as secular principles of individual religious freedom have worked against tribes seeking to limit the rights of businesses and New Agers to either commercialize or appropriate native ceremonies and sacred icons.

Other repercussions of the religification of Pueblo doings are becoming visible more gradually. In a secular society, religion tends to be regarded not just as a matter of individual choice but also as a matter of theological inheritance, handed down from the past, as opposed to a set of innovative responses to changing conditions. Hence, new religious rituals and institutions typically gain legitimacy by hiding their novelty behind the argument that they are, in fact, a return to a doctrinal core or basic foundational principle of a faith. Practically speaking, this means that Pueblo and other Native American communities are only really able to enlist the discourse of religious freedom in regard to sacred places, objects, images, or practices that have been demonstrably sacred for hundreds of years. Thus, the members of Taos Pueblo may have been successful in regaining control of Blue Lake, long viewed as their place of original emergence from the underworld, but they would have a very difficult time gaining legal support were they to attempt to draw a *new* landscape into the religious life of the tribe.

In precolonial times, Pueblo doings were necessarily responsive to the evolving network of people and things. Lock them into the realm of "tradition," make them a matter of preserving the past rather than intervening in the present, and doings are sapped of a good deal of the worldly power they once had. Of course, these are precisely the sorts of restrictions and limitations that give religion its shape and definition in secular societies: true religion is made to stand apart from realpolitik by deflecting religion's focus away from the material concerns of the present and redirecting spiritual attention toward purely mythohistorical or eschatological questions—first comings and second comings. Religion becomes, then, a connection with the past that prepares one for the future, leaving the quotidian push and shove of immediately pressing political issues to the politicians.

Native American religions had little choice but to become "traditional" in this way. Take the language of something like the American Indian Religious Freedom Act of 1978—key legislation in the battle for native rights—in which it is asserted that "the traditional American Indian religions, as an integral part of Indian life, are indispensable and irreplaceable." The statement was well intentioned, but consider its deeper implications. As elsewhere in the document, we are told specifically that "traditional" native religions will be protected by the act, presumably in an effort to distinguish them from Christian religions, which, while not traditional to Native America, are important to many communities. The distinction runs deeper than this, however. "Traditional" stands apart not just from "Christian" but also from "the modern" more broadly. Are there any protections in the act for whatever new and inventive religions might be developed within Native America in the future? Presumably not. Indeed, there is no space to even pose such a question. This is one of the reasons why the assertion that "the traditional American Indian religions" are "irreplaceable" is such a double-edged sword: it builds respect for existing native religions by quietly establishing that the era of native religious innovation has ended. A Pyrrhic victory indeed. Doings have gained certain protections by being encased in amber, legally at least.

Doings, Religion, Place, History

Although Pueblo doings early on were presented as inoffensive "customs" to protect them from the Spanish and then were rebranded as authentic "religions" to protect them from the Americans, this is not to say that doings ever ceased to operate as doings within native communities, nor is it to say that the Pueblos' strategic efforts to translate and retranslate their doings have fully stabilized. New translations are always waiting in the wings. Native commentary on ancestral ruins is particularly telling in this respect. While such sites are typically referred to as "sacred," one increasingly encounters Pueblo statements that appeal to nonreligious logics as well. Writing from a Hopi perspective, Ferrell Secakuku observes:

> Hopis do not view cultural resources such as ruins, as abandoned or as artifacts
> of the past. To a Hopi, these villages were left as is when the people were given a
> sign to move on. These homes, kivas, storehouses, and everything else that makes

a community, were left exactly as they were because it is our belief that Hopi will someday return. Our people are still there. Today the Hopi designate these ruins as a symbol of their sovereign flag. Potsherds are left in abundance, usually broken into small pieces with the trademarks showing. These are the footprints of the occupants. Hopis believe that ruins should remain untouched because when anything is taken it breaks down the value of holding the village in place. (Quoted in Gulliford 2000:92)

Secakuku's metaphors are significant. Ruins are described as symbols of the Hopi's "sovereign flag" in an effort to draw upon the inviolability of nationalistic rather than religious icons. The implication is that the destruction of ancestral sites is comparable to flag burning (which most Americans—and state governments—regard as a crime even if the Supreme Court does not). However, Secakuku's statement also gestures toward the legal protections in neoliberal economic systems. Potsherds at ancestral sites, he suggests, display Hopi "trademarks." By implication, the rights accorded to American businesses should be extended to tribal nations, a move not unrelated to what Comaroff and Comaroff (2009) have glossed as the recent corporatization of ethnicity.

Hence, in their struggles to protect ancestral sites, which have always been key locations for Pueblo doings, a variety of strategies are employed. Most often, an appeal is made to the way Pueblo commitments to specific places are like other people's religious commitments to sacred things. Occasionally, ancestral sites are portrayed as akin to the foci of nationalistic or capitalistic commitments as well. None of these translations are made insincerely, but none are fully adequate either, precisely because Pueblo doings continue to be neither religion nor politics, nor economics. As Curtis Francisco of Laguna Pueblo put it during protests to prevent uranium mining on Mount Taylor (a key focus of his tribe's doings), "We don't look at [Mount Taylor] just as a shrine. We look at it as life itself" (quoted in Linthicum 2008). "Shrine"—the language of religion—now proves too weak when confronting the capitalist forces of secular modernity; and in the search for a meaningful translation, the Pueblos increasingly have no recourse but to invoke "life itself," although such statements do little more than signal the complete breakdown of translation. Certainly, they are illegible from an orthodox legal standpoint. What we are seeing in all these shifting references, however, are indigenous efforts to find discursive leverage within a dominant society that is still unwilling to accept Native American alterity on its own terms.

A few Pueblo scholars have begun to explore a new and potentially much more powerful translation, referring to doings as "native science," following a book of that same title by Gregory Cajete (2000) of Santa Clara Pueblo. One must take care in using such terms, of course. Malinowski (1935:460) may have been the first anthropologist to write about "native science" as such, and he did so in the service of an implicit project to conceptually align anthropological notions of primitive magic with modern secular notions of rational inquiry (see chapter 1). Needless to say, Cajete and his colleagues (e.g., Deloria 1992; Dyck 2001) are arguing something different.

Principally, they are observing that there are core affinities between doings and the scientific study of ecological systems. Consider the comments of James Lujan, a member of Taos Pueblo and dean of instruction at Southwestern Indian Polytechnic Institute, as he reflected on his career:

> I actually decided to study science as a result of my time in the Kiva society. It was during my education in traditional knowledge that I became fascinated with plants and animals, which led me into the courses I later pursued in formal mainstream education. During my cultural apprenticeship at Taos Pueblo, I studied rocks, springs, tiny animals, and big animals. One of the things I noticed was that when animals get sick they often cure themselves by eating certain types of plants. I wanted to know what those plants did for those animals and how. So from my education in Indian ways, I learned that there were things I wanted to study in school. Even during my college days, I tried to learn science by associating and connecting it with what I had learned in the Indian way. "Transference" you could call it. (Lujan 2001:77)

You could also call it an important new attempt at cultural translation. Lujan observes that Pueblo kiva doings are, in large part, about the empirical realities of the world: "rocks, springs, tiny animals, and big animals." Anthropologists have repeatedly made this observation as well. "The Zuni lexicon of sensuous symbols," noted Barbara Tedlock (1983:93) in an essay on Zuni doings, "includes clays, minerals, herbs, flowers, seeds, cornmeal, corn pollen, sun, moon, stars, birds, reptiles, mammals, gems, feathers, flutes, drums, dances, melodies, gestures, postures, wands, puppets, masks, costumes, chants, myths, prayers, prayersticks, altars and shrines." Considered as elements of a religion, one might be led to focus on things like myths, prayers, altars, and wands. Considered as elements of a science or ecology, one is led to focus instead on clays, minerals, reptiles, and mammals. The main point is that doings provide scope for a great diversity of translations.

From customs to religion—and now to science? The latter comparison at least improves upon the false understanding of doings as mere belief in the supernatural. Like science, doings are indeed an empirically grounded and authoritative means of acting in the material world. Should we, then, attempt to write an archaeology of pre-Columbian scientific practice rather than of Pueblo ritual? Useful though this would be as a way to complicate and challenge existing orthodoxy, such a project would ultimately pervert our understanding of doings no less than the study of pre-Columbian "religion." Science has its own purified position within the secular modern imaginary, kept ideologically at arm's length from political and moral issues, and it would not clarify matters to impose this on the Pueblo past.

In the end, we are forced to work through and not around language. The alterity of something like Pueblo doings can only be approached by measuring the dissonance that ensues when we use familiar categories to describe the unfamiliar. Call them religion, or science, or politics, or whatever else you like; then pull out your seismometer and record the amplitude of the shaking as these woefully inadequate modernist categories rub up against the nonmodern phenomena of interest. How much ground has been displaced? Where is the epicenter of the disruption? Where do the aftershocks reverberate? These become the key questions that drive analysis and provide a modicum of cross-cultural insight.

One of the most perceptive cultural seismologists in this sense was Vine Deloria Jr. (1994, 1998), who devoted a significant portion of his research to monitoring what happens when the Western category of religion is used to describe Native American societies. His key text, *God Is Red*, is embarrassingly absent from most conversations in the anthropology of religion, continued evidence of Deloria's own observation that Western anthropologists still prefer Western statements about natives to the self-reflexive statements of the natives themselves. Be that as it may, *God Is Red* is a study of the extensive system of fault lines that separate Native American doings from the Abrahamic religions that have been thrust in their midst as part of the European and Euro-American missionary project. As such, it is a study of a basic binary opposition—though not in a totalizing, structuralist sense. The binary examined by Deloria is a local historical product, born of colonialism and Native America's unique confrontation with Christianity. It is a real, on-the-ground face-off that interests Deloria, in other words; from this perspective, the tremors between Catholics and Protestants or the battles of both against Jews and Muslims become insignificant in comparison to the profound rift separating all four from Native America.

Deloria's analysis is best appreciated as a rejoinder to prior theories of religion, notably Mircea Eliade's influential essays on what he regarded as the rupture separating the religions of "archaic humanity" from the Abrahamic tradition that has unfolded over time to produce the modern age. (Eliade, unlike Deloria, did indeed regard the primitive-modern binary as a totalizing, global opposition; see chapter 1.) The fundamental variable for Eliade was how each dealt with the alleged "terror of history": the constant threat presented by the tendency of time to undermine our ontological hold on the world. Archaic societies, concluded Eliade, grapple with the terror of history by denying it entirely through their repetition of timeless archetypes:

> This refusal to preserve the memory of the past, even of the immediate past, seems to us to betoken a particular anthropology. We refer to archaic man's refusal to accept himself as a historical being, his refusal to grant value to memory and hence to the unusual events (i.e., events without an archetypal model) that in fact constitute concrete duration. In the last analysis, what we discover in all these rites and all these attitudes is the will to devaluate time. Carried to their extreme, all the rites and all the behavior patterns that we have so far mentioned would be comprised in the following statement: "If we pay no attention to it, time does not exist; furthermore, where it becomes perceptible—because of man's 'sins,' i.e., when man departs from the archetype and falls into duration—time can be annulled." (Eliade 1974:85–86)

The religions of the book, Eliade continues, have adopted an opposite strategy, vesting their identity in the directional passage of time itself and conquering history by turning it to their advantage: "Without finally renouncing the traditional concept of archetypes and repetitions, Israel [attempted] to 'save' historical events by regarding them as active presences of Yahweh" (106–107). For Eliade, Judaism was the first truly historical religion and so bore witness to humanity's great theological break with the archaic past: namely, the birth of monotheism, which is understood to have given rise both to religious imperialism and to the notion of a truly transcendent God who is withdrawn from the material present precisely because he inheres in, and is revealed through, the unfolding of history itself (cf. Assman 2008).

I am not concerned with the fine print of Eliade's argument, much of which should not be separated from the immediately postwar existential crisis to which he was responding. But I do want to use Eliade to demonstrate just how important Deloria's intervention was and continues to be. Whereas Eliade drew together the vast array of non-Western "archaic societies" and described them as being in collective denial of a historical reality that only the Western, Abrahamic tradition has come to accept—that is, whereas Eliade defined non-Western religions in negative terms as lacking a Western temporality—Deloria promoted an understanding of Native American religions in positive terms: as an alterity rather than an absence. Accepting that Abrahamic religions have a distinctive historical character, Deloria argued that Native American religions are not so much lacking this character as they are focused on a very different set of *spatial* priorities. "The fundamental problem," he argued, is "whether we consider the reality of our experience as capable of being described in terms of space or time—as 'what happened here' or 'what happened then'" (Deloria 1994:78):

> [T]he fundamental difference is one of great philosophical importance. American Indians hold their lands—places—as having the highest possible meaning, and all their statements are made with this reference point in mind. [European] immigrants review the movement of their ancestors across the continent as a steady progression of basically good events and experiences, thereby placing history—time—in the best possible light. When one group is concerned with the philosophical problem of space and the other with the philosophical problem of time, then the statements of either group do not make much sense when transferred from one context to the other without the proper consideration of what is taking place. (63–64)

The problem of translation identified in this passage lies at the heart of the difference between religion and doings, as these categories have been used in the present study. Pueblo doings, as we have seen, are predominantly concerned with the material interconnections between people, animals, rivers, mountains, corn, architecture, stones, and so on. There is no future orientation, no elaborate preparation for the soul's afterlife, no cult of named ancestors; significantly, there is very little focus on mortuary traditions at all, just unadorned bodies returned to the earth in simple pits. And while many doings invoke the past, either through the recitation of oral histories or the visiting of ancestral sites, there is no past orientation either, no focus on a return to origins (see Ortiz 1972:143). When past and future enter into doings, they do so more as *places* than as historical epochs.

Deloria underscores this point by highlighting the distinction between Western and Native American understandings of revelation. For those coming out of the Abrahamic tradition, revelation is a matter of coming to know a divine plan or design, which is only communicated to the faithful once they have arrived at the appropriate historical level of preparedness to accept the new knowledge. Christian revelation, then, happens in history and reveals a plan for history. Revelation within Native American traditions tends to be very different:

> The structure of [the Native Americans'] religious traditions is taken directly from the world around them, from their relationships with other forms of life. Context is therefore all-important for both practice and the understanding of reality. The places where revelations were experienced were remembered and set aside as locations where, through rituals and ceremonials, the people could once again communicate with the spirits. Thousands of years of occupancy on their lands taught tribal peoples the sacred landscapes for which they were responsible and gradually the structure of ceremonial reality became clear. It was not what people believed to be true that was important but what they experienced as true. Hence revelation was seen as a continuous process of adjustment to the natural surroundings and not as a specific message valid for all times and places. (Deloria 1994:67)

Doings, in this sense, are a kind of relational revelation grounded in the material experiences of particular places.

Does this mean that in their attentiveness to the evolving present, Pueblo doings deny history? Not at all. In fact, it is precisely due to their spatial, this-worldly concerns that Pueblo communities have developed a much more *linear* notion of historical progress than comparable accounts in the Western theological tradition. Consider the Hopi origin story, in which the past is recounted as a successive movement upward through four distinct worlds. In the first world, the people dwelt as insect-like creatures; in the second world, they were transformed into animals plagued by frequent warfare; in the third world, the people assumed human form and learned to cook food and farm, albeit ineptly; in the fourth world, society achieved its present appearance (Courlander 1971). Hopi cosmology even acknowledges that a fifth and as yet unknown world lies ahead of us—or, rather, above us, in the spatialized conception of Hopi historiography. The same sort of radically nonteleological account of linear progression upward into new bodily forms and new landscapes characterizes most Pueblo traditions. And we are left to wonder: where is the myth of return, the circularity, the elision of history that is meant to keep "traditional man" in his enchanted condition? To the great surprise of the Western analyst, perhaps, it simply isn't there. On the contrary, there is an almost Darwinian sensibility to the Pueblos' claim that they have evolved from insect form, to animal form, to human form over time.

The paradox is striking. By attending to interconnected phenomenal landscapes of people and things in the present, the Pueblos are far more inclined to see time as a directional progression, similar to Gell's (1992:149–155) "A-series" temporality, where time becomes immanent in the passage of materially experienced phenomena. (Again, it is not "what happened then" that is important but "what happened here.") In contrast, by making history transcendent and permitting time to stand apart from place, Western thought is, ironically, far more likely to fall back upon circular models in which the future comes to be understood as a return to a quasi-original condition. One can only convince oneself that the future will look like the past when history is set adrift and detached from the sensuous specificity of things. Only when one has vested one's identity solidly in an unfolding narrative rather than in one's material surroundings is it possible to go back to the first world. In contrast, Hopi society seems to be forever moving toward new material realities; there is no illusion that the future will again be insect-like.

Doings, then, are to religion as place is to history. A number of implications follow from this, of which I will emphasize four.

First, when one privileges place over history, one's focus tends to be directed toward questions of immanence rather than transcendence, presence rather than absence. If we choose to continue the anthropological tradition of talking about Pueblo doings as a species of religion, then we must consistently remind ourselves that doings are not a religion in the sense of being a set of strategies for mediating the transcendent, the unseen, or the supernatural. The anthropology of religion has recently rallied around mediation as a core concept (Engelke 2010), and while it would be possible to draw upon this literature to help think through certain aspects of Pueblo doings—for instance, the Northern Tiwa prohibition on katsina depiction (see chapter 6)—it would be entirely misleading to conclude that mediation was or is the dominant concern of doings more broadly. Generally speaking, Pueblo doings deal in what we might call "material connections" rather than signs, traditionally conceived. Theirs is a sensuous semiotics, a way of bringing places into being as situated networks of people and things (see chapter 5). Doings neither represent nor mediate; they make.

Second, to ground identity in place rather than in history is to commit to a localism that is entirely antithetical to the rubric of "world religions." To a great extent, Native American doings are situated; they do not travel, nor could they. This is why there are no kivas or other comparable institutional presences of American Indian "traditional religions" in New York City despite the fact that New York has the largest Native American population in the country. Synagogues, mosques, and churches all travel and can be erected with minimal attention to the ground on which they sit.

Doings are different. They cannot be exported. To change landscapes is to alter one's doings at a basic level. Western individuals frequently do not appreciate this, coming as they do from a proselytizing cultural tradition in which religions have been expressly designed for dissemination:

> Take the plea from Tuwaletstiwa [a Hopi consultant] that outsiders, from campers to conservation fund-raisers, stop sentimentalizing indigenous peoples. For years outsiders have streamed into Hopi land. "They come by the thousands," hoping to find spiritual sustenance, he says. "They're not going to get it from us." "What they do not understand is that you cannot export the Hopi religion," he explains. "It can exist only here, where we have our shrines, springs, landmarks, materials, animals, plants, and hundreds and hundreds of years of belief and practice." Someone living away from the tribal land "cannot practice the Hopi religion," he says. (Milius 1998:92)

As archaeologists, we should think long and hard on this. Is there not a certain folly in our efforts to track pre-Columbian Pueblo migrants across the landscape by tracking their practices, the assumption being that nonlocal people will do things in nonlocal ways? Is it any wonder that, even when we can clearly see populations decline in one region and rise in another, we are typically unable to find "site unit intrusions," as it is so often put? If we take the alterity of Pueblo doings seriously, then we must build from a very different premise: namely, that when ancestral Puebloans migrated to a new landscape, they became new people.

This, perhaps, is why pueblos like Taos are able to acknowledge the geographically expansive set of migration pathways by which different kiva groups came to settle in their present village while simultaneously asserting that the entire community also emerged in place at a specific point in the local landscape. There is only a logical contradiction here if one assumes that identity transcends place and so can intrude into new landscapes—an impossibility within the world of doings. To understand the difference, consider the experience of driving across country while listening to the radio. During one's travels, the car radio is still the car radio, but it sounds entirely different in each place. The radio, in other words, is necessarily local—fully indigenous—at every point. Pueblo doings might be understood similarly as a means of "tuning in" to one's material surroundings. Doings necessarily refashion immigrants on local terms; they remake them as indigenous, as when the Summer People transformed the recently arrived Water People from fish into humans (see chapter 6). Viewed in this way, the community at Taos Pueblo did indeed emerge out of the ground right there in the Taos landscape: as a specific people, they have always been there and can never be separated from it. This also helps us understand why it is not just disrespectful but also downright illogical for someone like a New Age enthusiast to take the prayers and dances witnessed at the pueblo and try to replicate them in Cleveland or Amsterdam. From the perspective of doings, such an undertaking would be as ridiculous as the tourist on holiday in Mexico who purchases a

Mexican radio because he likes the songs and wants to listen to them back home in his Philadelphia apartment.

Third, as doings establish primary linkages between place and identity they also establish the logic according to which social change becomes possible. It goes without saying that within the Western tradition, dramatic historical changes can unfold at a given place. Nothing would seem more obvious than this. Has not the Parisian landscape shifted over time from Roman imperial outpost, to Frankish capital, to a center of Catholicism, to the world's most aggressively secular society? Have not European nations been able to occupy the same physical space as they became reformed, enlightened, industrialized, digitized, and so on? Of course. But our traditional way of talking about such phenomena implies much more than this. It implies that place holds little sway over the form society takes and that historical events flow forward with a force of their own, rushing over geography as a river rushes over pebbles. In the Western tradition, place is a comparatively neutral ground upon which history plays out its dramas.

None of this is self-evident from the perspective of doings. Certainly, Pueblo villages have witnessed major social transformations over the course of their occupation. This does not mean, however, that Pueblo philosophy regards the relationship between history and place in the same manner as the Christian tradition does. On the contrary, the Pueblo past is replete with efforts to bring about social transformation by physically moving to a new landscape, thereby becoming a new people. Origin stories discuss this explicitly. In the typical story, a crisis of some sort arises— for example, a community fails to attend to its doings or, worse yet, falls prey to witchcraft—and rather than undertake the needed reforms in place, Pueblo leaders invariably set the community off in search of a new home, a new center or middle place, where things will be different. These migrations, which fill native accounts of the past, are transformative; they create new Pueblo subjects defined by new relational networks of people and things. They are also plenty evident in the archaeological record: most pre-Columbian villages were only occupied for a generation or two before a decision was made to move on.

The most spectacular archaeological evidence of this strategy is found in the movement away from Chaco Canyon in the middle of the twelfth century and from successor settlements in the northern San Juan at the end of the thirteenth (see chapter 3). Chaco was one of the Southwest's rare pre-Columbian experiments in overt social inequality, and it is significant that the eventual rejection of this experiment and the instantiation of a newly asserted egalitarianism was undertaken through the literal distancing of the Pueblo people from the former Chacoan heartland, which was, for all intents and purposes, empty of Pueblo people by the time of the Spanish invasions. Reflecting on Chaco, Hopi artist Victor Masayesva has commented, "in our history there are recollections and commemorations of our leaving the previous world to emerge here, following moral corruption and the devastation of our environment" (2006:61), and he relates this to the movement away from Chaco, which, following oral history, Masayesva interprets as a place that had become plagued by sorcery. "This is why good-hearted people left Chaco, leaving the *popwakt* [sorcerers] to their devices" (65). It was a striking reformation of pre-Columbian Pueblo society enacted through a change in geography (Fowles 2010a, 2012).

In a world of doings, then, time does not flow over place; past and present are laid out spatially, not temporally. The past exists over there or in the world beneath this one. Migrations make history; new landscapes constitute new futures. Change the land, change the people. Since the imposition of the reservation system, this logic has been forced into dormancy, but it still governed Pueblo action well into the colonial period. Presumably, this was why so many communities of the Pueblo Revolt era did not find it enough to end colonialism by running the Spanish off their existing landscapes. Some physically relocated and established new settlements adjacent to the ruins of ancestral sites; others left the colonial landscape of the Rio Grande valley altogether, opting to settle in the Hopi area, where the Spanish had never made significant inroads. Revivalism through relocation (see Liebmann et al. 2005).

All of this stands in marked contrast to the situation in predominantly Christian societies, where historical narratives tend to make of places what they will. In his analysis of civil religion in the United States, Robert Bellah (1967) noted the persistent tendency in presidential discourse to portray America as a new Israel: "Europe is Egypt; America, the promised land." Latour (2009) has highlighted the same tradition in the United Kingdom, notably in the chants of the British Labour Party whose delegates ritually invoke Blake's poem "Jerusalem" at the close of each meeting: "Nor shall my sword sleep in my hand, / Till we have built Jerusalem, / In England's green and pleasant Land." The ideological imposition of an Israeli landscape on an American or British landscape is more than rhetorical flourish; it lies at the heart of the coloniality of biblical monotheism, as Deloria (1994) was at pains to point out (see also Martin 1992:64–66). Indeed, this is the same privileging of history over place that permitted the sixteenth-century Spanish to equate their conquest of the New World with the reconquest of Iberia. For Christians, it is the story line that matters most.

Hence, the fourth and perhaps the most important implication: because doings are necessarily local, they are noncolonial; one might even say anti-colonial.

The Future of Doings

What, then, is the future of doings? Throughout this study, the discussion has awkwardly moved between past and present tenses, the implication being that the heyday of doings are over and that ongoing colonialism will continue to undercut the Pueblos, drawing them ever more deeply into the American secular project. But the Pueblos have already held their ground well beyond the bleak nineteenth-century prophecies of their inevitable disappearance, and while Western systems of categorization have performed their alchemy time and again, it is clear that the transmutation of doings into religion is far from complete.

In a postsecular age, might doings do more than just struggle to survive? Might they expand? Might they provide assistance as we attempt to think in new, nonmodern ways about the future, both Western and non-Western? Native intellectuals have long argued precisely this. Take a now-classic statement by Chief Luther Standing Bear of the Sioux, who wrote in the 1930s:

> The white man...does not understand America. He is too far removed from its formative processes. The roots of the tree of his life have not yet grasped the rock and soil. The white man is still troubled with primitive fears; he still has in his consciousness the perils of this frontier continent, some of its fastnesses not yet having yielded to his questioning footsteps and inquiring eyes. The man from Europe is still a foreigner and an alien. (Standing Bear 1978[1933]:248)

Yet, he added: "America can be revived, rejuvenated, by recognizing a native school of thought. The Indian can save America" (255).

Deloria and other native scholars have continued to reiterate this argument. What interests me about Standing Bear's statement, however, is the way his philosophy of place unfolds into a temporality that runs entirely counter to the dominant Western discourse of Native American primitivity (see also chapter 6). Concepts like progress and development, observes Standing Bear, can be evaluated according to two very different yardsticks. In the eyes of most Euro-Americans, native societies have been considered undeveloped, as measured by their position within an imagined evolutionary narrative of ever-increasing social scale, complexity, and technological capability. What matters most, from this perspective, is society's relative location in history. Standing Bear, however, proposes an alternative yardstick, replacing the Westerner's transcendent historical imaginary with the immanent realities of place. Reckoned in this manner, the Euro-American is young and naive, childlike in relation to a landscape he has not yet come to know, much less respect. He remains a foreigner who has yet to learn how to become indigenous.

When Standing Bear implored America to embrace a "native school of thought" —for all intents and purposes synonymous with "doings," as used here—he was arguing a decidedly postsecular position. We need to recognize it as such, in part to remind ourselves that what comes after secularism doesn't have to be resurgent religion. Secularism's critique need not send Europe running back to its Christian roots; militant Iranian-style theocracy is not the only option for a postsecular Middle East; and history books in the United States need not be rewritten to turn George Washington into an evangelical or the Declaration of Independence into a strategy to protect religion from the state rather than the other way around. On the contrary, postsecularism can be imagined as something distinct from *both* secularism and presecular religion.

Part of the problem is that most postsecular thought thus far has been wedded to a narrative of return no less than its predecessors in the Western tradition. Take

Stephen Toulmin's visionary set of essays, *The Return to Cosmology: Postmodern Science and the Theology of Nature* (1982), in which he offered at once a history of science, a diagnosis of the ailments of modernity, and a prescription for the future. At the heart of Toulmin's argument was a deep sympathy for the project of "natural religion"—that is, for a mode of premodern European inquiry in which scientific exploration was also theological exploration, and cosmology was a radically integrated project drawing together the rational and the moral, the celestial and the terrestrial, the human, the natural, and the divine. "Whatever became of natural theology and natural religion, as a result of the changeover from medieval to post-Renaissance scientific thinking?" he asked longingly (231). For Toulmin, the mid-nineteenth-century fragmentation of cosmological inquiry into discrete, autonomous disciplines was a dangerous transgression leading humanity away from pressing matters regarding the relations between cosmos and polis. His solution? A return to theological science and scientific theology. A Renaissance reborn. Significantly, Toulmin found cause for hope in the ecological sensibilities of the late twentieth century (see also Toulmin 1990), but the dominant image he offered was of a renewed covenant with a deeper Christian tradition that modernity has, in his opinion, wrongly abandoned.

Today, nearly thirty years on, Latour (2009) offers a similar argument, although Latour's endorsement of premodern Christianity is even more explicit than Toulmin's. In part, the difference springs from the fact that Toulmin was writing in the wake of the 1970s with its surging environmental consciousness, while Latour now writes from a twenty-first-century position in which ecological crises have massively intensified and the idea of "going green" has become disfigured to the point that a disturbingly large percentage of consumers seem convinced they can "organically" buy their way into a sustainable future. Enter Latour's own plea for a renewed covenant:

> [R]eligion, in its Christian instantiation at least, presents itself as a rather plausible alternative to an ecological consciousness whose ethical and emotional drives do not seem to have enough petrol (or soybeans) to carry us through the tasks it has burdened upon us.... we should not forget that the appeal to renewing everything, here and now, and in this world, is first of all a religious passion—and a Passion it is.... Whereas ecological consciousness has been unable to move us, the religious drive to renew the face of the earth just might. (Latour 2009:463)

And he continues: "Perhaps we can postpone this seemingly inevitable [environmental] Apocalypse: religion could become a powerful alternative to modernizing and a powerful help for ecologizing, provided that a connection can be established (or rather re-established) between religion *and Creation* instead of religion *and nature*" (464, emphasis in original). "Eco-theology," then, is Latour's effort to arrange an unlikely marriage between medieval Christian understandings of God's creation and the constructivism of contemporary science studies.

One could excuse Native Americans for balking at the suggestion that we should recapture the animating logics of the Renaissance. Or for shuddering when Latour writes of the "necessity" of again being "seized by the religious urge radically to transform that which is given into that which has to be fully renewed…to seize, or seize again, this world, this same, one and only world" (2009:473). Surely it says a great deal about the current scholarly distaste for secular modernity that premodern Catholicism—with its deep-seated colonial agenda that legitimized the genocide of native peoples and the seizure of their lands—is now being resuscitated as a plausible alternative.

Suppose we follow Standing Bear's native school of thought instead. Suppose we take seriously Vine Deloria's plea that Euro-Americans finally undergo the hard work of becoming indigenous, giving up the fetishization of history and committing themselves to the ecological realities and responsibilities of place. Rather than resuscitate "religion," might we imagine a postsecular future that draws inspiration from the struggles and hard-won lessons of doings? Perhaps then we could find a way out of the persistent tendency to turn global warming into a quasi-biblical, end-of-days narrative of things to come when we should be addressing it as a material phenomenon of the present that must be dealt with in the present. It is the West's particular religious heritage that has led it to mistake a crisis of landscape for a crisis of history. And it is unlikely that a deeper engagement with this heritage will provide a solution.

I am fully aware that by suggesting that mainstream American society has lessons to learn from Native American philosophy I risk being dismissed as a misguided neoprimitivist naively idealizing the tribal world. But the irony of this spurious critique could not be greater, insofar as it entirely depends on an evolutionism that situates native communities like those of the Pueblos at the beginning of a master narrative that culminates in the modern industrialized state. Let me emphasize, in contrast, that it is precisely this evolutionary optic—this crude historicity—that is being contested. Doings are part of the pueblos' past, not Europe's. If, as Deloria and others have suggested, the late twentieth-century environmental movement began to inch mainstream society closer toward a native position, it is not because something primitive was being recaptured. Far from it. Standing Bear's point remains valid: with respect to the North American landscape, Europeans remain adolescents with primitive fears and much to learn. Perhaps the greatest tragedy is that by its continuous redevelopment of the landscape, industrial society runs the risk of becoming trapped in a perpetual immaturity, changing its places even before it has gotten to know them.

But I do not intend to proselytize for or against any particular postsecular future. As I see it, the archaeologist's intellectual charge in such matters is twofold. First, we must continue to root out teleological interpretations of the past that make the future seem inevitably one way or another. In the Western tradition, there is a powerful magnetic pull toward stories with three chapters defined by (1) an original purity,

(2) a subsequent corruption or fall from grace, and (3) a renewed covenant that promises to return humanity to its true and proper nature: $A^1 \rightarrow B \rightarrow A^2$. I will not revisit this model or its critique (see chapter 1), except to underscore the obvious point that it amounts to little more than the backward projection of modern concerns into premodernity. Grasping analytical categories like strings, we hold religion in one hand, politics in another, and economics clenched firmly in our teeth, confident that these will serve as able guides as we move back into the past, beyond the tangled world of medieval and archaic states to the point where the threads eventually separate again and reveal to us an original nature: the primitive anchors to which our categories have supposedly always been tied. Needless to say, this is a spurious string theory, and it encourages us to play the past like a puppet. The greater worry, however, is that such puppetry, uncritically performed, has the potential to turn back upon us, tugging at the present and limiting our possibilities for the future.

If the struggle against teleology is a struggle to keep our future open and untethered, then the second archaeological task is to find ways of bringing to light the varied alterities of the past so that our open future can be imagined more creatively. Archaeologists often argue for the relevance of their discipline by noting that 95 percent of the diversity of human organization is only accessible via the archaeological record, and there is something to this. But if we are to have any success in unearthing novelty we must do more than place comfortable categories in dialogue with the material remains we pull from the ground. As I have repeatedly stressed, an important step in the right direction would be for archaeologists to come clean regarding the deep problems of translation involved with using terms like "religion" and "ritual." If we have been slow to develop an archaeology of religion, let us acknowledge that this is not due to the difficulty of studying a transcendent or immaterial phenomenon via a material record. Given the obvious materiality of all contemporary religions, this has never been a compelling excuse anyway. Premodern religion isn't just hard to excavate, in other words. Nor does our difficulty stem from religion's entanglements with politics, economics, kinship, and so on; the problem is not that religion simply had fuzzier boundaries in antiquity. Let us acknowledge, finally, that premodern religion isn't there to be found at all. Freed of this category, we stand in a better position to be surprised by the past and to learn something new about it.

Easier said than done. The disciplinary attachment to religion as a universal aspect of the human condition runs deep. As we have seen, this is partly because the anthropology of religion has long participated in a laudable effort to counter colonial accusations that the indigenous victims of European conquest were godless heathens lacking their own systems of social and moral order. But the stakes involved in defending religion's universality have grown far too high. Twentieth-century anthropology presented us with an image of religion as the very thing that affirms the world's orderliness and relative predictability, without which one would be, as Geertz (1973:99) put it, "a kind of formless monster with neither sense of direction nor power of self-control, a chaos of spasmodic impulses and vague emotions."

The implication is that whatever irreligious hiccups may occur here and there in the course of history, humanity will always return to its sacred project. I disagree. Human communities need not make the false Geertzian choice between religion and the monstrous spasms of a world without religion, any more than anthropologists need to choose between describing their subjects as pious or heathen, or contemporary society needs to choose between secularism and religious resurgence. The world has a greater spectrum of possibilities.

Notes

Chapter 1

1. Schleiermacher effectively inverted what Assman (2010) calls the Mosaic distinction: namely, the distinction between the one true God and the swarm of false religions, the latter of which become intolerable within an orthodox monotheistic logic. If the Judeo-Christian tradition was born a "counterreligion," as Assman would have it, defined through the negation of an older paganism, then Schleiermacher and his contemporaries could be said to have helped clear space for a "counter-counterreligion," one that has left a strong mark on the modernist historical imaginary.

2. The irony of equating modern and primitive in opposition to the medieval was not lost on Tylor. This is evident, for instance, when he notes how easily modern science can reawaken a primitive fetishism: "I will venture to assert that the scientific conceptions current in my own schoolboy days, of heat and electricity as invisible fluids passing in and out of solid bodies, are ideas which reproduce with extreme closeness the special doctrine of Fetishism" (1913[1871]:2:147). Indeed, the modern's uneasy proximity to the primitive was a repeated theme in fetish discourse during the nineteenth and early twentieth centuries (Masuzawa 2008).

3. The antiquarian study of the Greco-Roman world also played an important role in shaping Enlightenment notions of history. Insofar as my goal is to establish an intellectual lineage for the theorization of religion in anthropological (rather than classical) archaeology, I have sidestepped the deep logics of return that also might be explored.

4. In Childe's account of human history, religion and capitalism are intertwined, part of a common ideology that legitimizes elite control of resources. Thus Childe focused on the rise of the temple economy and the emergence of God as "a great capitalist" whose temple had become a "city bank" (Childe 1948[1936]:154). "The [Christian] idea of humanity as a single society, all of whose members owe one another common moral obligations," wrote Childe (1964[1942]:221), "is an ideological counterpart of an international economy based on the interchange of commodities between all its parts." It is reasonable to conclude that Childe did not regard the rise of modern capitalist states as liberation from the theocracies of old, but rather as the culmination of a process begun during the Iron Age.

Chapter 2

1. Taos's hostility toward anthropologists, and Anglos in general, only intensified when the US government stripped the tribe of control over Blue Lake, Taos's deeply sacred place of emergence and the location of much ritual attention. Blue Lake was lost in 1906—the same year as Stevenson's arrival—when it was made part of the National Forest system and opened to the general public for fishing and camping. This painful episode in Taos's history ended in 1970 when Blue Lake was finally returned to the tribe in what continues to be regarded as a seminal postcolonial reparation not just for Taos, but for Native Americans generally (see Gordon-McCutchan 1995).

2. Stevenson's Taos notes are currently on file at the National Anthropological Archives in Washington, DC; for most of the twentieth century, they were unknown to anthropologists working in New Mexico. While it is clear that Hodge (1912) received much of his information from Stevenson and that Jeançon (1930) had access to at least a portion of these notes, neither published anything close to a synthetic picture of the community. All major statements on Taos society following 1930 were written without access to Stevenson's notes, with the sole exception being Bodine's (1988) essay on the Taos pilgrimage to Blue Lake.

3. The traditional role of the cacique in Taos leadership is clouded in uncertainty, the result, I suspect, of the Pueblos' success in shielding important information from inquisitive outsiders. Parsons (1936:77) was given the impression that the cacique was a Spanish introduction but that a position of Water Man existed as a native tradition, the Water Man being the leader of both the Water Kiva and the southside kiva group. (The issue was confounded further by the fact that at the time of Parsons's research, a single individual apparently served as both cacique and Water Man.) In light of Stevenson's (1906–1907:file 3.1) earlier information, however, it is more likely that the cacique was indeed a *native* position of great importance.

4. Brandt (1980:138) also identifies a third "in-between" category that she describes as the "Middle People," although there is no known Northern Tiwa term for this category. The Middle People consisted of individuals who underwent an abbreviated form of kiva initiation and so were able to act as assistants to the lulina. Similarities with the religiously based class system of the neighboring Tewas are striking (cf. Ortiz 1969) and suggest close cultural relations.

5. Historically, women could assume ritual roles as "kiva mothers" and perhaps also a number of other positions. Nevertheless, these female ritualists appear to have had very circumscribed tasks and were not formally involved in community decision making.

Chapter 3

1. "Life is a road," observe the Pueblos. Road and movement metaphors have permeated Pueblo thought historically and undoubtedly did so a thousand years ago during the Chacoan era, when large formal roads were constructed across many parts of the San Juan basin (Fowles 2011).

2. Ridge Ruin and the many other important Sinaguan sites established west of the Little Colorado River during the twelfth century (Elden Phase) were not formally Chacoan even though the presence of turquoise, macaws, shells, and so on indicate that they participated in a common prestige goods exchange network. Distinctive architectural features, such as ball courts, point to a southern derivation for Sinaguan culture. Viewed regionally, however, the Sinaguas and the Chacoans shared a common pattern of strongly marked leadership to which later Pueblo peoples reacted.

3. Parsons was given somewhat different information. According to her informants, "Winter People" was another name for the Big Hail Society that oversaw the important ceremonies in the middle of winter (Parsons 1936:114; 1996b[1939]:934). This contradicts Stevenson's (1906–1907:file 3.2) more detailed records on the Big Hail Society as linked to the Abalone Shell (Big Earring) People. I have followed Stevenson.

4. Late tenth- and early eleventh-century potters in both the Piedra and Taos regions produced unpainted storage vessels with direct rims, little or no shoulders, and relatively conical
bases. Piedra vessels were typically adorned with banded decorations below the rim (see, for example, Roberts 1930:pl. 13). Banding in the Taos region was identical and came to be accompanied
by vessels with linear incised decorations below the rim that imitated banding (Fowles 2004:847–
888). The only other comparable vessels in the northern Southwest appear in twelfth-century
deposits in the Gallina district, which lies between the Taos and Piedra regions. A historical
connection between the Piedra and Gallina districts has long been suggested (in part based upon
such ceramic similarities); here, I merely suggest that an eastern migration out of southwestern
Colorado began somewhat earlier and extended farther east (see also Ortman 2010:759).

5. A sherd decorated with a proto-katsina mask stands out in the eleventh-century ceramic
sample from the Taos region and deserves separate consideration (see chapter 6).

Chapter 4

1. The jar has strong parallels with the Mogollon region and appears to be akin to the
Tularosa B/W tradition. It was misidentified by Wetherington (1968:50, fig. 26c) as a locally
produced "Taos B/W" vessel.

2. The original narrative recorded by Stevenson (1906–1907:file 2.29) variably refers to the
Winter People and the Ice People, but there can be little doubt that these are two names for the
same group. For clarity, then, I have substituted "Winter People" in those places where Stevenson's
informant referred to the "Ice People."

3. With a tree-ring cutting date at 1147 CE, significant evidence of rebuilding, and trace
amounts of imported Santa Fe B/W in deeply buried contexts, the final occupation of LA 102068
may be confidently placed at the very end of the twelfth century.

4. In this sense, the Pueblos' conception of witches differs significantly from that of, say, the
Azandes in which witchcraft is only considered to manifest through hatred and is therefore considered as fleeting as that emotion. An Azande may be born with the seed of witchcraft but keep
it in remission and thereby avoid social stigmatization (Evans-Pritchard 1976[1937]:48). Among
the Pueblos, however, the mere whiff of witchcraft is enough to spoil an individual's reputation
for life and effectively exile him from the community (Dozier 1970).

5. In a sense, of course, the Northern Tiwas never stopped occupying the site. Today,
many hundreds of years after the village was reduced to ruin, its descendants still visit T'aitöna.
Local tradition indicates that a pre-Columbian foot trail between Taos and Picurís over nearby
McGaffey Ridge included a formal extension that led down to the site, and elderly individuals
at Picurís Pueblo still relate stories of having been brought to the ancestral ruin as children for
semi-ceremonial picnics. Even as recently as 2002, an offering of native tobacco, tightly wrapped
in brightly colored cloth, hung from one of the centrally located junipers at the site. The mag-
pies—T'aitöna's current residents—have since gotten the better of this offering, but it highlights
the continued importance of the place in the native traditions of both Taos and Picurís.

Chapter 5

1. The total solar eclipse observed in the skies of the Taos district in 1259 was preceded by
a partial solar eclipse two years earlier. Such a rapid succession was unique in Pueblo prehistory,
a fact that becomes even more significant when we note that these were two of the eight most
visually impressive eclipses in the American Southwest between 700 and 1700 CE (Wade 1997).

2. The massive eruption of Sunset Crater in the late eleventh century was undoubtedly
the most dramatic "celestial" event experienced by pre-Columbian peoples in what is now the
American Southwest. An ash plume twelve kilometers high, a fire fountain shooting into the air,
thunder, and lightning would have turned the sky into an impressive theatrical stage (Elson et

al. 2002). Some archaeologists have begun to argue that the eruption may have played a critical role in bringing about, or solidifying, the Pueblo understanding of katsina spirits.

3. It is striking to note the affinity between Durkheim's sociology of religion and the theological writings of Schleiermacher (1996[1799]) over a century earlier. Schleiermacher also stressed the emotive aspects of religion. "I wish I could draw you a picture," he wrote, "of the rich, luxuriant life in this [ideal or original] city of God when its citizens assemble, all of whom are full of their own power, which wants to stream forth into the open, all full of holy passion to apprehend and appropriate everything the others might offer them." In such assemblies, the individual's "heart and the heart of each are but the common stage for the same feeling" (1996[1799]:75). This is very close indeed to Durkheim's later discussion of religious effervescence—with one important exception. While for Durkheim, God emerged out of the experience of the social, for Schleiermacher it was the social that emerged out of the experience of God. "Once there is religion, it must necessarily also be social," he argued (1996[1799]:73). Schleiermacher's suggestion was that it is natural for individuals both to intuit the divine and to desire to communicate this understanding with others as part of a religious community. Thus did society emerge out of religious experience, precisely the inverse of the Durkheimian model.

4. In writing of Zuni, Jane Young (1985:27) makes this same point, but draws instead upon a notion of *reciprocity*: "Zuni religious belief is thus based, not on a notion of the ability of humans to cause things to happen, but on one of reciprocity between humans and other more powerful beings who do have this ability to effect change in the physical world.... Thus, the core of Zuni religion may be said to be a belief, not in magic, but in the efficacy of reciprocal relations, the belief that if ritual activities are carried out in the proper manner, with a 'good heart,' the desired result will be obtained. The central issue here, then, is the power of ritual activity and related visual imagery, but only as they exist within this framework of reciprocity."

5. I am unaware of other archaeological examples in which seeds have been found in the floor adobe of a kiva, but Zuni stories include at least one reference to seeds that were "planted" in the center of the floor of a room that was intended to house specific ceremonial functions (Bunzel 1992[1932]:523–524). Tedlock (1983) also notes that seeds were planted in the floor of roomblock kivas at Zuni at various points during the ritual cycle.

6. Or willow (*Salix* spp.). These two species could not be distinguished in the analysis, but this makes little difference to the observations made above. Both are riverine species found in the same microenvironments in the Rio Grande del Rancho valley.

7. The three-and-a-half-month-old dog was placed upon the floor well after the roof of Room 822 had been collapsed. A pit was dug into the structure's fill, the dog was interred and covered with trash deposits, and the pit was then ceremonially filled with white ash and capped with a deer pelvis. I include this dog in the discussion of floor objects because it appears to have been a later addition to the floor assemblage, included by those who were well aware of the objects already interred (see Fowles 2004:619–625 for a more detailed discussion).

8. In her review of the T'aitöna mortuary assemblage, Whitley (2009:188) implies that the Room 822 burial was violently interred and so was not an "intentional burial." This is incorrect. Though the infant's body was not formally flexed, it was covered first by stone slabs, then by what may have been a bison hide, and finally by a pile of refuse that was clearly brought in for this purpose. Moreover, the entire assemblage of floor artifacts within the room must be interpreted as accompanying grave goods of sorts. The child's death may have been violent (on this point, we can only guess), but the child's burial was performed with great care.

9. The only remaining evidence of a bison robe is the presence of two bison third phalanges (hoofs) found roughly on opposite sides of the infant's remains. Bison are not local to the region and their bones are rare. We do know that bison hides were prized commodities throughout the northern Southwest and that bison phalanges were often left attached to the hides, as handles

of sorts. A decayed robe, then, would leave just the sort of pattern encountered in Room 822. Indeed, there are no other ready explanations for the presence of these bones in the kiva.

10. I am grateful to Lisa Young (personal communication 2000) for identifying these distinctive wear patterns.

11. Identification of the digging stick tip was made by Richard Ford (personal communication 2001).

12. My argument regarding shrine dualism would have been stronger had we discovered south and north shrine complexes, rather than south and *west* complexes. Nevertheless, ethnographic research clearly indicates that Pueblo communities can be flexible in such spatial matters (see Ortiz 1969). It is entirely possible, in other words, that T'aitöna's occupants located their "northern shrine complex" on the western side of the village.

13. Creamer's (1993:109) map of the large rock circle shrine south of Arroyo Hondo Pueblo details a similar small circle of rocks in the shrine's interior. While not described in the text of her report, this feature appears to have been part of a northern Rio Grande Pueblo IV shrine style extending at least from Santa Fe to Taos.

Chapter 6

1. The Hopis have been the most public in their efforts to guide humanity toward a better place. Ferrell Secakuku thus writes that "the future of the Hopi is a great burden to them because we must live a life of spiritual meditation and humbleness in order to take this corrupt world, which will get worse, into the better world. Yes, we believe in the fifth world" (quoted in Gulliford 2000:91–92). The fifth world will transcend this, the fourth world of the present. The community at Taos Pueblo is more secretive about such matters, but it shares a similar ethics and cosmology.

2. Matthew Tafoya (Diné/Navajo) and Colleen Lloyd (Tsa-la-gi/Tuscarora) have both taken credit for the original design of the "Homeland Security" T-shirt. For Lloyd's account, see http://westwindworld.com//store/index.php?main_page=page_2.

3. Twenty-four unit pueblos dating to the early thirteenth century (Pot Creek Phase, 1190–1260 CE), each with five to ten surface rooms and one or two pit structures, have been located during survey work in this area. The subsequent construction of T'aitöna as well as twentieth-century logging operations have likely obscured the traces of additional sites.

4. For brief but useful discussions of the Northern Tiwas' nonparticipation in katsina doings, see McGuire 1995:58 and Ware and Blinman 2000:402.

5. At Taos, the katsina have been recorded as *ła'tsina* or *łachina* (Parsons 1936:109), t'lächina (Stevenson 1906–1907:file 2.6), "Cloud People" (Stevenson 1906–1907:file 3.2), and "Cloud Boys" (Parsons 1936:109). Scott Ortman (personal communication 2011) has studied George Trager's notes on Taos linguistics and reports that Trager recorded the term *łaciseonem*, roughly translated as "tobacco-talk old men." Regardless, Parsons (1936:110) is unequivocal in stating that "there is no doubt that in the *łachina* we are meeting the kachina-katsina-koko of the other pueblos." At Picurís, the katsina appear to be referred to as *łacci* (Parsons 1939).

6. Across the Pueblo world, the katsina are considered to have a close connection with some, if not all, of the deceased within a given community. The katsina are the ancestors, then, but it would be incorrect to portray the Pueblos' veneration of the katsina as evidence of an "ancestor cult," in the classic anthropological sense. The katsina are corporate or community ancestors rather than the named ancestors of particular lineages or clans, and they dwell in a generalized underground realm that mirrors that of the living, periodically traveling to the upper world to provide rain, blessings, and occasional punishments to humans.

7. Stevenson used the term "Ice People" rather than "Winter People" in this portion of her notes. The terms appear to be interchangeable.

8. The translation of this term was not included in Stevenson's notes. It may refer to the Picurís round house or one of the pueblo's kivas.

9. The sherd is alternately classified as Talpa B/W (Wetherington 1968:56) or as Santa Fe B/W (var. Taos; Fowles 2004). Either way, the coarse, unslipped surface of the sherd and the distinctively heterogeneous paste (with quartz, sandstone, and biotite inclusions) leave little doubt that it was locally produced. Based on chronological research in the region, the katsina design could have been painted at any point during the thirteenth or early fourteenth centuries (Fowles et al. 2007). The precise excavation context of the sherd has been lost, frustrating stratigraphic efforts at chronological refinement.

10. One fragment of a Kwahe'e B/W duck pot was recovered from late twelfth-century deposits at the Cerrita Site (see figure 3.7G), a short distance southwest of T'aitöna, suggesting, once again, that knowledge about the katsina in the Taos region may be quite deep and quite old.

11. In the Pueblo tradition, zigzag motifs are often regarded as symbols of water serpents as well. Here, I interpret zigzag motifs as lightning following Parsons (1936:104, 110–111) who found little local recognition of a water serpent deity and instead noted a deep cultural attention to lightning. This is not to say that zigzag motifs did not index both lightning/katsina and water/serpent for some of the ancestral Northern Tiwas. In fact, one late pre-Columbian or early colonial kiva mural at Picurís Pueblo includes a lightning bolt with upraised horns, similar to Rio Grande water serpent (awanyu) imagery (see Crotty 1999:164).

12. In a version of this story told to Espinosa (1936:133), the Water People were said to have come "over the mountain streams to the Santa Fé River. Then they swam up the Taos River and to the Ranchos de Taos creek until they arrived near the place where the Fiadaina [Feather, or Summer, People] and the Holdaina [Day, or Winter, People] were living together."

13. The image of the Water People clinging to the corn stalk as they were drawn up from the river references Hopi origin stories in which the final migrants from the third world held onto a bamboo shoot while seeking to climb upward into the fourth world. In the Hopi account, however, it was witches who clung to the bamboo shoot, and they had to be shaken off by the warrior twins so that they would not ruin things in the new land (Courlander 1971:26). This raises the possibility that the Water People were being implicitly linked to the threat of witchcraft in the story.

Chapter 7

1. I am referring specifically to the Eastern Pueblos of the Rio Grande valley. The history of colonialism has been quite different in the Western Pueblo area, where geographic distance from Spanish settlements made it possible to reject missionization entirely.

2. The careful reader will note that in chapter 3 and elsewhere (Fowles 2010a) I readily participate in the tradition of comparing Ancestral Pueblo communities with American Protestants. In doing so, however, my aims are very different, for I have sought instead to critique and remake the existing discourse of "Pueblo Protestantism" that is implicit in much of the literature. Rather than viewing Pueblo doings as a pure and originary form of true religion, I have suggested we use the Protestant metaphor to underscore the degree to which Pueblo doings must be understood as reactionary formations that are highly evolved and historically contingent. Another way of putting this is to say that if the Pueblos are to be fitted into a return narrative of $A^1{\rightarrow}B{\rightarrow}A^2$, then they are better placed in the position of A^2, a position typically reserved for the modern West alone.

References

Adams, E. Charles. 1991. *The Origins and Development of the Pueblo Katsina Cult.* Tucson: University of Arizona Press.

Adams, Jenny L. 1993. Toward Understanding the Technological Development of Manos and Metates. *Kiva* 58(3):331–344.

Adler, Michael A. 1989. Ritual Facilities and Social Integration in Nonranked Societies. In *The Architecture of Social Integration in Prehistoric Pueblos*, edited by William D. Lipe and Michelle Hegmon, pp. 35–54. Cortez, CO: Crow Canyon Archaeological Center.

———. 1993. Why Is a Kiva? New Interpretations of Prehistoric Social Integrative Architecture in the Northern Rio Grande Region of New Mexico. *Journal of Anthropological Research* 49(4):319–346.

———. 2002. Building Consensus: Tribes, Architecture, and Typology in the American Southwest. In *The Archaeology of Tribal Societies*, edited by William A. Parkinson, pp. 155–172. Ann Arbor, MI: International Monographs in Prehistory.

Adler, Michael A., and Richard H. Wilshusen. 1990. Large-Scale Integrative Facilities in Tribal Societies: Cross-Cultural and Southwestern U.S. Examples. *World Archaeology* 22(2):133–144.

Akins, Nancy J. 2001. Chaco Canyon Mortuary Practices: Archaeological Correlates of Complexity. In *Ancient Burial Practices in the Southwest*, edited by Douglas R. Mitchell and Judy L. Brunson-Hadley, pp. 167–190. Albuquerque: University of New Mexico Press.

Akins, Nancy J., and J. D. Schelberg. 1984. Evidence of Organizational Complexity as Seen from the Mortuary Practices in Chaco Canyon. In *Recent Research on Chaco Prehistory*, edited by W. J. Judge and J. D. Schelberg, pp. 89–102. Albuquerque, NM: Division of Cultural Research, National Park Service.

Alberti, Benjamin, and Tamara L. Bray. 2009. Introduction to "Animating Archaeology: Of Subjects, Objects and Alternative Ontologies." *Cambridge Archaeological Journal* 19(3):337–343.

Alberti, Benjamin, Severin Fowles, Martin Holbraad, Yvonne Marshall, and Christopher Witmore. 2011. "Worlds Otherwise": Archaeology, Anthropology and Ontological Difference. *Current Anthropology* 52(6):896–912.

Alberti, Benjamin, and Yvonne Marshall. 2009. Animating Archaeology: Local Theories and Conceptually Open-Ended Methodologies. *Cambridge Archaeological Journal* 19(3):345–357.

Anderson, Frank Gibbs. 1951. The Kachina Cult of the Pueblo Indian. PhD diss., University of New Mexico.

———. 1955. The Pueblo Kachina Cult: A Historical Reconstruction. *Southwestern Journal of Anthropology* 11:404–419.

Anschuetz, Kurt F. 1998. Not Waiting for the Rain: Integration Systems of Water Management by Pre-Columbian Pueblo Farmers in North-Central New Mexico. PhD diss., University of Michigan, Ann Arbor.

———. 2007. The Valles Caldera National Preserve as a Multi-Layered Ethnographic Landscape. In *More than a Scenic Mountain Landscape: Valles Caldera National Preserve Land Use History*, edited by Kurt F. Anschuetz and Thomas Merlan, pp. 129–162. Fort Collins, CO: U.S. Department of Agriculture, Forest Service, Rocky Mountain Research Station.

Asad, Talal. 1993. *Genealogies of Religion.* Baltimore, MD: Johns Hopkins University Press.

———. 2003. *Formations of the Secular: Christianity, Islam, Modernity.* Stanford, CA: Stanford University Press.

Assman, Jan. 2008. *Of God and Gods: Egypt, Israel and the Rise of Monotheism.* Madison: University of Wisconsin Press.

———. 2010. *The Price of Monotheism.* Palo Alto, CA: Stanford University Press.

Babcock, Barbara A. 1988. At Home, No Women Are Storytellers: Potters, Stories, and Politics in Cochiti Pueblo. *Journal of the Southwest* 30:356–389.

Bandelier, Adolph Francis. 1976[1890–1892]. *Final Report of Investigations among the Indians of the Southwestern United States, Carried on Mainly in the Years from 1880 to 1885*, parts 1 and 2. New York: AMS.

———. 1984[1885–1888]. *The Southwestern Journals of Adolph F. Bandelier 1885–1888*, edited by Charles H. Lange, Carroll L. Riley, and Elizabeth M. Lange. Albuquerque: University of New Mexico Press.

Bandy, Matthew S. 2004. Fissioning, Scalar Stress, and Social Evolution in Early Village Societies. *American Anthropologist* 106(2):322–333.

Barrowclough, David A., and Caroline Malone, eds. 2007. *Cult in Context: Reconsidering Ritual in Archaeology.* Oxford: Oxbow.

Barth, Fredrik. 1961. *Nomads of South Persia: The Basseri Tribe of the Khamseh Confederacy.* Boston: Little, Brown.

———. 1969. Introduction. In *Ethnic Groups and Boundaries*, edited by Fredrik Barth, pp. 9–38. Boston: Little, Brown.

Bauer, Brian S. 1996. Legitimization of the State in Inca Myth and Ritual Source. *American Anthropologist* 98(2):327–337.

Bellah, Robert N. 1967. Civil Religion in America. *Daedalus* 96:1–21.

Bennett, Jane. 2004. The Force of Things: Steps toward an Ecology of Matter. *Political Theory* 32(3):347–372.

Benson, Larry, Linda Cordell, Kirk Vincent, Howard Taylor, John Stein, G. Lang Farmer, and Kiyoto Futa. 2003. Ancient Maize from Chacoan Great Houses: Where Was It Grown? *Proceedings of the National Academy of Sciences* 100(22):13111–13115.

Berger, Peter L. 1999. The Desecularization of the World: A Global Overview. In *The Desecularization of the World*, edited by Peter L. Berger, pp. 1–18. Grand Rapids, MI: Eerdmans.

Bernardini, Wesley. 1996. Transitions in Social Organization: A Predictive Model from Southwestern Archaeology. *Journal of Anthropological Archaeology* 15:1–31.

Bernardini, Wesley, and Severin Fowles. 2011. Becoming Hopi, Becoming Tiwa: Two Pueblo Histories of Movement. In *Movement, Connectivity, and Landscape Change in the Ancient Southwest*, edited by Margaret Nelson and Colleen Strawhacker, pp. 253–274. Boulder: University Press of Colorado.

Bertemes, François, and Peter F. Biehl. 2001. Introduction. In *The Archaeology of Cult and Religion*, edited by Peter F. Biehl and François Bertemes, pp. 11–26. Budapest: Archaeolingua.

Biehl, Peter F., and François Bertemes, eds. 2001. *The Archaeology of Cult and Religion*. Budapest: Archaeolingua.

Bloom, Lansing Barlett. 1936. Bourke on the Southwest. *New Mexico Historical Review* 11(3):245–282.

Bodine, John J. 1979. Taos Pueblo. In *Handbook of North American Indians*, vol. 9, edited by Alfonso Ortiz, pp. 255–267. Washington, DC: Smithsonian Institution Press.

———. 1988. The Taos Blue Lake Ceremony. *American Indian Quarterly* 12(2):91–105.

Bourdieu, Pierre. 1990. *The Logic of Practice*. Palo Alto, CA: Stanford University Press.

Boyer, Jeffrey L., James L. Moore, Daisy F. Levine, Linda Mick-O'Hara, and Mollie S. Toll. 1994. LA 70577. In *Studying the Taos Frontier: The Pot Creek Data Recovery Project*, edited by Jeffrey L. Boyer, James L. Moore, Daisy F. Levine, Linda Mick-O'Hara, and Mollie S. Toll, pp. 175–228. Santa Fe: Museum of New Mexico, Office of Archaeological Studies.

Bradley, Bruce A. 1996. Pitchers to Mugs: Chacoan Revival at Sand Canyon Pueblo. *Kiva* 61(3):241–255.

Brandt, Elizabeth A. 1977. The Role of Secrecy in a Pueblo Society. In *Flowers of the Wind: Papers on Ritual, Myth and Symbolism in California and the Southwest*, edited by T. C. Blackburn, pp. 11–28. Socorro, NM: Ballena.

———. 1980. On Secrecy and Control of Knowledge. In *Secrecy: A Cross-Cultural Perspective*, edited by S. Tefft, pp. 123–146. New York: Human Sciences Press.

———. 1994. Egalitarianism, Hierarchy, and Centralization in the Pueblos. In *The Ancient Southwestern Community: Models and Methods for the Study of Prehistoric Social Organization*, edited by W. H. Wills and Robert D. Leonard, pp. 9–23. Albuquerque: University of New Mexico Press.

Brown, Donald Nelson. 1973. Structural Change at Picuris Pueblo, New Mexico. PhD diss., University of Arizona, Tucson.

————. 1979. Picuris Pueblo. In *Handbook of North American Indians*, vol. 9, edited by Alfonso Ortiz, pp. 268–277. Washington, DC: Smithsonian Institution Press.

————. 1999. Picuris Pueblo in 1890: A Reconstruction of Picuris Social Structure and Subsistence Activities. In *Picuris Pueblo through Time: Eight Centuries of Change at a Northern Rio Grande Pueblo*, edited by Michael A. Adler and Herbert W. Dick, pp. 19–41. Dallas: Southern Methodist University Press.

Brück, Joanna. 1999. Ritual and Rationality: Some Problems of Interpretation in European Archaeology. *European Journal of Archaeology* 2(3):313–344.

Brumfiel, Elizabeth M. 1998. Huitzilopochtli's Conquest: Aztec Ideology in the Archaeological Record. *Cambridge Archaeological Journal* 8:3–13.

Bunzel, Ruth L. 1992[1932]. Introduction to Zuñi Ceremonialism. *Forty-Seventh Annual Report of the Bureau of American Ethnology 1929–1930*, pp. 467–544. Washington, DC: Smithsonian Institution Press.

Cajete, Gregory. 2000. *Native Science: Natural Laws of Interdependence*. Santa Fe, NM: Clear Light.

Calhoun, Craig, Mark Juergensmeyer, and Jonathan VanAntwerpen, eds. 2011. *Rethinking Secularism*. Oxford: Oxford University Press.

Cameron, Catherine M., and Robert Lee Sappington. 1984. Obsidian Procurement at Chaco Canyon, AD 500–1200. In *Recent Research on Chaco Prehistory*, edited by W. James Judge and John D. Schelberg. Albuquerque, NM: Division of Cultural Research, National Park Service.

Cauvin, Jacques. 2000. *The Birth of the Gods and the Origins of Agriculture*. New York: Cambridge University Press.

Childe, V. Gordon. 1944. *Progress and Archaeology*. London: Watts.

————. 1948[1936]. *Man Makes Himself*. London: Watts.

————. 1964[1942]. *What Happened in History*. Baltimore, MD: Penguin.

Clastres, Pierre. 1989. *Society against the State*. New York: Zone.

Cole, Sally J. 1989. The Homol'ovi Research Program: Investigations into the Prehistory of the Middle Little Colorado River Valley. *Kiva* 54(3):313–329.

Comaroff, John L., and Jean Comaroff. 2009. *Ethnicity, Inc.* Chicago: University of Chicago Press.

Comte, Auguste. 1880[1830]. *The Positive Philosophy of Auguste Comte*. Chicago: Belford-Clarke.

Corman, Catherine A. 2004. 9/11 and Acoma Pueblo: Homeland Security in Indian Country. *Common-Place* 5(1). http://www.common-place.org/pastimes/200408.shtml (accessed March 2, 2010).

Coulam, Nancy J., and Alan R. Schroedl. 2004. Late Archaic Totemism in the Greater American Southwest. *American Antiquity* 69(1):41–62.

Courlander, Harold. 1971. *The Fourth World of the Hopis*. Albuquerque: University of New Mexico Press.

————. 1982. Introduction. In his *Hopi Voices: Recollections, Traditions, and Narratives of the Hopi Indians*, pp. xi–xli. Albuquerque: University of New Mexico Press.

Creamer, Winifred. 1993. *The Architecture of Arroyo Hondo Pueblo, New Mexico*. Santa Fe, NM: SAR Press.

Crotty, Helen K. 1999. Kiva Murals and Iconography at Picuris Pueblo. In *Picuris Pueblo through Time: Eight Centuries of Change at a Northern Rio Grande Pueblo*, edited by Michael A. Adler and Herbert W. Dick, pp. 149–188. Dallas: Southern Methodist University Press.

Crown, Patricia L. 1991. Evaluating the Construction Sequence and Population of Pot Creek Pueblo, Northern New Mexico. *American Antiquity* 56:291–314.

Crown, P., and T. Kohler. 1994. Community Dynamics, Site Structure, and Aggregation in the Northern Rio Grande. In *The Ancient Southwestern Community: Model and Methods for the Study of Prehistoric Social Organization*, edited by W. Wills and R. Leonard, pp. 103–117. Albuquerque: University of New Mexico Press.

Crown, P., J. Orcutt, and T. Kohler. 1996. Pueblo Cultures in Transition: The Northern Rio Grande. In *The Prehistoric Pueblo World, AD 1150–1350*, edited by Michael A. Adler, pp. 188–204. Tucson: University of Arizona Press.

Darling, Andrew. 1998. Mass Inhumation and the Execution of Witches in the American Southwest. *American Anthropologist* 100(3):732–752.

Dawkins, Richard. 2006. *The Root of All Evil?* Channel 4 documentary, United Kingdom.

de Angulo, Jaime. 1985. *Jaime in Taos: The Taos Papers of Jaime de Angulo*. San Francisco: City Lights.

Deloria, Vine, Jr. 1988. *Custer Died for Your Sins*. Norman: University of Oklahoma Press.

———. 1992. Ethnoscience and Indian Realities. *Winds of Change: American Indian Education and Opportunity* 7(3):12–18.

———. 1994. *God Is Red: A Native View of Religion*. Golden, CO: Fulcrum.

———. 1997. *Red Earth, White Lies: Native Americans and the Myth of Scientific Fact*. Golden, CO: Fulcrum.

———. 1998. *For This Land: Writings on Religion in America*. New York: Routledge.

DeMarrais, Elizabeth, L. C. Castillo, and Tim Earle. 1996. Ideology, Materialization, and Power Strategies. *Current Anthropology* 37(1):15–31.

Derrida, Jacques. 1982. Différance. In *Margins of Philosophy*, translated by Alan Bass. Chicago: University of Chicago Press.

Dick, Herbert W., Daniel Wolfman, Curtis Schaafsma, and Michael A. Adler. 1999. Prehistoric and Early Historic Architecture and Ceramics at Picuris. In *Picuris Pueblo through Time: Eight Centuries of Change at a Northern Rio Grande Pueblo*, edited by Michael A. Adler and Herbert W. Dick, pp. 43–100. Dallas: Southern Methodist University Press.

Dickson, Bruce D. 1979. *Prehistoric Pueblo Settlement Patterns: The Arroyo Hondo, New Mexico, Site Survey*. Santa Fe, NM: SAR Press.

Douglas, Mary. 1982. *Natural Symbols, Explorations in Cosmology*. New York: Pantheon.

———. 1988[1966]. *Purity and Danger*. London: Routledge and Kegan Paul.

Dozier, Edward P. 1958. Spanish-Catholic Influences on Rio Grande Pueblo Religion. *American Anthropologist* 60(3):441–448.

————. 1970. *The Pueblo Indians of North America*. New York: Holt, Rinehart and Winston.

Durkheim, Emile. 1965[1915]. *The Elementary Forms of the Religious Life*. New York: Free Press.

Duwe, Samuel. 2011. The Prehispanic Tewa World: Space, Time, and Becoming in the Pueblo Southwest. PhD diss., University of Arizona, Tucson.

Dyck, Lillian. 2001. A Personal Journey into Science, Feminist Science, and Aboriginal Science. In *Science and Native American Communities: Legacies of Pain, Visions of Promise*, edited by Keith James, pp. 22–28. Lincoln: University of Nebraska Press.

Earle, Timothy. 2001. Economic Support of Chaco Canyon Society. *American Antiquity* 66(1):26–35.

Echo-Hawk, Roger C. 2000. Ancient History in the New World: Integrating Oral Traditions and the Archaeological Record in Deep Time. *American Antiquity* 65:267–290.

Eddy, Frank W. 1966. *Prehistory in the Navajo Reservoir District, Northwestern New Mexico*. Santa Fe: Museum of New Mexico Press.

————. 1974. Population Dislocation in the Navaho Reservoir District, New Mexico and Colorado. *American Antiquity* 39(1):75–84.

————. 1977. *Archaeological Investigations at Chimney Rock Mesa: 1970–1972*. Boulder: Colorado Archaeological Society.

Eggan, Fred. 1950. *Social Organization of the Western Pueblos*. Chicago: University of Chicago Press.

Eliade, Mircea. 1961[1957]. *The Sacred and the Profane: The Nature of Religion*. New York: Harper and Row.

————. 1974. *The Myth of Eternal Return*. Princeton, NJ: Princeton University Press.

Ellingson, Ter. 2001. *The Myth of the Noble Savage*. Berkeley: University of California Press.

Elliot, Michael A. 2006. Indian Patriots on Last Stand Hill. *American Quarterly* 58(4):987–1015.

Ellis, Florence Hawley. 1954. Comments. *American Anthropologist* 56(4):678–680.

————. 1974[1962]. Anthropological Data Pertaining to the Taos Land Claim. In *Pueblo Indians*, vol. 1, pp. 29–150. New York: Garland.

————. 1988. *From Drought to Drought*, vol. 1. Santa Fe, NM: Sunstone.

Ellis, Florence Hawley, and J. J. Brody. 1964. Ceramic Stratigraphy and Tribal History at Taos Pueblo. *American Antiquity* 29(3):316–327.

Elson, Mark D., Michael H. Ort, S. Jerome Hesse, and Wendell A. Duffield. 2002. Lava, Corn, and Ritual in the Northern Southwest. *American Antiquity* 67:119–135.

Emerson, Thomas E. 1996. Cahokian Elite Ideology and the Mississippian Cosmos. In *Cahokia: Domination and Ideology in the Mississippian World*, edited by Timothy M. Pauketat and Thomas E. Emerson, pp. 190–228. Lincoln: University of Nebraska Press.

Engelke, Matthew. 2010. Religion and the Media Turn: A Review Essay. *American Ethnologist* 37(2):371–379.

Engels, Frederich. 1902[1884]. *The Origin of the Family, Private Property and the State*. Chicago: Charles H. Kerr.

Espinosa, Aurelio M. 1936. Pueblo Indian Folk Tales. *Journal of American Folklore* 49:69–133.

Evans-Pritchard, E. E. 1976[1937]. *Witchcraft Oracles and Magic among the Azande*, abridged ed. Oxford: Clarendon.

Fabian, Johannes. 1983. *Time and the Other: How Anthropology Makes Its Object.* New York: Columbia University Press.

Fallon, Denise, and Karen Wening. 1982. Howiri, Excavation at a Northern Rio Grande Biscuit Ware Site. *Laboratory of Anthropology Notes* 261b. Santa Fe: Museum of New Mexico.

Fenton, William N. 1957. *Factionalism at Taos Pueblo, New Mexico.* Washington, DC: Smithsonian Institution, Bureau of American Ethnology.

Fewkes, Walter. 1922. Ancestor Worship of the Hopi Indians. In *Annual Report of the Board of Regents of the Smithsonian Institution Showing the Operations, Expenditures, and Condition of the Institution for the Year Ending June 30, 1921*, pp. 485–506. Washington, DC: Government Printing Office.

Fitzgerald, Timothy, ed. 2007. *Religion and the Secular: Historical and Colonial Formations.* Sheffield, England: Equinox.

Fogelin, Lars. 2006. *Archaeology of Early Buddhism.* Lanham, MD: AltaMira.

———. 2007. The Archaeology of Religious Ritual. *Annual Reviews in Anthropology* 36:55–71.

Fogelin, Lars, ed. 2008. *Religion in the Material World.* Carbondale: Southern Illinois University Press.

Fowles, Severin M. 2004. The Making of Made People: The Prehistoric Evolution of Hierocracy Among the Northern Tiwa of New Mexico. PhD diss., University of Michigan, Ann Arbor.

———. 2005. Historical Contingency and the Prehistoric Foundations of Eastern Pueblo Moiety Organization. *Journal of Anthropological Research* 61(1):25–52.

———. 2006. Our Father (Our Mother): Gender, Praxis, and Marginalization in Pueblo Religion. In *Engaged Anthropology*, edited by Michelle Hegmon and Sunday Eiselt, pp. 27–51. Ann Arbor: University of Michigan Press.

———. 2008. Steps toward an Archaeology of Taboo. In *Religion, Archaeology, and the Material World*, edited by Lars Fogelin, pp. 15–37. Carbondale: Southern Illinois University Press.

———. 2009. The Enshrined Pueblo: Villagescape and Cosmos in the Northern Rio Grande. *American Antiquity* 74(3):448–466.

———. 2010a. A People's History of the American Southwest. In *Rethinking Complexity in Native North America*, edited by Susan Alt. Salt Lake City: University of Utah Press.

———. 2010b. People without Things. In *The Anthropology of Absence: Materialisations of Transcendence and Loss*, edited by Mikkel Bille, Frida Hastrup, and Tim Flohr Sørensen, pp. 23–41. New York: Springer.

———. 2011. Movement and the Unsettling of the Pueblos. In *Rethinking Anthropological Perspectives on Migration*, edited by Graciela Cabana and Jeffrey Clark, pp. 45–67. Gainesville: University Press of Florida.

————. 2012. The Pueblo IV Village in an Age of Reformation. In *Oxford Handbook of North American Archaeology*, edited by Timothy Pauketat, pp. 631–644. Oxford: Oxford University Press.

————. forthcoming. On Torture in Societies against the State. In *Violence and Civilization*, edited by Rod Campbell. Providence, RI: Joukowsky Institute, Brown University.

Fowles, Severin M., and Katherine Heupel. forthcoming. In the Absence of Modernity. In *Oxford Handbook of the Archaeology of the Contemporary World*, edited by Paul Graves-Brown, Rodney Harrison, and Angela Piccini. Oxford: Oxford University Press.

Fowles, Severin M., Leah Minc, Sam Duwe, and David V. Hill. 2007. Clay, Conflict, and Village Aggregation: Compositional Analyses of Pre-Classic Pottery from Taos, NM. *American Antiquity* 72(1):125–152.

Fox, Robin. 1967. *The Keresan Bridge, A Problem in Pueblo Ethnology*. London: Athlone.

Frazer, James George. 1955[1911–1915]. *The Golden Bough: A Study in Magic and Religion*, 3rd ed. London: Macmillan.

French, David H. 1948. *Factionalism in Isleta Pueblo*. New York: J. J. Augustin.

Friesen, T. Max. 1999. Resource Structure, Scalar Stress, and the Development of Inuit Social Organization. *World Archaeology* 31(1):21–37.

Fritz, John M. 1978. Paleopsychology Today: Ideational Systems and Human Adaptation in Prehistory. In *Social Archeology: Beyond Subsistence and Dating*, edited by Charles Redman, Mary Berman, Edward Curtin, William Langhorne, Nina Versaggi, and Jeffery Wanser, pp. 37–59. New York: Academic.

Garwood, Paul, David Jennings, Robin Skeates, and Judith Toms. 1991. Preface. In *Sacred and Profane: Proceedings of a Conference on Archaeology, Ritual and Religion*, edited by Paul Garwood, David Jennings, Robin Skeates, and Judith Toms, pp. v–x. Oxford: Oxbow.

Gauchet, Marcel. 1999. *The Disenchantment of the World*. Princeton, NJ: Princeton University Press.

Gaukroger, Stephen. 1991. *The Uses of Antiquity: The Scientific Revolution and the Classical Tradition*. New York: Springer.

Geertz, Clifford. 1973. Religion as a Cultural System. In his *The Interpretation of Cultures*, pp. 87–125. New York: Basic.

Gell, Alfred. 1992. *The Anthropology of Time: Cultural Constructions of Temporal Maps and Images*. Oxford: Berg.

————. 1998. *Art and Agency: An Anthropological Theory*. Oxford: Clarendon.

Glowacki, Donna M., and Scott Van Keuren, eds. 2011. *Religious Transformation in the Late Pre-Hispanic Pueblo World*. Tucson: University of Arizona Press.

Goldfrank, Esther Schiff, ed. 1962. *Isleta Paintings*. Washington, DC: Smithsonian Institution Press.

Goody, Jack. 1996. A Kernel of Doubt. *Journal of the Royal Anthropological Institute* 2:667–681.

Gordon-McCutchan, R. C. 1995. *The Taos Indians and the Battle for Blue Lake*. Santa Fe, NM: Red Crane.

Graeber, David. 2004. *Fragments of an Anarchist Anthropology*. Chicago: Prickly Paradigm.

Grant, Blanche C. 1976[1925]. *The Taos Indians*. Glorieta, NM: Rio Grande Press.

Graves, Michael W., Sally J. Holbrook, and William A. Longacre. 1982. Aggregation and Abandonment at Grasshopper Pueblo: Evolutionary Trends in the Late Prehistory of East-Central Arizona. In *Multidisciplinary Research at Grasshopper Pueblo, Arizona*, edited by William A. Longacre, Sally J. Holbrook, and Michael W. Graves, pp. 110–121. Tucson: University of Arizona Press.

Greeley, Andrew M. 1972. *Unsecular Man: The Persistence of Religion*. New York: Schocken.

Green, Ernestene L. 1976. *Valdez Phase Occupation Near Taos, New Mexico*. Dallas: Southern Methodist University Press.

Gulliford, Andrew. 2000. *Sacred Objects and Sacred Places: Preserving Tribal Traditions*. Boulder: University Press of Colorado.

Gutiérrez, Ramon A. 1991. *When Jesus Came, the Corn Mothers Went Away: Marriage, Sexuality, and Power in New Mexico, 1500–1846*. Palo Alto, CA: Stanford University Press.

Hall, Robert L. 1997. *An Archaeology of the Soul: North American Indian Belief and Ritual*. Champaign: University of Illinois Press.

Haraway, Donna J. 1988. Situated Knowledges: The Science Question in Feminism and the Privilege of Partial Perspective. *Feminist Studies* 14(3):575–599.

———. 2008. *When Species Meet*. Minneapolis: University of Minnesota Press.

Harman, Graham. 2009. *Prince of Networks: Bruno Latour and Metaphysics*. Melbourne: re.press.

Harris, Max. 2000. *Aztecs, Moors, and Christians: Festivals of Reconquest in Mexico and Spain*. Austin: University of Texas Press.

Harvey, Byron. 1963. Masks at a Maskless Pueblo: The Laguna Colony Kachina Organization at Isleta. *Ethnology* 2(4):478–489.

Hawkes, Christopher F. 1954. Archaeological Theory and Method: Some Suggestions from the Old World. *American Anthropologist* 56:155–168.

Hawley, Florence. 1950. Big Kivas, Little Kivas, and Moiety Houses in Historical Reconstruction. *Southwestern Journal of Anthropology* 6(3):286–302.

Haycock, David Boyd. 2002. *William Stukeley: Science, Religion, and Archaeology in Eighteenth-Century England*. Rochester, NY: Boydell.

Hayden, Brian. 1987. Alliances and Ritual Ecstasy: Human Responses to Resource Stress. *Journal for the Scientific Study of Religion* 26:81–91.

———. 2003. *Shamans, Sorcerers, and Saints: A Prehistory of Religion*. Washington, DC: Smithsonian Institution Press.

Hays, Kelley Ann. 1994. Kachina Depictions on Prehistoric Pueblo Pottery. In *Kachinas in the Pueblo World*, edited by Polly Schaafsma, pp. 47–62. Albuquerque: University of New Mexico Press.

Hays-Gilpin, Kelley. 2000a. Gender Ideology and Ritual Activities. In *Women and Men in the Prehispanic Southwest: Labor, Power, and Prestige*, edited by Patricia L. Crown, pp. 91–136. Santa Fe, NM: SAR Press.

————. 2000b. Beyond Mother Earth and Father Sky: Sex and Gender in Ancient Southwestern Visual Arts. In *Reading the Body*, edited by Alison E. Rautman, pp. 165–186. Philadelphia: University of Pennsylvania Press.

Hays-Gilpin, Kelley, and David S. Whitley, eds. 2008. *Belief in the Past: Theoretical Approaches to the Archaeology of Religion*. Walnut Creek, CA: Left Coast Press.

Hegmon, Michelle, Scott G. Ortman, and Jeannette L. Mobley-Tanaka. 2000. Women, Men, and the Organization of Space. In *Women and Men in the Prehispanic Southwest*, edited by Patricia L. Crown, pp. 43–90. Santa Fe, NM: SAR Press.

Heidegger, Martin. 2001. The Thing. In *Poetry, Language, and Thought*, pp. 165–182. New York: HarperCollins.

Heitman, Carrie C., and Stephen Plog. 2005. Kinship and the Dynamics of the House: Rediscovering Dualism in the Pueblo Past. In *A Catalyst for Ideas: Anthropological Archaeology and the Legacy of Douglas W. Schwartz*, edited by Vernon L. Scarborough, pp. 69–100. Santa Fe, NM: SAR Press.

Henshilwood, Christopher. 2009. The Origins of Symbolism, Spirituality, and Shamans: Exploring Middle Stone Age Material Culture in South Africa. In *Becoming Human: Innovation in Prehistoric Material and Spiritual Culture*, edited by Colin Renfrew and Iain Morley, pp. 29–49. New York: Cambridge University Press.

Herold, Laurance C. 1968. An Archaeological-Geographical Survey of the Rio Grande de Ranchos. In *Papers on Taos Archaeology*, edited by Laurance C. Herold and Ralph A. Luebben, pp. 9–42. Talpa, NM: Fort Burgwin Research Center.

Hesse, Father Jerome. 1916. The Missions of Cochiti and Santo Domingo, N.M. In *The Franciscan Missions of the Southwest*, vol. 4, pp. 27–30. Saint Michaels, AZ: Franciscan Fathers.

Hill, W. W. 1982. *An Ethnography of Santa Clara Pueblo, New Mexico*. Albuquerque: University of New Mexico Press.

Hodder, Ian, ed. 2010. *Religion in the Emergence of Civilization: Çatalhöyük as a Case Study*. New York: Cambridge University Press.

Hodge, Frederick W. 1912. *Handbook of American Indians North of Mexico*. Washington, DC: Smithsonian Institution Press.

Howell, Todd L. 2001. Foundations of Political Power in Ancestral Zuni Society. In *Ancient Burial Practices in the American Southwest: Archaeology, Physical Anthropology, and Native American Perspectives*, edited by Douglas R. Mitchell and Judy L. Brunson-Hadley, pp. 149–166. Albuquerque: University of New Mexico Press.

Howells, William. 1948. *The Heathens: Primitive Man and His Religions*. New York: American Museum of Natural History.

Huckell, Lisa. 1993. Plant Remains from the Pinaleno Cotton Cache, Arizona. *Kiva* 59(2):147–203.

Hume, David. 1976[1757]. *The Natural History of Religion*, edited by A. Wayne Colver. Oxford: Clarendon.

Ingold, Tim. 2007. Writing Texts, Reading Materials: A Response to My Critics. *Archaeological Dialogues* 14(1):31–38.

————. 2008. When Ant Meets Spider: Social Theory for Arthropods. In *Material Agency*, edited by C. Knappett and L. Malafouris, pp. 209–215. New York: Springer.

Insoll, Timothy. 1999. *The Archaeology of Islam*. London: Routledge.

Insoll, Timothy, ed. 2001. *Archaeology and World Religion*. London: Wiley-Blackwell.

Irwin, Lee. 1997. A Brief History of Native American Religious Resistance. *American Indian Quarterly* 21(1):35–55.

Jeançon, Jean Allard. 1911. Explorations in the Chama Basin, New Mexico. *Records of the Past* 10:92–108.

————. 1923. *Excavations in the Chama Valley, New Mexico*. Washington, DC: Smithsonian Institution Press.

————. 1930. Taos Notes. *El Palacio* 18(1–4):3–11.

Johnson, Gregory A. 1982. Organizational Structure and Scalar Stress. In *Theory and Explanation in Archaeology*, edited by Colin Renfrew, M. J. Rowlands, and B. A. Segraves, pp. 389–421. New York: Academic.

Judd, Neil M. 1954. *The Material Culture of Pueblo Bonito*. Washington, DC: Government Printing Office.

Jung, Carl G. 1973[1961]. *Memories, Dreams, Reflections*, recorded and edited by Aniela Jaffé, translated by Richard Winston and Clara Winston. New York: Vintage.

Kantner, John. 2004. *Ancient Puebloan Southwest*. New York: Cambridge University Press.

————. 2006. Religious Behavior in Post-Chaco Years. In *Religion in the Prehispanic Southwest*, edited by Christine S. VanPool, Todd L. VanPool, and David A. Phillips Jr., pp. 31–52. Lanham, MD: AltaMira.

Keane, Webb. 2007. *Catholic Moderns: Freedom and Fetish in the Mission Encounter*. Berkeley: University of California Press.

Kennard, Edward A. 1938. *Hopi Kachinas*. New York: J. J. Augustin.

Knapp, A. Bernard. 1988. Ideology, Archaeology and Polity. *Man*, n.s., 23(1):133–163.

Kosse, Krisztina. 1990. Group Size and Societal Complexity: Thresholds in the Long-Term Memory. *Journal of Anthropological Archaeology* 9:275–303.

————. 1994. The Evolution of Large, Complex Groups: A Hypothesis. *Journal of Anthropological Archaeology* 13:35–50.

————. 1996. Middle Range Societies from a Scalar Perspective. In *Interpreting Southwestern Diversity: Underlying Principles and Overarching Patterns*, edited by Paul R. Fish and J. Jefferson Reid, pp. 87–96. Tempe: Arizona State University Press.

Kroeber, Alfred L. 1917. *Zuni Kin and Clan*. New York: American Museum of Natural History.

Kroeber, A. L., and Clyde Kluckhohn. 1952. Culture: A Critical Review of Concepts and Definitions. *Papers of the Peabody Museum of American Archaeology and Ethnology* 47(1).

Kuijt, Ian. 2002. Reflections on Ritual and the Transmission of Authority in the Pre-Pottery Neolithic of the Southern Levant. In *Magic Practices and Ritual in the Near Eastern Neolithic*, edited by H. G. K. Gebel, B. Dahl Hermansen, and C. Hoffmann Jensen, pp. 81–90. Berlin: Ex Oriente.

Kuwanwisiwma, Leigh J. 2001. Introduction: From the Sacred to the Cash Register—Problems Encountered in Protecting the Hopi Cultural Patrimony. In *Katsina: Commodified and Appropriated Images of Hopi Supernaturals*, edited by Zena Pearlstone, pp. 16–21. Los Angeles: UCLA Fowler Museum of Cultural History.

Lakatos, Steve. 2007. Cultural Continuity and the Development of Integrative Architecture in the Northern Rio Grande Valley of New Mexico, A.D. 600–1200. *Kiva* 73(1):31–66.

Lange, Charles H. 1967. Problems in Cochiti Culture History. In *American Historical Anthropology: Essays in Honor of Leslie Spier*, edited by Carroll L. Riley and Walter W. Taylor, pp. 69–100. Carbondale: Southern Illinois University Press.

Lape, Peter V. 2005. Archaeology of Islam in Island Southeast Asia. *Antiquity* 79:829–836.

Latour, Bruno. 1988. Irreductions. In his *The Pasteurization of France*, pp. 153–238. Cambridge, MA: Harvard University Press.

———. 1993. *We Have Never Been Modern*. Cambridge, MA: Harvard University Press.

———. 2002. What Is Iconoclash? or, Is There a World beyond the Image Wars? In *Iconoclash: Beyond the Image Wars in Science, Religion, and Art*, edited by Bruno Latour and Peter Weibel, pp. 16–38. Cambridge, MA: MIT Press.

———. 2004. Why Has Critique Run Out of Steam? From Matters of Fact to Matters of Concern. *Critical Inquiry* 30(2):225–248.

———. 2005. *Reassembling the Social: An Introduction to Actor-Network-Theory*. New York: Oxford University Press.

———. 2009. Will Non-Humans Be Saved? An Argument in Ecotheology. *Journal of the Royal Anthropological Institute* 15:459–475.

Lawrence, D. H. 1982. *D. H. Lawrence and New Mexico*, edited by Keith Sagar. Salt Lake City, UT: Gibbs M. Smith.

Leach, Edmund R. 1964[1954]. *Political Systems of Highland Burma*. London: Athlone.

Lekson, Stephen H. 1988. The Idea of the Kiva in Anasazi Archaeology. *Kiva* 53:213–234.

———. 1999. *The Chaco Meridian*. Walnut Creek, CA: AltaMira.

———. 2002. War in the Southwest, War in the World. *American Antiquity* 67(4):607–624.

———. 2005. Complexity. In *Southwest Archaeology in the Twentieth Century*, edited by Linda S. Cordell and Don D. Fowler, pp. 157–173. Salt Lake City: University of Utah Press.

———. 2006. Lords of the Great House: Pueblo Bonito as a Palace. In *Palaces and Power in the Americas: From Peru to the Northwest Coast*, edited by Jessica Joyce Christie and Patricia Joan Sarro, pp. 99–114. Austin: University of Texas Press.

———. 2009. *A History of the Ancient Southwest*. Santa Fe, NM: SAR Press.

Lekson, Stephen H., and Catherine M. Cameron. 1995. The Abandonment of Chaco Canyon, the Mesa Verde Migrations, and the Reorganization of the Pueblo World. *Journal of Anthropological Archaeology* 14:184–202.

Lévi-Strauss, Claude. 1966. *The Savage Mind*. London: Weidenfeld and Nicolson.

Levy, Jerrold E. 1992. *Orayvi Revisited: Social Stratification in an "Egalitarian" Society*. Santa Fe, NM: SAR Press.

Lewis-Williams, David. 2010. *Conceiving God: The Cognitive Origin and Evolution of Religion*. London: Thames and Hudson.

Lewis-Williams, David, and David Pearce. 2005. *Inside the Neolithic Mind: Consciousness, Cosmos and the Realm of the Gods*. London: Thames and Hudson.

Liebmann, Matthew, T. J. Ferguson, and Robert W. Preucel. 2005. Pueblo Settlement, Architecture, and Social Change in the Pueblo Revolt Era, A.D. 1680 to 1696. *Journal of Field Archaeology* 30(1):45–60.

Lightfoot, Dale R., and Frank W. Eddy. 1993. The Effects of Environment and Culture on the Distribution of Prehistoric Dwellings at Chimney Rock Mesa, Colorado. *Geographic Journal* 159(3):291–305.

Lightfoot, Kent G., and Steadman Upham. 1989. Complex Societies in the Prehistoric American Southwest: A Consideration of the Controversy. In *The Sociopolitical Structure of Prehistoric Southwestern Societies*, edited by Steadman Upham, Kent G. Lightfoot, and Roberta A. Jewett, pp. 3–32. Boulder, CO: Westview.

Linthicum, Leslie. 2008. Fight over Mountain Emotional. *Albuquerque Journal* (online edition), June 15. http://www.abqjournal.com/news/state/311324nm06-15-08.htm (accessed March 16, 2011).

Lipe, William D. 1995. The Depopulation of the Northern San Juan: Conditions in the Turbulent 1200s. *Journal of Anthropological Archaeology* 14:143–169.

Lipe, William D., and Michelle Hegmon. 1989. Historical Perspectives on Architecture and Social Integration in the Prehistoric Pueblos. In *The Architecture of Social Integration in Prehistoric Pueblos*, edited by William D. Lipe and Michelle Hegmon, pp. 15–34. Cortez, CO: Crow Canyon Archaeological Center.

Lipe, William D., and Michelle Hegmon, eds. 1989. *The Architecture of Social Integration in Prehistoric Pueblos*. Cortez, CO: Crow Canyon Archaeological Center.

Lippmann, Walter. 1929. *A Preface to Morals*. New York: Macmillan.

Locke, John. 2003[1685]. A Letter concerning Toleration. In his *Political Writings*, pp. 390–436. Indianapolis, IN: Hackett.

Lomawaima, K. Tsianina. 2004. An Interface between Archaeology and American Indian Studies. In *Identity, Feasting, and the Archaeology of the Greater Southwest*, edited by Barbara J. Mills, pp. 139–151. Boulder: University Press of Colorado.

Lubbock, Sir John. 1892[1865]. *Pre-Historic Times as Illustrated by Ancient Remains, and the Manners and Customs of Modern Savages*, 5th ed. New York: Appleton.

Lujan, James. 2001. Education as a Tool for American Indian Community Development. In *Science and Native American Communities: Legacies of Pain, Visions of Promise*, edited by Keith James, pp. 76–82. Lincoln: University of Nebraska Press.

Lukes, Steven. 1975. Political Ritual and Social Integration. *Sociology* 9(2):289–308.

———. 2005. *Power: A Radical View*, 2nd ed. New York: Palgrave Macmillan.

Mahmood, Saba. 2004. *The Politics of Piety: The Islamic Revival and the Feminist Subject.* Princeton, NJ: Princeton University Press.

Mahoney, Nancy M. 2000. Redefining the Scale of Chacoan Communities. In *Great House Communities across the Chacoan Landscape*, edited by John Kantner and Nancy M. Mahoney, pp. 19–27. Tucson: University of Arizona Press.

Majid, Anouar. 2009. *We Are All Moors: Ending Centuries of Crusades against Muslims and Other Minorities.* Minneapolis: University of Minnesota Press.

Malinowski, Bronislaw. 1922. *Argonauts of the Western Pacific.* New York: Dutton.

———. 1935. *Coral Gardens and Their Magic*, vol. 1. London: Routledge.

———. 1948[1925]. Magic, Science, and Religion. In his *Magic, Science, and Religion and Other Essays*, pp. 17–92. Garden City, NY: Doubleday.

Malone, Caroline, David A. Barrowclough, and Simon Stoddart. 2007. Introduction. In *Cult in Context: Reconsidering Ritual in Archaeology*, edited by David A. Barrowclough and Caroline Malone, pp. 1–7. Oxford: Oxbow.

Malville, J. McKim, ed. 2004. *Chimney Rock: The Ultimate Outlier.* New York: Lexington.

Mann, Barbara Alice. 2003. *Native Americans, Archaeologists, and the Mounds.* New York: Peter Lang.

Mann, Barbara Alice, and Jerry L. Fields. 1997. A Sign in the Sky: Dating the League of the Haudenosaunee. *American Indian Culture and Research Journal* 21(2):105–163.

Marshall, Michael P. 1997. The Chacoan Roads: A Cosmological Interpretation. In *Anasazi Architecture and American Design*, edited by Baker H. Morrow and Vincent Barrett Price, pp. 62–74. Albuquerque: University of New Mexico Press.

Martin, Calvin. 1992. *In the Spirit of the Earth: Rethinking History and Time.* Baltimore, MD: Johns Hopkins University Press.

Marx, Karl. 1990[1865]. *Capital*, vol. 1. New York: Penguin.

Masayesva, Victor, Jr. 2006. *Husk of Time: The Photographs of Victor Masayesva.* Tucson: University of Arizona Press.

Masse, W. Bruce, and Fred Espenak. 2006. Sky as Environment: Solar Eclipses and Hohokam Culture Change. In *Environmental Change and Human Adaptation in the Ancient American Southwest*, edited by David E. Doyel and Jeffrey S. Dean, pp. 228–280. Salt Lake City: University of Utah Press.

Masuzawa, Tomoko. 2005. *The Invention of World Religions; or, How European Universalism Was Preserved in the Language of Pluralism.* Chicago: University of Chicago Press.

———. 2008. Troubles with Materiality: The Ghost of Fetishism in the Nineteenth Century. In *Religion: Beyond a Concept*, edited by Hent de Vries, pp. 647–667. New York: Fordham University Press.

McGregor, John C. 1943. Burial of an Early American Magician. *Proceedings of the American Philosophical Society* 86(2):270–298.

McGuire, Randall H. 1995. The Greater Southwest as a Periphery of Mesoamerica. In *Centre and Periphery*, edited by T. C. Champion, pp. 39–62. London: Routledge.

McGuire, Randall H., and Dean J. Saitta. 1996. Although They Have Petty Captains, They Obey Them Badly: The Dialectics of Prehispanic Western Pueblo Social Organization. *American Antiquity* 61:197–216.

Micklethwait, John, and Adrian Wooldridge. 2009. *God Is Back: How the Global Revival of Faith Is Changing the World*. London: Penguin.

Milius, Susan. 1998. When Worlds Collide. *Science News* 154(6):92–94.

Miller, Angela. 1994. "The Soil of an Unknown America": New World Lost Empires and the Debate over Cultural Origins. *American Art* 8(3–4):8–27.

Miller, Daniel, and Christopher Tilley. 1984. Ideology, Power and Prehistory: An Introduction. In *Ideology, Power and Prehistory*, edited by Christopher Tilley and Daniel Miller, pp. 1–16. New York: Cambridge University Press.

Miller, Merton Leland. 1898. A Preliminary Study of the Pueblo of Taos, New Mexico. PhD diss., University of Chicago.

Mills, Barbara J. 2000. Gender, Craft Production, and Inequality. In *Women and Men in the Prehispanic Southwest*, edited by Patricia L. Crown, pp. 301–343. Santa Fe, NM: SAR Press.

———. 2008. The Establishment and Defeat of Hierarchy: Inalienable Possessions and the History of Collective Prestige Structures in the Pueblo Southwest. *American Anthropologist* 106(2):238–251.

Mills, Barbara J., ed. 2000. *Alternative Leadership Strategies in the Prehispanic Southwest*. Tucson: University of Arizona Press.

Mindeleff, Victor. 1989[1891]. *A Study of Pueblo Architecture in Tusayan and Cibola*. Washington, DC: Smithsonian Institution Press.

Mitchell, W. J. T. 2005. *What Do Pictures Want?* Chicago: University of Chicago Press.

Mithen, Steven. 1996. *The Prehistory of the Mind*. London: Thames and Hudson.

———. 2009. Out of the Mind: Material Culture and the Supernatural. In *Becoming Human: Innovation in Prehistoric Material and Spiritual Culture*, edited by Colin Renfrew and Iain Morley, pp. 123–134. New York: Cambridge University Press.

Mobley-Tanaka, Jeannette L. 1997. Gender and Ritual Space during the Pithouse to Pueblo Transition: Subterranean Mealing Rooms in the North American Southwest. *American Antiquity* 62(3):437–448.

Moore, James L., Linda Mick-O'Hara, Mollie S. Toll, Daisy F. Levine, and Jeffrey L. Boyer. 1994. LA 2742. In *Studying the Taos Frontier: The Pot Creek Data Recovery Project*, edited by Jeffrey L. Boyer, James L. Moore, Daisy F. Levine, Linda Mick-O'Hara, and Mollie S. Toll, pp. 75–156. Santa Fe: Museum of New Mexico, Office of Archaeological Studies.

Morgan, Lewis Henry. 1965[1881]. *Houses and House-Life of the American Aborigines*. Chicago: University of Chicago Press.

———. 1974[1877]. *Ancient Society*. Gloucester, MA: Peter Smith.

Naranjo, Tessie. 2009. Discussant Comments. New Mexico Archaeological Council Meetings, Hibben Center, University of New Mexico, November 14.

Neitzel, Jill E. 2003. Three Questions about Pueblo Bonito. In *Pueblo Bonito: Center of the Chacoan World*, edited by Jill E. Neitzel, pp. 1–9. Washington, DC: Smithsonian Institution Press.

Nequatewa, Edmund. 1967. *Truth of a Hopi*. Flagstaff, AZ: Northland Press.

Newman, Jay R. 1997. Patterns of Lithic Procurement and Utility in the Rio Grande del Rancho Valley of the Northern Rio Grande Region, New Mexico. PhD diss., Dallas: Southern Methodist University Press.

Oates, Joan. 1978. Religion and Ritual in Sixth-Millennium B.C. Mesopotamia. *World Archaeology* 10(2):117–124.

Olsen, Bjornar. 2010. *In Defense of Things: Archaeology and the Ontology of Objects*. New York: AltaMira.

Orcutt, Janet D. 1999a. Chronology. In *The Bandelier Archeological Survey*, vol. 1, edited by Robert P. Powers and Janet D. Orcutt, pp. 85–116. Santa Fe, NM: Intermountain Cultural Resources Management.

———. 1999b. Demography, Settlement, and Agriculture. In *The Bandelier Archeological Survey*, vol. 1, edited by Robert P. Powers and Janet D. Orcutt, pp. 219–308. Santa Fe, NM: Intermountain Cultural Resources Management.

Ortiz, Alfonso. 1969. *The Tewa World*. Chicago: University of Chicago Press.

———. 1972. Ritual Drama and the Pueblo World View. In *New Perspectives on the Pueblos*, edited by Alfonso Ortiz, pp. 135–161. Albuquerque: University of New Mexico Press.

Ortman, Scott. 1998. Corn Grinding and Community Organization in the Pueblo Southwest, AD 1140–1550. In *Migration and Reorganization: The Pueblo IV Period in the American Southwest*, edited by Katherine A. Spielmann, pp. 165–192. Tempe: Arizona State University Press.

———. 2010. Genes, Language and Culture in Tewa Ethnogenesis, A.D. 1150–1400. PhD diss., Arizona State University, Tempe.

Pagden, Anthony. 1982. *The Fall of the Natural Man: The American Indian and the Origins of Comparative Ethnology*. New York: Cambridge University Press.

Pandey, Triloki Nath. 1977. Images of Power in a Southwestern Pueblo. In *The Anthropology of Power*, edited by Raymond D. Fogelson and Richard N. Adams, pp. 195–215. New York: Academic.

———. 1994. Patterns of Leadership in Western Pueblo Society. In *North American Indian Anthropology: Essays on Society and Culture*, edited by Raymond J. DeMallie and Alfonso Ortiz, pp. 328–339. Norman: University of Oklahoma Press.

Parker, Douglas R. 2004a. Changing Settlement Patterns. In *Chimney Rock: The Ultimate Outlier*, edited by J. McKim Malville, pp. 51–60. New York: Lexington.

———. 2004b. Petrographic Analysis of Chimney Rock Ceramics. In *Chimney Rock: The Ultimate Outlier*, edited by J. McKim Malville, pp. 73–88. New York: Lexington.

Parsons, Elsie Clews. 1936. *Taos Pueblo*. Menasha, WI: George Banta.

———. 1939. Picurís, New Mexico. *American Anthropologist* 41:206–222.

———. 1974[1929]. *The Social Organization of the Tewa of New Mexico*. Millwood, NJ: Kraus Reprint.

————. 1996a[1940]. *Taos Tales*. New York: Dover.

————. 1996b[1939]. *Pueblo Indian Religion*. 2 vols. Lincoln: University of Nebraska Press.

Pauketat, Tim. 2011. Getting Religion: Lessons from Ancestral Pueblo History. In *Religious Transformation in the Late Pre-Hispanic Pueblo World*, edited by Donna M. Glowacki and Scott Van Keuren, pp. 221–238. Tucson: University of Arizona Press.

Peacock, Sandra, Severin Fowles, and David Bleckley. 2001. The Ethnobotany of a D-Shaped Kiva. Poster presented at the 66th Annual Meeting of the Society for American Archaeology, Philadelphia.

Peckham, Stewart. 1979. When Is a Rio Grande Kiva? In *Collected Papers in Honor of Bertha Pauline Dutton*, edited by Albert Schroeder, pp. 55–86. Albuquerque: Archaeological Society of New Mexico.

————. 1990. *From This Earth*. Santa Fe: Museum of New Mexico Press.

Peckham, Stewart, and Eric K. Reed. 1963. Three Sites near Ranchos de Taos, New Mexico. In *Highway Salvage Archaeology*, vol. 4, assembled by Stewart Peckham, pp. 1–27. Santa Fe: Museum of New Mexico and New Mexico State Highway Department.

Pepper, George H. 1909. The Exploration of a Burial-Room in Pueblo Bonito, New Mexico. In *Putnam Anniversary Volume: Anthropological Essays*, pp. 196–252. New York: G. E. Stechert.

Perry, Elizabeth M. 2009. Agency and Gender in Prehispanic Puebloan Communities. In *The Social Construction of Communities*, edited by Mark D. Varien and James M. Potter, pp. 89–108. New York: AltaMira.

Plog, Stephen. 1995. Equality and Hierarchy: Holistic Approaches to Understanding Social Dynamics in the Pueblo Southwest. In *Foundations of Social Inequality*, edited by T. Douglas Price and Gary M. Feinman, pp. 189–206. New York: Plenum.

————. 2011. Ritual and Cosmology in the Chaco Era. In *Religious Transformation in the Late Pre-Hispanic Pueblo World*, edited by Donna M. Glowacki and Scott Van Keuren, pp. 50–65. Tucson: University of Arizona Press.

Plog, Stephen, and Carrie Heitman. 2010. Hierarchy and Social Inequality in the American Southwest, A.D. 800–1200. *Proceedings of the National Academy of Sciences* 107(46):19619–19626.

Plog, Stephen, and Julie Solometo. 1997. The Never-Changing and the Ever-Changing: The Evolution of Western Pueblo Ritual. *Cambridge Archaeological Journal* 7(2):161–182.

Potter, James M., and Elizabeth M. Perry. 2000. Ritual as a Power Resource in the American Southwest. In *Alternative Leadership Strategies in the Prehispanic Southwest*, edited by Barbara J. Mills, pp. 60–78. Tucson: University of Arizona Press.

Price, Neil, ed. 2001. *The Archaeology of Shamanism*. New York: Routledge.

Rappaport, Roy. 1971. Ritual, Sanctity, and Cybernetics. *American Anthropologist* 73:59–76.

————. 1999. *Ritual and Religion in the Making of Humanity*. New York: Cambridge University Press.

Reid, J. Jefferson, and Barbara K. Montgomery. 1999. Ritual Space in the Grasshopper Region, East-Central Arizona. In *Sixty Years of Mogollon Archaeology*, edited by Stephanie M. Whittlesey, pp. 23–29. Tucson, AZ: SRI.

Reilly, F. Kent, and James F. Garber, eds. 2007. *Ancient Objects and Sacred Realms: Interpretations of Mississippian Iconography*. Austin: University of Texas Press.

Renfrew, Colin. 1985. *The Archaeology of Cult: The Sanctuary of Phylakopi*. London: Thames and Hudson.

———. 1994. The Archaeology of Religion. In *The Ancient Mind: Elements of Cognitive Archaeology*, edited by Colin Renfrew and Ezra B. W. Zubrow, pp. 47–54. New York: Cambridge University Press.

———. 2001. Production and Consumption in a Sacred Economy: The Material Correlates of High Devotional Expression at Chaco Canyon. *American Antiquity* 66(1):14–25.

———. 2004. Chaco Canyon: A View from the Outside. In *In Search of Chaco: New Approaches to an Archaeological Enigma*, edited by David Grant Noble, pp. 100–106. Santa Fe, NM: SAR Press.

———. 2007. Ritual and Cult in Malta and Beyond: Traditions of Interpretation. In *Cult in Context: Reconsidering Ritual in Archaeology*, edited by David A. Barrowclough and Caroline Malone, pp. 8–13. Oxford: Oxbow.

Renfrew, Colin, and Iain Morley, eds. 2009. *Becoming Human: Innovation in Prehistoric Material and Spiritual Culture*. New York: Cambridge University Press.

Renfrew, Jane M. 2009. Neanderthal Symbolic Behaviour? In *Becoming Human: Innovation in Prehistoric Material and Spiritual Culture*, edited by Colin Renfrew and Iain Morley, pp. 50–60. New York: Cambridge University Press.

Robbins, William J. 1941. Some Aspects of Pueblo Indian Religion. *Harvard Theological Review* 34(1):25–47.

Roberts, Frank H. H. 1930. Early Pueblo Ruins in the Piedra District, Southwestern Colorado. *Bureau of American Ethnology Bulletin* 96.

Rorty, Richard. 2005. Anticlericalism and Atheism. In *The Future of Religion*, edited by Santiago Zabala, pp. 29–42. New York: Columbia University Press.

Rountree, Kathryn. 2002. Goddess Pilgrims as Tourists: Inscribing the Body through Sacred Travel. *Sociology of Religion* 63(4):475–496.

———. 2007. Archaeologists and Goddess Feminists at Çatalhöyük. *Journal of Feminist Studies of Religion* 23(2):7–26.

Routledge, Carolyn. 2008. Did Women "Do Things" in Ancient Egypt? In *Sex and Gender in Ancient Egypt*, edited by Carolyn Graves-Brown, pp. 157–177. Swansea: Classical Press of Wales.

Ruscavage-Barz, Samantha M. 1999. Knowing Your Neighbor: Coalition Period Community Dynamics on the Pajarito Plateau, New Mexico. PhD diss., Washington State University, Pullman.

Sahlins, Marshall D. 1968. *Tribesmen*. Englewood Cliffs, NJ: Prentice Hall.

Saile, David G. 1989. Many Dwellings: Views of a Pueblo World. In *Dwelling, Place and Environment: Towards a Phenomenology of Person and World*, edited by David Seamon and Robert Mugerauer, pp. 159–181. New York: Columbia University Press.

————. 1990. Understanding the Development of Pueblo Architecture. In *Pueblo Style and Regional Architecture*, edited by Nicholas C. Markovich, Wolfgang F. E. Preiser, and Fred G. Sturm, pp. 49–63. New York: Van Nostrand Reinhold.

Saitta, Dean J. 1997. Power, Labor, and the Dynamics of Change in Chacoan Political Economy. *American Antiquity* 62(1):7–26.

————. 1999. Prestige, Agency, and Change in Middle-Range Societies. In *Material Symbols: Culture and Economy in Prehistory*, edited by John Robb, pp. 135–149. Carbondale: Southern Illinois University Press.

Sang-Hun, Choe. 2007. Shamanism Enjoys Revival in Techno-Savvy South Korea. *New York Times*, July 7, p. A3.

Sassaman, Kenneth E. 2001. Hunter-Gatherers and Traditions of Resistance. In *The Archaeology of Traditions*, edited by Timothy R. Pauketat, pp. 218–236. Gainesville: University Press of Florida.

Satterthwaite, Linton. 1945. Another Subterranean Passage Legend. *American Antiquity* 4:387–388.

Schaafsma, Polly. 1994. The Prehistoric Kachina Cult and Its Origins as Suggested by Southwestern Rock Art. In *Kachinas in the Pueblo World*, edited by Polly Schaafsma, pp. 63–80. Albuquerque: University of New Mexico Press.

————. 2000. *Warrior, Shield, and Star*. Santa Fe, NM: Western Edge Press.

Schaafsma, Polly, and Curtis F. Schaafsma. 1974. Evidence for the Origins of the Pueblo Kachina Cult as Suggested by Southwestern Rock Art. *American Antiquity* 39(4):535–545.

Schachner, Gregson. 2001. Ritual Control and Transformation in Middle-Range Societies: An Example from the American Southwest. *Journal of Anthropological Archaeology* 20:168–194.

Schillaci, Michael A., E. G. Ozolins, and Thomas C. Windes. 2001 Multivariate Assessment of Biological Relationships among Prehistoric Southwest Amerindian Populations. In *Following Through: Papers in Honor of Phyllis S. Davis*, edited by R. N. Wiseman, T. C. O'Laughlin, and C. T. Snow, pp. 133–149. Albuquerque: Archaeological Society of New Mexico.

Schleiermacher, Friedrich. 1996[1799]. *On Religion: Speeches to Its Cultured Despisers*, translated by Richard Crouter. Cambridge: Cambridge University Press.

Sciolino, Elaine. 2008. By Making Holocaust Personal to Pupils, Sarkozy Stirs Anger. *New York Times*, February 16, pp. A1, A6.

Scott, David, and Charles Hirschkind. 2006. *Powers of the Secular Modern: Talal Asad and His Interlocutors*. Palo Alto, CA: Stanford University Press.

Scully, Vincent. 1972. *Pueblo: Mountain, Village, Dance*. New York: Viking.

Sebastian, Lynn. 1992. *The Chaco Anasazi: Sociopolitical Evolution in the Prehistoric Southwest*. New York: Cambridge University Press.

Sekaquaptewa, Emory, and Dorothy Washburn. 2004. "They Go Along Singing": Reconstructing the Hopi Past from Ritual Metaphors in Song and Image. *American Antiquity* 69(3):457–486.

Shanks, Michael. 2010. Archaeological Manifesto. http://documents.stanford.edu/michaelshanks/112 (accessed December 2, 2010).

Sharlet, Jeff. 2006. Through a Glass Darkly: How the Christian Right Is Reimagining U.S. History. *Harper's Magazine*, December, pp. 33–43.

Shorto, Russell. 2010. How Christian Were the Founders? *New York Times Magazine*, February 11.

Silverberg, Robert. 1986. *The Mound Builders*. Athens: Ohio University Press.

Slackman, Michael. 2007. A Quiet Revolution in Algeria: Gains by Women. *New York Times*, May 26.

Smith, M. Estellie. 1967. Aspects of Social Control among the Taos Indians. PhD diss., State University of New York, Buffalo.

Smith, Watson. 1952. *Kiva Mural Decorations at Awatovi and Kawaika-a*. Cambridge, MA: Harvard University Press.

————. 1994. *When Is a Kiva? and Other Questions about Southwestern Archaeology*. Tucson: University of Arizona Press.

Smith, Wilfred Cantwell. 1978[1962]. *The Meaning and End of Religion*. New York: Harper and Row.

Snead, James E. 2008. *Ancestral Landscapes of the Pueblo World*. Tucson: University of Arizona Press.

Snead, James E., and Robert W. Preucel. 1999. The Ideology of Settlement: Ancestral Keres Landscapes in the Northern Rio Grande. In *Archaeologies of Landscape*, edited by Wendy Ashmore and A. Bernard Knapp, pp. 169–197. Oxford: Blackwell.

Spicer, Edward H. 1954. Spanish-Indian Acculturation in the Southwest. *American Anthropologist* 56:663–678.

————. 1962. *Cycles of Conquest*. Tucson: University of Arizona Press.

Standing Bear, Luther. 1978[1933]. *Land of the Spotted Eagle*. Lincoln: University of Nebraska Press.

Stein, John R., and Stephen H. Lekson. 1992. Anasazi Ritual Landscapes. In *Anasazi Regional Organization and the Chaco System*, edited by David E. Doyel, pp. 87–100. Albuquerque: University of New Mexico Press.

Stevenson, Matilda Cox. 1906–1907. Unfinished Manuscripts and Notes on File at the National Anthropological Archives, Washington, DC.

————. 1915. Ethnobotany of the Zuñi Indians. In *30th Annual Report of the Bureau of American Ethnology, 1908–1909*, pp. 31–102. Washington, DC: Bureau of American Ethnology.

Stewart, Omer C. 1987. *Peyote Religion*. Norman: University of Oklahoma Press.

Straughn, Ian B. 2006. Materializing Islam: An Archaeology of Landscape in Early Islamic Period Syria. PhD diss., University of Chicago.

Stuart, David E., and Rory P. Gauthier. 1988[1981]. *Prehistoric New Mexico*. Albuquerque: University of New Mexico Press.

Stukeley, William. 1740. *Stonehenge: A Temple Restor'd to the British Druids*. London: W. Innys and R. Manby.

———. 1763. *Palaeographia Sacra; or, Discourses on Sacred Subjects*. London: J. Baillie.

Sweet, Jill D., and Karen E. Larson. 1994. The Horse, Santiago, and a Ritual Game: Pueblo Indian Responses to Three Spanish Introductions. *Western Folklore* 53(1):69–84.

Swentzell, Rina. 1985. An Understated Sacredness. *MASS: Journal of the School of Architecture and Planning* (Fall):24–25.

———. 1990. Pueblo Space, Form, and Mythology. In *Pueblo Style and Regional Architecture*, edited by N. C. Markovich, W. F. E. Preiser, and F. G. Sturm, pp. 23–30. New York: Van Nostrand Reinhold.

———. 2004. A Pueblo Woman's Perspective on Chaco Canyon. In *In Search of Chaco: New Approaches to an Archaeological Enigma*, edited by David Grant Noble, pp. 48–53. Santa Fe, NM: SAR Press.

Talayesva, Don C. 1942. *The Sun Chief: The Autobiography of a Hopi Indian*, edited by Leo W. Simmons. New Haven, CT: Yale University Press.

Taussig, Michael. 1998. Crossing the Face. In *Border Fetishisms: Material Objects in Unstable Spaces*, edited by Patricia Spyer, pp. 224–244. New York: Routledge.

Taylor, Charles. 2007. *A Secular Age*. Cambridge, MA: Harvard University Press.

Tedlock, Barbara. 1983. Zuni Sacred Theater. *American Indian Quarterly* 7(3):93–110.

Toulmin, Stephen. 1982. *The Return to Cosmology: Postmodern Science and the Theology of Nature*. Berkeley: University of California Press.

———. 1990. *Cosmopolis: The Hidden Agenda of Modernity*. Chicago: University of Chicago Press.

Trager, George L., and Felicia Haren Trager. 1970. The Cardinal Directions at Taos and Picuris. *Anthropological Linguistics* 12:31–37.

Trigger, Bruce G. 1990. Maintaining Economic Equality in Opposition to Complexity: An Iroquoian Case Study. In *The Evolution of Political Systems*, edited by Steadman Upham, pp. 119–145. New York: Cambridge University Press.

Tylor, Edward B. 1913[1871]. *Primitive Culture*. London: Murray.

Underhill, Ruth. 1938. *First Penthouse Dwellers of America*. New York: J. J. Augustin.

UNESCO. 1992. Advisory Body Evaluation, no. 492 rev., Taos. http://whc.unesco.org/en/list/492 (accessed June 4, 2006).

Upham, Steadman. 1982. *Polities and Power: An Economic and Political History of the Western Pueblo*. New York: Academic.

———. 1989. East Meets West: Hierarchy and Elites in Pueblo Society. In *The Sociopolitical Structure of Prehistoric Southwestern Societies*, edited by Steadman Upham, Kent G. Lightfoot, and Roberta A. Jewett, pp. 77–102. Boulder, CO: Westview.

Van Dyke, Ruth M. 2007. *The Chaco Experience: Landscape and Ideology at the Center Place*. Santa Fe, NM: SAR Press.

VanPool, Christine S. 2003. The Shaman-Priests of the Casas Grandes Region, Chihuahua, Mexico. *American Antiquity* 68:696–717.

VanPool, Christine S., Todd L. VanPool, and David A. Phillips. 2006. Introduction: Archaeology
and Religion. In *Religion in the Prehispanic Southwest*, edited by Christine S. VanPool, Todd
L. VanPool, and David A. Phillips Jr., pp. 1–16. Lanham, MD: AltaMira.

VanPool, Christine S., Todd L. VanPool, and David A. Phillips Jr., eds. 2006. *Religion in the
Prehispanic Southwest*. Lanham, MD: AltaMira.

Van Zandt, Tineke. 1999. Architecture and Site Structure. In *The Bandelier Archeological Survey*,
vol. 2, edited by Robert P. Powers and Janet D. Orcutt, pp. 309–388. Santa Fe, NM:
Intermountain Cultural Resources Management.

Verhoeven, Marc. 2002. Ritual and Its Investigation in Prehistory. In *Magic Practices and Ritual
in the Near Eastern Neolithic*, edited by H. G. K. Gebel, B. Dahl Hermansen, and C.
Hoffmann Jensen, pp. 5–40. Berlin: Ex Oriente.

Vickery, Lucretia D. 1969. Excavations at TA-26, a Small Pueblo Site Near Taos, New Mexico.
Master's thesis, Wichita State University, Wichita, KS.

Vivian, R. Gwinn. 1990. *The Chacoan Prehistory of the San Juan Basin*. San Diego, CA: Academic.

Voltaire. 1974. An Important Study by Lord Bidingbroke; or, The Fall of Fanaticism. In *Voltaire
on Religion: Selected Writings*, translated by Kenneth W. Applegate. New York: Frederick
Ungar.

Wade, Cam. 1997. Total Eclipses of the Sun in the Anasazi Country, AD 700–1700. In *Layers
of Time: Papers in Honor of Robert H. Weber*, edited by Meliha S. Duran and David T.
Kirkpatrick, pp. 99–114. Santa Fe: Archaeological Society of New Mexico.

Walker, William H. 1998. Where Are the Witches of Prehistory? *Journal of Archaeological Method
and Theory* 5:245–308.

Wallis, Robert J. 2003. *Shamans/Neo-Shamans: Ecstasies, Alternative Archaeologies and Contemporary
Pagans*. New York: Routledge.

Warburg, Aby. 1995. *Images from the Region of the Pueblo Indians of North America*. Ithaca, NY:
Cornell University Press.

Ware, John A., and Eric Blinman. 2000. Cultural Collapse and Reorganization: The Origin and
Spread of Pueblo Ritual Sodalities. In *The Archaeology of Regional Interaction*, edited by
Michelle Hegmon, pp. 381–409. Boulder: University Press of Colorado.

Warner, Michael, Jonathan VanAntwerpen, and Craig Calhoun. 2010. *Varieties of Secularism in a
Secular Age*. Cambridge, MA: Harvard University Press.

Watt, W. Montgomery. 1953. *Muhammad at Mecca*. Oxford: Clarendon.

Weber, Max. 1946. *From Max Weber: Essays in Sociology*, translated and edited by Hans H. Gerth and
C. Wright Mills. New York: Oxford University Press.

Webster, L. 1997. Effects of European Contact on Textile Production and Exchange in the North
American Southwest: A Pueblo Case Study. PhD diss., University of Arizona, Tucson.

Wendorf, Fred. 1953. Excavations at Te'ewi. In *Salvage Archaeology in the Chama Valley, New Mexico*,
assembled by Fred Wendorf, pp. 34–98. Santa Fe, NM: SAR Press.

Wenger, Tisa. 2009. *We Have a Religion: The 1920s Pueblo Indian Dance Controversy and American
Religious Freedom*. Chapel Hill: University of North Carolina Press.

Wetherington, Ronald. 1968. *Excavations at Pot Creek Pueblo.* Talpa, NM: Fort Burgwin Research Center.

White, Leslie A. 1937. Review of "Taos Pueblo." *Journal of American Folklore* 50(196):198–200.

———. 1942. *The Pueblo of Santa Ana, New Mexico.* Menasha, WI: American Anthropological Association.

———. 1959. *The Evolution of Culture.* New York: McGraw-Hill.

Whiteley, Peter. 1998. *Rethinking Hopi Ethnography.* Washington, DC: Smithsonian Institution Press.

Whitley, Catrina Banks. 2009. Body Language: An Integrative Approach to the Bioarchaeology and Mortuary Practices of the Taos Valley. PhD diss., Dallas: Southern Methodist University Press.

Whitley, David S. 2000. *The Art of the Shaman: Rock Art of California.* Salt Lake City: University of Utah Press.

———. 2008. Cognition, Emotion, and Belief: First Steps in an Archaeology of Religion. In *Belief in the Past*, edited by Kelley Hays-Gilpin and David S. Whitley, pp. 85–104. Walnut Creek, CA: Left Coast Press.

Whitley, David S., and Kelley Hays-Gilpin. 2008. Religion beyond Icon, Burial and Monument: An Introduction. In *Belief in the Past*, edited by Kelley Hays-Gilpin and David S. Whitley, pp. 11–22. Walnut Creek, CA: Left Coast Press.

Wilcox, David R. 1993. The Evolution of the Chacoan Polity. In *The Chimney Rock Archaeological Symposium*, edited by J. M. Malville and G. Matlock, pp. 76–90. Fort Collins, CO: Rocky Mountain Forest and Range Experiment Station.

Williams, Lucy Fowler, Isabel C. Gonzales, and Shawn Tafoya. 2007. WaHa-belash adi Kwan tsáawä: Butterflies and Blue Rain: The Language of Contemporary Eastern Pueblo Embroidery. *Expedition* 49(3):20–29.

Wittfogel, K. A., and E. S. Goldfrank. 1943. Some Aspects of Pueblo Mythology and Society. *Journal of American Folklore* 56(219):17–30.

Wolfman, Daniel, and Herbert W. Dick. 1999. Ceremonial Caches from Picuris Pueblo. In *Picuris Pueblo through Time: Eight Centuries of Change at a Northern Rio Grande Pueblo*, edited by Michael A. Adler and Herbert W. Dick, pp. 101–119. Dallas: Southern Methodist University Press.

Woosley, Anne I. 1986. Puebloan Prehistory of the Northern Rio Grande: Settlement, Population, Subsistence. *Kiva* 51(3):143–164.

Yinger, J. Milton. 1970. *The Scientific Study of Religion.* London: Collier-Macmillan.

Yoffee, Norman. 2001. The Chaco "Rituality" Revisited. In *Chaco Society and Polity: Papers from the 1999 Conference*, edited by Linda S. Cordell and W. James Judge, pp. 63–78. Santa Fe: New Mexico Archaeological Council.

———. 2005. *Myths of the Archaic State.* New York: Cambridge University Press.

Young, M. Jane. 1985. Images of Power and the Power of Images: The Significance of Rock Art for Contemporary Zunis. *Journal of American Folklore* 98(387):3–48.

Index

Abalone Shell People, 171, 266n3

Abrahamic religions/traditions, 15, 25, 33, 237, 252–254

Acoma Pueblo, 208

Adler, Michael, 150–151

afterlife, 8, 27, 57–58, 253

agency, 10, 98, 156, 195, 207, 235

aggregated villages, 91, 111, 141, 146, 148, 152, 199–201, 206

agriculture, 63, 105, 152, 235; artifacts relating to, 169–170; ceremonies for, 239; and clay pipes, 154–155, 157; cotton, 232; development of, 28–29; vs. hunting, 47, 112, 148; intensified, 111–112; and irrigation, 154, 157, 181, 209, 236; and the katsina, 204, 207; offerings for, 209; and Pueblo doings, 160, 177; and rainfall, 103; and southside of villages, 52, 133, 175; and stone shrines, 179, 181; of Summer People, 109, 113; and T'aitöna, 183, 197; in Taos district, 87–88; and Taos Pueblo religion, 53. *See also* farming

Alberti, Ben, 9–10

American flag, 191, 193, 195–196, 236

American Indian Religious Freedom Act, 249

American Museum of Natural History, 75

ancestral: sites, 91, 153, 157, 159, 167, 249–250, 254, 258; spirits, 158, 161, 169, 182–183

Ancestral Puebloans, 26, 43, 45–46, 51, 60, 64, 67, 70, 75–76, 81, 86–87, 90–91, 96–97, 107, 112, 123–124, 141, 158, 169, 178, 256, 270n2

ancient religion, 5–6, 32, 34, 237–238, 252

Ancient Society (Morgan), 14

Angulo, Jaime de, 43–44

animal remains, 7, 164–165, 168–170, 268n7

Anschuetz, Kurt, 179

anthropological diplopia, 76, 107, 122, 236

anti-clericalism, 16, 20, 28, 84, 86

Apaches, 43, 196–197, 201

archaeological sites, 23–27, 33–34, 87, 124, 182. *See also* specific sites

archaeology, 43; Anglophone, 26; antiquarian beginnings of, 23, 25; and data sets, 27–28; of primitive religion, 23–35; professionalization of, 27; of religion, 5, 7, 30, 262; study/methods of, 5–6, 10–11, 24, 27–28, 42, 60–61, 63–64, 262

architecture, 79, 82, 84–85, 87, 89–90, 106; adobe, 40–42, 86, 88, 160, 162, 182–184, 193; aggregated pueblo, 111, 146, 199–201; burning of, 233; centerpost/basin complexes, 172–173; and the cosmos, 158; D-shaped pueblos, 130–131, 159; and female practices, 174; kiva hearth complexes, 219; masonry, 92; multipurpose, 150–151; multistory, 78, 81, 128–130; orientated towards sun, 132–133; patterns of, 113; and Pueblo doings, 253; sacred vs.profane, 150–151, 172; of Sinaguan sites, 266n2; spatial organization of, 172, 175; surface roomblocks, 129, 141, 150, 152, 159, 175, 179, 232, 269n3; of T'aitöna village, 112, 124–126, 128–130, 132–134; unit pueblos, 86, 88, 113, 117–118, 174, 182, 200, 269n3. *See also* plazas; specific pueblos; specific types

Archuleta Site, 211

Arizona, 42. *See also* Hopi people/villages

arrowheads, 169

Arroyo Hondo, 64, 87, 224

Arroyo Hondo Pueblo, 64, 269n13

Arroyo Seco, 87

artifacts, 7, 9, 59, 176, 266n2; biographies of, 164–165, 169; burial, 80–83; of Chaco Canyon, 79–83, 92, 94; and katsina doings, 217–218; ornamental, 81–82, 85; spatial relations of, 164–165, 168–170; study of, 23–25, 110; at T'aitöna, 161, 163–171, 174, 177–178, 217–218, 228, 233; of Taos district, 94–95, 118. *See also* specific types

Asad, Talal, 2, 4–5, 11–12, 98, 102, 120–121

atheism, 20, 33, 70

Avebury (England), 23, 26

Awatovi (Hopi village), 154

axes, 164, 168–170, 179

Aztecs, 10, 79

Balance, 47–48, 58, 148–149, 158, 166, 171, 174–175, 178, 183, 197
Bandelier, Adolph, 48, 50, 140
Baptists, 239–240
Barth, Fredrik, 72, 123, 147
Basket Dance, 209
Basseri nomads, 72
belief, 103; and action, 36; in beings/powers, 9; collective, 30, 240; end of, 34; free from, 70–72; in immortality, 19; important role of, 73; individualized, 3; local, 139; networks of, 119; private/individual, 24, 28, 97–98, 240; in supernatural, 5, 8, 20, 70–71, 73, 241, 251; systems, 9–10, 15; and unbelief, 74, 84; in unseen order, 8–10, 147, 244, 255
Bellah, Robert, 240, 258
Benedict, Ruth, 44
Bennett, Jane, 152
Bent, Charles, 193
Bernardini, Wesley, 234
Bertemes, François, 7
Biehl, Peter, 7
Big Earring Kiva, 47–49, 56, 171
Big Earring Man, 48, 55–56, 58
Big Earring People, 50, 144, 266n3
Big Hail People/Society, 52, 208, 266n3
Binford, Lewis, 29
bird effigy vessels, 217–218, 270n10
birth, 166
Black Eyes People/Society, 52, 192–193, 195, 209
"Blessing of the Corn" ceremony, 173–174
Blue Lake, 48, 166, 209, 248, 266n1–2
bodily adornment, 81–82, 88
Borges, Jorge Luis, 123
Bourke, John G., 238
Bradley, Bruce, 130
Brandt, Elizabeth, 54, 58–59, 266n4
Brave New World (Huxley), 42
Brück, Joanna, 9
Bunzel, Ruth, 54
Bureau of Indian Affairs, 244
burials, 79–83, 85, 92, 94, 120, 167–169, 183, 254, 268n7, 268n8. *See also* mortuary complexes/traditions
Bursum Bill, 245

Caciques, 48, 54–56, 58, 61, 236, 266n3
Cajete, Gregory, 250–251
Cameron, Catherine, 206
capitalism, 11, 33, 59, 86, 92, 99, 102, 143, 148, 166, 250, 265n4
Catholic Church, 40, 47, 166, 193–194, 202, 229–230, 238, 245
Catholicism, 17, 23, 237–241, 244–246, 252, 257, 261
celestial phenomena, 138, 141, 260, 267n1–2
celestial powers, 171–172
ceramics, 187, 199, 206–207, 236, 250; ceremonial, 94–95, 104–106, 154–155, 173, 176, 187–188, 217–219, 221, 270n10; at Chaco Canyon, 78, 80, 85, 92, 94–95; clay used for, 154–155, 160–161, 204, 211, 219, 251, 270n9; and cloud/lightning icons,

219–220; of Gallina region, 73, 267n4; Gallup black-on-white, 85; with katsina images, 210–212, 214, 216, 224, 267n5, 270n9; Kwahe'e black-on-white, 85, 87, 90, 95, 125, 127–128, 212, 270n10; and mineral-based paint, 125; miniature, 94–95, 104–106, 219, 221–222, 267n1; Neolithic, 39; Pot Creek Phase, 116; Red Mesa black-on-white, 85, 87, 90; at Ridge Ruin, 81; of Rio Grande Valley, 85, 87; Santa Fe black-on-white, 113, 125, 127–128, 212, 220–221, 267n3, 270n9; at T'aitöna, 104–106, 112, 114, 125–128, 210–212, 217–219, 221, 224, 233; at T'aitöna kiva, 161, 163–165, 169–170; of Taos district, 111, 113–116, 220, 267n4–5; unpainted, 87, 90–91, 111, 113–115, 128, 217, 220, 267n4; Valdez Phase, 90, 95, 116; and vegetable-based paint, 113, 125–126, 128. *See also* pipes
ceremonial: adoption, 51; architecture, 78, 130, 133, 268n5; hegemony, 74; knowledge, 59, 62–63, 235; landscapes, 178; life, 49, 63, 145; objects, 94–95, 176, 268n7; order, 47; paraphernalia, 229; practice, 62, 65, 99, 103, 129, 149, 179; prescriptions, 48; responsibilities, 49, 148; sodalities, 87; systems, 46–51, 53, 58. *See also* ceramics
ceremonies, 32, 44–45, 53, 81–82; aligned with Catholicism, 238; collective, 149; commercialization of, 248; control of, 235; as cultural attraction, 246; of katsina, 198, 202, 204–207, 209; in kivas, 51, 239; peyote, 229–230, 248; the pole-climb, 161, 192–193, 195, 236; protection of, 238; right to engage in, 62–63; sun and moon, 171–172; of Winter People, 266n3. *See also* specific names
Cerrillos mines, 85
Cerrita Site, 89–90, 95, 116, 119–120, 122, 270n10
Chaco Canyon, 111, 183, 188; architecture of, 76–80, 82, 84, 86, 92, 130–131, 159; as "big idea," 75–86; disintegration of, 83–85, 92, 116; and economy, 78, 84, 93; extravagant lifestyles of, 79–84, 94; importance of, 76; influence of, 74–75, 79, 85–86, 92–93, 130–131, 158–159; interpretations of, 75–78; kivas at, 79, 82, 89, 94–95; migration away from, 257–258; and politics, 76, 78, 93; power of, 116; as regional center, 76, 79–80, 84–86, 92, 123; and religion, 74, 78, 93–94, 100; and shrines, 177–178; and Sinaguan culture/people, 266n2; social differentiation in, 79–80, 83–84; and social inequality, 257; and Taos Winter People, 91, 93, 95, 98. *See also* Pueblo Bonito; roads; Room 33 burials
Chaco Culture National Historical Park, 76, 80
Cherbury, Lord, 16
Chetro Ketl, 77
Cheyennes, 229–230
chiefdoms, 30, 33, 61, 65, 93
Childe, V. Gordon, 28–30, 91, 265n4
Chimney Rock, 91–92, 129
Christianity, 4, 9, 15–17, 25–27, 107, 242–243, 252, 265n4.; European, 194, 259; and history/place, 257–258; iconography of, 222; and kivas, 149; and original innocence, 20; premodern, 12, 260; and Pueblo religion, 238, 240, 245–249; pure original form of, 21, 23–24; and revelation, 254; and

secularism, 35–36, 259 See also Catholicism; God; Protestants
church and state, 16, 35–36, 42, 193–194, 240–241
Church of England, 23–24
Cimarron district, 123
circular histories, 14–15, 18, 21, 23–25, 254–255
civilization, 11, 14, 18, 25, 27, 71, 199, 241–242
clans/clanship, 45–46, 49, 51, 82, 102, 202, 205, 227, 236
Clastres, Pierre, 61, 93
clerical: corruption, 33; reform, 16
clericalism, 84–86, 93, 99, 247
clothes/costumes, 29, 171, 209, 232, 239, 247, 251
"cloud blowers": See pipes
Cloud People, 269n5
clowns, ceremonial, 129, 192, 195
Collier, John, 246–248
colonial: violence, 193–194, 196
colonial period, 40, 43, 56, 173, 201, 204, 210, 219, 222, 224, 232, 234, 238, 240–242, 244
colonialism, 11–12, 26–27, 99, 102, 166, 193–194, 196, 243, 245, 252, 258, 261, 270n1
Comanche raiders, 40
Comaroff, John and Jean, 250
commodification, 205
copper bells, 78–79, 94
Corman, Catherine, 196
corn: ceremonial storage of, 173–174; and clay pipes, 154–157, 160; ground by women, 133–134, 146, 174–177; and katsina spirits, 154; left behind, 63, 233; offerings of, 209; and origin stories, 270n13; planting of, 244; and Pueblo doings, 236, 251, 253; remains of, 113, 164, 169–170, 172; transport/trade of, 79; used in ceremonies, 160, 173, 219. See also mealing rooms
Corn Mother, 52, 173–174
corruption narrative, 15–16, 20–21, 23, 26–28, 30, 33, 42, 65, 84, 257, 262
cosmic: balance, 166, 171; boundaries, 177; directions, 105; intermediaries, 192–193; order, 142, 168, 170, 184, 187–188; powers, 96; rebirth, 22; reverberations, 199; unity, 197
cosmology, 119, 122, 157; of Chaco Canyon, 78; of the Hopi, 254, 269n1; of Northern Tiwas, 57–58, 139–140, 166; and Pueblo doings, 104, 192; of Rio Grande valley, 178; study of, 260; of Summer People, 128; of Taos Pueblo, 269n1; and twin war gods, 129; of Winter People, 96, 99, 110
cosmos, 141, 176–178, 184, 201, 260; access to, 230; and cotton textiles, 232; depiction of, 189; and the katsina, 204, 208; and kivas, 149, 158, 162, 171; and Pueblo doings, 102, 104–106, 157–158, 192, 195–196; of T'aitöna village, 216
cotton textiles, 232–233, 236
cottonwood, 161–162, 182, 188
counterculture, 86, 92, 98, 100, 109, 111
craft items, 62, 79, 81, 95
craft production, 54, 235
Crotty, Helen, 222–223
Crown, Patricia, 199, 231, 233–234
cults, 7, 31–34, 75, 202, 206–207, 210, 226, 253, 269n6
cultural: alterity, 228; beliefs, 103; contexts, 99;

development, 91, 93; differences, 115; hegemony, 79, 83, 98; identity, 128; imaginary, 59; integration, 30; isolation, 206; links, 85–86; practices, 58, 80, 123, 238; property, 205; reproduction, 63; tradition, 230, 256; translation, 242, 251
curing, 51–52, 64, 140, 229, 239, 251

Dances, 103, 157, 175; and Chacoan system, 78; as "doings," 242, 251; katsina, 202, 205–207, 209–210, 215, 244; in kivas, 50; masked, 202, 205–207, 209–210, 215, 218, 245; at Picurís Pueblo, 161, 209; in plazas, 129, 171, 218; restrictions on, 244–245; at Taos Pueblo, 62, 140, 161, 171, 209; viewed by visitors, 256; and white ash, 161
Darwin, Charles, 22, 26
Darwinism, 17–18, 148, 255
Dawkins, Richard, 2, 9
Day Kiva, 47–51, 171
Day People, 50–51, 91, 270n12
de Niza, Fray Marcos, 243
death, 5, 19, 58, 122, 166, 168, 170, 192, 208, 232. See also burials
decision making, 52, 57, 64–66, 69–70, 142, 144, 162, 190, 233–234, 236, 240, 266n5
deities, 15, 29, 42, 55, 87, 155, 188
Deloria, Vine, 103, 242, 252–254, 258–259, 261
democracy, 14, 16, 18, 20–21, 24, 30, 33–34, 74, 95, 98, 148, 240–241
Derrida, Jacques, 147
devil worship, 243
Dick, Herbert, 188, 220, 222
digging sticks, 164, 168–170
disease, 43, 53, 140
divine kings, 28–29, 33, 54, 60
domesticated plants, 29, 39
Dorantes, Esteban, 243
Douglas, Mary, 71–72, 74
Dozier, Edward, 238–239
drought, 84, 103, 119
Druidic religion, 23, 25
drums, 230–231
dualism, 46–48, 123–124, 129–131, 166, 176, 178, 180, 183–184, 187, 269n12
Durkheim, Emile, 2–3, 17, 18–20, 28, 30–31, 65, 145–149, 189–190, 240, 268n3

Eagle People, 109
Earth Mother, 47, 108–109, 158, 173, 177, 192
ecological approach, 31–33, 171, 260
ecology, 72, 103, 148, 152, 155, 158, 177, 188, 202, 204, 251
economics, 13, 28–29, 31–33, 99, 139, 172, 262; and agriculture, 169; and "doings," 104; of Hopi people, 205; organization of, 142; and power, 76; practices of, 105; premodern, 5–7; production of, 78, 244; of Pueblos, 39, 41, 60, 62–63, 66–67, 78; and religion, 5, 69, 76, 107, 174, 235; systems of, 250
effervescence, 24, 145–148, 152, 162, 171, 189–191, 195, 268n3
Egypt, 24–25, 60, 79, 102
Eliade, Mircea, 22, 252–253

nature, 5, 10, 20, 27, 29, 31–32, 56, 103, 260, 262
nature and culture connections, 103–106, 110
Navajo Nation, 196, 201, 269n2
Navajo Reservoir area, 92
Neitzel, Jill, 76
Neolithic peoples/times, 10, 27–29, 33, 39, 87, 91, 93,
    107, 141–142, 145, 200
Neolithic revolution, 190, 199
New Mexico, 39, 42, 44, 70, 73, 98, 105, 108, 152,
    193–194, 227, 243–244, 246, 266n2
New People, 54, 58
New World, 73–74, 99, 242–244, 258
Newton, Sir Isaac, 24–25
non-Western societies, 4–6, 9–10, 19, 70–73, 98, 122,
    139, 150, 241–242, 253
North House (Hlauuma), 47, 148, 192
north-south divisions, 182–184, 187, 197
Northern Tiwas: and balance/complementarity, 148;
    ceremonial landscapes of, 178; ceremonialism of,
    54; collectivity of, 123; community organization
    of, 135; early history of, 46; ethnographic insight
    into, 43; and factionalism, 53; identity markers
    of, 172–173; and the katsina, 206–211, 214–216;
    and materiality of doings, 161; origin/emergence
    stories of, 48. See also Ancestral Puebloans; Summer
    People; T'aitöna Tiwa village; Taos Pueblo; Winter
    People

Oates, Joan, 73
"Offering of the Plant Shields," 108–110, 122, 128
offerings, 57, 81, 103, 108–109, 128, 157, 184, 209, 233,
    267n5
Ohkay Owingeh Pueblo, 184, 221, 238
Oklahoma tribes, 229–230, 248
Old Axe Kiva, 47–49, 52, 171
On Religion: Speeches to Its Cultured Despisers
    (Schleiermacher), 16–17
On the Origin of Species, 26
Oñate, Juan de, 194
ontology, 4, 10, 22, 24, 106, 119, 146, 156, 176, 178, 183,
    197, 233, 252
oral histories, indigenous, 45–46, 51, 53, 86–87, 91,
    97, 108–112, 119–120, 123–124, 141, 192, 220,
    227–228, 254
origin/emergence stories, 35, 48, 87, 96, 110–111, 119,
    141, 158, 166, 192, 200, 227–229, 247, 254,
    256–257, 266n1, 270n13
Origin of the Family, Private Property and the State, The
    (Engels), 14–15
orthodoxy, 74–75, 83–84, 86, 92–93, 95, 100, 111, 149,
    174, 211, 251
Ortiz, Alfonso, 46, 131–132, 177, 184, 187
Ortman, Scott, 113, 269n5

Pagans/paganism, 34, 40, 194, 237–238, 243–247, 265n1
Pajarito Plateau district, 113, 201
Paleolithic peoples/times, 27–29, 33, 36, 91
Pandey, Triloki, 241
papacy, 15, 23, 25, 241, 247
Parsons, Elsie Clews, 44–45, 48–51, 56–57, 62–63,
    116–118, 141, 184, 207–211, 216–217, 226–229,
    266n3, 269n5, 270n11
patriotism, 193, 195–196
Pearce, David, 8–9, 34
Peckham, Stewart, 73
Pecos Pueblo, 188
Peñasca Blanca Pueblo, 80
people and things relationship, 10, 161–162, 173, 188,
    190, 195, 202, 205, 233, 248, 253–255, 257
Pepper, George, 80
Perry, Elizabeth, 235
personhood, 10, 190, 197
petroglyphs, 212–215, 224–226. See also rock art
peyote ceremonies/church, 229–230, 239–240, 248
Picurís Pueblo, 49, 53, 55, 141; architecture of, 43, 183,
    270n8; and centerpost/basin complexes, 172–173;
    and ceramics, 105, 220–222; ceremonies at, 139,
    161, 209; and clay pipes, 155; emigration from, 201;
    and katsina, 221–222, 269n5; kiva murals at, 222–
    225, 270n11; kivas at, 163, 188, 219, 232, 270n8;
    migration to, 220, 230, 236; and ruins at T'aitöna,
    267n5; and "spirit channels," 188. See also kivas
Piedra district, 91–92, 267n4
pilgrimages, 48, 53, 76, 78, 80, 91, 101, 157, 209, 242,
    266n2
pipes, 94–95, 152–158, 160–161, 171, 204, 218, 221, 236
pithouses, 120, 129, 182, 199, 269n3; become kivas,
    150–151, 174; cosmological significance of, 96;
    "D" of LA 102064, 113–119, 122; in northern Rio
    Grande, 85–86; and population estimates, 200;
    purpose of, 150–152; in Taos district, 87–89, 91,
    94, 96–97, 111–113
plant remains, 164, 169–170, 183
plazas, 82, 129–130, 171, 177, 187, 216–218, 232,
    234–235
political: action, 42; authority, 13, 69; ecology, 31–32;
    economy, 63, 67; exploitation, 28; formations, 199;
    gain, 28; interconnection, 138; oppression, 29–30;
    organization, 41, 142; power, 31–32, 66, 76, 108,
    143, 194, 240; practices, 67, 105, 122; sovereignty,
    246; subordination, 40
politics, 5–8, 15, 17, 30–32, 120, 143, 194; and burial
    objects, 82; desecularization of, 2–3; not separated
    from religion, 16, 42, 57, 66–67, 76, 97, 100; and
    premodern religion, 69, 107; at Pueblos, 52, 57–58,
    76, 151; separated from religion, 5, 16, 26, 35, 41,
    178, 193, 235, 240–241, 249, 262
polities, 31, 60, 76
polytheism, 17, 24
population, 46, 112, 145; decrease in, 43, 91–92,
    198–201, 234, 256; density, 90, 142, 199; disloca-
    tions, 116, 131; estimates of, 89, 200; increase in,
    87, 92, 113, 142–144, 151, 198–200, 234, 256;
    movements, 105, 111, 113, 182; pressure, 119; and
    religiosity, 142–143; scale, 142–143, 198. See also
    scalar stress; scale
post-Chacoan, 82, 111–112, 115, 123, 125, 130–131, 135,
    141, 178
post-Reformation, 4, 8, 42, 76, 102, 122, 241
postcolonial period, 42, 98, 156, 266n1

phenomenon, 8–9; original nature of, 15–16, 21, 24, 107; origins of, 5, 26, 28, 33, 146; and other spheres of life, 5–7, 31; politicization of, 33, 36, 65, 100; private/individual, 16, 24, 28, 30, 35, 99–100, 248; restrictions on, 249; resurgence of, 263; rigid structure of, 16–17, 28; specialized, 13; universality of, 5, 10, 19, 25, 34–35, 70, 99, 262. *See also* "false" religion; "true" religion; belief

religion-politics divide, 122

religious: architecture, 64, 95–96, 149–151, 158, 255–256; authority, 13, 83; battles, 26; contexts, 176; crusades, 243; freedom, 246–249; hierarchy, 62, 247; ideology, 120, 122; meaning, 67; organization, 142; persecution, 166; phenomena, 204, 235; power, 2, 58–59, 66, 76, 190; practice, 15, 66, 78, 101, 104–105, 143, 244, 248; reforms, 12–13; secrecy, 58–59, 61; tolerance, 17–18, 24, 33, 74, 99, 248; traditions, 52, 253–254; training, 54–55, 58; unmusical societies, 71–74, 94. *See also* knowledge: religious; Pueblo doings

Renfrew, Colin, 7–8, 30, 75, 78

return, logic/myth of, 12–23, 18, 24, 26–28, 31, 33, 35–36, 246, 254–255, 262, 265n3, 270n2

Return to Cosmology: Postmodern Science and the Theology of Nature, The (Toulmin), 260

revelation, 254

Ridge Ruin, 81–83, 266n2

Rio Grande del Rancho, 87–89, 92, 96, 115–118, 125, 179, 183, 199–200, 212, 227–228, 233, 268n6

Rio Grande gorge, 90, 121, 211, 213–215, 224–226

Rio Grande River, 211–212, 245

Rio Grande Valley, 201, 227; ceremonial landscapes of, 178; and Chacoan system, 74–75, 85, 93; migration away from, 258; migration to, 99, 111–113, 116, 123, 131, 202, 218; moieties of, 131; shrines of, 178, 184, 187

Rio Lucero, 154

Rito de la Olla, 181–182

ritual, 64, 103, 139, 146, 198, 241; architecture, 73, 94–96, 104, 149–151, 268n5; control over, 235; definition of, 7–8, 72, 151; feasts, 149; importance, 57; important role of, 73; individual, 47–48; negligence, 84; objects, 9, 63, 82, 94–95, 109, 149, 156, 169, 183; poverty, 72; power, 132, 268n4; practices, 57–58, 78, 94, 99, 107, 145, 157, 169, 175; secret, 45, 48–49, 58–59, 61, 101; and the secular, 9; societies, 45–48, 172; specialists, 78; structures, 65, 142, 144, 234; study of, 7, 234; symbolism, 56, 72; systems, 46–48, 64; training, 62; violence, 31, 122. *See also* knowledge: ritual

roads, 78–79, 85, 179, 182–183, 188, 192, 204, 266n1

Robbins, William J., 240

rock art, 120–121, 204, 206; and katsina images, 211–215, 218, 220, 224–226; site LA 166891, 224–226; site LA 75747, 224–225

Rome, 17, 23–24

Room 33 burials, 80–82

Room 822: *See* kiva (Room 822, T'aitöna)

Rowlands, Henry, 24

ruins, 182–184, 193, 199, 249–250, 258, 267n5

rupture narrative, 15–16, 21, 23–24, 35, 36, 252

Sacred, 7–8, 190; directions, 96, 105, 132, 139–140, 166, 171, 188; forces, 32; icons, 248; idiom, 45; images, 248; middens, 169; objects, 31, 58–59, 62–63, 67, 69–70, 94, 104, 248; places/lands, 58, 78, 91, 129, 248–250, 253–256, 266n1; and profane, 102, 149–150, 166, 172, 174, 176; societies, 70; spaces, 31, 194; waters, 188. *See also* knowledge: sacred

Sahlins, Marshall, 29, 71, 102

Saile, David, 188–189

Saitta, Dean, 61–62, 78, 235

San Geronimo de Taos Church, 193–194

San Geronimo Feast Day, 192–193

San Juan basin, 75, 85, 89–92, 95, 97, 99, 113, 122, 130, 159, 178, 227, 257, 266n1

Sand Canyon Pueblo, 130–131

Sangre de Cristo Mountains, 87

Santa Clara Pueblo, 238, 247

Santa Fe district, 85, 113, 123, 269n13

Santo Domingo Pueblo, 238

Sassaman, Kenneth, 97

scalar stress, 142–144, 148, 198, 233–234

scale: community, 199–200; decrease in, 198–201; economy of, 162, 202; increase in, 189–190; and religiosity, 144–145; social, 31, 259. *See also* population

Schaafsma, Polly and Curtis, 206

Schleiermacher, Friedrich, 16–17, 265n1, 268n3

science, 5, 8–10, 17, 24, 27, 34, 145, 265n2; of culture, 17; and magic, 19–20, 35; and politics, 251; professionalization of, 74; and Pueblo doings, 250–251; and religion, 34–35; and shamanism, 32; sheds religious illusions, 21; theological, 260

scientific: archaeology, 28; cosmology, 189; exploration, 260; practice, 251; rationality, 20–21, 72; research, 34; revelations, 25; theology, 260. *See also* knowledge: scientific

Secakuku, Ferrell, 249–250, 269n1

secular: definition of religion, 5–6; futures, 35; governance, 16; humanism, 73; irreligion, 107; liberals, 3; modern imaginary, 5; modernity, 250, 261; narrative of religion, 141; peoples, 99; politics, 13; power, 66; principles of religious freedom, 248; scholarship, 35; society, 245–246, 248–249, 257; tradition, 103; tribes, 72–73, 99

secularism, 94, 258–259, 263; anthropology of, 99; and artifacts, 9; critical analysis of, 10–11; critics of, 145; definition of, 4, 11–12; emergence of, 15–16, 23, 36; and logic of return, 31, 35; of modern society, 71, 74, 99, 240; narratives of, 12, 31, 65; notions of, 20–21; and religion, 6, 121; and skepticism, 70; Western, 120

secularization, 1–2, 4, 24, 28, 34–37, 241

sedentary villages, 39

seeds, 160, 204, 236, 251, 268n5

Service, Elman, 29

settlement, patterns of, 111–113, 118, 125, 141, 182, 201, 212

shamanism, 3, 30, 32–33

shamans, 9, 29, 31–35, 94, 103, 120–121
Shamans, Sorcerers, and Saints: A Prehistory of Religion
(Hayden), 31
Sharlet, Jeff, 35
shells, 79–82, 94, 171, 266n2
shields, plant, 108–111, 122, 128
shrines, 78, 81, 91, 169, 188–189, 250–251; of bermed
earth/rocks, 178, 181, 184–187; cupule, 129,
178–180, 187, 230; of Hopis, 256; orientated
towards sun, 132; and Pueblo ruins, 182–183; of
rocks/boulders, 178–183, 187, 269n13; systems of,
177–178, 187, 269n12; of T'aitöna village, 178–183;
of upright stones, 184–186
Sierra Blanca, 188
Sinaguan sites, 81, 266n2. *See also* Ridge Ruin
Sioux, 259
sipapus, 81–82, 89, 96, 158, 160–161, 230
Small Olivella Shell People, 171
Smith, M. Estellie, 56
Smith, Wilfred Cantwell, 15, 244
smoking, 152, 157, 218, 221. *See also* pipes
Snead, James, 183
social: action, 66–67, 70; bonding, 32; change, 112,
257; constructions, 98; deviance, 119; differences,
65–66, 79–80, 83–84, 147; dissension, 198;
diversity, 143, 146; division, 46–48; "doings," 104;
domination, 110; evolution, 31, 142; harmony,
66; hierarchy, 56, 116, 123, 205, 230; integration,
30, 52, 64–65, 148, 150–151, 195, 198, 206, 230,
234–235; intensity, 190; life, 5, 20, 46, 48, 51; networks, 177; order, 97, 103, 143, 262; organization,
39, 45, 46, 141, 144, 230, 234; patterns, 143–144;
phenomena, 138–139, 141, 199; polarization, 132;
power, 54, 100, 148; relations, 10, 124, 205, 228;
simplicity, 93, 97–98, 247; solidarity, 146–147,
151; tradition, 105; transformation, 143, 198, 257;
turbulence, 92; world, 147, 149, 151, 164
society, 130–131; ancient, 40, 69; archaic, 252–253;
ceremonial, 51–52; complex, 31–32, 51, 61, 64–65,
93, 97, 235; dissolution of, 14; egalitarian, 143,
257; evolution of, 26, 91; of the fourth world, 254;
fragmented, 42, 63; future course of, 17; hierarchical, 42, 56; large-scale, 60; original nature of,
96; origins of, 40; and place, 257; progression of,
14; Puebloan, 51–52, 57, 60–61, 66–67, 79; and
religious experience, 268n3; secret, 28; small-
scale, 30–31, 41–42, 70, 143, 195, 199; solidarity
of, 28–30, 32, 42, 64; state-level, 61, 143, 240;
study of, 76–77; tolerant, 35; traditional, 70, 98;
transegalitarian, 32
sociocultural anthropologists, 6–7, 10–12, 28–30, 36, 42,
70, 151, 241
solar eclipses, 137–141, 267n1
solar observations, 132–133, 140
Solomon's Temple, 25
songs, 45, 152, 171, 208, 251
South House (Hlaukwima), 47, 148
Southern Methodist University, 124
Southern Tiwas, 184, 227
Spanish settlers, 39, 56, 83, 92, 194, 199, 204, 242;

arrival of, 43, 123; conquest of, 79, 224, 257–258;
and katsina tradition, 206; missionization efforts
of, 238, 243, 245, 270n1; oppress Puebloans, 201;
Puebloans submit to, 43; and Pueblo politics/
religion, 240–241, 243, 249; wage war on Pueblo
"rebels," 243–244
Spencer, Herbert, 26
Spicer, Edward, 238
spirit beings, 155, 186, 188, 202, 244; ancestral, 81, 122,
158, 161; communication with, 152, 254; and kivas,
149, 158; and masks, 204, 218–219; and Northern
Tiwas, 141; priests as, 58; and stone shrines, 184.
See also katsina
spirit world, 29, 72, 81, 106
spiritual: innocence, 42; mediation, 269n1; power, 29,
54; realm, 29, 33; relationships, 139; terrorism, 98;
traditions, 239
spirituality, 20, 24, 33, 35, 103, 135, 246
squash blossom/seeds, 160
Standing Bear, Chief Luther, 259, 261
states, 27, 29–30, 76, 93, 98; archaic, 31, 33, 262; hierarchical, 33; indigenous, 27, 61, 65; and mediation,
12; modern, 13, 261; and religion, 31, 34–35, 259
status, 60, 80–82, 94, 205
Stein, John, 78–79
Stevenson, Matilda Cox, 44–45, 48–51, 54–55, 57,
105, 110, 119, 124, 154–155, 167, 171, 173, 188,
207–209, 227–228, 266n1–3, 267n2
Stone Knife People, 171
stone tools, 14, 29, 39, 224
Stonehenge (England), 23, 25, 33
Strathern, Marilyn, 241
Stuart, David, 112–113
Stukeley, William, 23, 25–26
Summer People, 112, 122, 132, 175, 208, 270n12; arrival
of, 111, 113–115, 150; defeat Winter People, 87,
109–110, 120, 130, 152, 200, 228; narrative about,
109–111, 119, 123–124, 130; plant shields of,
109–111, 128; powerful medicine of, 52, 109–110,
228; at T'aitöna, 141, 144, 148, 200, 229; and
Water People, 227–228, 256
summer solstice, 188
sunrise, 132, 140, 166, 177, 179
supernatural, 5, 8, 20, 27, 34, 57, 70–71, 73, 172, 230,
241, 243–244, 251, 255
superstition, 16, 28, 71
Swallow Bird Boy, 152
Swentzell, Rina, 82, 187–188, 192
symbolism, 5, 47, 52, 56, 72, 96; and ceramics, 73,
155–157, 187; of east-west division, 166, 168–170;
and katsina, 203, 208; of landforms, 91, 129; of
north-south division, 133, 148, 166, 168–171, 175,
178, 180; and religion, 7, 66; of squash blossom/
seeds, 160
sympathy, 19, 156–159, 168–169, 171–173, 187–189, 195,
204

Tafoya, Matthew, 196–197, 269n2
Tafoya, Shawn, 232
tai'na (peoples), 46

T'aitöna Tiwa kivas, 124, 130, 132, 141, 149, 158–171, 175, 182, 184, 197, 230–234, 236. *See also* kiva (Room 822, T'aitöna); T'aitöna Tiwa kivas

T'aitöna Tiwa village, 112, 114, 190, 267n5; abandonment of, 184, 201, 220, 230–231, 233–234, 236; architecture of, 124–126, 128–130, 132–134, 141, 152, 180, 217; burials at, 167–168, 268n7–8; centerpost/basin complexes at, 172–173, 192; ceramics of, 90, 104–106, 125–128; clay pipes made at, 152–154, 221; diverse peoples of, 146, 229; divides surrounding landscape, 182–184; doings at, 124, 141, 158, 161–162, 165, 169, 172, 177, 189, 197–198, 206; founding of, 216; great kiva of, 230–234; importance of, 267n5; katsina images at, 210–212, 214, 216; layout of, 216; leaders of, 234; mealing rooms at, 124, 130, 133–134, 174–177; migration to, 200–201; north-south division of, 175, 178, 180, 183–184, 187, 197; orientated towards sun, 132–133; religiosity of, 135; shrine network of, 178–187, 230, 269n12; social organization of, 144, 201, 234; women at, 133–134, 146, 174

Talpa Phase, 125, 270n9

Taos district: architecture of, 86–88, 90–91, 94–97, 152; ceramics of, 87, 90–92, 113–115, 267n4; and Chaco Canyon, 74–75, 86; Chacolessness of, 93–95, 98–99; cultural development of, 91; description/map of, 87–88; early occupation of, 74, 86–87, 90, 92, 99–100, 109–110, 124, 141; and katsina, 270n10; katsinalessness of, 206–207; pre-Columbian archaeology of, 106; and religion/politics, 100; and shrines, 269n13; during turbulent 1200s, 111–112, 122. *See also* Summer People; T'aitöna Tiwa village; Taos Pueblo; Winter People

Taos Elk Dance, 62

Taos Plateau, 87–88, 90, 215

Taos Pueblo, 251; and 1847 massacre, 193–194, 216; and Antelopes and Hawks story, 116–118; anti-modernist stance of, 102; architecture of, 40–41, 43, 47–48, 130–131, 148; and centerpost/basin complexes, 172; ceramic practices at, 105, 111, 154, 204; ceremonial societies of, 51–52; ceremonies of, 108–111, 139–140, 149, 161, 171–174, 177, 192–193, 195; and east-west division, 166; emigration from, 201; and ethnographers, 43–46, 48–50, 56, 58–59, 140, 208, 266n1, 266n2; and gender, 197; governance at, 240; historical accounts of, 90–91, 97, 111, 119, 123–124, 140; leaders of, 48, 55–58, 139, 266n3; lulina of, 55, 230; migration to, 220, 230, 236, 256; name of, 46; and nearby shrines, 177–178; oppose anthropologists, 45; organization of, 141, 148; origin/emergence of, 110–111, 119, 187–188, 200, 248, 256, 266n1; peoples of, 43–46, 50–52; and peyote ceremonies, 229–230, 248; and relations with US, 40; religious leaders of, 51–60; religious makeup of, 53, 237, 239–240, 247; ritual life of, 46–49; ruins of, 183, 193; and secrecy of religion, 45, 208, 215, 218, 266n3, 269n1; social division in, 46, 46–48; three-tiered structure of, 52; Turtle Dance at, 209, 216–217, 228; underground connections at, 188; and UNESCO

designation, 40, 43; visitors to, 139, 266n3. *See also* Blue Lake; Summer People; Winter People

Taos Pueblo kivas, 46–53, 58, 87, 130–131, 148–149, 219, 222, 228–229, 237, 240, 256, 266n3

Taylor, Charles, 22

technology, 14, 26–29, 39, 104, 113, 128, 139, 166, 259. *See also* ceramics

Tedlock, Barbara, 188, 268n5

Te'ewi female figurine, 179, 186

temples, 33, 76, 149, 151, 265n4

Tewas, 54, 62, 167; and ethnographers, 208; flee to Hopi mesas, 92; initiations of, 197; and katsina glyphs, 213; kivas of, 158–159; moieties of, 46, 131–132; and prayer bowls, 219; religiously based class system of, 266n4; shrine system of, 177–179, 183–184, 186–187; villagescape of, 189

textiles, 39, 80, 232–234

theocracy, 3, 24, 30, 60, 96, 240–241, 259, 265n4

Toulmin, Stephen, 157, 260

tourists, 39–40, 101–102, 166, 192, 195, 202, 205, 246, 256

trade, 43, 76, 78, 85, 207, 235, 266n2

transcendence, 11–12, 20, 24, 27, 70, 147, 176, 178, 190, 195, 253, 255, 259, 262

trash deposits. *See* refuse

tree-ring dating, 132, 231, 267n3

tribal: government, 240, 247–248; humanism, 73, 107; land, 43; nations, 250; religion, 108, 151, 247–248; ritual, 151; societies, 19, 41–42, 61, 70–73, 99, 205–206; sovereignty, 196, 240

Trinidad district, 123

"true" religion, 15–17, 23–26, 30, 41–42, 65, 97, 204, 244, 249

turquoise, 62, 78–82, 85, 92, 94, 266n2

Turtle Dance, 209, 216–217, 228

turtle shell rattles, 217, 228, 236

Tylor, Edward, 17–18, 137, 143–144, 146, 265n2

Underhill, Ruth, 247

UNESCO, 40, 43

United States: ancient inhabitants of, 26; Christian Coalition in, 107; colonial violence of, 193–194; forts of, 236; heritage of, 40; and political subordination of Taos, 40; politics of, 3, 16, 53; protects religion from state, 259; recognizes Pueblo religion, 247–249; takes control of New Mexico, 43, 194, 244

Upham, Steadman, 65–66

Upper Paleolithic, 32

Utes, 43

Valdez Phase, 86–90, 95, 97, 111–116, 118–120, 200

Van Dyke, Ruth, 235

Victorian era, 14, 26

villagescapes, 178, 180, 183–184, 187–190

violence, 43, 76, 83, 85, 111, 113, 115–120, 122–123, 144, 167, 193, 216, 243, 268n8

Voltaire, 25–26

Walpi (Hopi village), 203

war societies, 202, 210

Warburg, Aby, 40

warfare, 12, 33, 51, 56, 81, 91, 98–99, 108, 203, 244, 254

Water Kiva, 47–49, 52, 171, 266n3

Water Man, 48, 266n3

Water People, 144, 171, 208, 210, 227–230, 256, 270n12–13

Watt, W. Montgomery, 73

We Have a Religion (Wenger), 245

wealth, 62–63, 81, 235, 244

weaving: *See* textiles

Weber, Max, 71, 143, 190

Wendorf, Fred, 186

Wenger, Tisa, 245–246, 248

Western: category of religion, 252; civilization, 241–243, 246; concepts, 15, 98, 242; historical imaginary, 36; ideology, 174; individualism, 148; narratives, 11–12; philosophy, 176; physics, 9; principles of governance, 241; religions, 33; scholars, 121, 172; scientists, 10; sense of place, 257; society, 9, 21, 246; state, 76; systems of categorization, 258; theological tradition, 254; theorists, 149

white ash, 161, 268n7

White, Leslie, 29–30, 44

Whiteley, Peter, 66

Whitley, David, 34–35, 133, 268n8

Williams, Lucy, 232

Winter People, 133, 266n3, 270n12; arrival of, 86–87, 90; bring snow and rain, 208; burials of, 88; ceramics of, 90, 94–95, 128; and Chacoan system, 91–94; defeated by Summer People, 87, 130, 152, 200, 228; narrative about, 87, 91, 109–111, 119, 123–124, 267n2; and pipe smoking, 152; pithouses of, 96, 114; population of, 150; religious/ritual life of, 94–99; settlements of, 86–89; at T'aitöna, 141, 144, 148, 229; violent death of, 115, 120, 122; and Water People, 227–228

winter solstice, 96, 132–133, 140, 177, 188

witches/witchcraft, 27, 79, 81, 103, 117–120, 122, 229, 257, 267n4, 270n13

women: and ceremonialism, 50; domestic labor of, 174–177; exclusion of, 54, 59, 205; great power of, 54; marginalization of, 53; as ritualists, 266n5; at T'aitöna, 133–134, 146, 174. *See also* corn: ground by women

Woosley, Anne, 91

World Heritage Site, 40, 76

World War I, 245–246

Yoffee, Norman, 76

Young, Jane, 268n4

yucca matting, 164, 169–170

Zuni Pueblo, 201; and arrival of Spanish, 243; and bird motif, 223; ceremonies of, 63, 204; "doings" at, 251; and ethnographers, 208; and katsina, 198, 202, 204–205, 209–210, 218–219; and kivas, 222, 268n5; prayersticks of, 188; priests of, 54, 60, 67; provides raw cotton, 232; religious beliefs of, 268n4; and theocracy, 241

Severin M. Fowles is an assistant professor in the anthropology department at Barnard College, Columbia University who lives and works part-time in Dixon, New Mexico. He has ongoing intellectual commitments to the landscapes and communities of the northern Rio Grande where he has directed archaeological fieldwork each summer since 1998. His research draws on the rich Native American, Hispano, and Anglo Heritage of New Mexico to develop new archaeological understandings of the evolutionary history of voluntary simplicity and the discursive role of religion in accounts of the human past.